MOROCCAN DIALOGUES

MOROCCAN DIALOGUES
Anthropology in Question

KEVIN DWYER

WAVELAND PRESS, INC.
PROSPECT HEIGHTS, ILLINOIS

For information about this book, write or call:

Waveland Press, Inc.
P.O. Box 400
Prospect Heights, Illinois 60070
(312) 634-0081

Contents

Detailed Contents
(Containing prepared questions)

Preface

When I went to Morocco in the summer of 1975 my aims were uncertain. I had been there twice before, for two years from 1969 to 1971 and for one month in the summer of 1973, both times to carry out research in social anthropology. Yet, ever since that first visit, when I began to tailor my experiences in Morocco to suit academic anthropology, I had found the fit unsatisfactory and had come to feel quite at odds with the main traditions within anthropology.

The anthropologist has two basic, customary styles to use to interpret his or her encounter with people of another culture. One is to interpret the experience according to the norms of "science" and to create an object for study (or, as the anthropologist might say, an "Other") that is strictly distinct from the subject who studies it (the "Self"). This done, the anthropologist may take substantial liberties in remodeling the object, organizing it into selected themes, neglecting "irrelevant" details, combining separate events and ignoring chronology—all in accord with the canons of science. Or, the anthropologist may reject science and insist on the unique and personal aspects of the experience, trying to recount that experience subjectively, in a manner somewhat akin to a novel.

Both styles seemed to me deficient: the scientific approach, I thought, radically distorted the experience because, at the very least, it overlooked the role played by the anthropologist in constructing the situations and eliciting the behavior that he or she later reported in ethnographic monographs or professional journals; the personal account, although placing the anthropologist within the experience, usually presented that experience "naively," without questioning the implications of the anthropologist's presence and comportment. Both styles, whatever their differences, were more like escapes from, than solutions to, the

problems of conveying the experience to people who had not participated in it.[1]

As I planned my coming summer visit to Morocco, I decided that, if
nothing else, I would confront my dissatisfaction directly. I did not
intend to carry out a research project thought out in advance; nor, at the
other extreme, would I make the hopeless attempt to "go native." I
would simply spend time with people I had come to care about and enjoy
myself with and who seemed to feel similarly toward me, I would try to
be sensitive to my needs and theirs, and I would seek to assess my doubts
about academic anthropology.

As the summer progressed, I became more and more aware that both
for me and for Faqir Muhammad, a Moroccan cultivator in his mid-
sixties with whom I had spent much time over the years, our most
satisfying activity together was a series of tape-recorded interviews.
These began provisionally and advanced spontaneously, tentatively. Initially, I simply intended to ask him a few general questions about his past
and about his attitudes toward his current problems, and I had only one
interview in mind. Our second interview was prompted by the unexpected visit of a regional leader of a religious brotherhood. Throughout
the rest of that summer, I continued to single out "events" almost without realizing it, and the Faqir remained more than willing (sometimes
suggesting it himself) to sit and talk with me about them.

My experience in Morocco that summer had, then, two sources: one in
my poorly articulated dissatisfaction with the limits of traditional anthropological approaches, the other in my desire to be sensitive to the
Other's "voice" at the earliest stage possible, to not stifle it within the
constraints of a rigid research project, and to respect its integrity. But
that experience gained its distinctive form and content as a product of
both my aims and the Faqir's: as the Faqir and I continued to discover in
one another a peculiarly attractive combination, perhaps impossible to
explain, of empathy and difference; as "events" provoked my questions
and the Faqir remained willing, even anxious, to answer; as I sensed that
something about this whole process was critical to the effort to understand and appreciate people of other cultures and therefore critical to
anthropology, which claimed to dominate that effort; and as the Faqir's
deeper aims, which I am in no position to summarize, were somehow
satisfied too.

I spent much of that summer and, as it turned out, a good part of the
next few years questioning this experience, the satisfaction it had given

---

[1]This distinction between a "scientific" and a "personal" style does not do justice
to the variety and complexity of anthropological genres. I examine these genres at some
length in chapters 12 and 13, where I also suggest that despite their apparent differences,
most share certain basic, mistaken assumptions.

me and Faqir Muhammad, and its relationship to my dissatisfaction with academic anthropology. As I did this, I found that concentrating on the "event + dialogue" motif helped me not only to examine my encounter with a person from another culture, but also to expose the deficiencies of the usual anthropological interpretations of such experiences and to suggest ways to convey this experience without repeating the deficiencies.

In the first place, the events and dialogues illustrate the structured inequality of the partners during their encounter: the anthropologist singles out "events" and poses questions; the informant answers, embellishes, digresses, evades. The anthropologist, in part for reasons and in a manner reflecting his own society's concerns, is pushed to impose form upon his experience, and his questions provide a skeleton designed to provoke the informant to respond; the informant's responses add flesh to this frame and dress it, often in unexpected ways. The events and dialogues do not hide this inequality but, instead, help to display it: as we look at the events in the text, we can begin to question how the anthropologist defines his experience; from the questions he asks, we gain some insight into the kind of understanding he seeks.

The partners' contributions are certainly complementary, but they are definitely not equal. This particular kind of inequality is not an accident of personal preference but is one aspect of a wider social confrontation between the West and the rest of the world that, in recent history, has never been symmetrical: the West has systematically intruded upon the non-West and reworked it, sometimes subtly, sometimes violently, according to the West's own needs. This asymmetry has its counterpart in the anthropologist's project: the Self's search for knowledge of the Other takes the form of a personal expedition into the Other's cultural and social territory, to seek a kind of understanding that has been defined by the needs of western institutions.

The personal expedition is thus inevitably tied to the interests of the society from which the anthropologist comes, and all he says and does— how he gives form to experience, how he shapes and directs his questions, how he interprets and proceeds from the answers he receives— provides a commentary on those interests. (With the tie between individual and society always in mind, I use the terms *Self* and *Other* in an extended sense throughout this book, to mean not only individuals involved in the encounter but also the cultural and societal interests that these individuals carry with them, deliberately or in spite of themselves. Therefore, wherever these terms occur, the reader should understand them in their extended meaning: individuals *and* societies are in question.[2])

----

[2]If, on occasion, I have written "the Self and its society," or juxtaposed Self and society in other ways, it is not to oppose Self and society to one another but to make certain

But the events and dialogues are an illustration of more than a particular instance of the structured inequality of Self and Other—the motif also illustrates the interdependence of Self and Other. In the dialogues, we see a complex process of adjustment and readjustment: false beginnings, hesitation and redirection, streaks of continuity and moments of rupture. In the confrontation between anthropologist and informant, each changes and develops while interacting with the other; during their actual encounter and in response to the other, each creates himself in part as a reaction to the other. The anthropologist who encounters people from other societies is not merely observing them or attempting to record their behavior; both he and the people he confronts, and the societal interests that each represents, are engaging each other *creatively*, producing the *new* phenomenon of Self and Other becoming interdependent, of Self and Other sometimes challenging, sometimes accommodating one another.

Consequently, the events and dialogues encourage us to question what is taken for granted under the familiar anthropological perspectives: the anthropologist's individuality, for we now see that the anthropologist is inextricably linked to his own society's interests (the term *Self* now embraces both the individual and the society whose interests the individual carries); and the Self's identity, for we now see that it has been touched and perhaps indelibly marked by the Other.

We are now led to a further, inescapable conclusion. In confronting the Other in so direct a manner; in seeking, however persistently, to define and give form to experience; in questioning other people again and again to refine and articulate their experience: in all this the Self confronts an Other who parries, extends, and reworks the questions, who counters the Self's view of the experience, who may even refuse to continue the direct confrontation. Now, the very power of the Self is called into question and the fundamental problem of the Self's "vulnerability" in the face of the Other is raised.

My aims could only be carried forward by finding some way to make the experience concrete, to turn it into a text and make it accessible to people who had not participated in it. Otherwise, the experience would remain a purely personal one, which, however worthwhile to the Faqir and myself, would serve an extremely limited critical function. Unfortunately, the experience is inevitably transformed in making it into a text. "Events" certainly lose their immediacy and are reworked in the mind of the writer as he writes them down. Less obviously, but just as certainly, much is lost in transcribing conversations into written dialogues: gestures do not appear, tone of voice is muted and mood is hidden, and

that society is not forgotten when Self is mentioned. In any case, it should be clear by now that although the terms *Self, Other,* and *vulnerability* may easily lend themselves to a personal, psychological interpretation, this is not the interpretation I have in mind.

Moroccan Arabic disappears as it is translated into English. And, of course, the apparently simple choice of presenting "events" and "dialogues" as an epitome of the experience is a complex one that entails a radical recasting of experience. Consequently, it would be absurd to claim that the events and dialogues either faithfully record the experience or fully communicate it.

If a faithful record, a full communication, of the experience is impossible, this is no excuse to reduce the effort to preserve in the text, and to convey to others, what one believes to be crucial in that experience. The effectiveness of this book should be judged, then, not in the light of a necessarily mistaken criterion of fidelity to experience, but in terms of the significance of taking certain aspects, rather than others, as essential, and the book's success in displaying them: here, the structured inequality and interdependence of Self and Other, the inevitable link between the individual's action and his or her own society's interests, and the vulnerability and integrity of the Self and the Other.

When I began to seriously envisage publishing a book in which the Faqir would be a major character and which would include his own words, I realized that I would first have to discuss the project with him. Although the Faqir knew as we recorded the conversations that his words might go beyond the two of us (the dialogues show that we both had students in mind, and I had some of my close friends in mind too), the wider and less predictable readership that a book would reach raised new problems. I was not able to return to Morocco until some three and one-half years after the interviews were recorded, for three weeks in the winter of 1978–79. I brought up the project with the Faqir and we had the following conversation:

You remember, don't you, all the recordings we did that other year?
Of course.
Well, I've been thinking of making a book out of those recordings and out of what happened that summer. But I said to myself, "Before I go through with this I must talk it over with the Faqir." Well, what do you think about this?
What do you mean? How are you going to make a book?
Well, you know, we talked then as we are talking now
                          I know, I know.
I've written down the words that we said, and now I would make that into a book. The book would have, "Kevin said such and such" and "The Faqir said such and such."
I see. So other people would have our words.
Well, the words would be translated; they would be in English.
You mean they would have a transcript, like in the court sometimes?
That's it, exactly.
Well, the matter is clear. Words that have to do with the government

shouldn't be in it. You know, it's not that we have said anything wrong, or anything bad about the government. It is that there are people who wish me ill, and people who wish you ill. Someone without good faith will take our words and twist them, and they will cause me trouble and they will cause you trouble.

But the things that happened—the events in Morocco that we talked about, and our ways of living, and our habits—all that is all right.
You're sure?
Sure. "The Faqir says . . . you say . . . whoever says." All that is all right.
O.K. Let's go over some of what we actually talked about that summer, and see what you think. We talked about Morocco's struggle for independence, and your time with the troops patrolling Casablanca.
That's fine, that's a good story. It should be in the book.
And the boys' circumcision? [The Faqir nodded assent.] And the religious brother-hood? Is it all right if I include details of the seance—the chanting and the recitations?
That's all fine.

What about the marriage of your daughter, which was then in a very bad state?
Oh, that's not so important, not important at all.
But we can leave it in, can't we?
Leave it in or leave it out, what's the difference? Sure, leave it in, it doesn't matter to me. Let it be transcribed; I've nothing against it.
And how about your youth and your first marriage? [The Faqir nodded again.] And your words on Berbers and Jews?
That's all fine.

How about the differences between you and your brother? Feelings between you were very cold that summer.
All that, our words, are fine.
Now you know if you wanted, I might be able to write the book in such a way that your name doesn't appear in it.
Look—just don't touch the government and you can put my name all over it. And even pictures if you want. But not the government. It will make trouble for me, and for you too. And for me, perhaps, a lot.

Because, this is all a question of trust. Look, I'm a Muslim and you are a Christian, and there is trust between us—we've been through a lot together. But as for others—you can't have trust in them, whether they are Muslims or Christians. They are just the same. If someone you don't know comes and gets the book, he can use it to do something bad for us, even if we haven't done anything wrong.

Look, you and I have been through a lot together. You know I would never cause trouble for you, and I know you would never make trouble for me. We've never dealt with one another because of money, or out of greed, or because of land, or because of an automobile. We're just to-

gether, with one another, in front of God, on our good faith. That's the thing.
O.K. We'll just leave the government out of it.
That's it. Everything else is fine, but the government stays outside. That's it.

The book is composed of two parts. Part 1, "A 'Record' of Fieldwork," begins with a prologue that provides some background to life in a southern Moroccan village and to my encounter with Faqir Muhammad; it then proceeds, in each succeeding chapter, to present an event that occurred during the fieldwork and a subsequent dialogue between me and the Faqir about it. Each dialogue is introduced by a brief interrogatory note in which I set out the questions I had that summer about my own aims and outline the questions I planned to ask the Faqir in the dialogue.

The Faqir and I managed between one and three interview sessions a week, and the duration of each varied according to the subject and to demands on the Faqir's time. The events and dialogues are presented in their actual chronological order. I wrote a rough draft of each event within a day or two after it occurred, except in those cases where the event itself is not so clearly defined (as in chs. 7 and 8). Once I had singled out an event, I prepared a number of questions for the Faqir (these prepared questions are indicated in the text by bold face italic type and are collected in the Detailed Contents); other questions came to mind as our talk proceeded. All the dialogues we taped that summer and all the questions and answers we exchanged during them appear in their original order.

I translated all the interviews from Moroccan Arabic. Otherwise, I edited them only by excising several sections in order to remain as faithful to the Faqir's expressed wishes as I could (these deletions are indicated by ellipses inside parentheses), by changing some names and eliminating others where I thought it appropriate, and by substituting names for pronouns in a number of places for the purposes of clarity. Pauses are indicated by a series of dots; interruptions are shown by speech beginning at midline. Aside from these changes, the dialogues are transcribed here just as they were recorded.

Part 1 contains, then, the questions I posed to the Faqir and to myself during that summer. Part 2, "On the Dialogic of Anthropology" (chs. 12 and 13), consists of an essay in which the questions raised as I later reflected on this experience are directly addressed to anthropology and to its claim to be a privileged means of reaching understanding of the Other. In chapter 12, "Disintegration and Fragmentation," I question at some length the familiar anthropological approaches and try to locate the deficiencies that prevent both a sound appreciation of the Other and a serious examination of the Self. In chapter 13, "Toward Reconstitution," I try to assess to what extent this book may point the way toward remedying these deficiencies.

The plan of this book thus mirrors, to some extent, the stages of the fieldwork experience. But I have not charted my fieldwork experience simply to record it for myself (although this undoubtedly is one of my aims), or to show how different, how changed the anthropologist had become at the end of the summer: how his knowledge of Islam had widened, his understanding of colonialism had broadened, his relationship with the Faqir had deepened; or to trace the subtle shifts in the anthropologist's personality or in his sense of self-assurance. While some of this may indeed have occurred and may even be visible (or rebutted) in portions of the book, for me the more significant change was my becoming convinced, during my encounter with the Faqir, that to take the Other seriously entailed conveying rather than concealing that moment when the Self directly confronts the Other, when the Self is most vulnerable and the Other closest to us. To do otherwise is not merely dishonest but is pernicious and self-serving, because it shields the Self and works to distance and disarm the Other.

The overall aim of this book, then, is not to treat theoretically the vulnerability and integrity of Self and Other, but to show them, as well as one can, in the anthropological encounter with the Other; not to categorize, label, and compare vulnerability and integrity, but to render them visible. It is in the march, course, and changing pace, in the successive rounds, of the Self's confrontation with the Other and not in its end result that the substance lies: in the mutually creative influence of Self and Other on one another, in the continuing dialectic between the individual's effort and the interests of his own society, in the exposure and opening of the Self's defenses to the Other's challenge.

I have little hope of being more than partially successful in my aims. I do hope, though, that this book will encourage readers to confront rather than disguise the vulnerability of the Self and its society in the encounter with the Other and to seek forms of encounter which allow the Other's voice to be heard at the earliest possible moment, addressing and challenging the Self. Alone, such confrontations may do little to influence the West's mission or to reduce the inequality and redress the imbalance that has characterized the Self's intrusion upon the Other; yet they are a necessary step in the effort to assess that mission and the way the Self has sought to sustain its control of the Other.

Paradoxically, then, this book is meant to be vulnerable to criticism. To the extent that the Self's conceit may be here more visible, the Self's defenses less hidden and more easily probed, the individual's ties to the interests of his own society more obvious and clearly exposed: to that extent should this book point the way toward a critique of interpretations of the Other where the immunity of the Self is more subtly promoted and, also, toward a critique of itself. To that extent, too, this book's failures should, perhaps, be counted in its favor. I do not say this to hedge my bets, but rather in the conscious recognition that, "In order to remain consistent with paradox itself, we must both accept and refuse it at one and the same time" (Goldmann 1964, p. 212).

Acknowledgments

Many people helped me to write this book. I would particularly like to thank Daisy Dwyer for sharing much of the time I spent in Morocco and for enabling me to experience that time with a milder sense of loss than separation from one's own society normally entails; Daisy, Brigitte Luchesi, and Lou for reading carefully the full manuscript at various stages and making many useful suggestions; Steve Barnett and Tom Dichter for their continuing friendship and for the many hours we spent over several years discussing the arguments I put forward in part 2; Talal Asad, Stanley Diamond (who published two early versions of my theoretical argument and who gave me the opportunity, in a seminar he directed in 1977, to develop my ideas further), Clifford Geertz, and Sidney Mintz for their comments on various versions of part 2; Richard Price for having confidence in the manuscript and encouraging its publication by the Johns Hopkins University Press, and Jane Warth for her attentive editing; my family and my close friends Matt, Joan, Bill, Michael, and Lou, for asking me, each in his or her own way, "What was it like in Morocco?" and for bearing with me while I, at my own pace, worked out this book in part as an answer for them.

It should go without saying—but I do not think it can be said too often—my deepest debt is owed to the Faqir and through him, to his family and friends. It is a debt I cannot repay.

A Note on Transcription

In transcribing Arabic into the Latin alphabet, I have kept the general reader rather than the specialist in mind, and have used the following rules:

1. Common Arabic names and words are written in their usual Anglicized form; for example, Ali, Muhammad, Omar, Abdallah, Hassan, sheikh.

2. ʿ indicates the Arabic letter ʿain, which is a strong, voiced, guttural consonant. Where the ʿain begins a name, the first Latin letter following it has been capitalized.
   kh is pronounced as the ch in the Scottish loch and the German Aachen.
   dh, as the th in the English the.
   sh, as the sh in the English shut.
   gh, as in the guttural (not the rolled) French r in gras.
   q, as a strong, guttural, voiceless k. There is no correlate in European languages.

3. l- is the definite article, the. It often precedes proper names and, in such cases, the first letter after the l- will be capitalized or, if that first letter is an ʿain, the next letter will be a capital; for example, l-Hajj, l-ʿAribi

4. I have not distinguished between emphatic and nonemphatic consonants, or between long and short vowels.

PART ONE

A "RECORD" OF FIELDWORK

Me-ti sagte: Unsere Erfahrungen verwandeln sich meist sehr rasch in Urteile. Diese Urteile merken wir uns, aber wir meinen, es seien die Erfahrungen. Natürlich sind Urteile nicht so zuverlässig wie Erfahrungen.

Es ist eine bestimmte Technik nötig die Erfahrungen frisch zu erhalten, so dass man immerzu aus ihnen neue Urteile schöpfen kann.—Brecht, Me-Ti

[Me-ti said: Our experiences usually transform themselves very quickly into judgments. We perceive these judgments, but we think they are experiences. Of course, judgements are not as reliable as experiences.

A certain technique is necessary to keep the experiences fresh, so that we can continually derive new judgments from them.]

Prologue

My wife and I first went to Morocco in 1969, each planning to carry out research leading to a doctorate in social anthropology. We spent two months in Rabat, the capital, studying Arabic and obtaining government permission for our research, and then six months in Taroudannt, a southern Moroccan town with a population of about twenty-five thousand and the urban center of the Sous Plain. The plain, which begins in the east, where seasonal mountain streams feed the westward-flowing *Oued* Sous (Sous River), is bordered on the north by the High Atlas Mountains; on the south by the Anti-Atlas Mountains, which separate it from the Sahara Desert; and on the west by the Atlantic Ocean. We chose this region primarily because, unlike the richer northern areas of Morocco, the Sous had not been the focus of colonial interest during the period of French rule in Morocco from 1912 to 1956 and had therefore been, we supposed, less affected culturally and economically. Not coincidentally, but significant for us, European and American social scientists had so far paid the region little attention.

The Sous, whose inhabitants first converted to Islam as early as the eighth century, has long been a vital prize in the contest for political control of Morocco. On several occasions the region was the first major conquest of groups that later went on to anchor their power and establish a sultan in the larger northern cities of Marrakech, Meknes, or Fez and to rule all of Morocco, at times even including parts of Spain. The Sous appears again and again in chronicles of the times, here as a center of resistance against the northern Sultanate, there as a faithful province (Lévi-Provençal 1934, pp. 568–69). Early Arab geographers described the Sous as a fairly rich region that produced large quantities of grain, as well as grapes, lemons, pomegranates, nuts, figs, and much sugar cane (Lévi-Provençal 1934, p. 568). Prosperity, however, was not constant and was affected by the region's turbulent politics, by the ravages of the

3

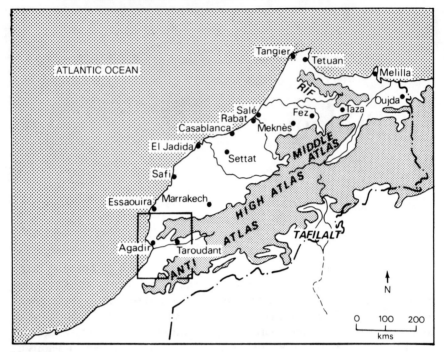

Morocco

plague and cholera (Valensi 1969, pp. 20–25), and, as always, by the climate.

There had been momentary European interest in the region already in the sixteenth century when the Portuguese attempted to establish an outpost on the coast, at Agadir. The inhabitants of the Sous, under the leadership of the Saadians who had come from farther south and established Taroudannt as their capital (the Saadians were later to rule Morocco from Marrakech), met the incursion with a *jihad,* a holy war, and drove away the Christian invaders in 1541.

Much later, in the second half of the nineteenth century, the Sous again attracted European interest, and European scientists and travelers began to note its intense commercial activity and numerous weekly markets (Gatell 1871; Foucauld 1888). At this time, the Sous was importing textiles, metals, and other European articles from Mogador (now Essaouira), exporting olive oil, argan oil, dates, and almonds northward, and exporting grains southward (Miège 1961, p. 133).

By the late nineteenth century, French interests had begun to outweigh those of the other European powers in Morocco. By the early twentieth century, after a series of agreements in which the European powers carved up most of Africa for themselves, the French had supplanted the other powers in Morocco and, through a series of economic and political maneuvers, succeeded in eroding the authority of the Mo-

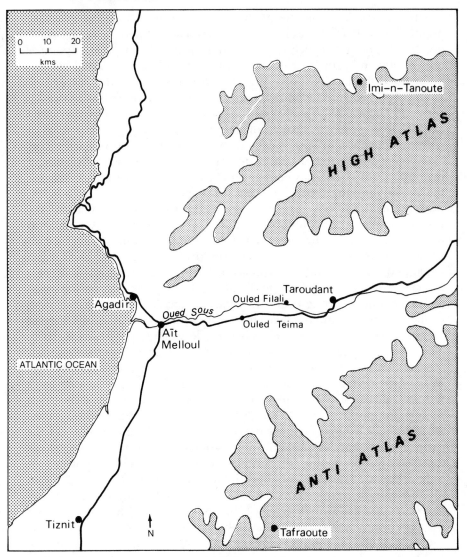

The Sous Plain

roccan sultanate. This culminated with the establishment of a French protectorate in Morocco, sealed in 1912 by the signing of the Fez Treaty.

Although the Sous Plain became fully integrated into the political structure of the protectorate within a decade, French settler and economic interest in the region remained slight throughout the protectorate period. As late as 1953, three years before Morocco regained its independence, only 128 of 5,903 colonial farms were in the southern province of Agadir, accounting for just 2 percent of the area cultivated under colonial control (Ayache 1956, p. 154).

The major inland centers of the Sous Plain are Taroudannt (whose population in 1975 was estimated at 25,000) and Ouled Teima (population 6,000), both of which depend administratively on Agadir (population 70,000 and growing rapidly). Agadir, on the plain's coastal border, maintained some importance as a port from the time of the Portuguese defeat until the construction of a port at Mogador in the mid-eighteenth century (Miège 1961, p. 143), after which it declined rapidly. Renewed growth during the last decades of the protectorate and the first years of independence was tragically halted in 1960 when a severe earthquake killed more than ten thousand people. However, substantial government investment since then has helped Agadir to grow quickly and to become the major shipping center and depot for goods imported into and exported from the Sous. Ouled Teima, known to most residents of the region as "44" (the number of kilometers between it and Agadir), was only a small village when the French made it into an important administrative center in the early years of the protectorate. Since then it has expanded steadily, and its expansion, both administratively and commercially, has enabled "44" to challenge the primacy of Taroudannt.

Taroudannt has long been the political, commercial, and population center of the Sous and the heart of activity within the region, although in recent years its preeminence has become less marked. Already in 1056, Taroudannt counted as a major step as the Almoravids expanded their control from the Saharan regions northward into Spain (Julien 1966, p. 80), and from that time onward the city clearly constituted the dominant military garrison, the richest source of fiscal revenue, and the most important population center south of Marrakech. As did the Sous region as a whole, Taroudannt also suffered from periodic epidemics and the turns of Moroccan political life and was destroyed several times, perhaps most completely in the late seventeenth century, when the armies of Sultan Moulay Isma'il killed all its inhabitants (Julien 1966, p. 229).

Taroudannt, eighty kilometers east of Agadir, was the sultanate's arm to extend control over as much of the Sous as it was able, through taxes on agricultural production, the mobilization of forced labor, and the more shameless forms of land seizure by government agents. In its own right, Taroudannt's economic importance was considerable, solidly based in extensive olive groves, a well-developed artisanry, and a saltpeter industry, as well as in its historic role as a way station for the trans-Saharan trade. Olive-growing and crafts still remain essential to the economic life of the city today.

During our six months in Taroudannt, my wife and I continued to learn Arabic and became acquainted with a number of Moroccans. Almost everyone we met during this period insisted on addressing me as "Monsieur," although I was certainly not French and was intent on speaking Arabic with them. This was true for the local officials who wanted to keep informed of my whereabouts, for the merchants whom I might meet once when buying furnishings for our apartment or whom I saw daily when buying food, for the children in the streets who, with little encouragement from me, would shout, "Bonjour monsieur, ça va monsieur?", and even for the otherwise unemployed agricultural laborer whom I specifically paid to speak to me in Arabic.

My wife intended to continue her research in Taroudannt; I planned to move to a village in the Sous Plain as soon as I had more than a rudimentary command of Arabic and some "feel" for what I thought was a "Moroccan way" of doing things. I began to ask some of the Moroccans I knew for suggestions. After visiting a number of villages, I settled on Ouled Filali for several reasons: it contained approximately one hundred households, which seemed a manageable size for an anthropologist; it was located near the riverbed of the Oued Sous, and villagers practiced both dry grain and irrigated vegetable cultivation—the region's two main agricultural methods; and the person who introduced me to the village seemed on good terms with many villagers, which I hoped would make my intrusion easier for all of us.

For the next eighteen months (during which I was disabused of many of my initial expectations) I lived in the village, returning to see my wife in Taroudannt about once a week, sometimes more, sometimes less, being given rides there by villagers I knew, according to their marketing schedule. I attempted to learn as much as I could about Ouled Filali in all its aspects, as my dissertation project required; to satisfy my narrower research proposal, I concentrated on the village economy.

The climate in the Sous Plain is Mediterranean in character, with a summer that is hot and dry and a cool winter that provides almost all the scant precipitation. The mean annual rainfall is less than that required to sustain dry-land farming, and precipitation varies greatly from year to year.[1] Farmers therefore need water sources other than rainfall, and they draw or pump water from wells, or have it brought to the land from seasonal rivers or from mountains to the north via a carefully maintained network of canals. The soils of the Sous Plain are fairly typical arid-zone brown and brown-red soils. Both are chemically rich, but the latter are richer in organic matter; neither, however, is rich in humus (Nuttonson 1961, pp. 14–15). These soils are relatively fertile, but are prey to water erosion in winter and erosion by the wind in summer.

The village of Ouled Filali is divided by one quite deep and sandy gulley into two main clusters of homes. In the western cluster lies the mosque, architecturally distinct from the one- or two-storied rectangular earthen houses only in the small protrusion on its eastern wall. In this

---

[1]Mean annual rainfall is 212 mm. (Nuttonson 1961, p. 90), placing the region in an "arid zone" category; in roughly one-third of the years, rainfall is less than 25 percent of the mean (Cote and Legras 1966, p. 23).

alcove inside the mosque, an old and respected villager leads the congregation in prayer. Outside the mosque, there is usually stacked a large pile of wood, collected from nearby forest land, which is used to heat water so that the men may wash in the anteroom, before they enter the mosque to pray.

All villagers are Muslims and subscribe to the Credo: "There is no God but God, and Muhammad is the Messenger of God." Many perform the five daily prayers, more conveniently in their homes or in the fields and usually not in the mosque. All villagers reaching puberty begin to observe the fast of the month of Ramadan, when neither food nor water may pass their lips during daylight hours. As Muslims, villagers should also give alms to the poor (methodically and systematically at harvest time, when one-tenth of the crop is set aside for the poor); and, if they possess the wherewithal, they should attempt the Pilgrimage to Mecca at least once in their lives.

Other buildings in the western part of the village include the two main stores, each little more than a small room that stocks sugar, tea, soap and other sundries. At the mosque and the stores, groups of friends congregate after work, toward sundown and the time of the fourth daily prayer. To the east of the gulley lie almost half of the village homes; a third, much smaller cluster of homes, is situated northward, a short five-minute walk away. A half-dozen dwellings are scattered outside these clusters.

Dirt roads traverse all sectors of the village, some just wide enough to permit a tractor or a pickup truck to pass, most little more than footpaths. The roads are all lined with thick and thorny gray hedges that also separate agricultural plots from one another; within the village, the hedges frequently reach higher than eye level. The plots furnish, for the most part, grains such as barley and wheat but, when the owner can irrigate them, either from a well or a canal, may provide instead a wide variety of vegetables and fruits, including gourds, tomatoes, peppers, carrots, cucumbers, and corn, as well as olives, apples, pears, and pomegranates.

The color that permeates this landscape, especially in summer, is that of the light-brown earth. Not only do the adobe houses match the soil, but as the grain crop matures, in late spring and early summer, it too turns light brown. And in mid and late summer, when strong and gusty winds blow frequently and often violently, the earthen color rises with them.

As older villagers tell it, the village was settled about two centuries ago when three men met by chance while each was searching for a place to settle. One was from the Tafilalet region and claimed descent from the Prophet Muhammad, another was from the Saharan region beyond the Anti-Atlas Mountains, and the third came from the foothills of the Anti-Atlas Mountains. Two were invited to the makeshift dwelling of the third; they got on well together and agreed to unite in their search. After some further exploration, they decided on the present site of Ouled Filali (literally, the sons of the Tafilalet region), where they found a number of houses abandoned, they assumed, as a result of a recent epidemic.

Villagers today are not all descended from the founders; in fact, fully one-third of Filali households have male ancestors who came to the village within the last eighty years. The nearby Oued Sous, in times of drought, attracts many High Atlas Berbers to the plains as seasonal laborers, primarily for the grain and olive harvests, but also as permanent settlers. Or, a young man from a slightly uplands village with no accessible water might seek work and become attached to a Filali household, marry one of the daughters, and become a full-fledged Filali. Perhaps a man from a neighboring village might marry a Filali woman and, if his new wife's rights to land far exceeded his, come to live with her family; or a man might move into the village to escape political and legal prosecution (although it is not as easy to escape now as it used to be).

Filalis, too, often move and many have been attracted to the cities of the Sous Plain, to the northern regions and, more recently, to Europe. Usually, one adult or young adult male emigrates and tries his success, and then perhaps sends for his family or simply returns home periodically when work permits. Since 1941, approximately forty Filali men have emigrated definitively; three went to France, six to neighboring villages, eighteen to Taroudannt and other regional cities, and twelve to the large cities of the north.

All who now live in the village, with the exception of those who moved there during their lifetime, clearly identify themselves as Filalis. Most refer to themselves, too, as "Houara," the name for the major tribal group living on the banks of the Oued Sous. As "Houara," they unambiguously distinguish themselves not only from other Arabic-speaking groups in Morocco, but also from the Berber speakers who populate the High Atlas Mountains to the north and the Anti-Atlas Mountains to the south.

The Houara are divided into five fractions and each of these, in turn, into subfractions; Filalis count themselves in the Ouled Sa'id fraction and the Ouled Brahim subfraction. The fraction and subfraction have little importance now, other than to provide convenient administrative groupings and, on occasion, units that are assessed a certain sum to pay for government celebrations. The Ouled Brahim and one other subfraction, which together have a population of barely ten thousand, are served by one sheikh aided by three moqaddems, all residents of the region and all directly responsible to the regional qaid, appointed by the Ministry of the Interior and with his office in "44."

Ouled Filali's population, grouped into ninety-five households and totaling 725 people, is a young one: over half are under twenty years of age and one-third are under ten. Of the almost two hundred males of working age (those who partake of the Ramadan fast and are thus approximately fourteen or older), one-third spend most of their time farming village land, usually their own land, but often in complicated partnerships, with specified portions of the crop allotted to the supplier of water, to the supplier of labor, and to the supplier of land. A little more than one-quarter work as agricultural laborers on the modern, mechanized farms that dot the region. Among the rest are merchants, craftsmen, day laborers, shepherds, workers temporarily abroad, chauffeurs, nonfarm wage laborers, and several government workers. Most families, however, also gain some revenue from their own land; only six of the ninety-five Filali households do not. (See figure 1.)

Almost all village land is clearly bounded and enclosed by hedge. Villagers exploit approximately five hundred hectares, of which slightly more than three-quarters is given over to dry grain farming, about one-seventh is irrigated from wells and primarily devoted to vegetables, fruits, corn, and pulses, and about one-fifteenth is oued land, irrigated from the oued via canals and producing mostly vegetables, corn, and some barley. Filalis own, in addition, about two hundred cows, six hundred sheep, twenty-five goats (held in other villages with free grazing land), three mules, two camels, and one show horse; many households also possess at least one donkey. Villagers own twenty-three fuel-driven irrigation pumps, as well as four tractors, three pick-up trucks, one large truck, and one flour milling machine. This wealth is distributed quite unequally: approximately 3 percent of the households control one-third of village wealth, and the poorer 50 percent, taken together, control only 6 percent.

The work of male villagers has changed noticeably over the years. (See figure 2.) In the period since 1941, the proportion of those working on village land has declined sharply, particularly in the years following independence in 1956. This decrease was mirrored, between 1956 and 1971, by an almost equal increase in the proportion of those working for wages on nearby mechanized farms, but this increase has now slowed, if not stopped. The proportion of villagers engaged in long-standing village occupations other than agriculture—trade (itinerants, market vendors, store owners) and certain crafts (carpenters, builders, curers, religious students, makers of reed mats, makers of grain storage bins, jewelers, traveling holy men)—also fluctuated, declining from 21 percent of the active male population in 1941 to about 12 percent in 1971 and back up to 15 percent in 1975; the decrease in that period is wholly attributable to a decline in the craft sector and the recent increase to greater numbers now engaged in commerce. The recent expansion in nonagricultural wage labor directly corresponds to an increase in factory

Figure 1.   Present-day (1975)
          Distribution of Labor.

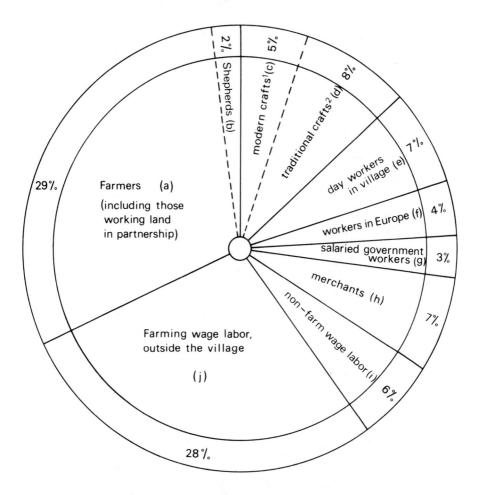

1   Modern crafts includes mechanics, chauffeurs, bicycle repairmen.

2   Traditional crafts includes carpenters, builders, religious specialists,
    makers of reed mats, grain storage bins, jewelers, etc.

labor now processing the products of large farms and to additional
people working as chauffeurs and mechanics.

  Accompanying these developments were moves toward mechanized
technology. In 1950, a well-to-do villager bought a fuel-driven grain mill
and began to mill flour from the corn and barley that villagers brought
to him. Some five years later, another villager bought the first mechan-

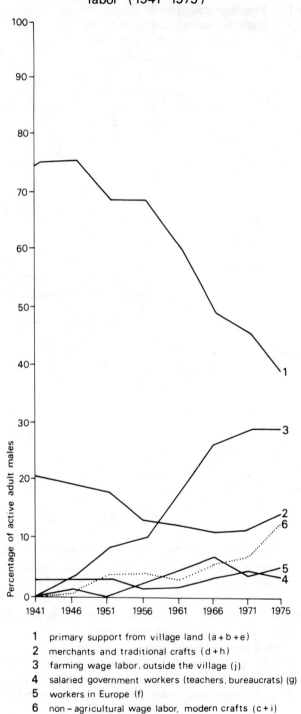

Figure 2 . Changes in the distribution of
labor (1941–1975)

1   primary support from village land (a + b + e)
2   merchants and traditional crafts (d + h)
3   farming wage labor, outside the village (j)
4   salaried government workers (teachers, bureaucrats) (g)
5   workers in Europe (f)
6   non – agricultural wage labor, modern crafts (c + i)

12

ical irrigation pump and many villagers have since followed this example. As the number of mechanical pumps increased, so did the production of vegetables for market and the need for transportation to bring the crops to market. In 1961, a Filali purchased a three-ton truck; this had to be abandoned after two years but meanwhile others began to buy pickup trucks and, then, two more large trucks. The first tractor was bought in 1965, and villagers now own three tractors.

In the course of my original research in Ouled Filali, I developed relatively close ties with perhaps a dozen villagers, a working relationship with some dozen more, a nodding or passing acquaintance with many, and a definite aversion to some. As I was getting to know people, their way of addressing me was a frequent topic of conversation and some of them obviously took pains to learn my name, a name not only unfamiliar to them but one that contained a consonantal sound, "v," unknown in Moroccan Arabic. Indeed, a leitmotif running through many of my initial meetings (and Moroccans are very fond of such leitmotifs) was a playful wager, which I almost always won, that they would not remember my name the next time we met.

Even after several years, many villagers continued to address me as "Monsieur," although some who knew me better tried the title *Fqih* (teacher, scholar), but admitted that somehow this did not fit or, as they would say, "It doesn't stick to you." Several others called me "M'allem" (craftsman, artisan), explaining that I possessed some trade, some particular skill. A few made an effort to assimilate my name to a standard Arabic one that they thought it resembled, such as Qebbor or Abdelkbir. I also heard that, behind my back, quite a few referred to me as "that Christian" or "that *Rumi*"; I later learned that some called me "spy." But Faqir Muhammad and others that I became close to gradually came to call me "Kevin" or, when they insisted on using an honorific title of some sort (a common practice in Morocco), "Si Kevin" (a term that connoted "a man of learning") or even, after they had asked for the American equivalent of "Monsieur," "Mr. Kevin."

Faqir Muhammad b. (*ibn:* son of) l-'Ayashi Sherardi's name, on the other hand, posed no problem; not for me, because I was in Morocco for the express purpose of learning such details and would carefully write them down in order not to forget them; certainly not for his compatriots, who, when he was absent, normally referred to him as "b. l-'Ayashi," and directly addressed him as "Faqir Muhammad" or, simply, "Faqir." The Faqir's father, l-'Ayashi, had been surnamed "Sherardi" (after Sherarda, his village of origin) when he first immigrated to Ouled Filali (otherwise, he might have received a name coming from some distinctive physical or character trait, or describing his occupation). He married a woman from Ouled Filali, and they named their first son Muhammad, as is common practice, in honor of the Prophet.

Muhammad b. l-'Ayashi Sherardi took the title "Faqir" when he joined a religious brotherhood in the late 1940s, as a man then in his mid-thirties. Those who take this title[2] view their membership in the brother-hood as an important step on the path to salvation. Some outside the brotherhoods, however, accuse the brotherhoods of sacrilege, believing that the privileged status claimed by the brothers is contrary to the Islamic tenet that all believers are equal before God; others, more char-itable, simply see the brotherhoods as a rather harmless distraction from more important worldly concerns.

As I spent more time in Ouled Filali, the Faqir and I frequented one another more and more and continued to enjoy one another's company. When I returned to Morocco two summers later, in 1973, I saw him more than any other villager, although I still had to visit many other villagers for research related to my dissertation. And then, in the sum-mer of 1975, I spent almost all my time in Morocco with him and his family, part of it recording the dialogues and setting down the events of the following pages.

The Faqir is now a man in his mid-sixties, and most of his life has been spent farming his land. From very humble beginnings—his mother pos-sessed only a small plot of land in the eastern village cluster and his father, an immigrant, none at all—the Faqir, together with his younger brother, Ali, labored strenuously over the years to secure the ample holdings they now possess. His is one of the few families in the village whose ascent has not depended upon some form of migration, often leading to work in Europe and access to European wealth.

The clearest symbol of the Faqir's accomplishment was his move in the mid-1950s from the village to a large plot of land he had just bought and cleared, and which was a fifteen-minute walk from the village. This gave him open space, which his mother's plot lacked, and, slowly and pains-takingly, he began to build a compound that is now quite spacious. Much of the compound is given over to animals: sheep, cows, bulls, rabbits, chickens, and, in one of the walls, bees. Otherwise, the house is divided into two parts: the *dar* (home), or family domain, where the women cook and care for the children and where most of the family eat and sleep; and the *dwiria* (little house), the guest's domain. The men spend much of their time in the dwiria, particularly when workers or guests are present. It was here, either in the courtyard of the dwiria or in the large guest room, that the Faqir and I did much of our talking and here, with some slight variations, that all of the dialogues in this book originally took place.

---

[2]The title "faqir" (literally, poor man, pauper) has its origins in the asceticism of the early Sufi mystics, of which the Moroccan brotherhoods are the indirect descendants. The title has lost much of this original meaning and now carries with it the connotation "old man," although a brotherhood member may indeed be young and still called "faqir."

The household consists of the Faqir and his brother, Ali, who is ten years younger (two sisters were born in between and both now live with their families in other villages); their wives, Fatima and Khadija; the Faqir's seven children (Mehdi, the eldest, is in his early twenties; three daughters, all younger than Mehdi, are married and now live elsewhere; a young son had died from the measles several months before I arrived in June 1975); and Ali's three children, aged one, four, and seven.

On a normal summer's day, we would all awaken with the sun, at about 6 A.M. After slowly drinking a large cup of hot corn porridge, the men (the Faqir, Ali, Mehdi, and a worker or two who might have been hired for a specific task) would set off for work in the fields. They would return before nine for breakfast, and then go back to the fields until between noon and one, depending on the heat of the day. After returning to the compound, the men would nap until lunch was ready at about three and then, once the meal had been eaten and the final glass of tea drunk, set off again for the fields. By shortly after sundown, everyone was back in the compound. We ate our evening meal after the fifth daily prayer, performed in summer at about 9:30 P.M. By eleven, the household was usually asleep for the night, although the boys might still be in the village with their friends and not return home until somewhat later.

But many days were disrupted by the need to market the crop and on those days—as often as three times a week or as rarely as none—the schedule depended on the unpredictable arrival of the pickup truck. The Faqir liked it to arrive before daybreak, allowing sufficient time to reach the marketplace and to assess the selling, but often it would not come till much later, angering the men. On some days, the crop might be transported late the previous night, some time between sundown and the early morning hours. On these days, we all had very little sleep; the Faqir, for one, was able to compensate for this somewhat by catching a few winks whenever the moment permitted.

Ali usually took charge of marketing the crops. But the Faqir often did this himself, particularly when other business required him to be at the marketplace: one day to pay taxes, another to settle an account with a debtor or creditor, another to attend a court session. The Faqir, in any event, was often away from home on such affairs. On these and similar occasions, the rest of the household would continue its normal day.

While living with the Faqir and his family during the summer of 1975, I spent much of my time setting down the events and recording the dialogues. I tried, of course, to tape the conversations without causing too much disruption in the Faqir's day. Usually, I had to seek him out, but occasionally he suggested that we talk, saying, "Well, I have a little time. What do you want to make noise about now?"

We most frequently talked after lunch, or before lunch if he did not feel like napping; sometimes in the early evening, between the prayer at sundown and the one just before supper. The dialogues proceeded undisturbed for the most part, although a couple of times the women of the house summoned him for a moment, or one of the children brought the tea utensils to us. One dialogue (in ch. 9) was interrupted and had to be continued the next day. Most of the time, the Faqir's attention was undivided, if not riveted, and his tone was definite but relaxed; during one dialogue he shaved, and he ended another, the last, by falling asleep.

An Approximate Chronology of the Faqir's Life

Date	Faqir Muhammad	Brother Ali	Village and Region	Morocco
1910	Born			
1912				Beginning of French Protectorate
1920		Born		
1922	Father dies			
1925			Beginning the rule of Qaid Bush'ib, who remains for thirty years	
1937	Begins to work on European's farm, staying three years			
1940	Tries without success to go to France.			
1941	First marriage		Rationing period begins	
1944	Divorces			
1948	Remarries Joins Tijanni brotherhood	Employed by Public Works for six months	Rationing period ends	
1949	Employed by Public Works, for three years	Marries		
1950	Buys large plot of land a short distance from the village			
1951	First child, a son, born			
1952	Leaves Public Works job Begins full-time farming			
1953	Taken to patrol in Casablanca	Divorces		Sultan (later King) Muhammad V exiled by French authorities

Date	Faqir Muhammad	Brother Ali	Village and Region	Morocco
1954		Remarries		
1955			First mechanical irrigation pump in the village	Muhammad V returns from exile
1956			Village run by its own leaders for two years (1956–58) Region has no qaid for two years (1956–58)	Morocco regains independence
1957	Family moves to land outside village Becomes village leader (*moqaddem*)			
1958	Begins to buy sheep			
1959	Buys another large field for farming			
1960			Earthquake in Agadir kills more than 10,000 people	
1961			First truck in village	Muhammad V dies; succeeded by his son, King Hassan II
1963	Mother dies		Local and national elections	
1964	Buys his first mechanical irrigation pump		First tractor in village	
1965				King Hassan II declares "state of exception" Opposition leader Ben Barka kidnapped and disappears in Paris
1967	Second mechanical irrigation pump			
1968	Leaves moqaddem position	First child, a son, born		
1970	My first visit to Ouled Filali, and to the Faqir and his family. I stay eighteen months.			
1971	I leave Ouled Filali			Assassination attempt on King Hassan
1972				Another assassination attempt
1973	I visit the Faqir and family for one month during the summer			
1974	Marriage of his daughter Zahara Death of his young son			
1975	I visit for two months during the summer			Fall: the "Green March" and the outbreak of war in the Western Sahara

Cast of Characters

1. The Faqir's Family

A. Faqir Muhammad b. l-ʿAyashi Sherardi

Fatima: his wife

Mehdi: the eldest son, now in his early twenties; works on the family land

Khadija, ʿAisha: two daughters, married and living in other villages

Zahara: a recently married daughter, living with her husband and his family in the Medina

Habiba: a fourteen-year-old daughter; often works on the family land

l-ʿAribi (diminutive of l-ʿArbi): a twelve-year-old son; works most of the time as the family's shepherd, and some time working on the family land

Mbiriku (diminutive of Mbaraka): a nine-year-old daughter

Kbibir (diminutive of Abdelkbir), Hmida (diminutive of Hmed), l-ʿAwiwish (diminutive of l-ʿAyashi): three young sons

Hisen (diminutive of Hsen): a young son who had recently died.

B. Ali: The Faqir's younger brother, now in his early fifties; works on the family land

Khadija: his wife

Hmida: his eldest son, age seven

Muhammad, Fatima: two younger children

2. Villagers

b. Sadiq: eighty years old, now inactive due to ill health; a Tijanni brother and close neighbor of the Faqir

bu Ruwwis: in his late fifties, a Tijanni brother, and seller of dates, figs, and nuts in regional markets

Faqir Hmed: almost fifty, and formerly a regular worker for the Fa-

19

qir; now works his own land in the village and does occasional jobs
for others (see ch. 7)

Hajj Hmed: old, very respected; went on the Pilgrimage to Mecca
before World War II; now oversees the village mosque

Hashim: in his mid-thirties; owner of one of the two successful village
stores; a frequent party-goer who loves to have a good time (see
ch. 10)

Hassan: in his late forties; has worked in France and now farms his
own land

Qebbor: a tea and sugar merchant in regional markets; in his early
fifties, and a very good friend of the Faqir's brother, Ali; extremely tall, robust, and lively

Sessy: an important figure in the village during the colonial period,
when he was the village leader (*moqaddem*) and inspired much
resentment; he is quite old now, and the hostility he generated
earlier has turned against him

Sessy b. Muhammad: old, infirm, nearly blind; a Tijanni brother.

Si Hassan: wealthy, about sixty years old; takes part in many of the
same social gatherings as the Faqir.

Saleh: thirty years old; once worked in France (see ch. 4)

3. Outsiders

A. Bukhensha: living in the Medina, he is the father of the Faqir's
daughter Zahara's husband (see ch. 8); he introduced me to the
Faqir in 1970

Muhammad b. Bukhensha: the Faqir's daughter Zahara's husband

Fatima: Bukhensha's wife

Mehjuba, 'Aisha: Bukhensha's two daughters

B. Others

Sidi Ali: a leader of the Tijanni religious brotherhood (see ch. 2)

Sheikh: an impressive man, in his mid-fifties; an important local
official and a good friend of the Faqir (see ch. 9)

Tahami: a man from another region who occasionally worked for
the Faqir (see ch. 6)

1

The First Dialogue

⊞ RESEARCH TASKS IN QUESTION

I arrived in Morocco in June 1975 with no specific research task planned. I suspected that a clear research project, designed to respond to current theoretical concerns in anthropology, would tend to suppress and severely distort the spontaneity and normal behavior of people I encountered, forcing them to fit into categories, modes, and aspects defined by the project. In particular, I had no intention to construct a "life history," an informant's "autobiography." I simply wanted to spend the summer with people I cared about and who seemed to care about me.

Several issues had perplexed me ever since 1971, when I first realized that my relationship with the Faqir had become important to both of us in a way that went beyond what were then the needs of my research. I wondered, first of all, what made this relationship important to both of us; what was the relationship between the Faqir, a Moroccan villager, and me, a New Yorker, built upon? Second, what significance did this relationship have for the practice of anthropology? After all, the relationship was born within the context of an anthropology that takes the encounter between individuals of different societies as its primary research tool, yet this relationship had had no explicit place in my dissertation nor, as far as I could see, any easy position in the genres other anthropologists had written in. Finally, I was dismayed that, with so much of my relationship with the Faqir expressed verbally, my written notes captured it so inadequately and most of it was quickly lost as my memory of it faded; and that, unlike other people I felt close to, the disruption imposed by long periods of absence could not be partially relieved by letter writing (except of the most rudimentary sort, because the Faqir is illiterate).[1]

---

[1] The Faqir felt this disruption too, although in a manner different from mine. There is some discussion of this in the dialogue in chapter 11.

With little more than these thoughts, poorly articulated, in the back of my mind, I thought I would try to record talks with the Faqir on tape, something we had not done much during my earlier visits to Morocco. For the first talk, I had no definite subject in mind, nor was I certain that either of us would have any desire to talk into a tape recorder again. I prepared only two specific questions (in "What do you think about . . . ?"), but also noted in key words a number of broad subjects that I intended to ask about in a vaguely chronological order (in "Work . . . marriages . . . Colonial period . . .).

✳ FIRST DIALOGUE

WHAT DO YOU THINK ABOUT . . . ?

Faqir, you spend a lot of time working out in the fields. What do you think about while you're working?[2]

I look at what I'm working at, and I'm concerned about what will come from it. Let's say that I'm beginning the plowing. You know, I'd like to see the crop come up well—corn, or barley, or farina, or gourds. I'd hope there would be enough of it to eat a bit in our home and to sell a bit, in order to be able to buy sugar.

In earlier times, you know, there wasn't the kind of work outside the homestead that there is today. Now, if you can send one son to work on the farms,[3] he'll bring back sugar, or he'll bring back soap, or something that he's bought for his wage. But in those times there was nothing outside of our own cultivation. Nothing. You'd have to get sugar from that, and soap, and clothes. You'd have to get a living from it—everything. All the men who were living in the house at that time would work in their fields or be shepherds. In the early years, there was no outside work on the farms. And even if you worked for someone else in the village, your pay was just the food for your stomach: work was paid cheaply.

If you think about your life, what do you see as important in it?

Well . . . [the Faqir paused] . . . I have a lot of thoughts. And during my life, every year, new thoughts, new ideas come to me: this is a question of

---

[2]This question and the following one are both general questions (I did not even ask, "What were you thinking about today?") and as such are symptoms of my lack of a clear topic for the dialogue. On the other hand, they illustrate two dominant interests of mine that motivate many of the questions occurring in this and ensuing dialogues: the importance I attach to "everyday" matters and to the Faqir's thoughts, rather than to what might be termed the "exotic" and empirical detail.

[3]I use *farms* to translate the Faqir's word *firma*, which always refers to large, relatively modern and mechanized agricultural enterprises. These were initiated in the region by Europeans during the period between the two world wars, and their number and size grew quickly after World War II. Most have by now come under Moroccan control.

age. But what is important to me now is the situation we are in now, the times that we are living in now.

What is important to you about this?

What's important is: I'm concerned that, after knocking myself out over work, I can get enough to eat. And, wait a second, there is more. I don't want to run around and eat out in the wilds; I hope not to steal, or to get into fights, or to cause the smallest problem. I hope to work as I am able, to sit on the ground and eat what God provides, as I am able; to be free, not owing anyone anything; and to be far away from places where there are arguments. And that if I have something to say, I will settle upon my words at home, before I go outside, and will not enter into a dispute with anyone.

There was a time, earlier in my life, when my only concern was to take what I made into the wilds. That is, eating at home gave me no joy: I enjoyed only those things that can be done outside, in other places, in places that aren't proper. What I ate in our home was no fun at all.

Did you have these thoughts when you were a boy?

No. When I was a boy, I had neither these thoughts nor the others. I didn't think about enjoyment on the outside, or about enjoyment in the home. I only thought about what I'd eat and what I'd wear.

And when did you begin to have those wayward thoughts?

When I reached the age of fasting, when I was fourteen or fifteen years old.[4] Then I began to think only of taking what I had to the wilds. Only that I be really good-looking, better than everyone else; and tougher than everyone else; and a bigger operator than everyone else. I hoped for all that. But I didn't work at this seriously. Most of my running around was a waste, it just passed. But then, I didn't have the thoughts I have now.

WORK... MARRIAGES... COLONIAL PERIOD...

When you began to fast, what kind of work were you doing?

Always in our own farming, for our house. You know, I never worked for someone in the village, unless I worked his land in partnership, or contracted for a special task. I never asked for day labor. When I worked for them, I was still free: when the work was finished, he and I would split up.

I did work for a time outside of our farming, on the first European farm that was set up in our region, that of Monsieur Friks. He came from Belgium and was sent here by some company. I worked for him for about three years and at the same time I worked on our own farming. My job was to dig the ditches for the orange trees.

---

[4]The Faqir is referring to the religious fast from sunrise to sunset that lasts throughout the month of Ramadan.

When was this?

Oh, about five years before the rationing period.[5]

What was this Friks like?

Friks, all in all, was all right. But he was a tough one!

How so?

Well, if he had dealt with you and had turned to go, he would never turn back, he would go straight ahead. And he would never glance sideways as do other Christians, or as the Arabs do: when he wanted to look sideways he would turn his whole body. And if he happened to pass you by, you had to run after him until you got in front of him: he'd never turn around. And if he said anything to you at all, don't answer him back, don't say, "No." Don't say, "It's not like that." Just say, "Good, fine." And do what he told you.

His wife was a crafty one. She'd turn around, come and bend down with the boys, look at the workers. She was crafty, his wife. But not Friks.

Why did you stop working for Friks?

Well, I left because my own farming was suffering and I had to return to it. At that time, you know, I only planted barley or corn. If I wanted to sow corn, for example, I'd have to wait until Saturday—we were off from the work on the farm Saturdays—and I'd have to ask for Friday off in order to do the plowing. And when it was my turn to irrigate my land from the canals, I'd have to ask for the day off in order to irrigate.

You didn't cultivate vegetables then?

I couldn't because the work on the farm kept me away, it didn't allow me the time to do vegetables.

Couldn't your brother have helped you?

He was too young, about Hmida's age [Hmida, the oldest son of the Faqir's brother, Ali, was about seven years old].[6] There was only me and my two sisters, and my mother.

You were still living in the village at that time, weren't you?

Yes, we lived on our family land in the village. I was born there, and, when I was small, we went to live for about two years in another village. I don't remember that at all. Then we came back here, and my father died just then. After our father died, we remained in the village a long time, until independence, when we moved here.[7]

After your father died, who took care of the house?

[5]The rationing period began during World War II and ended some six years later, in 1948. Most Moroccans in the Sous Plain refer to this period as *l-bo*, from the French word *bon*, meaning rationing coupon.

[6]From other information, Ali was probably slightly older, perhaps from ten to thirteen years old, at the time the Faqir worked on the Friks farm, between 1936 and 1939.

[7]Shortly after independence, which villagers associate with the return of the exiled King Muhammad V to Morocco on 18 November 1955, the Faqir's family moved to a home they had built on a large plot of land about a fifteen-minute walk from the village.

I did. My mother would tell me what to do and I'd go and do it. I'd go to market to sell clarified butter and I'd carry it in my cupped hands like this. I wouldn't even go on a donkey.

Didn't your mother or anyone else help in the farming?

No, I was the one who did the farming. I'd struggle with a pair of cows for the plowing when I was just l-'Aribi's age [one of the Faqir's sons, age twelve]. Even that small, I'd struggle with them. My mother would just tell me, "Go there," or "Do this" or "Do that". And I couldn't tolerate that at all, that she would direct me. Even at l-'Aribi's age, I couldn't stand that. So I did what I wanted, myself.

Then too, I'd deal with outsiders. I'd work their land in partnership, and if guests came to visit I'd host them myself. And when taxes were due, I'd go to friends of my father to borrow. I'd say to them, "Let me have some money to pay the tax," and they'd give me money. When it was due, I'd pay it back. And if I had a calf to sell, I'd take it to market and I'd ask someone to help me drive it there. But I'd sell it myself, alone. They'd try to get the better of me and I'd try to get the better of them. That's how things were until I grew up and things settled down.

And you hadn't yet married?

No, not yet. After I got back from working on that European farm, I farmed here for a while, and then the rationing period came. As that started, I got married.

Whom did you marry?

A woman from the Medina,[8] from the neighborhood of the Grand Mosque.

How did you get to know her?

You know how! It was during those wayward years that we were talking about before. Well, for a long time before that I had been wasting my time; and then I had gotten to know this woman in the Medina. But I didn't want to get married and I was getting sick and tired of running around. I didn't know what to do.

So I said, "Let me try to go to work in Bordeaux." I went to Rabat, but with no luck. The war with Germany had just started, and they stopped taking people to Bordeaux to work. So I came back here, absolutely broke. I had nothing. And nothing to do. Nothing, nothing, nothing. When I got back here the corn hadn't yet been sowed, so I sowed it, and began to work at settling down a bit. I usually managed to get together enough money for sugar; if not, I didn't drink tea at all.

How did you make that money?

Well, I'd get some by selling a bit of clarified butter from the cow, or a bit of argan oil, or some argan nutshells. Or I'd sell grass feed in the

---

[8]Most villagers refer to Taroudannt simply as the *Medina*, the Arabic word for *city*. I have followed their usage throughout.

markets. And I'd bring back a bit of sugar with that. As for food, I'd bring it in from the farming. And then, I got married.

Why did you get married then?

Well, I said to myself, "It's not good for this fooling around to go on much longer." I was beginning to get some sense. And my mind had been divided between here and the Medina, my head was too heavy, it wasn't in harmony. So I said, "I'll bring here what is holding my mind in the Medina."

So you brought the woman here. How long did she stay?

For three years.

And there were no children?

No. No children. She stayed here for three years, and it came to nothing. And I divorced her.

Why did you divorce her?

We fought.

About what?

A lot. A lot. [The Faqir's responses were terse, and he seemed very pensive.]

About something specific?

She wasn't happy, she wasn't happy at all. She would say that she didn't like it here and I couldn't accept that.

Was she a Medina woman originally?

Yes, she was a Medina woman—she didn't speak Berber. She was born in the Medina and died in the Medina, that's all.

Did she take to the work out here?

She took to the work and knew it all; but it didn't go easily with her. And we say, "What is built without foundation, falls."

What does that mean?

Well... a marriage without good roots is no good. You know, our acquaintance wasn't made in the right way, it was made in the street. We got to know each other the wrong way. It wasn't nice, not nice at all.

So your mother didn't know this woman?

No, my family didn't know about her until I told them, until I told them that I wanted to bring her home. But, in fact, they had known something, they had suspected something. They had asked me about it until they tired of it. And I kept saying, "There is no one. I don't know anyone." Well, this thing was dragging on, and they told me that if I really needed that woman, that I must bring her home. They saw that the noise in my head was too much. So I went and brought her here.

What do you mean, "The noise was too much"?

They'd say, "You have something outside," and I'd say, "Nothing. I don't know anyone." And they'd say, "What's the matter with you? If you've gotten to know someone, bring her here. We'll all partake of what

God has given." So that I wouldn't leave work undone, or take everything and spend it in the wilds. And so that there would be children, and that my mind would be centered on the home. Well, when they spoke to me in this way, I thought things over. I saw that there was no way for me to let the woman go, no way to break up with her. So I married her.

You know, we had been together for three years, she and I. And I found her good, she had taken root in me. She didn't hold herself back from me, she didn't cheat on me, and she was very fond of me. For a time, I was looking for a way to break with her but I couldn't find one. I was looking for a reason to let her go, for some defect in her, but I couldn't find one. She was fine. She would do whatever I'd tell her, and she was very fond of me. That's why she stuck in my mind.

Perhaps she had put a spell on you?[9]

Perhaps. You don't know, one can't know that. The most powerful spell is one that works on your will. If the woman is insolent and does sorcery that's a different thing. But the real spell is one that works on the will.

So this woman said to me, "Wherever you tell me to go, I'll go." And she left her family, and came to us here. That is what I desired. I was tired of getting nowhere, of having nothing for her. You know, I would go to her broke, with nothing, and she would bring food for us from her family's house.

And she was very fond of you?

Very much, much more than is usual. We were entangled, tied together, that's all. Just as you and I are tied together now. That's it. I couldn't break with you, I couldn't say, "Get out, you American. Out of the way!" I couldn't do that, now. I couldn't, even if I were to die.

So much the better.

Well, you know we're not lying, by God. You and I have partaken of so much, so much. It is now inscribed, with God.

Well, that's the reason.

When you married, whom did you live with?

With my mother, and my brother and sisters; and with the family of my mother's brother. Our family was together then, on our land in the village. But each had its own hearth.[10]

Did your wife get on well with your mother?

Yes.

---

[9]Without intending to, I had phrased this question so that I appear to accept the effectiveness of witchcraft and spells.

[10]The Moroccan term *kanun* (hearth) indicates both the earthenware hearth over which food is cooked, and the group of people served from one collection of cookware. By extension, *kanun* may also refer to all family members who compose one economic unit and whose resources are shared, even if they do not strictly cook and eat together.

Did they fight at all?

Yes, a bit, she and my mother fought a bit. My mother would say to me, "No children. There are no children." And I was worrying, I too was worrying that my life was going by and that there were no children. I was worried about that and my wife probably overheard something. She understood what was meant and she probably said to herself, "There are no children, and these people perhaps don't want me here any more." Then she said to me, "Take me home." And I took her home.

So she wasn't happy here?

No, not with those words that she had heard. She was happy—wherever I was, she could be happy. But she understood that because there were no children, people would be disrespectful toward her.

Were you of the same opinion, that you should bring her back to her house?

Well, if the commotion was going to continue, then I had to take her away. If it had quieted down, I wouldn't have taken her away. But with all the disturbance—it was too much.

What was on your mind at that moment?

When the noise became too much, I thought, "Enough, I'll take her home." And the first time, we had gotten as far along the road as that first riverbed when she said, "Let's return. I don't want to leave. I want to go back with you." And I brought her back to my home.

Then, a second time, I took her away. This time, just as we reached the city walls, she kissed my head: "Don't tell my father or mother. Just tell them that we've come to see them." I went and bought some sugar, and we went to visit them. Just as you have come to us now. And we didn't say anything. My head was turning this way and that. Anyway, we kept quiet and stayed with them two or three days, and her family gave us corn flour and a container of olive oil, and they slaughtered a chicken for us. Then we came back here.

And then, about five months later, I brought her to her house again, just the same way. And again she changed her mind and kissed the top of my head: "Don't tell them anything, please." Again we stayed two or three days and came back here.

The final time—wait, I forgot something. On that occasion I just mentioned, after she had gone out of her house, I returned to her father. I said to him: "You shouldn't think that when we visited you months ago, we visited you freely. We came for this reason and for that. But when we got here, your daughter pleaded with me. We didn't want to ruin your pleasure, and we kept quiet, and went back to our land. Now, again, we have not come to you freely."

What did her father say, God rest his soul? He said to me, "My son." I answered, "Yes?" He said: "That day, no one brought you two together, you got to know one another yourselves. And now, she is my only daughter, and I love her very much. I couldn't hit her. She is now grown up, and she no longer fears me. If you decide to continue together, the two of you, thank God and God bless you. If you no longer have the same good humor as you had in those days, then split up. But you mustn't think that you are no longer welcome here. Believe that you are my son and she is my daughter. If you take her, you are always welcome here; if you don't take her, you are always welcome here. Now go and come to an agreement, or else separate." That was the second time.

Finally, the third time, I just brought her into their house, and I ran away. I beat it and came back here, and that was that.

Did you ever return to their house after that?

I never went there again. After I came back here, I sold some sheep in order to get the one thousand two hundred rials for the dowry;[11] one thousand two hundred rials at that time was difficult. I sold the sheep and went to her mother's sister's son. I said to him, "Listen friend, you must go to this woman and tell her that we have to meet at the scribe's."

Why didn't you go to her house to tell her?

I didn't want to embarrass her father. For her father had told me: "If you stay together, you should have only the best; but if she wants to separate, I can't force her to stay. If you separate, whenever you want to come here, you're welcome." So her mother's sister's son went for her, and we met at the scribe's.

The scribe asked her, "Does this man owe you anything; has he taken anything that was yours?" Because she had brought some things to our house from her first marriage—a light rug, one heavy rug, a brass kettle and brazier, and a table. The scribe said to her, "Hasn't he taken anything from you?" She said "No." He said, "Does he owe you anything?" She told him, "No." He said, "You're not carrying a child?" She said, "No." He said, "Well, do you two want a divorce now?" And she said, "Well, sir, that's what he wants." That's what she said. And he said, "Here's your money."

Was she actually in agreement about the divorce?

She had to, of necessity. But she could no longer speak. She began to cry.

Didn't she say anything?

What could she say? Could she say, "I want him against his will?" Well, when we split up there, I gave her that dowry of 1,200 rials, she was given her divorce paper, and that was that.

I came home, and I remained unmarried for about four years.

---

[11]The dowry is a sum of money settled upon by the fathers of the spouses when the marriage contract is drawn up. This sum must be given to the bride's family by the groom's in the event the couple divorces. (See ch. 8 for further discussion.)

The Moroccan currency system is based on the dirham, which is divided into one hundred francs. In common speech, the unit of account is the rial, which is equal to five francs, although the rial is not recognized officially in currency terminology. Between 1969 and 1975, the official exchange rate for one dirham varied between twenty and twenty-five cents U.S. One rial was therefore worth between one and one and one-quarter cents U.S.

Did you think about her afterwards?

Yes. I still think about her. It's painful, it's painful. For three years, perhaps four, I remained unmarried.

Did you see her at all after the divorce?

No, not until about two years later. Then, when we'd see one another in the marketplace, she'd come and greet me, or I'd greet her. Anyway, after those four years, I got married again.

Did she marry again too?

No, she didn't marry again. She did nothing. She stayed until I got married again and then she died, just then. I had just been remarried for three months or so when she died.

During those four years when you were single, did you associate much with your friends in the village?

I had friends, but I cut them off, cut them all off. There was all that ill will during the rationing period, and then I had that unhappiness from the divorce. I cut down on everything. For two years, I couldn't even bear talking to people. For two years. I'd go down to do my farming, early in the morning, and I'd come back at sunset. I'd see no one and no one would see me.

After that divorce, it was exile! There was misery from one direction, for at that time there wasn't a good crop, and that separation from the other. I was in anger. For two years, I couldn't stand talking to anyone. I don't know whether it was a spell, as you said, I don't know. I was like an animal, I didn't want people, no one at all. No one at all.

What did you work at during those years?

Farming, that's all. Just farming. I grew some vegetables, a bit of watermelon, some gourds, corn, and fava beans. We'd substitute the fava beans for the corn sometimes, because they gave a high yield and we'd sell them, not eat them much at all. And I'd sell clarified butter and argan oil.

But you didn't have much land then?

I had some of my own, and I worked some parcels of others.

When did you begin to think of marrying again?

Three years went by and then, during the next year, I was looking to get married. How did I look?[12] I said, "All that has gone before was worth nothing. What I need . . .

What had been worth nothing?

All that noise, all that waste, that wild life. I needed, for myself, to become humble, to make do with what is here. And to marry someone humble. That is how I saw things then. And by then my sister had married, and her husband had a sister, and I married her.

So, before getting married that second time, you thought you wanted a woman who

---

[12]The Faqir, here, was anticipating what he thought would be my next question.

who was, you know, of a small mind, without the build or the style of a city woman. You know the type. She should be a country woman and humble like us. This one was an orphan; her father was dead and so was mine. Well, those were the reasons. And I said to myself, "This way, I'll be in peace."

When you were a married man, did you used to gather with other villagers?

No, very rarely, and only with those I knew well. I didn't hang around with street friends. I was married and they weren't, so I didn't go around with them. Once I got married, I didn't sit around with people.

You didn't go to parties?

No. If there was a general village party, to which everyone went, all right. But special parties, like those with peers—no, nothing. I stayed out of friendship circles.[13]

When you did get together with your friends, in those times, what did you talk about?

Well, we'd talk about what so-and-so did, or we'd joke around; and we'd drink tea, that's all. Like the gatherings of Qebbor.[14]

Did you talk about colonialism, or about France?

No. We didn't comprehend "colonialsm" then or know much about the French. And we couldn't say either, "Frenchmen" or "colonialism." Nothing.

You couldn't say the words?

No, never, Words about the government couldn't be said. Someone might hear you and that would mean punishment. And the government kept us busy with work; we'd have to work fifteen days, and then again four days, each year. Then, right after the war with Germany, they began to work us fifteen days every two months. And there was always work to be done for the qaid.[15] Whenever they found you, whenever

---

[13]In addition to celebrations marking significant stages in the life cycle (e.g., circumcisions and weddings) and those associated with important religious events (such as the traditional Muslim feast of 'id l-Kbir, or the festivals of local saints), there are two other sorts of party within the village: village-wide parties (*rma'*), which used to be held at least once a year but are now held very occasionally, less than once a year, at no set time; and small, weekly gatherings (*zerda*) of a small circle of friends, consisting of between five and ten people, not all of whom need be villagers. At the weekly gatherings, each friend takes his turn hosting and providing the food and refreshment.

[14]A villager whose parties I regularly went to.

[15]The major officials in the present local administrative system are the qaid, the sheikh, and the moqaddem. The qaid, appointed by the Moroccan Ministry of the Interior and generally not a native of the region, is the highest official to whom villagers have direct access. Sheikhs, several of whom serve under each qaid, are appointed by the qaid in consultation with important local figures and with the inhabitants. Moqaddems are of two sorts: those who work directly under the authority of the sheikh and are chosen by him and do his bidding; and those who are informally chosen by the people in each village to lead them, and whose functions are essentially social.

In the colonial period and well into the independence period too, the qaid's word was

you went out on the road, the sheikh might find you and say to you, "Get wood and bring it to the qaid's house," or "Get some grass feed to the qaid's."

And was that work paid for?

Never. Whenever they found you—it could be today and then again tomorrow—you were never given anything, except some punishment perhaps. I'd just try to stay near the house and do my own work. Trouble came from every direction.

What was the rule of the qaid like in those days?[16]

In the beginning it was good—he would judge with the Law. You'd say to him, "Rule over me by God and by Islamic Law," and he'd clout you and tell you, "I am myself the Law." He would judge then and there, and if you owed a rial you'd pay it right then. Or go to prison until you paid. None of this shilly-shallying. No delaying, not even one hour. The money, or prison.

And the Qaid Bush'ib would look at the guy from afar and know what was in his head. If he didn't see this at first, he'd say, "Go back and return to me again." When the guy would return to him he'd know what was in his head. Sometimes the qaid would put his hand on the fellow's and from that know what was in his head. Amazing work there.

So, he ruled alone?

He ruled alone, for thirty years. From the time I was l-'Aribi's age [about twelve]. Toward the end, just before independence, the French control officer was with him. And for a while, earlier, a captain, a fellow of Jewish origin.

Was that fellow actually a Jew?

He had been a Jew, but he had become French. He was a shrewd one, very shrewd. Whenever he thought the sheikhs were giving him problems, he would remind them, "Listen, sheikhs. You know that the Qaid Bush'ib and I are holding the cow by the horns for you, and that you are milking it." That is, "We're holding the government and you're taking turns milking it." He had some manner! He was short, very very short, too.

In any event, when that French control officer came on the scene, the qaid began to grab for money. In his early days, he'd never take money, and he'd be concerned for the poor people—he was Number One. But

---

law, the sheikh's power considerable, and the moqaddem's importance in the village very substantial, both socially and politically. The force of each of these positions has become somewhat weaker in recent years, although the qaid still wields great power.

[16]We were talking about Qaid Bush'ib, who was the dominant political figure in the region throughout the colonial period. Bush'ib became qaid in the mid-1920s and remained in the post until the last days of colonial rule, in 1955. For those adults who remember the colonial period, their memory of it is intimately tied to the rule of this single individual. (See also ch.4.)

toward the end, when the control officer ruled with him, when his command was divided, it was as though the government no longer had faith in him, as though he no longer had its confidence. So he began to grab for money. And then, too, the nationalist movement was clearing the terrain.

What was the nationalist movement about?

Morocco began to make noise, to have organizations. People began to get together at night: "Let's get so-and-so. We want to do this. We want to speak for ourselves. We want to be free." It was concerned with freedom, and it had been going on for a long time before we found out about it, for twenty-six years before independence. Part of the movement was here, part in Casablanca, part in every region. But it was led from Casablanca. And whenever anyone in it was discovered, they were arrested, or killed, or beaten.

Wait, let's go back a bit, to your second marriage.[17] *How did that wedding proceed?*

We registered it, but we had no big celebration, no entertainment. We were poor and weak and, besides, all that celebration serves no purpose. We say that only those with no sense do it, that it is worth nothing. That boisterousness, those amusements, we say it's sinful.[18] And also, we were poor.

And when did you begin to have children?

About a year and a half or two years later. I was concerned. And I was very happy to have children, and my mother was very happy. The first was a daughter who died. Then came Mehdi, who is the oldest of all. Then my daughter who is married here in the village. Between each of them was about one and a half years.

This was right after the rationing period ended. What was life like during the rationing period?

Things were pretty tough, tough with respect to food, and sugar, and clothes. *Gar nichts,*[19] nothing. No clothing materials at all! We'd wear that coarse wool, and the women would wear that and all kinds of rags. No materials, none at all.

---

[17] I wanted to return to a proper chronology; I was perhaps wrong to be unhappy with the conversation but, at that moment, it seemed too formless to me.

[18] Later that summer, I learned that the Faqir had clashed with the family of his daughter's husband on just this issue: the degree of ostentatiousness of his daughter's wedding (see ch. 8). Did his remarks here reflect that dispute?

[19] The Faqir had only very few non-Arabic words that he saw as such in his vocabulary. These included (from the French): *Je m'en fous* (I don't give a damn), *fatigué* (tired), *fou* (crazy), *toujours* (always), and *non* (no). There were many other words that, although borrowed from European languages (primarily French and Spanish), had been fully integrated into Moroccan Arabic. I have kept the former in their foreign form but have translated the latter into English. How the Faqir came to know the German term *gar nichts* (nothing at all) is a question I never asked.

And how was it otherwise?

As for food: we'd get sugar, sometimes half a kilo a month, sometimes three-fourths; sometimes, if there was a lot, one kilo. Per head. But the merchants would always make off with some of that. And we'd get a bit of tea, leftovers. And soap, one or two soap bars, from month to month. And we had a book that would be punched every month. Grains were scarce, too. Scarce. Sometimes a small bit of wheat was given out, but rarely. Food was really lousy, it was no good at all.

What were your thoughts during this time?

What was I thinking? I was thinking... like now, you know, with the Sahara. The Sahara problem has made tea more expensive for us.[20] Then, I was saying, "Let God settle things over there in Europe so that we can have our things here." That's what I said.

Things were tough, much worse than now. Now, everything can be had, but then times were tough. With the black market then, a sugar cone would cost a thousand francs, a thousand francs at a time when there was no money around. That's one hundred rials a kilo, twenty rials for 100 grams. And a man would watch over his sugar, hoard it until he had 100 grams, and then he'd bring it to provide drink for ten or twelve people. Today, with 150 grams, we provide drink for just one. There was even a time when instead of sugar, we used dates. We'd drink tea, and suck on a date instead of using sugar. Then dates got expensive and everybody began to try and deal in dates. I did that for a while, too.

Did you make any profit from it?

What I made I drank up. It passed quickly. For about a year, people were using dates with tea. It was tasteless.

Well, things went that way for a while, until my brother had grown up a bit. Then he began to sell feed grass for us, and I began to do a lot of farming, on my mother's brother's plots. I'd work three or four of his gardens. I had four donkeys and, at the time of the crop, I'd sell gourds, watermelons, and so on.

And when did your brother get married?

He got married... about two years after the rationing period ended, to the daughter of my mother's brother.

Was it your brother who said to you, "I want to get married."?

No, it was my mother and I who said to him, "You must get married." He said, "All right." We told him, "Your mother's brother's daughter."

[20]The Western Sahara was still under the control of the Spanish in Summer 1975. In the fall of 1975, as the Spanish departed, King Hassan II and the Moroccan government organized the "Green March," in which several hundred thousand Moroccans marched into the Western Sahara to claim it, or reclaim it (depending on one's point of view) for Morocco. The area is now claimed by both Morocco and the Polisario Front; the latter seeks recognition for an independent state.

And he said, "All right." Then, we were just he and I, and my mother, and the two women. My two sisters had already married by then.

Your brother divorced his first wife. How did that come about?

After a while, they no longer got on together. And her mother came and told her, "Don't knuckle under to them. Your father has a lot and can support you." That is, "Don't work hard for them, don't get upset." My brother heard this and told her, "Get out, I don't want to see you. Go to your father if he has so much." And she left.

I went to my brother and I told him, "You must take her back." But he said, "No, I'm not taking her back. Never, never." So I left it.

And after your sisters married, did you often go to visit them?

Of course.

When you saw them, did you ask them . . .

No, I don't ask. I don't question them. But when I see them, I say, "How are you. Is everything well?" That's all, that's it. Even with my daughter now, I don't question her at all.[21]

Why don't you?

It would be shameful. What would I ask her? I've nothing to say to her.

But, I mean, if you were concerned about her, might you ask her whether she was happy in her new home, or whether they were treating her well?

No. "Hello, how are you?", that's all. She'd say nothing but that, and I'd say nothing else to her.

And to her mother? Would she be embarrassed in front of her mother?

Her mother can question her. She will tell things to her mother. To me, no. I couldn't ask her.

That's enough. That's all now.

[21]The Faqir was referring to his daughter Zahara, who recently married and now lived in the Medina (see ch. 8).

2

A Meeting
of the Religious
Brotherhood

One Friday morning in mid-June, the Faqir asked me to go outside the compound, to greet someone sitting in the shade of the pear trees. I recognized Sidi Ali immediately from a distance: I had met him only once before, but he was very corpulent and not easily forgotten.

Sidi Ali was the second son of a man who had been the regional leader of the Tijanni religious brotherhood.[1] Many years earlier, Sidi Ali's father had emigrated from Fez, where the brotherhood's central lodge is located, where its largest library is housed, and where pilgrims assemble annually at the tomb of the founding saint, Hmed al-Tijanni. His father established a Tijanni lodge in Taroudannt. Upon his death, the mantle of Tijanni leadership in the Taroudannt region passed to the eldest son, and Sidi Ali moved to Marrakech, where he married and now lives. There, he has no position in the Tijanni hierarchy.

Sidi Ali has not allowed his regional brotherhood ties to lapse, but actively renews them twice each year when he returns to the southern plains to visit Tijanni brothers: he travels from village to village, spending a day or two in the homes of the more generous faqirs, and accepting as his due whatever alms they offer him. He used to make these rounds on a donkey or mule, but now he is more often relayed from one brother's motorcycle to another's pickup truck to another's tractor. His round ends in the Medina, where he spends some weeks with his brother's

---

[1]The Tijanni are one of a number of Moroccan religious brotherhoods, each of which claims to follow the particular path to Islamic salvation laid down by its own founding saint. In comparison to other brotherhoods, the Tijanni appear especially pious and puritanical. In Ouled Filali, there are about ten Tijanni brothers; the only other brotherhood in the village, the Derqawa, is much larger, with approximately thirty-five members. The Derqawa also have a separate branch in the village for Derqawa women.

For further information on the Tijanni, see Abun-Nasr (1965). For a study of a contrasting, "ecstatic" brotherhood, see Crapanzano (1973).

family and other kinfolk, and he then returns by bus to Marrakech to bide time until the next cycle.

I had been sent outside to keep Sidi Ali company while the Faqir laid out his best rugs in the guest room. My sentiments, as I approached him, were mixed. At times, Sidi Ali could be very witty, and his views on religious matters, which he offered only rarely and then in a condescending manner, were taken to be authoritative. But more frequently, his self-assertive, arrogant style would impose rather long silences, which he would interrupt in order to collect bits of gossip that might serve him at his next stopover or to relate those that he had culled at his last. Then, too, he might awake from a doze with an abrupt request, "Well, let's have some walnuts and almonds!" or, "Don't forget to bring back a beautiful watermelon from the fields!" His presence also meant that, as long as he stayed, I would have no chance to talk with the Faqir.

When I reached him, Sidi Ali was seated under the pear trees upon an inverted wooden crate, which serves more commonly to package farm produce; occasionally, as it did then, it enables distinguished visitors to avoid sitting on the ground. Sidi Ali had spread his small, red prayer rug over the crate. He and I exchanged greetings and he introduced me to Sidi Hmed, a brother whose title indicated that he claimed descent from the Prophet Muhammad, but who was here simply because he had brought Sidi Ali on his motorcycle.

A short time later, we entered the guest room. Sidi Ali took for himself a disproportionate number of pillows, stretched himself out at full length on the rug, and began to doze. Other Tijanni villagers whom the Faqir had sent for began to arrive: the Hajj Hmed, an old man who had made the Pilgrimage to Mecca by boat long before it became common to do so by airplane; Bu Ruwwis, a middle-aged seller of nuts and dates whose quick cackling laughter often made me feel that I had missed a joke; Sessy b. Muhammad, old, enfeebled, and nearly blind; b. Sadiq, a close neighbor whose son had married the Faqir's second daughter; and Hassan, a village cultivator.

The Faqir's eldest son, Mehdi, brought in the tea utensils and the Faqir's brother, Ali, initiated the verbal fencing that often determines who prepares the tea, saying, "Set them down in front of Sidi Hmed."

"Make it yourself!" Sidi Hmed retorted.

Ali parried, "But I don't make it well."

"We'll drink it however you make it," responded Sidi Hmed. "God will show you the way. Besides we're tired."

The last words weakened Sidi Hmed's otherwise strong defense. Ali, who had just returned from a hard half-day's work in the fields, saw the opening and replied, "It's obvious that we're more tired than you are."

This was decisive. Sidi Hmed conceded and said simply, "Give it here."

We drank the tea before and after a small snack of barley bread and clarified butter. It was by now almost time for the mid-afternoon prayer, and this would lead directly into the weekly Tijanni group seance (*dhikr*). Ali and Mehdi returned to the fields to work and the other men, in turn, left the guest room in order to ritually wash themselves with warm water in preparation for the prayer and seance. I overheard Sidi Ali bluntly remark to the Faqir, "When will you finally build that small room in which one can wash? It is no good like this: people may see us from the roof."

Inside the guest room, Sidi Ali led the afternoon prayer, and then, with the sun now lower in the sky, the brothers moved into the shaded courtyard. They sat down on a reed mat, in an elliptical formation, and began the special Friday afternoon seance, which continued, with one short break in the middle, for about an hour and a half. It was completed, as required, before the time of the sunset prayer. The first part of the Friday seance consists of the office (*wadifa*), a series of recitations that must also be performed by every Tijanni at least once a day. During the second part, the formulaic *Hailalah* is chanted. In addition, twice daily the Tijannis perform another litany (*wurd*), once in the morning, and once in the evening. These specifically Tijanni duties do not replace the ritual obligations incumbent upon all Muslims; rather, they are said to be without value unless the basic Islamic obligations are carried out.

The seance began and most brothers, but not all, closed their eyes. All were extremely intent. They chanted in unison, rhythmically. The formula for penitence was repeated thirty times; count was kept on a hand-held string of beads: "I ask forgiveness of Allah, the Great, than whom there is no other God, the Living and the Self-subsisting."[2] Then the *Salat al-Fatih* (the Opening Prayer) was repeated fifty times: "O God, bless our master Muhammad, who opened what had been closed, and who is the seal of what had gone before; he who makes the Truth victorious by the Truth, the guide to Thy straight path, and bless his household as is the due of his immense position and grandeur."

In the middle of this recitation, the Faqir got up, brought a white cloth from the guest room, and carefully spread it out within the ring of brothers.

The Hailalah was repeated one hundred times: "There is no God but Allah."

The next recitation, the *Jawharat al-Kamal* (the Perfect Jewel), is the centerpiece of the Tijanni prayer. Hmed al-Tijanni claims that it was taught to him directly by the Prophet. It was repeated twelve times:

O God, send benediction upon and salute the source of divine mercy, a true ruby which encompasses the centre of comprehensions and meanings, the son of Adam, the possessor of divine Truth; the most luminous lightning in the profitable rain-clouds which fill all the intervening seas and receptacles;

[2]This and the following translations are taken from Abun-Nasr (1965).

Thy bright light with which Thou has filled Thy universe and which surrounds the places of existence.

O God, bless and salute the source of Truth from which are manifested the tabernacles of realities; the source of knowledge, the most upright; Thy complete and most straight path.

O God, bless and salute the advent of the Truth by the Truth; the greatest treasure, Thy mysterious Light. May God bless the Prophet and his household, a prayer which brings us to knowledge of him.

This was followed by a brief silent prayer, and then a ten-minute rest period. Two people had entered during the seance; they were now greeted, and some normal conversation was carried on.

Then, the second portion of the seance began. This was shorter and took about twenty minutes. "There is no God but Allah," was repeated six hundred times; "Allah" was chanted six hundred times, another silent prayer was mouthed, and the brothers terminated the seance by signaling their return to worldly affairs with the characteristic Muslim greeting, "Peace upon you."

Throughout the seance, I had tape-recorded the litany. The Faqir had requested this and Sidi Ali admitted that it was a worthy idea: it would permit the brothers to hear and enjoy a collective litany whenever they wished. I did not think that this would be so soon. Indeed, just as the seance ended, with the chanting rhythm of the six hundred "Allah"s having hardly subsided, the Faqir said, "Let us hear the litany." I played back a sample. "No," the Faqir insisted, "Let us hear all of it." For another hour and a half, the litany that Hmed al-Tijanni had given to his followers again echoed in the courtyard. This, of course, silenced almost all conversation, but it did not distract from the evening prayer, which was performed at the proper time, to the accompaniment of the tape-recorded litany. When it ended, the visitors from the village left, and we ate our evening meal and then prepared to sleep.

In the evenings, before going to sleep, I had the habit of talking for a while with either Ali or Mehdi. We would meet outside the compound, sit in the cool, open air, recount the village gossip, and joke with one another. It was a pleasant time and a change from the Faqir's righteous concerns; he was usually performing the evening Tijanni litany at that very moment.

Mehdi's first remark that night was, "Did you get your fill of noise today?" This cut in two directions: he was referring to the fact that the litany, for which he had (as yet) no use, had been repeated, and alluding to the occasional disturbance that my "always making noise with questions" generated. Mehdi insisted, in an apt metaphor of size, that Sidi Ali was "puffed-up and overblown. Ask him anything, and he always says, 'I know.' He's too haughty and has no shame. He is always coming through here and is never too embarrassed to take the money that my father offers." And he added, showing that such metaphors may work in unexpected ways, "He is what we call an 'Ant Faqir': he leaves the hay and carries away the grain."

A pickup truck was to come the next morning, at about 7 A.M. to take Sidi Ali to "44," the commercial center of the region, which, in its role as the major marketing depot for crops destined for the north and Europe, was appropriately named for the number of kilometers that separated it from the nearest port. By 9 A.M. the driver had not arrived, and Sidi Ali was already impatient. The Faqir attempted to mollify him, saying, "He probably took an early load to the Saturday market as he said he might."

But Sidi Ali knew the region well. "If so, he would have been back already. He's probably gone and taken another load from there to '44.'"

By 11 A.M., Sidi Ali was agitated. The Faqir sympathized: "These modern fellows, never put any confidence in them. They put on European trousers and a French jacket, and they think that with a little knowledge of mechanical things, they're big shots." The air is hot by 11 A.M., and traveling over the dirt roads at this hour produces an unpleasant mixture of sweat and dust. Conversation lagged now even more than usual. The Faqir was himself annoyed at the driver who had, as he said, "thrown Sidi Ali upon me when I have my own work to do."

At about 2 P.M., as we began to eat a midday meal of barley garnished with gourds, the barking of the dogs signaled the pickup's arrival. "If he has made that extra trip to '44,' I'm going to tell him off," said Sidi Ali. The Faqir shook his head sternly and said, simply, "No."

The driver entered and rinsed his hands. A place was made for him at the table. We ate for a long time in silence. Sidi Ali's eyes and mine were the only ones that moved from face to face; all others were fixed upon the meal.

As we licked our fingers after the meal, Sidi Ali asked, in a matter-of-fact manner, "So, everything was all right this morning? No problems with the police?"[3]

The driver said, "No problems."

"How was the Saturday market? Was it busy?"

The driver replied that it was as usual, nothing special.

"Then I suppose," Sidi Ali continued, "that you couldn't find a load to take to '44'?"

"To the contrary," the driver answered, either brash or unsuspecting, "I took one load there, and then another from there to the Medina."

This still did not account for all the time between sunrise and 2 P.M. and, for me, it raised several questions: "Hadn't you agreed to come

---

[3]Pickup truck drivers are constantly harrassed by the police on the roads. Legally, the drivers are allowed to carry produce but not passengers; however, they frequently carry both. Should they encounter a police roadblock when they have passengers, the drivers, on rare occasions, may have to pay a stiff fine. More commonly, the drivers avoid the fine by simply giving a small amount of money (usually referred to as *qahwa* [coffee]) to the police.

here early? How much money were those two extra loads worth, that you were willing to inconvenience all of us? Are you sure that you didn't spend a couple of hours in the Medina just amusing yourself?" Others may have had similar questions, but none of us posed them.

Little was said after that. The driver drank his final glass of tea quickly, and we followed him as he went to put cold water into the pickup's radiator. Sidi Ali wiped the sweat from his forehead with a handkerchief and unrolled his red prayer rug on the dust-covered seat of the cab. The Faqir bid him good-bye, wished that his trip would be peaceful, and slipped two hundred rials ($2.50) into his hand. The pickup's departure left the dust swirling.

🎴 WHAT TO DO?

I was not happy with the first dialogue. Although it noted a number of prominent events in the Faqir's life and provided some insight into his thoughts about them, it seemed to lack focus, to be too diffuse. Also, the Faqir had appeared somewhat disinterested, except at moments in his talk about his first wife. Perhaps the dialogue made this impression because I had arrived only a few days earlier; perhaps, too, the questions were too general or too boring and the dialogue needed more forethought and direction.

The first dialogue had ended, conveniently, by bringing the past up to the present, but I did not readily see where our talk might go from there. I considered choosing a series of topics such as religion, family life, agriculture, and so on; I might prepare a set of relevant questions and the Faqir and I could, then, systematically discuss each topic in turn. But I felt little enthusiasm for such an approach: it seemed at once too coercive, because it would force the Faqir's thoughts into categories he had no say in forming, and too arbitrary, because the categories themselves would have no necessary pattern, no definite beginning or end, no strong tie to our mutual experience. At that moment, I was neither optimistic about finding subjects for future dialogues nor even certain I would seek to hold them.

In any case, during Sidi Ali's visit private conversation with the Faqir was impossible. But the visit, the seance, and the accompanying incidents invited a number of questions that I thought appropriate for a taped dialogue. Here, at least, was a fairly well-defined event that we had both witnessed and that we could easily discuss together.

I prepared a number of questions. First, I was interested in how the Faqir came to be a Tijanni ("Becoming a Tijanni..."). I was also interested in how Islam, a religion in which all believers are said to be equal before God, could accommodate "saints" who not only attain privileged status themselves but who, by their example, help to confer a similar privilege upon their followers; and how, in such a system, the

Faqir would compare his brotherhood with the Derqawa brotherhood, which was dominant in the village and very different from the Tijanni ("Between man and God"). Finally, I had some questions on more practical matters, touching upon his attitude and that of others toward Sidi Ali ("Sidi Ali ... the driver ... the Faqir's brother ...").

▓ SECOND DIALOGUE

BECOMING A TIJANNI ...

I'd like to talk to you about the Tijanni Brotherhood. When did you take up the performance of the Tijanni litany?
There were about eight years left to the protectorate, or maybe ten [1946–48].
And why that litany and not another?
Well, that is god's beneficence (*rezq*), you know. I'd sit with those of that litany, and I saw that its light was for me. I said to myself, in my mind, "It is better." I liked their litanies of praise ... , and I saw that in the books it was preferred.
What was preferred?
That Sheikh Tijanni is to be preferred over all sheikhs.
Why is he preferred?
For example, our Holiness the Messenger of God is the Seal of the Prophets. That is, he is better than all the other prophets. The other, let's say, is the seal of the ... uh ... saints. My mind provides me with that comparison. In other words, he is the seal of the saints. Do you understand my language now?
I'd listen, and I'd see, and from what is in the books.
Did you hear this litany when you were young, or only when you got older?
Even though I heard it when I was young, I had no interest in it, because I saw no purpose to it. Then, when I reached a certain age, I had to. How would it enter my mind when I was young, if I saw no purpose to it?
When did you begin to pay attention to it? How did you begin, because when you were small you were unconcerned with it?
I didn't care about it. Well, we say that it was written, inscribed, in early times. Inscribed, written. What the Lord inscribes for you comes to appear.
When I heard the litany, I would be sitting with them, I was as old as Hmida [age seven]. In the beginning, the Brothers would come to my uncle's, in another section of our compound, only about once a year. His friends would come and stay with him for a week, and they would have a feast, a party that was one week long, from year to year. His friends would come, those who were his partners in commerce, those who were his partners in money, those who were his partners in livestock.

And they'd come. And they'd gather near the well, in the shed near the well, and they'd begin to have their feast. He'd go to the Saturday market and bring back Saturday's meat and innards; he'd go to Wednesday's market and bring back meat and innards; and he'd go to the Sunday market in Menizla and bring back meat and innards from Menizla. For a week, anyway.

And who would assemble?

Would assemble one from Hmer, and another, and another; and another from Deshra,[4] the father of that Si Omar whom you know; and another, whose son you saw at Hussein's tent at the last Tuesday market. About four or five of them, that's all.

Were there no other Tijannis from your village?

No, just my uncle at first, just him. Sometimes his brother. You didn't meet him; when you came here he had already died. He would be here, he'd come from Sherarda and be here.

After a while, they started to grow. A little later, a man returned from the Gharb,[5] and he was a Tijanni; then another from Bida, who was contracted here to be the mosque teacher, became the leader of the Brothers. And we began to gather more, until we became many, up to fifteen or sixteen.

This was during the colonial period, when I took it up. And we used to get together in that small upper room of ours; we'd meet there on Fridays, at our house. We'd fill up the porch.

[It was almost time for the midday meal, and his young son entered the room with the tea utensils.]

Put them down there, put it down! There. O.K. Go. And tell them to distribute the grass to the cows, in the shade!

At that time, had you heard the litanies of the other Brotherhoods, the Derqawa for example?

There were always many Derqawa. Sometimes there would be forty of them, outsiders would come, and the son of the sheikh would often come. But they agitate themselves during their litany. But, in the true path it is said, "Praise the Lord in your place," praise and stay still.

The Derqawa, in their seance, begin slowly, then faster, faster, faster, and faster. Then they... [here the Faqir stood up and began to rock back and forth progressively more rapidly, chanting]... "The Living One, the Living One." That's how they do it. They call this the Foundation (*'imara*), they call this the Foundation.

The Tijanni just sit still; they don't act that way.

You've seen that.

---

[4]Both of these, as well as Sherarda and Bida (mentioned later), are other villages in the Sous Plain.

[5]The Gharb is the rich northern plains region of Morocco, containing major urban centers such as Rabat and Casablanca.

There are other paths too, such as the Qadiri, and the Nasiri.

The Qadiriyin, at times, meet together with the Derqawa, but they do not have the bad practices that the Derqawa have. They just sing praise and remain quiet. And the Nasiriyin too, they sing praise, that's all; they don't practice that Foundation. The Derqawa are the ones who do the Foundation.

Do you know the litanies of the Qadiri and the Nasiri?

The litanies must be memorized. Each brotherhood has its own Way. And all of the others are easy; it is the Tijanni litany that is difficult. The others don't know ours. That "Jawharat al-Kamal," the one at the end, that final portion, they don't know it. It is very difficult if you haven't practiced it. Theirs are easy.

How much practice does it take until you learn it?

Well, it depends on your mind. If my mind is fine, I'll learn it quickly. I'm talking now of the "Jawharat al-Kamal," because all the others are easy. "There is no God but God," is known by everyone. The "Salat al-Fatih" is a little difficult, but not very. That final portion, the "Jawharat al-Kamal," is pretty difficult. And it is prohibited to say it at all, if you haven't done your ablutions, if you haven't ritually washed.

And the Tijanni, when performing their daily recitations, must speak to no one. Never. Nothing. To no one. With the other paths, this is not so. They work with their beads, and they may still talk. Or they begin to do the Foundation, and they might still talk. All of them, in all their litanies. With us, no.

Aside from the litany, what in your life makes you a Tijanni and not a Derqawi?

Our religion, ours or theirs, is all one. I work on my concerns, and there is no problem. But always my mind is focused on my sheikh. We say, you know, that there are three benedictions. There is that of God, there is that of your parents, there is that of your sheikh. And there is that of God.

If you have the benediction of your parents, your sheikh will bless you. And if you have the blessing of your parents and your sheikh, you will have the benediction of God. And if you don't have the blessing of your parents, neither your sheikh nor God will intercede on your behalf. Do you understand? Primary school, that's your parents. And secondary school is the sheikh. And the baccalaureat,[6] or whatever it's called, is God.

There are people who call the Tijannis severe and the Derqawa permissive.[7]

The Derqawi does as he likes and talks when he wants to. I told you

---

[6]An examination taken at the end of secondary school.

[7]The epithet commonly used to refer to the Tijanni is *diyyeq* (literally, tight, narrow); to the Derqawa, *wase'* (loose, wide). These were the Arabic words used in the

they were permissive. He takes out his beads and he might still be talking to you. He talks to you while singing praise! That *is* permissive.

But aside from the litany, is their path wider?

How could it be wider, wider than our path? Our Master is the same for all of us. "Wide" refers only to the litany of their sheikh. But that sheikh's path doesn't concern me. What is important to you is the path that you are in. The path may be called loose or narrow, but the people aren't, nor are their lives. No, it is only the practices that one performs that are called "wide" or "narrow."

For example, take the sunset prayer and the evening prayer. The sunset prayer must be done on time. The evening prayer can be done any time before the sunrise prayer. If you haven't had the occasion to do it, wait until it's almost time for the sunrise prayer and then do it. But the sunset prayer must be done at its time! That is difficult, so it is severe, narrow, like Tijanni practice.

The Tijanni doesn't begin his litany until he finishes, you know, all his work. He finishes it, and then he becomes silent; he won't talk to anyone. Unless a child is going to fall into the fire, or fall into a well, or in other words is going to die. Then the Tijanni may break his litany, may speak during it.

It is also said that the Tijannis are intolerant.

Yes, they are intolerant. You know, the books that he bestowed upon the Brothers are always standing firm on the limits. They allow no meddling with them.

For example, what is speech? Speech guards everything. A sin, if I'm going to commit it, I start by speaking. Isn't this so? I can't commit it if I haven't first spoken. Suppose I want a woman. What can I do if I haven't first spoken to her?

Nothing.

So there you are! Tijanni stands firm in his books, you see. You must learn them, and you must do this, and do this, and do this. If you see something and see yourself falling into it, you must turn away, or even run away, immediately. Don't remain watching it until it enters your bones.

Let's say that I feel tempted and I see the person who can satisfy me. I must draw away right away. If you are the one who is no good and I begin to talk to you, that means that I am going to transgress. I must keep away from you from the first, I must keep from talking to you. That is the meaning.

Are the Derqawa like that?

---

paragraphs that follow. Another distinction sometimes drawn, which I do not pursue here, is that between *nqi* (clean) brotherhoods and *mussekh* (dirty) ones; the Tijanni are at the clean end of the scale (see Geertz 1980, pp. 156–58).

Well, the Derqawa, no. The Derqawi will see what he wants and will then call it "healthy." Yet, their Way is an acceptable one. Yes, it is acceptable, but they find it hard to obey restrictions.

BETWEEN MAN AND GOD...

There are those who say that there is no one between men and God, that because we are all the same...

We are all children of Adam and the origin of each of us is with God. But for God to show me what is inside your head, or to show you what is inside mine—that doesn't happen. However, the Lord knows all that is inside our heads, and he sets us in motion, and we play around as we wish.

So how can someone, such as Sidi Hmed Tijanni, come between us and God?

From piety. He worshiped God. He worshiped God until God opened the way for him. And the Lord began to speak to him, to send him messages, through Mustafa, the Messenger of God,[8] and through our Holiness Gabriel. They say, you know, that Mustafa the Messenger of God does nothing until the Call comes. He can't do anything alone. Haven't you heard that he is the most powerful in matters of fighting, and in other matters? As he was in the matter of our Holiness Ali and all that. It was he who commanded our Holiness Ali during those Holy Wars. You know who our Holiness Ali was?

The Prophet's father's brother's son?[9]

Yes. But our Holiness Ali could do nothing until the Prophet sent him. And the Prophet wouldn't send him, until the representative from God would come to the Prophet. The Prophet wouldn't simply tell him, "Go!" No. He'd stay still until the Call from God would come, saying, "Send him, with the praise of God."

Did the Call from God come to Sidi Hmed Tijanni?

[8]The Prophet Muhammad, whom Muslims take to be the last of the prophets, the seal of the prophets, and to whom God is believed to have communicated the holy word of the Koran, is variously referred to as "the Prophet," "the Messenger of God," and "Mustafa" (the chosen one).

[9]Upon the death of the Prophet Muhammad in 632, his cousin and son-in-law Ali claimed the right, as the Prophet's closest relative, to succeed to the leadership of the Islamic community. This right was challenged (particularly by the Prophet's wife, 'Aisha), and others seized the leadership. It was not until 656 that Ali was able to assert his claim effectively, establishing the Islamic caliphate in Kufa, Iraq. His rule was neither long nor even fully accepted within the Islamic community. Renewed disputes broke out over the caliphate, and in 661 Ali was assassinated in the Kufa mosque. Ali's descendants and followers continued to struggle but were unable to regain clear supremacy except in certain regions. The followers of Ali, known as the Shi'a, continue to be of great importance in selected areas in the Middle East (but not in North Africa), including Lebanon, Syria, Iraq, Iran, and several of the Gulf states.

It came from the Mustafa, from the Prophet Muhammad. You know it is not only what comes through him which is from God. Everything is from God, but this came to Sidi Hmed Tijanni by means of the Mustafa, through the religion. And the Mustafa told him, "Do this and do this," and so Sidi Hmed Tijanni praises God and praises the Mustafa in his litany of praise. The litany that we recite now, Sidi Hmed Tijanni recited until he succeeded, until God the Almighty came to answer him. Then he imposed it upon his followers. And similarly for the Derqawa, and for the others. In the same way. And that is why they praise God in their ways.

Do you, as a Tijanni, believe that the Sheikh of the Derqawa reached God?

Well, in any event, the saints, all of them, all of them were answered by God the Almighty. He answered them. He answered them, for example, in dreams, and there are those to whom He sent messages. You know, our Holiness Muhammad the Messenger of God says to the saint, "Go and do this." For example: our Holiness Gabriel brings the message from Our Master and tells it to our Holiness the Messenger of God; our Holiness the Messenger of God tells the sheikh to perform that act. That is what it is about.

If the saint doesn't actually see the Prophet, he might dream of him, see him in dreams, side with him; then they conclude their pact. And the Prophet would say to him, "Do this." And the saint would know if it was the Devil who had come, or if it was our Holiness the Messenger of God who had come.

If you see a man on the road, do you know whether he is a Tijanni or a Derqawi?

The Derqawa have one obvious characteristic: they always have their rosary showing, so that they can be distinguished from others. And their rosary has thick beads. And there is something else: if you don't recognize him from his beads, watch how he greets someone. If he uses a special handshake, you know he is a Tijanni; if he kisses and bows as toward God, you know he is a Derqawi. They do one thing, those Derqawa: they kiss the head. We don't. We just use a special handshake.

And now they have hung upon us a name. They call us, "the ones who bow." But they are the ones who do that. No, our practice is just to grasp one another's hand, and there is nothing wrong in that. There is no reason to . . . you should bow to no one but God.

Are the Tijannis better than the Derqawa?

Well, in any event, it is in this matter as it is said in the books: "Is the Prophet, God bless him and grant him salvation, better, or are his companions?" They are all good, they are all fine. But the Prophet was preferred by the Lord. He was the Prophet before he was born.

All the saints, I mean all of the prophets, for example, their prophecies settled upon them only after they had already been born, when they were alive. But the Prophet, God bless him and grant him salvation, people were putting themselves under his protection and he was not yet born. Because he is the last of the saints, I mean the last of the prophets, the last of the prophets. And people were uniting under him, were committing themselves to him and he was not yet born. Because of that power of God's that he displayed. And, as with the Prophet and the prophets, so with Sidi Hmed Tijanni and the saints, as I showed you before.

But, how does it happen that I say Tijanni is good, the other says Derqawi, and so on?[10] Let's say, I'm sitting with you, an American; but destiny brought you here. Similarly, someone else might come to sit with a Frenchman, someone else to sit with an Egyptian. And the two go around together, and they begin to talk as we did, and he develops a great fondness for the other. That's the reason.[11]

And also, we say, "What precedes and what follows is only God's knowledge." That is, it was inscribed in earlier times. It was inscribed on the page that we, you and I, were going to meet one another. So it is that, in early times, those who were learned and who reached God found that even their marriages had been inscribed. Do you understand what I'm saying now?

Understood.

That is the meaning of, "What precedes and what follows is only God's knowledge." That is the meaning brought by this string of words. Me, I didn't know you at all. You know, we're now showing the meaning in order to get a comparison with the Tijannis.

Now, the Tijannis: I met with them, and went to their seances for three or four months before I formally took up their duties. Their manner pleased me, their style, and their meetings. They don't require, as the others do, an accounting where, "You give this, and you give that." Each person, according to his capabilities, or according to his belief, brings his due. There are no problems.

Are the Tijannis closer to you than your other friends?

Of course. They are called "brothers," brothers under the sheikh. That is, it is as though he is the son of my father the sheikh. He and I are both sons of the sheikh.

Yet, when there was the dispute over the road, the faqirs no longer came together for the Friday seance.[12]

---

[10]The Faqir here seems to pose a question, rhetorically, perhaps indicating that he anticipates such a question from me.

[11]The Faqir, at this point, brings our relationship directly into the conversation, as an example of a close tie, a "great fondness." He had done something similar in the previous dialogue (see ch. 1).

[12]I was alluding to a dispute that had created great bitterness in the village. (This dispute is referred to again in chs. 7 and 11.)

B. Sadiq and I no longer went and they held no Friday seances. But once Bu Ruwwis joined, they began to meet without us. I did what my duty was, at home, by myself, without a group.

Did you say to yourself, "It is a pity that we no longer meet"?

Yes, I said, "It is a pity that we no longer meet," because, for the prayers and the litany, if there are many people, the reward is greater. We say that he who prays with others will receive twenty-five gold coins in the hereafter. And he who prays alone will receive one. That is what we say.

But, from a certain standpoint, it's better to forgo a reward than to seek it in a place where you may cause trouble. In those situations you might subtract from your trust.

I didn't understand that too well.

Suppose I've arrived, and I want us to laugh together, or I want to tell you about religion, or to tell you to do something that is good. Then, it is said, "We have trust." And suppose that I expect that there will be some trouble, that someone and I are going to fight: it's better that I don't come with him to you, better that I do not harm that trust.

But concerning that trouble over the road, I was happy with respect to what was between God and me; I wasn't happy with what was between me and those people. Both together.

Of the Tijanni faqirs, only Bu Ruwwis is able to speak out. But he was on the side of B. Hussein.[13] The others are spineless, they are unable to say anything and, even if they could, they do not recognize the truth when they see it. They couldn't speak up and they didn't know anything.

Bu Ruwwis was saying, "Bn Hussein is on the just road." But B. Hussein was completely off course. The dispute went on and on and Bu Ruwwis finally woke up and discovered his error. So the brothers came to me here and brought me two sugar cones. Bu Ruwwis and three others, they brought me two sugar cones and said, "Return to us."

But I kept at them, I gave it to them, saying: "The wrong was this, and this, and this, and this. Finally, you brought evil into the Brotherhood meetings and, at a time when there is such ill will, why keep going? *You* did this wrong deed, and you, and you, and you." I showed up each of them. "You, you wouldn't speak to me once they told you, 'Ignore him!'" And, "You, you go to talk with them rather than talk with us. Why should I go? There is no reason. I don't owe anyone anything."

And even after they came for me, I still stayed away for a long while, for some three months after they had brought me the sugar. Later, I relented. I began to be concerned. B. Sadiq and I would sit together, and we talked back and forth, "Let's go back." "Let's not go back." Finally, we decided we would go back. And again we began to meet.

---

[13]Opponents of the Faqir in the dispute.

Where do you meet? In the douar (village)?

Yes, we have our own lodge. We built it a while ago, just as I was about to become a faqir, during the colonial time. We built it on the land of another faqir. This land will now always belong to the Tijannis.

The Derqawa have just built one this year, adding one wing to the douar's mosque. Their lodge is on the side of the mosque where the prickly pears grow and those few olive trees. To the east, where the mosque teacher leads the prayer.

What do you think about that, that the Derqawa have built their lodge as a wing to the mosque?

Well, in any event, their lodge must not remain occupied at the time of the prayers. That is, the people must not leave the mosque to pray separately in the lodge. They must pray in the mosque and then go to the lodge. And they mustn't say, "In this lodge, people will pray as though it were the mosque." To empty the mosque at the profit of the lodge, that is not proper. They must pray in the mosque and then go to the lodge.

Now, this is not yet a problem, because the mosque has the ablution facilities, the heating. They have to pray in the mosque and, even though they may want to do what I said, it hasn't happened. The lodge doesn't have the facilities, it has just a room.

SIDI ALI . . . THE DRIVER . . . THE FAQIR'S BROTHER . . .

What do you think of Sidi Ali?

Well, he holds to his religion and heeds its schedule. But he makes his living off the backs of the faqirs.

Is that good?

I don't know. I suppose it is all right. There is nothing the matter with it, I suppose. I suppose.

What about his behavior?

Well, he's clean, quite clean. And although his arrival does cost you a bit, his manner is good with respect to the prayers and with respect to what Our Master has spoken. And with respect to joking.

Is he modest?[14]

Of course he is modest. Why wouldn't he be modest?

As I see him, he is not very modest, he says . . .

His words are harsh. But he jokes, there is joking in it.

But he says, for example, "Give me, give me, give me."

That is straight talking! Yes, he does say, "Bring me, if you have some,

---

[14]The Arabic word is *hshem*, which variously connotes modesty, shame, deference, embarrassment. For an extended discussion of the meaning of this term in Morocco, see Eickelman (1976, pp. 138–141).

bring me." That is talking straight. He is unable to hold things back. Others are unable to speak like that, but you don't know what is in their hearts.

What about that driver who said he was going to come at seven o'clock and didn't?

He's no good.

Is he shameless in front of Sidi Ali?

He wasn't telling the truth. He was lying. He has shame but he lies.

If the driver was a religious man, and thought that Sidi Ali was a good man, would he have acted that way toward him?

He wouldn't have. But these modern youth do nothing. They only care about themselves, whether they're following religion or following something else. They put no value on others.

And it is not just the modern youth who do that. It all depends on what you think, on your thoughts. The driver sees only his own objectives. There are those who work only when there are others present. Let the other move away from that spot just a little bit and the work stops. There are those who won't work to improve even their own position, if no one watches them. That is common.

But if I care about my own standing, I must do what I have told you I will do, whether you are present or absent. The time arrives, and I do it. Whether you're gone, whether you're in New York, wherever you are. The deal we made has to be carried out.

But someone who behaves like that driver might even consume something given to him in trust. If you sent him with something to me, he might consume it. Or if I sent him with something to your home, he might consume it. Because he does not keep a vow. A trust, in our Law, is not to be opened, you are not even to know what is in it. That is, in the trusts of earlier times. But today, there is a lot of scheming with these trusts. You know, nowadays you shouldn't take a trust; there is too much scheming.

Someone, for example, might want to send marijuana to Taroudannt, to get it inside Taroudannt. He'll say to you, "Oh, Monsieur Kevin, take these prickly pears to Taroudannt, for me." Or something else. No, you have to watch out for such things. You have to look into it, to watch out for such scheming, if you've been too modest to refuse.

But in a true trust, you don't look into it. And you don't know what is in it, yet you take it to its destination. If you can't do this, you tell the owner, "No." This is in our religion. Among people who are closely related this is done. If someone can't, he tells you, "No, no, I can't do it, I have this to do, and this, and this." There are those who will say, "Give it to me," and then they won't follow through. They are too ashamed to say "No," but they are ashamed only when you are looking at them. As soon as he is out of you sight, he might send it with someone else.

Do you think that your brother might become a faqir?

It depends on him, on what is in his head. But he hangs around with everyone. He might even want to become a faqir, but he says to himself, "All that is worthless." This is because my brother, you know, blasphemes. He tells you, "That is worthless, this is worthless, and that is worthless." Well, you heard what he said yesterday evening about the span of life?

No, I didn't.

He said, "A person's life span can be increased." You didn't hear him? Well, what do you think? Can your life span be increased? There is no adding to it! Its term is bounded. That's all. Pain and illness can be treated. Illness—there are those who can ease it. But no one can alter your life span. And if one doesn't have the illness treated, it stays with you. After a while he heals; or he stays sick until he dies, until his term is up.

Are there many who are like your brother now, yet later they become faqirs?

This happens to many such people. But it must wait until he begins to sit with the faqirs, until he opens his mind and begins to see clearly, to notice what is in the books and to know that the hours of play are past. He must hold to the right path, at all costs, and perfect himself.

Are there, among the faqirs, those who had been ignorant and who turn faqir the next day?

There are. As if, once, one was a Christian and then became a Muslim; or, once, one was a Jew and then became a Muslim. Like that. He was once a faqir; today he is nothing. Or today a faqir and tomorrow nothing! There are many like that. That Omar was a faqir and is no longer. He does the things that boys do, and it's unlikely that he ever performs the litany at all. Everything can be found.

There are those who are faqirs, who strongly adhere, with the rosary, and on schedule, and this and that. And his actions are devilish. He does nothing good.

Is this more common among the Derqawa or...

It's common. In every brotherhood, in every one, everything can be found. The children of Adam—we are all alike.

On the other hand, there are some who you think do nothing. But when you leave him and observe him from afar, you find him holding to God's way. And he seems to be nothing, you'd say he does nothing.

It is like everything else. There is no one above us, except God.

3

The Circumcision

The Faqir came back from the distant Saturday market in mid-afternoon. He had departed that morning at sunup on a donkey fully laden with gourds, but he returned with the donkey bearing just him and one live goat. The gourds had been a pretext for that day's marketing; more pressing was the Faqir's desire to find b. l-Hajj, one of the few regional circumcision specialists. Four of the Faqir's sons, ranging in age from twelve to one, his brother's two sons, and several neighbor's boys would undergo the operation, if b. l-Hajj agreed to perform it. When the Faqir asked me to help him slaughter the goat, I realized that not only had he indeed encountered b. l-Hajj, but that guests would soon be arriving and that the circumcision would probably take place the next day.

I recalled a circumcision ceremony I had attended in the Medina shortly after I arrived in Morocco. The wealthy craftsman whose sons and nephews were to be circumcised had invited a group of some fifteen men to the ceremony. A male nurse from the city hospital was hired for the operation, which was performed in an anteroom adjoining the second-floor guest parlor where the men gathered. Beneath us, the women congregated in the first-floor kitchen, preparing the food and comforting the children.

No one in the guest room was able to see the actual operation. But the wailing of the boys conveyed the stages of the operation only too faithfully. As the wailing began, the men broke into a prolonged sequence of Koranic chants which continued until the last boy had been circumcised. Throughout, the two fathers chanted considerably more intensely than the rest, or so it seemed to me. Punctuating this unsettling performance was the occasional laughter and merriment that rose to us from the women below.

The Faqir and I finished slaughtering the goat, skinned, eviscerated, and quartered it, and brought it to the women for cooking. The Faqir was performing the late afternoon prayer when b. l-Hajj arrived and they did not greet one another until he had completed it. B. l-Hajj was quite an old man, well past sixty, but with decisive hands, which I could not help but notice. By the time of the sunset prayer, three other guests had arrived.

Among the men, the evening passed quietly, normally, and the easy silence was broken by small patches of conversation. News from the region of the Saturday market was much the same as from ours: it was an "empty" year, and the barley crop (the region's staple) would be hardly worth harvesting. It would not even supply, for most farmers, the seed for next fall's sowing. In addition (and more ominous in the long run), the level of the underground water was sinking, in some places as much as several meters. Not only would more work have to be done on the wells, but more powerful irrigation motors and pumps might be necessary. Money was scarce this year and this would make the first task difficult; the second, for almost all small farmers, would be practically impossible.

Meanwhile, in the central compound, the children were being prepared for the next day's events. The true purpose of these preparations was hidden from them as long as possible. The Faqir's brother Ali talked to the children as though he was planning for the Festival of the Saint Bu Moussa, which was to be held the next day: the men and the children would all be going, and it was for this reason, and no other, that each of the children must be especially well scrubbed. Each would also be getting a new white *fuqiya* (a long, loose overgarment), which they would wear to the festival. The sheikh would also be coming the next morning, and they would all ride to the festival together in a pickup truck. The man who had come to visit that afternoon was an old friend of the sheikh; he would stay over that evening and would accompany them on the next day's outing.

L-'Aribi, at twelve years old the oldest, told me several days later that he had been suspicious from the very beginning, when he noticed that the guest had long nails. The morning after the guest's arrival, he asked his mother and his uncle's wife if the visitor was the man who performed circumcisions. Their laughter, although accompanied by denials, only confirmed his suspicions. He became firmly convinced when two neighboring mothers arrived, each with one son, without the fathers. Over breakfast, l-'Aribi whispered the news to the other boys. The young ones seemed to take no notice and Abdallah, who had come with his mother (the Faqir's sister) early that morning from their home in a neighboring village, was already casually blocking the doorway, preventing the older ones from running away and hiding. Years before, the Faqir's oldest son, Mehdi, had been able to delay his circumcision (he too was quite old when it was performed) by climbing unnoticed up to the roof and hiding inside the large earthen vessel used for barley storage. It had taken half a day to find him.

This morning, despite Abdallah's attentiveness, the Faqir's five-year-old son, Hmida, vanished for a time. He was discovered a short while later, partly hidden behind a wooden clothes trunk. Throughout all this, l-'Aribi and the older sons were obviously upset; a neighbor's four-year-old, on the other hand, was all aglow as he proudly displayed himself in his bright new *fuqiya*.

In the guest compound, the men were served a copious morning meal of goat meat. As the meal ended and as the final glass of tea was drunk, the Faqir abruptly left. His brother Ali disappeared a minute later.

B. l-Hajj seated himself in the courtyard, on a reed mat, close to a shaded wall. In front of him he placed a little pouch containing a reddish powder and a piece of goat dung the size and shape of a small marble. He also took out a pair of scissors from its case.

L-'Aribi, the oldest, was first. He violently resisted. Abdallah grabbed him by the wrist and began to drag him from the central compound into the guest portion. L-'Aribi cursed him and vainly tried to bite his arm. Upon entering the courtyard, he mastered his fear. As he said later, "My heart was swollen," but he knew that "If you restrain yourself and don't cry, then the pain is less and you heal more quickly." He was "old enough to have some sense."

As l-'Aribi was brought before b. l-Hajj, Abdallah grabbed him around the shoulders, from the back, and with his right hand pushed l-'Aribi's chin up so that he could not look down. Another man grasped him around the legs. L-'Aribi, still standing, tightly closed his eyes, "in order not to feel the pain." B. l-Hajj placed the goat dung on the head of the penis and pulled the foreskin over it. He pinched the foreskin firmly with his nails and then quickly cut the foreskin off with the scissors. (l-'Aribi said later that the pinch hurt so much that after it he hardly felt the scissors cutting off the foreskin.) B. l-Hajj then picked up the pouch of red medicine and dipped the penis into it. The operation was over, and l-'Aribi walked out of the courtyard and into the central compound under his own steam, without crying, although clearly in great pain. He went into the room that had been set aside for the children and was given some hard-boiled eggs and honey to eat. He then went outside, walked around for a few minutes, returned to the room, lay down, and waited for the others.

Eight boys in all were circumcised. After l-'Aribi's circumcision, the others reacted with less "sense." Kbibir, eight years old, whimpered only a little, but the younger ones wailed for hours afterwards. Ali's son Hmida fought savagely, biting and drawing blood from the arm of the man holding him, and was made to submit only with great difficulty. He cursed incessantly throughout, particularly his father. As each boy's ordeal came to an end, his white fuqiya stained with blood, he was served and cared for by the Faqir's sister, who gave each about ten rials (about twelve cents) to ease the pain.

L-'Aribi healed quickly, knowing that if he ate well he would soon be back to normal. The others took longer; some suffered pain three weeks later, particularly when they urinated. For the youngest boys, the memory of the operation did not fade naturally, for they were frequently taunted by the other kids, and by adults as well, with threats such as, "Watch out, or I'll take you to the circumcisor." For weeks afterward, it was not uncommon for me to be asked, within earshot of the youngest, whether I had brought scissors with me. Such teasing was very effective, and the children would immediately burst into tears. In addition, the young ones remained for some time in terror of the courtyard in which the circumcision had been performed and stubbornly, almost in a tantrum, refused to enter it.

▨ A PROJECT VENTURED: EVENTS AND DIALOGUES

The circumcision took place only a few days after Sidi Ali's visit. By now, I was thinking that the sequence "event + dialogue" might be worth continuing: I would write a draft of the event soon after it occurred, to make what happened clear to me; that event, which the Faqir and I shared and which took place in the normal course of the Faqir's life, would furnish a clear focus for discussion. The discussion would extend, in a natural way, a relationship that had been nurtured on questions and answers, as one would expect in the interaction between anthropologist and informant.

I prepared for this dialogue as I had for the previous one. I came up with questions about details of the circumcision and the Faqir's views on the practice of circumcision ("The circumcision..."); about the Faqir's attitude toward his children, particularly toward a young son who had recently died ("Your children..."); and about his opinions and practices in raising children ("Parents and children ...").

▨ THIRD DIALOGUE

THE CIRCUMCISION ...

I'd like to ask you today about the circumcision that you did for the children, just four days ago. Why did you do it then?
When the moment is ready, you do it.
What do you mean, "ready"?
When you have the time, when we have the time.
Who is the fellow who performed the circumcision?
A faqir; he's called Faqir Muhammad b. l-Hajj.
Has he been doing this for long?
He's always been doing it, for about twenty years, or even thirty.
Is there anyone else in the region who does this?
There's one up there in the mountains, but he's too haughty.

Why did you seek out b. l-Hajj, and not the other one?

B. l-Hajj is ... humble, he doesn't bargain with you, and he doesn't make demands of you.

What do you mean, he "doesn't make demands of you"?

That other one, from the mountains, he tells you, "Bring flour," and he fills up his mule with flour from people. If there are four boys, four boys without a fifth, he says, "Bring a cock." This one, b. l-Hajj, says, "That is prohibited." And our Brotherhood says, "That is prohibited." He must do his work, and if someone offers, he may receive, but that is all.

And he is a faqir?

He is a faqir, but I don't know of what order. I didn't ask him.

Isn't l-'Aribi quite old to be circumcised? You know, I've heard it said that if the son isn't circumcised by the age of seven, then everything he does for the father after that is an offense, a sin.

He's old. But what are we to do? We waited, passed the time, until he grew old. Both l-'Aribi and Kbibir are old.

And l-'Ayashi, isn't he too young [he was one year old]?

Even if he is young [and the Faqir chuckled], it's better that he goes through it young.

At what age should it be done?

It's good to do it at two, then it's good, like Rhayyem [a neighbor's two year old]. At two it's very good, or at three, until four it's good. Also at five it's fine. But if he's past eight, like l-'Aribi, or seven, it becomes of some difficulty. He begins to show modesty, that's the problem, and then you can't put medicine on him. He begins to be modest, and you too. And they run away; some completely disappear. If an older one catches on, he can really run away.

Why was the circumcision done in the morning?

He does it whenever he can. But the morning is best, best because the blood isn't hot. The blood is cold, motionless, and stops flowing right away. If the children wait until the air warms up, and they have been coming and going, they'll give up a lot of blood.

Why did you disappear before the operation was performed?

Well, they would begin to look at me and cry. And they begin to curse their fathers. So I got out of there, to cut grass for the livestock. And my brother went to irrigate the watermelons.

Why did l-'Aribi go first?

In order of age, l-'Aribi was first. We were afraid they'd run away.

Had they been told beforehand that the circumcision would be performed?

No, not until they saw b. l-Hajj. Until then, they didn't know.

Did l-'Aribi know beforehand?

He caught on. But he lowered his eyes and steeled himself ... went out and steeled himself. For him, it wasn't too bad.

With the guests that you had, and the food we ate, would you call this a party, a celebration?

Yes, we had a celebration, yes. We slaughtered a goat, one that I had bought for one thousand eight hundred rials.

And all the while, were the women in the house?

And where would they go, the women? They were in the house over there.

What were they doing, the women?

Well, they were cooking, they were. They were cooking for us to eat. What would they be doing?

They were doing what they always do?

Yes.

Weren't they having a celebration?

As us, as them. They too were having a celebration. We were celebrating and so were they celebrating. And once they had cooked and sent the food over to us, they gave food to their children.

How much time do you think all the circumcisions took?

Well, perhaps a half an hour, or not even that long. You could do twenty in half an hour.

How much was b. l-Hajj paid?

I gave him 1,400 rials, 1,000 for our six boys, and 400 for the other two.

Why do you have the children circumcised?

We have... you know we have... it's a duty.

Is it good for their health, or is it good from a religious standpoint?

It's good from the standpoint of religion and perhaps, also, for health. They say that he who is bitten by a scorpion, and hasn't yet been circumcised, dics. If hc's not circumcised, the poison may be very potent. They say. I've heard that.

YOUR CHILDREN . . .

Would you call your children good, a little bad, or very bad?

Well, not bad... , not bad... they could use some manners. It's not badness, but they're not mannerly.

What do you mean, "not mannerly"?

They don't have the propriety that God wants in us.

Who is good among them, leaving aside Mehdi, who is much older than the others? Who appears rather good to you, and who appears rather rowdy?

None of them are really bad, there's no real badness there. They are just bad when they don't see me around. If I go from their side, they do what pleases them. Kids today are much worse than in the old days. In the old days, if a kid did something bad, out in the street, any adult might clout him. But then, under the colonial period, if you hit someone else's child, the father would threaten to prosecute you and take you to court. So now the kids are much worse. When their fathers aren't present, they will say anything in the streets.

And who among your kids does that a lot?

Qbibih [the Faqir laughed at this pun on Kbibir's name, and the word for rowdy, *qbih*], but it's just that he forgets, he doesn't know any better.

And who is rather good?

Well, that Hisen, God rest his soul, was rather good. Yes,... he was ... even though he was a little hard-headed. All in all, he was fine, *quand même.*

In your mind, did you prefer Hisen a bit over the others?

Hisen ... was a little tough nut. A little tough one. And his eyes. I'd just look at him sternly and he'd do this. [The Faqir lowered his head and then looked at me through his eyebrows, expressing fright.]

Was he a bit like you?

I don't know, I don't know.

Does it still hurt you to talk about him?

Uh-huh.

Would you rather not continue on this subject?

Well, it hurts. Whenever I think of him, it hurts me. [The Faqir sniffled.] But what can we do?

I was going to ask you how it happened, but if it hurts, we'll skip it.

Well, how it happened was this. The measles came, you know. Those to whom it came weren't too badly off. But Hisen, God rest his soul, from the moment he fell sick, he never got up again. Until... until he died. That's all.

Did you see this disease from its beginning?

Yes.

Did you do something for it?

We did nothing.

Don't people say there is some medicine for it?

We make fava beans for them; we do for them a mixture of fava beans. But if your term is completed, it is completed, that's all. Yes. Hmida was even sicker than Hisen was, but.... They all became sick, every one, from that. All of them. The measles reached all of them, together. But a fever came to the others, and perhaps it was that fever that made it easier for them.

What did you do when Hisen died?

When he died, I was just alone here, I was alone. The others had all gone, gone to the Festival of Sidi Mbarek near the Medina. I was all alone. A neighbor came by with the pickup truck, he was going to "44" or somewhere, and I sent him for the *tallib*.[1] He couldn't find the *tallib*, but brought someone else back, and we washed the body and brought it to the cemetery of Sidi Youssef. That's all. What could we do?

What do you do when you wash the body?

Well, we wash it like in the ritual ablutions. With warm water. And then we take it to the cemetery of Sidi Youssef.

And how do you bury it?

We dig him a grave, we put stones on the grave, and we turn the earth over upon him. That's all, what else? And on top, we cover it with brush.

Do you read something over the dead?

We pray over it, two movements. The *tallib* prays two movements over him.

Is the prayer the same for someone old as for a child?

Just the same. There is just one prayer for the dead.

And, in your thoughts, if a child dies so young, does it go to heaven or to hell?

According to the thoughts that are told to us, that the books tell. These are not my thoughts. Children, they say, have no Reckoning, they have no . . . there are no sins, they have no sins. Those of us, you know. who have grown up, and cheated, and lied, and stolen, and seen with our eyes, for us it is a misfortune. The children, they owe nothing. Born, died. They are, it is said but only God knows, among the bridegrooms of heaven. They are the group that . . . you know, the youths of heaven.

PARENTS AND CHILDREN . . .

When parents raise their children, who does the most, who has the strongest influence on the children, the father or the mother?

Everyone who does something is going to have an effect. It depends on what they do. There are those who are raised by their fathers. There are those who are raised by their mothers. There are those whose fathers never even speak to them, throughout their whole lives. There are those also whose mothers never even speak to them: from the day he begins to talk, he'll be with his father. People aren't all alike.

Does the father provide something that the mother doesn't?

No, it's the same. What this one gives, that one gives.

Well, who does a child like more, the father or the mother?

There are those who like their fathers more than their mothers, and there are those who like their mothers more than their fathers. There

---

[1]The *tallib* is an individual trained in religious matters who performs religious tasks for the villagers, such as teaching children the Koran, washing the dead, and so on. He is often hired from outside the village and is supported by a fee from each household proportional to the number of males of fasting age in it.

are those who like neither their mothers nor their fathers, and there are those who like their mothers and their fathers. The world is mixed, it's the same, all the world is the same.

And really, with respect to the parents, they are loved by all the children. If you hit them, then you're not at all loved, they don't love you only at the time you hit them. When they are at their pleasure with you, eating, then you are loved by them.[2]

If a child does something wrong, what do you do?

All things considered, if he got me very angry, I'd hit him.

With what?

With my hands, or with a stick, or with a belt, with whatever; with a piece of wood, or with a clump of earth. And if my heart is still a bit forebearing, I might spit on him, and that's all.

And if he does something good?

Well...

... you mean, he doesn't?

Yes, he does, sometimes, sometimes he does. Of course. Then I say to him, "Thank you my child, thank you."

And if you're angry, and want to yell at him, what do you say? I often hear you but I sometimes can't understand what you yell.

I tell him, "Hurry up, you're not moving at all," and "Hurry with that donkey, or there will be hell to pay," or some such. Or, "Watch the hell out, I'm coming for you," or "by God, I'm coming for you, watch the hell out or I'll clout you." That's what's in it, what else is in it?

If the father is good, what should he do for his child?

He must buy clothes for them, and bring meals for them, and must bring them what is needed from outside the home, because what comes from the home gets consumed right away. Also, that he satisfy their wishes, that he not hit them, and that he be patient. That is what is good. What else? That's all.

Has he no religious obligations?

And he must see that the child is circumcised, that he studies with the *tallib* in the mosque. And the father must see the son through his wedding. These are the father's obligations.

But you don't send the boys to either the mosque school, or to the primary school.

No, we haven't sent any of them. You know, they are still needed to watch over the livestock, and the schools are far from us [one was a thirty-minute walk away, another a forty-five minute walk.] So far, we haven't sent any of them.

Do you think there is nothing to be gained from such studies?

From our traditional studies, there is benefit, and good works. From

---

[2]I was trying to elicit a "rule," but the Faqir was reluctant to provide one.

the other studies, there is just worldly benefit, that's all. You become skillful, you come to earn money, but only if you are patient and hang on. But as for a guy who is energetic and impatient, whose heart is thus, he won't succeed in those studies. You must give money here, and give money there, and be patient and so on, until you succeed. Otherwise, you just get near the certificate for... for secondary school, and they boot you out. And what can you do with them? Nothing.

But he who is patient, and who gives money, and does things this way and that, he may succeed. But the benefit will just be of this world, that's all.

So, according to you, if there is still farming work to be done, it's better if he remains...

No. What's better... it's better if he... better that he studies until he can write, and until he knows what is proper. That's all right. Or, it's even better if he goes to study in our mosque, until he becomes learned. That's fine, even if he doesn't work at all. As for modern studies, he should study until he understands enough to write, until he understands arithmetic, and then he should become a farmer. Then he can do all together. That's what's good, the best of all.

Then why haven't you sent the sons to study in the mosque?

As for the kids, I've told you, they're needed to shepherd the livestock. The others are just beginning to grow up, as Hisen was, God rest his soul, and as Hmida [age seven]. But I'm hoping for it, hoping to send at least some of them, a bit.

Are there children now who study in the mosque?

There are, but they no longer make anything out of it. The *tallib* no longer does anything, neither the one we have now, nor the one before him. They do nothing. Leave the kid there for fourteen years, or fifteen years, and he comes back knowing nothing. As for the primary school, if he studies there for three years he begins to know something. Even after one year, if the kid is smart, he may begin to know how to write and do arithmetic. Like my nephew's son. He writes, and he adds, and he totals. He sits in the store and does everything there.

You've had a lot of children, haven't you?

God be thanked.

Can you still

Well, let's see what our strength accomplishes. That depends on strength. If a man has his belly full, and is healthy and willing, he can't help but make children.

Why, in the countryside, do people have so many children?

We, the Arabs, we produce many children, whether we're in the countryside or in the cities. We don't have the instruments to prevent having children. You, you have the instruments. And this was especially so in

the past. Nowadays, if someone is aware, and has the money, and isn't limited to the countryside, he will also have the tools that you have.
I suppose that's true.

But, you know, we're still... we're still blundering. If the man is strong, and the woman is strong, we like to make children. What can they do?
Well, first you say that it's because of the instruments, and then you say that anyone who cares to can find out about that.

We say that however many children we have, it is good. You [pl.] don't say that.
Why are children good?

They serve the person, they help him, and... oh, a lot of things. They serve your interests. And he who adds to Islam does well. According to us, he who produces many offspring has good works. He has these with respect to God. And if the Almighty takes them, he need not worry.

And one son may become a craftsman, another will plow, one will do the irrigation, one will be a smith, that's fine. Another will gather reeds, that's fine too. If this happens, if each brings in one kilo of meat, wouldn't there be ten kilos here in the evening? Is that the same as just one kilo?

Do you prefer a son or a daughter?

Well, all things considered, the son belongs to the outside as well as the inside; the daughter is just of the inside. As for the daughter, you only benefit from her until the day she leaves. That's that.

But, whatever our share is, it is provided to us by God. In God's beneficence, and in God's guidance, if the portion accorded to us is wide, how many people may be supported by just one daughter? But that's called, "living under another's protection." We, we can't at all tolerate being supported by a daughter. And we don't tolerate that a daughter work outside.

But today there are some who have even begun to rejoice in their daughters. The daughters come home from school, and they come together with friends. The father takes her allowance and says to you, "I have a daughter who studies." [The Faqir's tone is now a mocking one.] We don't at all tolerate a girl to study. Because a girl is just a girl.
What do you mean, "a girl is just a girl"?

The girl is just a girl, she must... she's like nothing. The girl, whatever the situation is, must remain in the house until she marries. That's what's proper.
And so you think it's no good to send a daughter to school?

No. You see what happens. You've seen how... she may meet with someone, and the father sees this. Or they all sit with one another in the class, in the room. What's that? And the father even comes to believe that she is knowledgeable. He says, "She talks about Lebanon," "She said this, she said that, she said that." And the father sits there like a sack, he knows nothing at all. That's what you see. "Let us know what time it is, daughter, let us see the time." Just an example, an example. Like Bukhensha and that daughter of his: "Daughter, let me know the time."

In your house the adult men are yourself, your brother, and your son Mehdi. If your children do something wrong, will your brother hit them?

Yes.

And if his son does something wrong, will you hit him?

Yes. I'll hit him.

Don't some disagreements arise over this?

Well, all things considered, there are some families in which disputes arise from this. As for me, I hardly speak at all to the children. But one of mine is now ailing on my brother's account. My brother hit him and sent his head spinning, and he hasn't been able to work for two days. But what am I going to say? My brother ordered something done, and it wasn't done.

Didn't you say something to him about this?

There is nothing to be said. If he had a good reason, there is nothing I can say. If I say something, it can only be, "Hit less brutally." What else can I say? It was for a reason. What, should he say, "Do this!", and then the boy doesn't do it? That can't be.

In your view, are his children like your children?

If I didn't think that way, we would no longer stay together. If I didn't think that my children were like his, we wouldn't be together.

You'd split up?

Yes. If he didn't want to touch my kids, yes. Just last year, he became stand-offish. He said that, as for his children, he wanted no one to touch them. He then began to leave my children alone. He no longer hit them at all, whereas he used to almost kill them. He had started to have his own kids, and they were taking hold [they were now seven, four, and one], and he began to hold back a little. He began to hold his hands back a bit.

And do the women of the house hit the children?

Yes, they hit them.

As hard as the men do?

They hit them more often. There are women who hit more often because they are the ones who are always watching over the children. They're always boiling water for them, and the children dirty the water, break utensils, spoil the floor, ruin... they hit them, that's all.

Do both the women in the house hit the other's children?

Yes.

And Mehdi?

No, they don't hit him... oh, you mean... yes, Mehdi hits all of them.

Does he hit the children as though he were playing with them, or as though he were a parent? In order to teach them or

When they don't want to do the thing that he told them to. That's all. Whether he's a parent or not. He says, "Do this!" and if it isn't done, he hits them. Or if he needs something. Or if the livestock get away from one of them and eat the crops.

And if the woman and the man are disputing, do they hit one another? Does the man hit the woman?

Yes. And there are women who hit the men. They fight on until she completely beats him up. Yes, there is that too.

How does a woman manage that?

Well, fighting with sticks, or with hands, or in any way. The man might be smaller. Or he might just be modest, and not want to hit her. It is as though he can't hit her.

4

The Mad Migrant

A heat wave had set in. The day before, in the late afternoon, the usual cooling breeze that brings Atlantic air from the west, had abated and given way to calm. By evening, a fitful eastern wind, the Qablaniya, had arisen, ushering in hot, dry air from the Sahara.

The evening and night remained warm. The rooms of the houses, their thick earthen walls providing good insulation, retained cool air and would do so for several days, despite the outside heat. After three or four days, however, the heat would penetrate the walls and invade the rooms, keeping the rooms very warm until a day or two after the heat wave had ceased. By then, the Faqir and I had usually moved into the courtyard to sleep and his brother would be sleeping on the roof. The heat indoors might have been lessened by cross-ventilation, but most farmers build windows into the same wall as the door and all give onto the central courtyard. Windows on the opposite wall, open to the exterior of the house, might provide an easy listening post for an outsider, or a thief.

As the sun rose the next morning, the day was already hot, which meant the normal workday in the fields would be altered. Work would still begin with the sun, but breakfast would come earlier, after a little more than two hours' work, by 8:30, rather than 9:00. After an hour of eating and drinking tea, the men would go back to the fields and return again to the house about an hour before usual, by noon. A short nap before lunch was common in any weather, but now, with the need for sleep intensified by the restless nights, the men would sleep longer, past 3. Lunch, consisting of barley and the vegetable in season, or sometimes corn gruel and milk, would finish between 4 and 4:30. The men would then sit around or busy themselves with some task in the house until the sun lowered in the sky and became more tolerable, toward 5 or 6. If a

66

hired day laborer was with them, they might force themselves back to the fields a little earlier.[1]

During these heat waves, the afternoon sun would often be shielded behind a dust-filled, brownish-gray sky, but this provided no relief from the heat. Intermittently throughout the day, the eastern wind would flare up, and its gusts, full of dust and sand, were sometimes so violent that work in the fields had to be stopped. The evenings and nights would not be much cooler as the wind from the east continued to blow.

As the heat wave wore on, the least essential farm tasks, such as the weeding of mature crops, began to be neglected. It was necessary, instead, to spend more time irrigating and, as always in summer, several hours each day collecting fodder for the cows. The preceding spring had been a cool one and the current heat wave was causing more damage than usual, for the crops and trees had been unable to adjust to the approaching summer.

If the heat persisted, some work would no longer be needed at all. Tomatoes and peppers, for example, would be burned white and yellow and would no longer be picked and marketed. Pears would turn red and spongy, and the pomegranates, still far from ripe, a crippled brown. Watermelons, although often spoiled, hid their injury better and would still be brought to market where buyers, all the more tempted the hotter the weather, might buy two or three in the hope of finding a delicious, sweet one.

As for livestock, sheep would, as always, huddle together, but now, where possible, in the shade. Cows, less gregarious, would also take care to stay out of the midday sun. But donkeys, apparently oblivious to the discomfort around them, would still stand or lie wide-eyed, and almost motionless, under the sun's hottest rays.

This particular heat wave had just started (it was to be especially long,

---

[1]The normal summer and winter schedules are approximately as follows:

Summer		Winter
6:00	sunrise	7:30
6:00	the men wake up	7:00
6:30	work begins	7:30
9:00–9:30	breakfast	9:30–10:00
9:30	work begins again	10:00
1:00	return from work	2:00
1:00–2:30	sleep	
3:00–3:30	lunch	2:30–3:00
3:30	work begins again	3:00
7:30	sunset	5:30
7:30–8:00	return from work	5:30–6:00
9:30	supper	7:30
10:30	sleep	9:00

lasting twenty-four days; daytime temperatures were officially reported to be 110°–125° in the shade). We set out for the fields shortly after 5 P.M. The task was to be a tedious one: weeding around the green pepper seedlings, which had been planted some weeks earlier and which were now about one-inch high. Manure fertilizer had been liberally mixed in with the soil and provided easy growth for weeds. The weeding required prolonged squatting and careful attention to the soil.

Mehdi had been working at this for an hour or so; I had been helping him, talking with him, and peppering him with questions. We were both pleased when a young man, no more than thirty years old, approached us, walking carefully to avoid the muddy canals. He was bare-headed with no turban, no skullcap, not even a round woolen ski cap, which in the last few years had become common among young men in southern Morocco; his hair was quite long, unlike the close-cropped and often even cleanly shaven hair styles of the region. He was barefoot, wore ragged European trousers and, with his shirt open to the waist, he was bare-chested too. His appearance was mild and pleasant, and Mehdi, knowing him well, seemed to anticipate some amusement.

Saleh crouched down with us, on his haunches, pulled a pipe from his pocket, and slowly filled its thimble-sized mouth with kif. Only then did he begin talking. His language was odd; it was filled with open syllables, which gave it a melodious, sing-song air, and lacked the initial consonant clusters that characterize Moroccan Arabic. Although reminding me of classical Arabic, it was certainly not classical because, among other things, it was studded throughout with French words, somewhat Arabicized. Nor was his speech close to colloquial Moroccan Arabic either, for Mehdi avowed that he did not understand much of it at all.

Saleh's talk rambled and for a long while brooked no interruption. Mehdi, between giggles, counseled that I not even try. Saleh frequently referred to "*jahennama*" and to "*l-'afiya*" ("hell" and "fire"). I began to piece together his story, little by little.

Saleh, the son of a village mat maker, had gone to France some years earlier to work in the coal mines, near Lille. His work was not as difficult as that of cutting the coal, and the wages were fine. But after a couple of years, the job became unbearable (he kept alluding to it with those very words, "hell" and "fire"). He was shifted to the task of watching over the coal belt, monitoring its operation. It was very monotonous, and he took to catnapping.

On one occasion Saleh was confronted by a Frenchman and an Italian, who called him a *fainéant* ("sluggard"). Saleh got angry: "I'm not a *fainéant*. This is just a lousy job, and I can't stand it." Tempers flared into a fight, and Saleh got caught between the moving belt and a wooden standpost. His ribs were crushed, and much of his stomach was severely damaged. He spent six months in the hospital. He showed me the scar in his neck where the doctors had inserted a tube in order to feed him during part of that time.

He now received two thousand rials a month from the insurance that workers carry while in the mines. Of this money, he spent about two hundred rials a week on kif, and he admitted that he had to buy a very poor, cheap variety. This left him little money for other things, and he spent most of his time walking around between "44" and the Medina, visiting farmers he knew, picking up a few vegetables from them, and usually sleeping in the open air.

Ali had by now joined us, to assist Mehdi with the seedlings. Mehdi's cousin Abdallah had come by to pick up some vegetables for his family's meals, and he also now helped with the weeding. Saleh's chatter still held my attention, but seemed to have become somewhat tedious for the others.

He talked about his desire to spend his life looking only at good things and not thinking at all of the bad. He had seen many bad things and to think of them made him angry and wrecked his spirit. This made a lilting refrain, "*Haja zina, mashi haja shina,*"[2] and it entered his speech at frequent intervals, contributing to the overall rhythmic, musical effect. He insisted on proving his literacy to me: he took my pen, wrote down part of the alphabet, and drew a picture of an object somewhat like a rocket, which he refused to describe any further. He then signed his name to the sheet of paper.

Later, he began to talk of religion and now his voice modulated slightly and assumed an incantatory tone. "God is present" he said, "for everyone who seeks him." His listeners nodded, following his speech, but not seeming to know where it would lead. "When we pray, we must not pray simply to be seen by others. Many pray only when they are with others, only from shame. Therefore we must pray alone, at night, when no one can see us. This is true prayer." Mehdi began to smirk. Ali attended to the weeding and appeared not to notice.

Saleh continued: "I go, on many nights, to that barren hill, and I pray, alone, to God. And several times He has made a sign to me that He is there, listening. He has even appeared to me, naked and headless, with hair on his body, and said to me that night is the best time for prayer, and alone is the best manner."

Abdallah, incensed, abruptly got up. "Now you've said something that has ruined everything that went before it." He took his vegetables and left.

The sun was about to set, and the fodder for the cows still had to be cut. The Faqir appeared in the distance on his donkey, surely expecting the fodder to be ready for loading. He yelled at us as he approached, "What kind of festival is this here!" and the rest of us split up.

[2]Literally, "Things beautiful, not things ugly."

⊠ OPENING QUESTIONS ABOUT EVENTS AND DIALOGUES

The encounter with Saleh in the fields provoked for me a number of questions, as had the two previous events, and I began to think about the ties between Morocco and Europe, between Moroccans and Europeans. But questions of a different kind also began to occur to me, and I now began to suspect that the sequence "event + dialogue" was not as straightforward as I had imagined. First of all, the encounter with Saleh was unlike both the visit from the brotherhood leader and the circumcision: the Faqir had not witnessed it, and it had few of the trappings and little of the clear definition of a "traditional" anthropological happening. I wondered whether my implicit, not clearly formulated, twin requirement—the event should be fairly well-defined and occur with both the Faqir and me present—might not be too rigid, like a carefully planned research project, and hide significant aspects of our mutual experience.

As I prepared questions for the dialogue, I also began to see that the questions themselves, although certainly provoked by the event, were tied as well to my own social and cultural situation. I had already thought about this, fleetingly, in the earlier dialogues, but these dialogues had not pushed me to concentrate on this: in the first dialogue, I had posed what seemed fairly matter-of-fact chronological and topical questions; in the second and third, most of my questions flowed quite naturally, I thought, from what seemed to be relatively uncomplicated events.

Here, however, I would be posing questions about relations between Europeans and Moroccans. My involvement with the Faqir was clearly one instance of these relations, and our questions and answers on the broader topic would inevitably comment on our ties with one another. If only indirectly, we would be talking about ourselves throughout this dialogue and I could no longer claim, even had I been so inclined before, that our dialogues were essentially an inquiry into external, "objective" events. More specifically, it did not seem accidental that I had singled out for attention an event that cast a very unfavorable light on Europe's role in Morocco. This certainly betrayed on my part an antagonism to colonialism and imperialism that could not help but influence the kind of questions I asked. Some questions, as I formulated them, seemed clearly designed to push the Faqir toward a condemnation of colonialism.

Yet, whatever the differences between this event and the preceding ones, and whatever effect our particular situation might have on the topic, I had questions about this event to which I wanted the Faqir to respond. I was interested in what the Faqir's actual contact with Europeans had been, both during colonial rule ("Christians, before independence... "); and in the postcolonial period ("Christians, after independence... "); in what he saw as the differences between Christian and

Muslim ("Christian and Muslim... "); in the specific experience of villagers, of whom Saleh was one, who had worked and lived in Europe ("Villagers in Europe... "); and in the Faqir's own attitude toward working in Europe ("Working in France... ").

▩ FOURTH DIALOGUE

CHRISTIANS, BEFORE INDEPENDENCE...

Who were the first people you saw who came from foreign lands?
Christians, that's all. The French.

Whom did you get to know of these French people?
We didn't deal with them, not enough to get to know them. I might know their names, hearing them. But there was one I dealt with, a captain, in the Medina. I was just about l-'Aribi's age [about twelve]. I wasn't yet able to buy and sell alone. I'd drive the animals to the Medina if my father couldn't, but I had to be accompanied by older people.

I remember that captain; we would bring him these thin tree branches, you know, the kind we use for our ceilings. Yes, they sure had some ignorant people among them. All the wood that we would bring from our region, he would buy, and he would come and pay, himself. He was tall, so tall! And he was French.

And after the captain?
Well, after him, things remained like that, you know. The captains were replaced, and we knew only of captains, or a few settlers. But other sorts of Christians we weren't acquainted with. They didn't deal with us and didn't even speak to us. Few of them spoke Arabic, very few. Very, very few.

And then the farmers began to come. And they kept on coming, one following another, then another following that one.

Were there any very poor foreigners, who had nothing, who walked through the Medina looking for something to do?
Ts, Ts, *non*! They never came here destitute. They didn't send us the poor. They all came with a position. Those who came already had a situation, or they came in some official capacity.

You mean, they didn't come of themselves?
No. They came under orders. They didn't arrive unattached as we do, the Arabs. They came with a position: a foreman, a director, a secretary, or... many positions.

Did you deal with them much? For example, when you worked on that colonial farm long ago?
We'd speak with the foremen—one was an Italian, another was French—they were foremen but small fry in any case. We'd speak with them but the boss, he wouldn't speak with you.

At that time, as you were growing up and becoming a man, those people, Christians, were settling the countryside. What did you think about them?

Well, we'd say to ourselves that their practices were fine, but ill will grew up between us and the northern Arabs, between the locals and the northern Arab officials. Because although the French were colonizing the country, and ruling, they used the northern Arabs as go-betweens, as qaids and sheikhs. The sheikhs had the loyalty of the moqaddems, the qaid had the loyalty of sheikh, and the French had the loyalty of the qaid. They all helped one another. As for the poor, they'd all beat up on us. Whatever they wanted to hang upon a poor fellow, they'd hang upon him.

What was your reaction to all of this? Did you want to get rid of the French, did you say, "They're not like us, they're sons of Adam but not like us"?

Well, in any event, at that time, there was ignorance. We didn't know about the wealth of the country. We didn't know about minerals, we didn't know.... We, the ordinary people, who wanted only sugar and tea, and to live, we'd say the Christians were good. But those Muslims who were ruling over us, who were telling us to do this and that, were saying to us, "The Christians want. . . ." But, in fact, the Christians didn't want that. The ruling Muslims were just filling their own needs, for themselves.

The moqaddem would come and tell you, "Hey, you're to go work for the qaid." And the Christians would never find out. If they found out, they would have confiscated everything. Or, on another occasion, he'd come and tell you, "You're to go to work for the captain," or, "for the officers," or for whomever. But it wasn't that at all. The moqaddem would be taking half the workers to work for him in his own house, and one half he'd take to the qaid. And the sheikh also would take a few. From that, we'd say the Christians weren't good.

On the other hand, there were those among us who were learned, who knew about the riches of the country, and who were thinking about how to . . . about throwing them out . . how to act to get the Christians out of the country. They understood the wealth of the country. At that time, we didn't know about such wealth; we didn't know that the earth could yield wealth. We cared only about what we had to give in taxes, and about the kind of work we knew of.

You mean wealth such as from mechanized farming?

No, no, no, no, no. That comes from toil. I mean wealth like minerals; that's what countries are now disputing over, you know, over minerals. But oranges and the like, that's the work of the hands, and you can do it with your own capital. I mean phosphates, and even commerce. You know, in the markets, the exchange of the markets, there is success to be had, there is profit there that we didn't know about then.

For example, the French would get hold of our merchandise and sell it. And then bring here some other merchandise, making a profit on that, selling it to us for whatever the French wanted. That's what we didn't understand then.

At the time you were working on that Christian's farm, did you see a lot of Christians?

No, only very few. Unless there was a squadron of the army or something, then you'd see a lot of Christians. Otherwise, you might see three Christians, or even four, in the Medina, in the large square.

And when did they begin to come, many of them?

There never were many of them here. Their presence was in Casablanca, but here, you wouldn't see them. And also, even those that did come, each would follow his own work. They didn't do as we do, gathering together and so on. They'd keep to themselves.

And just one Christian would stand over the Muslim officials?

Yes. In "44" there was just the captain and his assistant. In all of "44." And even then, he would go to the coast, he'd go and stay away for two days or three and he might not even return for the day of the court session.

Is there any difference in the words you use for Christians? Sometimes you say rumi *and sometimes* nasrani.

Well, there are so many names, *rumi, nasrani,* all of them mean the same thing. That's all, that's that.

Does one of them have a better meaning than the other?

No, no. It's all the same. *Nasrani* is the same as *rumi.* Except that those of them who had some knowledge, who were smart, if someone said to him, *nasrani,* he would answer, "No, don't call us *nasrani, nasrani* means 'hunger.'" Because we used to say, "A *nasrani* is an infidel; he's someone who won't feed you if you are starving, and won't give you to drink if you are thirsty." Those with some knowledge, they would tell us that they are *rumi.* And what is the meaning of *rumi?* They "fix" things.[3] That's why one type was called *rumi,* someone who will get something done, if it is possible.

And if you called someone rumi, *did that have a good meaning?*

Just as *French,* as *nasrani.* Under the term *nasrani,* we bring everything together, American, French, everything under *nasrani.*

But at first, when you would think about a Christian, would you think to yourself, French?

Then, we knew nothing except the French, period. Even if you were an old man, you didn't know anything about other countries.

[3]The Faqir sees a tie between *rumi* and the Arabic word *ruwwem* (to fix, repair). The actual etymology for *rumi* appears to be its derivation from *Romaean* (Wehr 1966, p. 369). The literal meaning of *nasrani* (derived from the adjectival form of Nazareth) is "Christian."

Didn't you know about Algeria?

No. Then we didn't know about it, we called them "in-betweens." We didn't call them "Algerians," we called them "in-betweens."

What did that mean?

In-between, between a Muslim and a Christian. The people, themselves, had become "in-between." Because they came close to becoming French.

Well, the French were in Algeria for 130 years.

And what about the Christians you met when you went to work for Public Works?

There, there were Christians of different sorts. There were Italians, there were Germans who were becoming French, there were Indonesians who are Muslims.

Did you work together?

Yes. But the French took their meals in a different room, by themselves. At meals, none of us would be with them. At work, each Christian would have four workers, or five, or twenty, or fifteen, according to the work. The team was led by a Christian. The Christian wasn't a worker, but gave orders.

Even if the Christian was an Italian, he wouldn't be a worker?

No. If he was skilled, skilled in some machine, he'd have one Moroccan behind him. He'd teach the Moroccan the machine, and then he'd rest, and begin to watch over him.

You mean, they wouldn't work alongside you?

What, with the pick and the shovel? No, *non!* Even if one was with you, in the pit, he would just cross his arms like this, and stand there, that's all.

Did you know those Americans who were at the aviation base, near the coast?

We'd see them, but we didn't deal with them. They came only after the war, a lot of them. And they came in droves to Casablanca.

What about the Moroccans who worked for the Americans?

Moroccans had their needs satisfied by the Americans, before they left. You'd only have to be an errand boy, and they'd give you something, like cigarettes, which would bring a lot of money. For those two years, those Arabs had their wants satisfied. People used to say to one another, "Hey, you're spending a lot of money, do you work with the Americans?" They had their wants satisfied. But then the Americans fell into bad practices.

How so?

In Casablanca they began to attack people.

What do you mean, they began to attack people?

They molested women, in Casablanca. I don't know whether it was the military, or civilians. I don't know. What they did was good for nothing.

And when you were taken to Casablanca, did you find a lot of Christians there?[4]

Yes, there were many, but they didn't show themselves much.

Why was that?

They were afraid, afraid that they would be attacked. They became wary; a Christian couldn't just walk around and deal with an Arab. No. He'd have to watch out for his skin.

How many of you were taken from here to Casablanca?

At first, we were four hundred, four hundred from the qaid's region. And then, after a month, they brought two hundred more.

And how many Christians were over you?

Six, or seven, at least.

At that time, in your own mind, what did you think about those French who had colonized and settled the country?

At that time, the heart was hardened... "Our nation at any cost, the nation at any cost." They must leave, even if there are Muslims who... "the country at any cost, the country at any cost."

The day we went to Casablanca—I now want to tell you about the Casablanca part.[5] That day, when we were to be sent to Casablanca, all of our region was summoned to "44," and the qaid began to select among the people.

Did the people want to go?

No, they didn't want to go. All those whom the sheikhs or the sheikhs' friends wanted to remain, or whom the moqaddems wanted to remain, were kept away. Those who went before the qaid were only those who had no one to stand up for them. And to some, whom the qaid knew very well, he said, "You must go." Because he wanted very much to have with him those who were loyal to him.

Then, we were brought into the qaid's residence, and locked in. That's it! There was no one to bring news, nothing. Locked. Until the next day, when we were brought arms and given ammunition. We were divided into groups and taken outside. The trucks came, we were loaded on, and began to travel.

We stopped once, after six or seven hours, and then drove on again. We arrived in Casablanca in the dead of night, about eleven o'clock, or maybe midnight. We were brought to the docks. We said to ourselves, "This must be Indochina." We thought we were going to be shipped to

[4]The Faqir was impressed into the army and taken to Casablanca as part of an expedition to keep order there, shortly after the uprising in December 1952, in Casablanca, in which more than 490 Moroccans lost their lives, according to official figures. Once before, as a youth, the Faqir had been forced into the army, that time as part of the French effort to pacify areas south of Taroudannt. I did not discuss this with the Faqir that summer.

[5]The Faqir, now clearly introducing this episode as a story, embarks upon what is to be his longest uninterrupted narrative in the dialogues.

Indochina. But the next morning, our group was assigned one section of Casablanca to control.

What would we do, you know? Well, we'd all go out, all four hundred, into one section, together. We'd leave only the guards at the port buildings. We'd approach the section by a road, and we'd put one of us, then one, one, one, one, until we surrounded the entire section. Standing. We'd just go three meters, and put one to stand. We'd surround it. The qaid would enter the section, and all those officers, and the women— they had women—would search the people. And we would be keeping watch.

And there would be one place through which there was entrance and exit. An officer would be there. And whoever wanted to enter or leave the section would have their papers examined. If he was a worker, and had a working card, they'd let him leave. And if he was returning from work, they'd let him enter. If he had no card, if he had nothing, there was the truck waiting near us, he'd be taken to it, and the truck would soon fill up.

After some days of this, the generals came, from abroad, and from other parts of the country, or wherever. And they brought journalists with them. We were put in four rows, and the qaid came to lecture us.

He said to us, "You understand, you are my children. And you understand that I, I have put my confidence in you. There are many other people, all over, but those in whom I don't have trust I didn't bring. And now, I have brought you here so that you can have some success, so that you will make a little money, so that you will hold the door for me.

"And me, the French government has put its confidence in me. After all, qaids are numerous, there are some five hundred qaids in our land. But they have chosen us, in whom they have confidence.

"And you know that what the agitators say isn't so. We and the French government are like this [the Faqir clasped his hands]. Our children, they are not separate, and their blood and ours are like this, and their treasury and our treasury are like this. And the French government, and ours, are the same, that's it. Don't believe that there is any difference between us.

"And know that the Casablancans are vicious. Watch where you pass when you're walking, and look behind you, for someone may be going to attack you. When you're walking, keep an eye out behind you. If you see that the earth has been disturbed, don't step on it. There will be a bomb there, or a grenade, or something.

"And be careful, and watch out for your own necks, and fight for your own lives. Don't think that you're fighting only for the government. Now, today, I'm telling you, 'Fight for the government.' But if something happens, fight for your own heads. Don't keep thinking about the government, just fight for your own skins. The best dog is saved by his own bark. And the Casablancans, watch out for the Casablancans!"

After those words were spoken, after he had heated us up, you know, with that electricity, the generals and the journalists left, and only those from his land remained with him. He said, "Sit down." We sat down. And those from his land sat in the middle, among us, sat during this difficult time in the middle. And he began to speak to them.

He said to them, "To me, now, the government, the French government, has given the garden. She has given me the key to it, and I'm sitting at the gate of the garden. I'm waiting for the order to arrive, and then I'll enter and look for what is ripe. I'll pick those that are ripe, and those that are still green I'll leave until they ripen." He was speaking to them in some other kind of speech, and we didn't understand. But among the northern Arabs, there were those who understood.

That is, he was telling them, "I am in charge of a garden, which is all of Morocco. And I sit at the gate, so that no one enters, no one exits. And when I enter, I'm the one who decides what goes and what stays." Well, when this moment was finished, the qaid left to bid the Christians goodbye, and the northern Arabs began to talk to one another, until they all understood what had been said.

Then the qaid came back to us and said: "You know that we used to work in large numbers. Now, we're going to begin working in smaller groups of one chief with his forty men. Now, this group must walk through the section of the city, until four hours are finished, and then another group will take its turn."

And each group had with it one man who knew the area, who would carry just a club, with no rifle. And one Christian, who would follow the guide; and the chief would follow the Christian. And then the men would follow, each ten men with one corporal, forty men in all. That was the order.

The qaid told us: "Your duty is: whoever approaches you in an automobile will not pass through the middle; whoever comes by bicycle will not pass through the middle. If they try, grab them. If someone has his hands in his pockets, seize him. If someone doesn't defer to you, seize him. That's the job. Don't search them, the Christian will do the searching, that's not your job. And anyone who's looking over the Christian, surround that person. You never know, there are guns around."

When we started on that job, none of the chiefs wanted to go first. So we drew straws, and we came in second. The men asked us, "What will we do, how are we going to do this?" We told them: "We have nothing to say yet, until we meet the first group. They'll tell us how the assignment went, and we'll take over for them."

When the first group returned, we met them outside in the garden, where you'd go if you had to relieve yourself, or whatever. "What did you do, how did you do?" They said, "We went around, no one spoke to us and we spoke to no one. And we didn't seize anyone."

And what about the Christian who was with them?

Even if he was. The Christian would keep a good distance from the Casablancans who would annoy and insult us. As if I said to you, "Ah, you American traitor!" By that time, the Christian would have already gone by, and he saw nothing at all.

So, the Casablancans used to insult you.

Yes! They'd call us traitors. As if you are an American, and the conqueror of America is giving you orders, and an American comes up to you and says, "Eeeh, you American traitor." Well, with the Christian way up front, we'd let the Casablancans talk. We didn't let it bother us. We only wanted to get the thing over with.

Well, in any event, we asked ourselves, "How are we going to do this job? The first group had no problems, but what about us? How can we work this?" We went aside, the three of us, the three corporals, to talk this over. After a moment, the man with the club came over to us. He was a black and had lived in Casablanca. He said, "I'll take part in your talk." We said, "All right." He said, "How do you plan to do this?" We told him: "Well, buddy, we're going to move out, and those who defer to us and are timid, God give them peace. Those who defy and bother us, we'll seize them."

He said, "We'll do a special kind of job." You see, as we'd leave the port area, we'd first enter the *mellah* [the Jewish quarter]. The *mellah* is very narrow, there are places where two of us abreast couldn't pass. And the Jews would be bold; they couldn't have cared less about all this. The black said, "Today, we'll work on the Jews."

"O.K. That's all right with us."

He said, "Well, I'll do it this way. As I go past them, I'll round them up with my club." Because the Jews were allowed to congregate, and there would always be three or four of them gathering together. But it was forbidden for the Arabs to gather, or talk together, or whatever. The Jews would be hanging around, joking.[6]

"If one flees, just let him go, don't try to seize him. Those who defy us, we'll... " What was our practice? Each two of us would put one Jew between us, and he'd go with us throughout the patrol. At least the patrolling would annoy him. But once we returned to the port, they would be let go. We said, "All right, that kind of work sounds fine."

In the event, when three or four Jews were sitting around, he'd go past them, turn around, and we would surround them. We didn't bother the Arab sections at all. Ah, ah! If one ran, he was gone. [the Faqir chuckled.] If he stayed and tried to answer us back, we'd put him between us, "Get going!" We had guns, and bayonets, and clubs, and

[6]There are clear hints here of some Moroccan attitudes toward Jews; also, of the manner in which French rule distinguished between Muslims and Jews. The Faqir discusses Jews in more detail in chapter 6.

ammunition, all of them hanging upon us like ornaments. We'd lead the Jew around until we finished our tour.

How many of them didn't run away?

Few. They all ran away, except for very few. We'd take them in, and then let them go. We'd tell them we just wanted to annoy them, let them spend the day working with us.

Well, in the event, the Muslims in Casablanca began, "Ts, ts, ay, ay, these southerners, these southerners, they know what's right, these southerners, ay, ay." You know, if we didn't want the government's bread, the people would give us their bread instead. And if we went to the bath house, they'd have everyone leave the bath house, they'd give us the key to it, and the bath house would be ours alone. Or we'd go to buy meat, and he [the butcher] would weigh a kilo and then add another quarter. Because of that work, that work of ours.

Well, we worked like that until we finished our tour. When the next team came out, we told them what we had done, they did the same, and the thing turned out well. Finally, we weren't bringing anyone in.

Then, the qaid told us: "Understand this. Now, you are no longer going out in groups of forty. You will go just in a group of ten, with one corporal. And the Christian will no longer go around with you."

Was that easy?

Easy? We were scared. It was easy when we were many, but now we were scared. Ten, what can it save you from? Just four guys come up to you and what will ten manage? Our group had to stand guard over the store owners in front of the stores. The merchants were no longer buying and selling; they were afraid of being killed.

At the end of three months, we gave back our arms. And we came back to our homes. But those last weeks, the work increased; they no longer kept us to our hours. More were dying.

Why was that?

They'd be shooting people, ambushing them, in the streets. Arabs were shooting at others, those who were militants, those who understood . . .

Were they shooting at you?

They'd shoot at those who lived there, the merchants, those who didn't want to work with the nationalists, and so on. But on the patrols, not one among us was shot, no one hit us, because we weren't hurting anyone.

Well toward the end we no longer had any rest. We'd just come back, sit down, and be about to eat, and be told, "Let's go, there was an incident in this place, or that." We'd go, wait until the police came, and then come back, sit down, and "Let's go, there's an incident in . . . " Like that. The troubles were too much for them.

Well, we came back here, and that was it. We had been paid a thousand francs a day, the chiefs, two thousand. You know, we cleared eighteen thousand rials for those three months. Some of us spent a lot, some of us spent nothing. They also gave us canned sardines and cigarettes. What we didn't consume, we sold. Some people bought rugs, and so on, and came back dressed in fine clothes.

So that those who had remained here, who hadn't been sent to Casablanca, who had had ties with the qaid or sheikh, began to say, "Eh, eh, I want to go." But then there was no place to go, and they became envious of us.

CHRISTIANS, AFTER INDEPENDENCE . . .

After independence, did the Christians remain in the region?
About a year after we came back, the qaid returned.[7] Over him was now a Frenchman called the control, no longer the captain. People would no longer pay the qaid any money. And they would no longer stand watch for him, at his residence. And no one would pay the fee at the marketplace. Finally, he sent an order to the coast, telling them, "Bring the army!" And the legion came to the marketplace, and the qaid said he was going to have everyone in the marketplace shot. But the control wouldn't let him. Well, people would no longer give the qaid anything.

After a while, we began to blockade the roads. The leaders of the nationalist movement—and I was one of them in our area—would tell the people, "To work, on the roads!" We'd pile stones and shrubbery so that a car couldn't pass. Impossible! If a Christian came, like you, one whom I knew, we'd take away the barrier. Otherwise, "Hey you, get out!" We blockaded the roads like this for fifteen days.
Were these blockades to help the government?
No, we were blocking the roads to help the Arabs, the nationalists, upon the orders of the movement. And the government's men, they wanted to come and fight with us. And the qaid, his eyes whitened. No one went to the court anymore, the sheikhs no longer could go to the qaid, and the qaid no longer received the sheikhs or the moqaddems. After a while, they could no longer even go out at all. What a time of trouble.
And what were the Christians around here doing at that time?
The Christian farm owners kept quiet, kept on working. They would

[7]I had tried, here, to move the Faqir's story ahead a few years, but the Faqir insisted on recounting events in 1953 and 1954, and did not allow me to jump ahead. For him, perhaps, these events all form a unit related to the struggle for independence in Morocco, what he might see as his "Casablanca story," and he did not wish to be deflected from it.

address us, "as-Sidi, as-Sidi" [a respectful term]. As for the Christian rulers, we never saw them anyway.

And after independence, did the behavior of those Christians who stayed change?

Yes, they changed. They began to take on workers who wanted to work, and to joke with the workers, and to give them a little better wage. Not, "Work, or I'll take you to the qaid!" Not the same at all. And they began to say, "God says . . . we understand that Morocco is winning its independence, we understand, we understand."[8]

And now you see all sorts of Christians, not only the French?

Now, all sorts. Then, there were only those French; the Christians weren't common. There weren't so many tourists.

But now there are. How do they appear to you?

Those who know the tourist's language know the tourists. Germans, or French, or, you know, Portuguese, or Americans.

But even if you don't talk to them, you see them in the Medina. **How do they appear to you?**

As for the kind of people they are, they are the children of Adam. Like us, like them; each has his own practices, and we ask that God help them, and that God help us, now.

But in those days, it was forbidden to meet a Christian and not to bow to him. Yeah, an army man or anyone with some leadership position might be following you, and if you didn't defer to the Christian, it was, "Hey, to prison!" Bwa, bwa, bwa! You think that was easy? There were times when in the marketplace they would round up three hundred or four hundred and take them to jail. That's how they were, the Christians.

And what about the hippies?

Now, there are many; then there were none.

And what is your view of them?

We don't understand them, these hippies. One type appears to be all hair, hair all around his head, and dirty. There are some who carry loads on their backs. There are some who have motorcycles, some who ride bicycles and who wear only shorts. And they eat while walking in the street! And sit wherever it suits them, they don't care. That's the hippie.

---

[8]According to the Faqir, then, the attitude of Christians toward Moroccans changed after independence and became more solicitous and understanding. Of course, the extent to which this change was sincere, or adopted simply in order to secure other goals such as continued control over basic resources, is an open question.

A related question, which I cannot ignore, is how this change may be tied to changes in the anthropologist's manner (and my own), changes from an era in which anthropology was, in many areas, closely tied to colonial institutions to one in which colonial rule has been squarely challenged. Have the anthropologists, too, become more solicitous and more understanding? Has this change been a sincere one, or adopted to secure other goals?

We used to say they were ruining the land, ruining piety, that they wanted to dirty the country. There are still some who say that. And some say, like your thoughts and mine, "They are just like the *hadawa*, each country gives forth some of these." That is what I say.[9]

CHRISTIAN AND MUSLIM . . .

After all this, what do you see as the difference between Christian and Muslim?

The difference between them is the Credo of the Prophet. That's the difference.

That's the difference?

And to the eye, it is their clothing that is different. And language. And the difference in piety, in "There is no God but God, and Muhammad is His Prophet."

And in their manner?

The Christians, in their dealings, deal with you fairly.

All of them?

All of them. Even if there are among them some thieves, they won't outfox you for something small. He'll be a big criminal, and in a special way, a special way. We, the Muslims, we'll scheme over something that's nothing.

Over a tiny watermelon?[10]

And we talk a lot, with no limit. Always talking, always joking, always passing the time even though it may be a complete waste.

And also, if there are just ten of us, the street isn't wide enough to hold us. With them, they could be thousands and they would still pass through. And they could be in a café, many of them, in a hotel or whatever, and each talks with his friend; they don't raise any commotion. With us, just ten of us, and we're all looking for horseplay.

They know the rules. And everyone knows his own customs, theirs and ours.

Can a Christian become a Moroccan?

No. There are some Jews who are Moroccans, but we've never seen a Christian Moroccan.

But now, under independence, there must be . . .

[9]The *hadawa* are itinerants, typically clothed in rags and with their head hair uncut, whose demeanor is, to most Moroccans, beneath contempt. The Faqir is echoing a talk he and I had earlier on the *hadawa*.

[10]I was alluding to an altercation that had occurred in the marketplace some days before when a buyer, having tasted a slice of watermelon and having been told by the seller that the very sweet slice was characteristic of all the watermelons in one pile (they all supposedly came from one field), quarreled with the seller after buying a watermelon that turned out to be tasteless.

No, Christians there aren't. There are no Christians who say the Credo... you mean who say the Credo?

No, not who say the Credo, but those who become Moroccan, you know, who... who are living here. There are some, there are. Like those in the cities who still have their property in the city. There are those.

Have you seen any convert to Islam?

No, we have never seen a Christian convert. The Jews, from year to year, a Jew might come to the large square in the Medina, and collect money from people, and testify to them that he was a Jew, and had become a Muslim. But Christians, never.

Why is it that Jews converted and Christians didn't?

I don't know. I don't know. I don't know.

VILLAGERS IN EUROPE...

Who went first, from the village, to work in Europe?

The first whom I remember—I was still small, about the age of l-'Aribi—was the Hajj Hmed. And the Hajj Abdallah, God bless him. They stayed there about twelve years, or more.

And when they came back... From France they went to Mecca, they made the Pilgrimage.

When was that?

Well, I don't want to tell you a lie. When they came back, they found me already plowing, and beginning to market.

And when they came back, did they come back with money?

Yes. They came back with money, bought cows, bought sheep, and took partnerships in the land of others, and built their compounds up, and married. They were very well off.

What did they say about the work in France?

They'd say that they had made a lot of money, that they had had good luck. As they do now.

As now?

No, then even more. Then, there was no money here, there were no francs. There was no paid work to be found. And those who came back, they were really well off, bought cows, bought sheep, and took land in partnership.

And when did people begin to go to work in France in large numbers?

Not until independence, until there were contracts. One group went from here, shortly after independence. Then, the large farmers got together with the government, and they said, "France is here in Morocco, there is much farming work to be done here." And they stopped allowing those from our region to leave. From that time, to go meant to go secretly, from the Medina, from the mountain regions, or from the coast. This is so even now. The contracts don't come for us. They're not allowed to come here. The large farmers got together and spoke with the officials. We didn't know about this, and they don't give a damn about us. They decided that in their meetings, meetings of those fat ones.

And did many go to France in the military?

Very many.

About ten?

No, more. And people also died in the military. Died here, and died there, and died in the north, and how many died in France, a lot. Muhammad, my mother's brother's son, for one.

Those who went in the military, did they go voluntarily, or did they go against their will?

No, they went voluntarily. There was nothing for them to do here, so they left.

Those who returned here from the military, what did they do?

When they returned? They farmed.

Didn't they return with money?

A little, a little, the military didn't bring in much money. Just a little.

Did you find them the same, in their manner, in their personality, as when they had left? Or had they changed?

Well, in any event, when they had just returned, their manner was different. But after only three or four years, they'd become just like us in the countryside.

How was their manner different when they first returned?

Well... when they left, they were ragged, and when they returned, they were cleaned up a bit. They had come to know about clothing, they knew a bit about... they had become acquainted with the government a little, they weren't so easily cowed. And we were cowed then, we wouldn't go to the government at all then. They were familiar with its workings. That's where the difference was.

And why were you cowed?

Ignorant. We were afraid of the government. You know, if a moqaddem or sheikh came to knock one of us around, we didn't know how to get away from it. Those military fellows, they came back tough. They didn't bow to either sheikhs or moqaddems. And the qaid allowed them great freedom.

How so?

They weren't forced to work for the officials, the way we were. They didn't have to do that.

And those who returned from working in France, had their manner changed?

They changed, yes. They were swelled up, become operators, they'd throw their wealth around. That's how they went beyond us.

But there were those who came back without money.

No. From France, all those who came back from France...

No, you know, like that Hummad.

Hummad is the only one who didn't bring money back. But everyone else who went to France came back well off. Hummad brought back nothing, He drank, and married a French woman. Then he fought with her, and they threw him out. He's a washout, period.

And what about Saleh, the mat maker's son?

As for him, he too was consumed by his drinking. And then he was injured, injured in the pits. The pit fell in on him. No. He was working in the mines with a machine, and the machine struck him. Some machine in the mine injured him.

And what about his mind?

I don't know. Some say that, while in the hospital, he spent his time reading *A Thousand and One Nights,* and from that his mind was damaged.[11]

And what about his brother, who also went to France?

That one, you know, just sits around drinking and gambling.

What about your sister's son, Milud?

He went there, worked there for six months, and fell ill. Because of the air, the air didn't agree with him. He was too weak.

Well, that's three or four now I've mentioned who...

Those are all, just those. But the others all came back well off. Ali went to France and came back with money; Hassan bought his pickup truck with money from France. That's not bad. [12]

And when they returned, did they deal with people as they had before they left?

Yes, of necessity. Why, they deal with others of necessity, both before they leave and after they come back.[13]

No, I mean did they put on airs?

All of them put on airs when they came back. Like Hassan. He says, "People are coming to me to cheat me out of my money. I won't lend to

---

[11]Many Moroccans believe a cause of unsound minds to be the reading of fantastical works, of which *A Thousand and One Nights* is one.

The Faqir's answers to questions about Saleh, the migrant who had visited us in the fields, showed a complete lack of concern. There seemed little point in pursuing his case.

[12]Despite the number of exceptions I have mentioned, the Faqir insists that the overall pattern has been beneficial; my search for a condemnation of this aspect of the colonial experience is thwarted. This happens again and again in the questions and answers that follow; the Faqir's view is consistently more nuanced.

[13]I have phrased my question poorly and the Faqir misunderstands me. What I meant was, "Did the manner in which they behaved toward others change?"

anyone." That's what those who've come back from France say. "Watch out that those from the countryside don't cheat you, don't go into partnership with them, don't... give them nothing, don't lend them anything. Their business is cheating." Well, they were a bit puffed up.

Did they keep apart from the locals?

No, they couldn't keep apart. How could they make a living and support the family if they stood apart? They couldn't remain separate.

And when they return, what do they say about their lives in those countries?

The Moroccans praise those countries: they have laws. If the government has its rules, and the people follow the rules, and they're living in good health, and you do what you're supposed to do, there is no one who will push you aside for someone else. And what you earn, you eat. That's all.

Don't they downgrade France at all?

No.

Don't they complain about it?

No.

Neither about the money, nor about the food, nor...

No. Everything about their treatment is good. They never speak badly about it, neither now, nor formerly.

And many people would want to go there?

They'd like very much to. If they could find a way, even the women would want to go.

Do people distinguish between France, and Belgium, and Germany, and Holland, and so on?

They say, "So-and-so is in France, so-and-so is in Belgium," and that each country has its own practices. But in all of them, they are treated well. Those of us here, we just say France, we call it all France. Because we haven't seen. But those who've gone there, they know the difference between France and Holland.

Which do they say is better, France or Holland?

As for money, and for *demokratiya*,[14] Holland. And France is a bit like Morocco, they say: there is forgiveness there.

What do you mean, "forgiveness"?

There aren't strict punishments. You know, if you did something wrong to me, I won't fight very much over it. I'll say, "This time, God watch over you." They forgive a little. In Holland, no.

In what respect is Holland demokratiya?

In Holland, if one does something wrong, he won't spend the night there. They throw him out, that's all.

[14]The word *demokratiya* will receive its specific meaning, which is quite unlike that of its French cognate, in what follows.

Is that good, or bad?

It's good. We'd very much like everything to be like that. He who makes trouble, throw him out, don't let him pass the night.

Throw him out, that's all, don't forgive at all?

Not at all.

But is such forgiveness good, or not good?

Well, one aspect... with respect to God, it is good. But forgiveness really makes for many more criminals.

And demokratiya *doesn't... ?*

No. If someone wants to commit a crime, he'll worry about the *demokratiya.*

Are there any who married Christians in France?

Among us, no. Except for Hummad, who was kicked out because he fought with her.

In your view, is it good for a man to go to France and to marry a Christian?

Well, if it pleases his will, fine. As for religion, I don't know what God Almighty says. In any event, each has his own religion. But the children, the children would be mixtures. I don't know.

WORKING IN FRANCE...

And you, did you ever want to go to France?

Yes.

What happened?

I went to the Medina and registered. Well, they gave me the passport, you know, in order to go to Rabat. I went to Rabat and came up against that war with Germany. And they kept us all back, not only me. Everyone. Well, we came back.

After that, you didn't try again?

No, I no longer wanted to. After that, I came back here and established my capital, and began to farm. I couldn't allow what was mine to run down, and I had gotten a bit of sense, and I couldn't leave what was mine.

Did you ever want to send Mehdi?[15]

Mehdi was looking for it himself, just last year. I didn't want that. But Mehdi knocked himself out looking for a way to go, until he was beaten back, until he found nothing.

Why do you think he wants to go?

I don't know his thoughts. Why... in my view, he just wants money, nothing more.

[15]This question was suggested by an earlier conversation I had had with Mehdi, who had told me that, the previous year, he had unsuccessfully tried to seek employment in France.

That's all, money?

Just wants money, and he doesn't want a boss, that's all. He wants to be free, on his own, he probably says.

Is it good for a son to think in that way?

No. If his parents don't want that, it's no good for him. He must wait until he can go with the approval of his father. Then, wherever he went God would protect him. If he doesn't have the approval of the parent, then God will not give His.

Could you send one of the other children?

If there are enough of them to take care of the work here, I could send one, if there is a way to do it. If the work is taken care of. But if there is work to be done here, I couldn't.

In your view, what is bad about a man going to work in France?

What is bad is if he went all the way there and failed, and brought back nothing. If he went out drinking, or gambling, or whatever. Or if he runs away from his responsibilities, stays there, you know, and never gets his capital together in order to return. That's what's evil. What is good is if he goes there, and works, and brings back money. That is good. As if he stayed here, and worked hard here. It's the same.

Let's say that a Muslim, who is used to the ways of this country, leaves here and goes there. Isn't there danger in that?

Danger with respect to religion?

Yes.

As for the religious way, it is all danger. If he holds to his religion, no one will take it away from him. France doesn't take your religion away. France, to the contrary, likes those who are religious. He who keeps to his religion, and brings back money, that is a good thing, he has done everything. Nothing has harmed him. But if it happened that he brought back money and shed his religion, that is perilous. All of that is perilous.

But, you know, a man there finds himself next to pork, next to liquor, next to all that is prohibited to him. Isn't it dangerous for a person to go and put himself in the middle of what is forbidden to him?

All that is forbidden is dangerous. All one's living is dangerous. And the Europeans don't force anyone to transgress. Like in Holland, Muslim meals are brought to them, not Christian meals. Those who transgress, transgress of themselves. He who is going to eat what is forbidden there will eat it here too. And he who is observant is able to eat either here or there.

In your view, how is it that those countries can hire Moroccans, pay for their trips, and pay them more than is usual in Morocco?

They get profit. They see profit in them; they make money from them.

Why then do they take workers from Morocco?

They take them from countries that have no work. These countries ask for contracts. The French nation will come to the government and ask, "Which region is it that needs work? And which has good people?" The government orders, "Go to Casablanca" or "Go to the mountains." And then the contract comes for the place that the government named.

So it's a relationship between governments?

Yes. Between Morocco and France. They guarantee it. And they use doctors; the workers must be passed by the doctors.

Why is that?

They look for disease. If the worker is sick, he doesn't go. It's like if I, let's say, want to buy a cow from the government, or a bull calf. If it's sick, I won't give my money for it. If I bought it and brought it all the way here, and it died on me, I'll really be losing out. They won't take sick ones.

Is there anything about this that I haven't asked you?

The practices that deal with what is between us and France, and between the nations, and on the subject of work, well, that's it. They looked to their needs, they looked for profit. And one government works with the other, sets up contracts, and takes the workers.

Do you see this as some favor from France, as some gift?

The gift from France, the help from France, is what you make of it, with your own sense. If you do good things with it, it's a help. If you don't do good things with it, it's no help.

Is France giving up something to provide this, or is she just satisfying her needs?

She satisfied her needs. And she did good things for those countries that dealt with her. It's as if I told you I did the best by you in hiring you to work on my land. She is satisfying her needs. If you don't get a profit from the worker, will you hire him? So there.

Close that up now.[16]

---

[16]The Faqir has no difficulty sympathizing with profit-making as a motive; after all, this is why he hires workers on his land.

This had been quite a long interview and the Faqir obviously had had enough.

5

The Festival

Only I was looking far forward to the annual festival, or Amouggar, of the saint Sidi Ahmad u Omar. I had been asking about it for several weeks and no one seemed to know when it would actually take place: answers were often uncertain and, taken together, contradictory. But everyone agreed that it could only occur after the much smaller Amouggar of Sidi Bu Moussa, which only the merchants from among the villagers would attend.

One evening during the week following the Amouggar of Sidi Bu Moussa, the sheikh arrived at the Faqir's compound on his motorcycle. The National Holiday of Youth would be in exactly two weeks, and the sheikh firmly advised the Faqir, as he had numerous other moderately successful men in the region, to attend the celebration at the administrative center, in "44." The Faqir should bring two rugs, his fine brass fuel burner and a suitable kettle; he should, as well, contribute one thousand rials, to defray expenses. And, by the way, since I had asked, the Amouggar of Sidi Ahmad u Omar would begin on the day following the National Holiday.

Two weeks later the Faqir attended, of course, the National Holiday of Youth celebration. The rest of the family stayed on the land, performing all the tasks of a normal day. The Faqir returned late in the afternoon and, right thereafter, Ali left to reserve a place at the Amouggar for the next day.

At 7:00 the next morning, the pickup truck that would take us to the Amouggar arrived, and we added our equipment—reed mats, several low, round wooden tables, earthen cookware (*tajines*), teakettle and teapot, tea glasses, some wood for fuel, and two timeworn but not yet threadbare rugs—to what the other passengers had already packed in. All of this was securely tied to the wooden frame of the pickup, and ten

90

adults and twelve children, all male, worked themselves into the remaining crevices.

We drove for almost an hour over dirt roads and reached the large, open field of the Amouggar at about 8:00. Some of the passengers left us then for different gatherings, but we greeted a few other villagers sitting with Ali, who had found space for all of us under an olive tree. This year the trees had not been well irrigated, their foliage was scant, and their shade would only partially block the sun. Even so, the space had to be rented, seventy rials for the day; up until three years ago, renting had never been the practice and one reserved a spot by marking it with a bit of wood.

The Amouggar juxtaposes religious and economic elements and this is no anomaly in Moroccan society, where merchants may build stores into the outer walls of mosques. It combines the festive aspects of a pilgrimage—the freedom from work and the day-long feasting—with the excitement of the marketplace—the crowds, the entertainment, and the lure of a wide variety of merchandise. The patronage of saint Sidi Ahmad u Omar, whose tomb is the locus for the rather limited ritual activities of the Amouggar, confers a privileged status upon the event as a whole, and the business transactions partake, in their own way, of the saint's blessedness, or *baraka*. The Amouggar attracts performers and itinerants of many sorts who depend upon the good spirits of their audience for contributions; it brings together, too, a vast number of merchants from whom the crowds buy all their day's food and numerous small presents for children. Prices for such things tend to be, if anything, slightly higher than usual, and buyers, although not inattentive to this, find a comfortable rationale in the little dose of *baraka* they obtain for the extra rial or two that they often have to pay.

By 9:30 we had bought a day's food for the twelve adults and seven children: a goat with about seven kilos of meat at a cost of 1,500 rials (its head and innards were later auctioned to one of us for 180 rials); sugar, mint leaves, a quarter of a kilo of the best tea, onions, cooking oil, black pepper, and paprika; and twenty-eight loaves of bread (ten of which were bought later, for lunch). The goat was promptly slaughtered—once the men had goaded Hummad into working on it—and eviscerated, quartered, parceled out into a number of *tajine*s and readied for cooking. In the meantime, tea had been prepared and, for want of a better sign, it was perhaps with the tea that the party proper can be said to have begun.

For the adults the occasion never became a boisterous nor even an overtly joyous one. Faqir b. Sadiq, oldest among us, used his *jellaba*[1] as a cushion and propped himself against the tree trunk, remaining prac-

---

[1]A jellaba is a hooded overgarment stretching almost to the ground, which may be made of cotton or wool and is usually a solid color, although it may have thin stripes.

tically motionless for the entire day. Another villager with us, Faqir Ali, also never left the space, spending much of the time glaring at Sessy, who was seated across the field from us and who had been trying for the last year to gain the right to cut a road through Faqir Ali's land. Faqir Muhammad, who had done much of the early marketing, spent most of the morning away from us, at a gathering of old friends from another village, and in this way avoided the restraint that his brother's presence imposed upon him. The other men spent most of their time resting, sleeping, or chatting, and each of them, at one time or another, left to make a tour of the market.

The younger children were scarcely to be seen, except at mealtimes. They each had some pocket money (some had up to one hundred rials), and they left in a horde for the market right after the first *tajine* meal was eaten. They did not return until the afternoon meal was about to be set on the tables.

The morning meal was prepared, cooked, and served by the older sons, three of whom did most of the work. After this, at about 11:00, Ali and I went up to the market area in order to, as he said, "freshen our eyes." The heat of the day was already oppressive, and the crowds, trucks, and livestock were kicking up dust. Aside from the more numerous than usual marketers—sellers of clothing, vegetables, fruits, and sundries—the Amouggar had drawn a variety of less frequently seen diversions: fortune tellers (women who, with a deck of playing cards, would recount the past and foretell the future, for four to ten rials); diverse collections of musicians (circles of seated, chanting *hadawi*s, accompanying themselves with the rhythmic beating of small drums, which they held on their left shoulder; some solo singers; several individual Berber singers, who also played violinlike instruments); a group of Aissawa practicing their well-known gift of charming snakes; and countless small, petty games of chance (which many Moroccans distinguish from gambling, which is prohibited in Islam, by noting that, in games of chance, everything is aboveboard and there is no room for deception).

As we moved into the market proper, the heat became more intense and, in some sections, the crowd was packed together like olives in a press. We searched out Qebbor, a village merchant who was one of Ali's best friends, and found him seated under his tent, visibly uncomfortable, selling tea and sugar. His business was a solid one: that day he would sell about 150 sugar cones (each weighing two kilos), making a profit of one or two rials on each one. Next to him, helping out, was his young son; several other friends had also sought relief under the shade of his tent. Qebbor, always an active and even at times rambunctious fellow, was bantering continually with buyers of his merchandise, with his friends nearby, and with passers-by. He was having an uncommonly difficult time remembering what he had sold to people when the time came to total their bills.

Ali and I then moved on, through the rows of vegetable sellers, into the clothing section. Here, under canvas roofing, there was no direct sunlight and less dust swirling, but the air was close and very hot. On the far side, the clothing section opened onto a vast livestock and animal market, for which the Amouggar is especially renowned. By this hour of the day, the animal market had passed its peak, but many camels, cows, bulls, horses, and mules remained to be sold. Ali patted some on their hind parts as we passed them by, just as he had patted some watermelons earlier—neither to test them nor to buy them, but just, it seemed, to establish direct, physical contact with the merchandise.

He asked the price of some of the animals and opened the animals' mouths to inspect their teeth and gums as he talked with the owners. "How much is that old woman?" he asked the owner of a large mottled cow of European stock. The owner was not amused and assumed (or feigned) injured honor: "Old woman? You don't know what you're talking about; you should keep your mouth shut rather than lie like that!" He seized the opportunity to become a focus of attention and began to show the cow's teeth to Ali, to point out its merits, all the while raising his voice. A small crowd began to gather. Ali, never quick with words, seemed beleaguered. As the owner continued to hound him, he yielded and said that he had only been joking. In any event, the price quoted was thirty-five thousand rials, quite a bit more than would have been asked for a cow of Moroccan stock.

We then retraced part of our route and made our way toward the central "spiritual" edifice of the Amouggar, the tomb of Sidi Ahmad u Omar. It is a small, white structure, crowned by a dome; inside, next to the stone that marks the saint's grave, visitors lay the money, sugar, or candles that they bring to pay him homage. These offerings are collected by the shrine's moqaddem, and the money may be used to repair the mausoleum or to restore its white coat. A courtyard, one side lined with a row of rooms open to visitors who wish to rest or perhaps sleep overnight, surrounds the mausoleum. Here, a bull will be ritually paraded and, after circling the tomb three times, slaughtered and served as a feast for the local residents who participated in the planning, preparation, and realization of the Amouggar. The entire complex is enclosed by a white wall, which opens to provide only one entrance into the courtyard. This opening bulges with alms seekers: the poor, holding out their right hands and repeating over and over the name of God; religious students and readers, reciting verses from the Koran; idlers and drifters, searching for rewarding activities and fulfilling the adage that, at an Amouggar, "half the people visit, and the other half roams."

Women were much more numerous in and around the shrine, within the outer wall, than elsewhere in the Amouggar, where they were, to all intents and purposes, absent. According to Ali, many of the women had come less to visit the tomb of Sidi Ahmad u Omar than to renew contacts with their male clients. One tall, thin woman, wearing a brown jellaba and no veil, was known to direct the activities of six prostitutes and was here to arrange their meetings with desiring men. Ali pointed out another; she was probably seeking small gifts from her male acquaintances who might number between twenty and forty. Such women made friendships, Ali said, the way they received money—not in the palm, where it could be firmly grasped but on the back of the hand; when a newcomer arrived, the old money, and the old friend, would just slide away.

It was almost 2:00 when we returned to the thin shade of the olive tree and watched Mehdi prepare and serve lunch. As he said to me later, "At these affairs, I always do most of the work. I'm like my father: when something has to be done, it might as well be done right away." We ate, napped, and chatted, and the children amused themselves with their new playthings: noisemakers, toy trucks, and, for one, plastic sunglasses. We expected to leave in the late afternoon, once the weather had cooled a bit. When the pickup truck did not arrive at the 'aser (the afternoon prayer), there was again talk of the irresponsibility of the driver and of youth in general.

As our group waited, more and more impatiently, itinerants, a singer, and the acrobatic Sons of Sidi Ahmad u Moussa visited us. Each walked away with between ten and twenty rials, given more or less willingly. When money was not spontaneously offered, a simple "Allah," addressed to a specific person, was enough to force him to dip into his leather purse.

In most of these encounters the itinerants took no notice of me. But one, a heavy old man of the Aissawa brotherhood, with a sharp and aggressive, yet winning, manner, turned to me after joking with several of the older men. "You and I," he said, "have been fighting with one another for many years now." I doubted that I had ever seen him before and was quite sure that we had never fought. I was even more certain that much of his meaning was escaping me, although his words were clear. But he looked me straight in the eye, defying me to answer, and I hazarded, "Yes, it has been such a long time that I don't even remember it." I was surprised when he then abruptly turned to someone else.

The pickup truck still had not arrived, and the restlessness of the adults was reflected in the growing freedom with which the children were now allowed to play. One, a son of a city dweller, had been spending the week with a farmer's family and had bought a small plastic ball, which he used for playing soccer. Mustafa began to play easily with the other boys, and it was clear from the outset that, although only eleven years old, he was much more practiced at the game and the others were no match for him. As they played, a challenge emerged: he could keep possession of the ball, soccer style, against any two of the others. Mustafa began deftly dribbling the ball with his feet but, almost immediately, two others jumped upon him and in seconds had gained possession.

Mustafa was hurt, but not physically. He tried again, but they jumped him again. By this time, a couple of younger boys had caught the spirit and, as Mustafa still stylishly tried to get the ball back, began to hurl stones at the players. The adults began to scold but this was almost as quickly drowned in their own laughter, as the older boys ferociously struggled with one another for the ball. They tumbled and tripped and pitched themselves onto one another with an almost inhuman abandon; as Ali described them, they were "like animals without a mind." We all could not help but laugh, and the laughter was very infectious.

Mustafa finally gave up and returned, sulking, to the mats. "They don't know how to play," he muttered. One of the fathers responded, "Well, you were the one who challenged them."

By now, the late afternoon wind had risen, from the direction of the sea, not from the hotter east. We hoped it would be signaling the end of the heat wave. The dust was beginning to swirl and now the boys were no longer allowed to play, because their antics only kicked up more dust. Everyone waited, a bit overwrought, for the pickup truck.

The pickup arrived, finally, shortly before sunset, and we all piled in. We reached the compound after dark. The Faqir greeted the women with angry words: "Look at the cows! They're dying of thirst, they look like they haven't been given feed or water all day. God burn you women up!"

▩ QUESTIONS AND ANSWERS IN QUESTION

Some of the problems I had begun to see in the sequence "event + dialogue" were put in abeyance by the Amouggar. Here, after all, was a well-defined event that both the Faqir and I had participated in, and an anthropologist might easily attribute to it a number of relatively clear stages, such as anticipation, preparation, performance, return, and reparation, for probing in the dialogue and for eventual analysis.

Yet I continued to be preoccupied by the kinds of questions I was asking the Faqir in the dialogues. They were certainly not flowing simply from an event but more, I thought, from my own personal, social, and cultural concerns: from my political beliefs; from an awareness, heightened by my encounter with the Faqir, of my Euro-American origins; from my partial knowledge of the academic literature on Morocco; from my previous experience in Morocco. Even questions that seemed purely descriptive were often called forth by other people's behavior that struck me as odd, that disappointed my own culturally based expectations (for example, the questions I was formulating about enjoyment at the

Amouggar were motivated by the boredom I myself felt there). And it was undeniable that although I was posing all these questions on my own, they were often tightly bound to the society within which I grew up and developed my interests.

The Faqir's answers, too, posed similar problems. I had been particularly struck when, during the previous dialogue, he had answered a simple question about Casablanca with an extended narrative, which I would have been rude to interrupt, and which was only indirectly related to the topic I wished to discuss; and when, in that same dialogue, he had answered what I thought to be a question that would open an important subject—that of the fate of the migrant worker Saleh—in a manner that left little room for further questioning.

In such ways, at least, the Faqir was not so much answering my questions as assessing them and commenting upon them, not merely satisfying my curiosity but reflecting upon his experience and forcing me, as he did this, to follow him in directions he thought important. In the give and take of question and answer, we were not really exploring the details of some "objective" event; rather, we were situating ourselves, each with regard to the other and to external phenomena that we defined and redefined, as our encounter proceeded.

In my questions on the Amouggar I was interested, first, in the extent to which the Faqir had enjoyed the Amouggar ("Enjoyment..."), then, in some of the specific incidents ("Specific incidents... "), and in the importance of Amouggars and Moussems ("Amouggars and Moussems... "). I also wanted to understand why the Faqir had scolded the women upon our return home ("Scolding the women... "). And I thought the occasion opportune for discussing the role of holy men in Moroccan society ("Holy men... ").

▧ FIFTH DIALOGUE

ENJOYMENT...

Well, Faqir, yesterday we went to the Amouggar. Did you enjoy yourself there?

Yes.

A little or a lot?

A little, no more, a little. Not the way that we used to.

Why, what was less enjoyable about this Amouggar?

We used to have a large tea kettle, and many rugs; and carpets, which we'd lay out all around us. That is, nowadays, we go to the Amouggar voluntarily. But formerly we *had* to go to it, and everyone *had* to have a more lavish party.

You mean you had to go against your will?

We were forced to go to the Amouggar. Our space had to be laid out with care and those that were next to the government's tent, next to the big tent, would have to be especially neat. And we'd stay there for three days. The large kettle, many carpets, the fine utensils—not like now, when we take the material just for the purpose of eating.

I still don't understand. Why did you have to go against your will?

The government wanted the Amouggar to be packed with people and wanted you to bring your best things, your finest things.

And if you didn't go?

If we didn't go, the qaid would be told, "There, so-and-so didn't go," and they'd take the fellow off to jail.

Was this during the independence period?

No, during the protectorate. After independence, it became a matter of choice. You could either go or sit home.

What benefit was it to the colonial government that you go, even against your will?

It would benefit from the crowded market: the marketers had to rent their selling places from the government. There would be taxes. And the government officials would come and see the people looking nice and proper. There would be lines of people, from the big tent all the way to the road. A crowd, not only at the tent itself.

And entertainment! Stallions! And Blacks! And the Aissawa! And musicians would come from all over, from Oujda and Ouezzane.[2] Everyone was there, packed from one end to the other.

And why has this changed since independence?

The government used to give money to support the Amouggar. Now they give nothing. And now no one says to you, "Come to the Amouggar," or even, "Don't come." The government used to go so far as to bring women to it, to dance, as part of the entertainment. Against their will, too.

And now the women no longer go?

No. There are some who go voluntarily. But none against their will, no.

What did you find enjoyable the day we went, and what didn't you find enjoyable?

There was no black market[3] and, as long as there is no thievery and no fights, all is fine. As for the entertainment, it has lessened, it is nothing now. We aren't involved in that anymore. We don't have anything to do with it now. Formerly, every gathering would create its own entertainment.

What kind of entertainment?

[2]Oujda and Ouezzane are distant cities, in the north of Morocco.
[3]The term *black market* has come to mean unexpectedly high prices.

You know, that kind of entertainment of ours that you've often seen: music-making, singing, and dancing. And religious chanters would be everywhere, together, chanting. Now you no longer can find any religious chanters at all sitting among the olive trees. They used to have some gathering! And people would come and give them money.

And now the musicians no longer come from such distant places. Some years ago, the kids began to break up the musicians' gatherings. A thief would be spotted somewhere in the market and the kids would begin to shout, "Woo, woo." All the people would run toward the disturbance and abandon the musicians. So now fewer and fewer musicians turn up.

So, since independence, the Amouggar has lost its attraction in all of these respects?

Hold it! It has lost in the things that were done by force. But the Amouggar still fills up and it always has. But those forced things have lessened since independence.

When you went to the Amouggar, what did you wear?

I wear everything that I have in the house. If I had four jellabas, I'd wear them all.

Why?

Why? Because I want to be good-looking too, of course.

What is so good-looking about wearing four jellabas?

I'd be dressed well, and be neat, with no problems. That is what is good about it.

What might someone who saw you wearing four jellabas say?

He'd say, "That one's dressed up, he certainly has clothes. He's a big wheel, a fine man, and neat." That's what he'd say. What else would he say?

Which jellaba do you wear on top?

If you have a black one and a white one, you wear the black one on the outside, and the white one underneath. If the weather is hot, you take off that black one, and leave on just the white one. That way you can stand up. That's the practice.

And how many do you usually wear?

At some periods I have only one, at others I have two, or perhaps three.

And the day of the Amouggar?

That day I had just two, that's all.

At the Amouggar, what did you enjoy, what didn't you enjoy?

That makes no sense—"Did you enjoy, didn't you enjoy?" How's that?

I mean, where did you find your enjoyment, and where didn't you?

There was nothing to annoy me, and I enjoyed everything. We wanted the kids to have a good time, and they were eating and drinking. We had the money to spend. There was nothing to bother us, nothing. No one said to us, "Get up from here," or "Go this way." If someone came over to annoy you, you wouldn't enjoy yourself. But now, we went there of our own free will, and the kids were eating away, filling themselves up, and the money that they were wasting, we had it to spend. No problems. That's that.

How about the Amouggar market? Did you find it good?

The market was good.

Did you enjoy it there?

I enjoyed it, of course. It's good, everything can be found there, what you want is there.

Did you go to the livestock section?

Yes.

How was that?

Everything was fine, but I didn't want anything from it.

Did you ask about prices?

Yes. I brought back the news. So that if someone asked me whether prices were high or low, I'd be able to tell him.

Even if you don't want to buy?

Yes, I'll always ask the prices.

You used to go for three days. Why do you go now for just one day?

Well, nowadays, it's just voluntary, and we're satisfied with just one day. And there is no longer the entertainment to hold people for three days. They used to say, "Now I'll get my fill of entertainment," and they'd stay for three days. Nowadays, there is little. The kids fill themselves with meat, and they all have a party, and then they go back home in the evening. That's all.

The day that we went, we sat all day on the mats, except for a short time visiting the market. We spent the whole day there, and did little else. Did you enjoy yourself, or would you say that you were bored?

No, nothing was boring us. Were we staying for three days, or even two, we'd get bored. But we had just come that morning, fooled around a little until we ate breakfast, had some fun for a bit, came back again and made our lunch; we never were bored. What's to bore us?

How about when we were waiting for the pickup truck?

Well, while waiting for the pickup, we were getting annoyed, that's true.

SPECIFIC INCIDENTS...

While we were sitting around, some people came by our group, like those acrobatic Sons of Sidi Ahmad u Moussa, and those Aissawa, and some others, all requesting money. Is that good?

It's good.

What is good about it?

Well, people are gathered there, and they too can thus get their portion of God's beneficience. If things like the Amouggar didn't occur, where would they find so many people? Better that they seek money at the Amouggar, and not come to people's houses.

Did you give money willingly to those people?

Yes.

I remember one person who came to whom no one wanted to give money.

That depends on the moment.

And then he said, "Allah."

There are occasions when ... when the fellow finds he has money to give, there are occasions when money seems scarce. Then there are people whose way of speaking just annoys you, and you won't give anything, even if you have money.

When might that happen?

For example, someone who has no manners.

Did we run across anyone like that?

That fellow who came jumping around until they gave him something. That very last one, that one in rags, going with his sandals upon the furnishings. That one didn't have manners.

Why was he given money then?

Well, each to his own thoughts.

In the beginning it seemed that no one would give him money.

But he stuck to them, "Allah, Allah, give me, Allah, our Lord."

He went from one to the other, and said, "Allah" until he got money. And then on to the next, and so on. It wasn't given willingly then, was it?

[The Faqir yawned.] You know, I say, "Here's four rials, or two rials," just for him to go away. Just to move on, let him not bother us.

You didn't give the money because of the word "Allah"?

He who begins to say "Allah" and is given the money, you know that God is between them. But if you say to him, "God make things easy," and he still doesn't leave, and then you give him money, you just want him to go away, you want him just to get far away from you.

And what is the meaning of, "God make things easy"?

It means, "I'll give you nothing. The Lord will make things easier for us and for you, someplace else."

And if he doesn't leave then?

When that's been said, if he doesn't leave, then he knows nothing, he's ignorant. At that time, you know, the meaning is apparent. When someone tells you, "God make things easy," are you going to keep at it and risk angering him?

And if you say "God make things easy" and he still sticks to you, and then you give him something, you're not giving willingly?

No.

Do you call that "alms"?

Alms against your will. Alms that are worth nothing.

Those alms won't be reckoned on your account?

It will be counted, but for little, not like what you give willingly.

Those who did the work for the meals at the Amouggar ... do you want to sleep now? [The Faqir had just stretched himself out at full length on the reed mat, and his head was now resting on a pillow.]

As long as I keep talking to you, do your work!

O.K. **How was it decided who would work at preparing the meals?**

Well, those who felt able, you know, worked.

At lunch, I saw Mehdi doing most of the work.

Mehdi, yes, Mehdi did.

The others did practically nothing. He cooked, and he served everything, he only didn't fetch the water.

Well, the Arabs around here, they just see that something has already started, and they like to sit around and watch it proceed.

Why did Mehdi do all that work?

He gave in (*hshem*) and knew that he'd have to do the work himself. And he didn't want to wait.

Why didn't he say to himself, "I'm always doing the work, and the others continue to sit around," and then stop?

Then, if Mehdi had wanted to sit around, we'd have said to someone else, "Get up!" and that person would have given in and done the work.

Does Mehdi act like you in those situations?

No. A little, not really. He can't ... he can't ... he can't really do things the way they should be done. He can't get up and serve properly.

AMOUGGARS AND MOUSSEMS ...

Do you usually buy a lot at the Amouggar?

Well, I buy according to the money I have, and according to what I need.

Do you buy things in order to bring back some of the saint's blessing (baraka)?[4]

I brought back some blessedness for the kids, some dates and chick-peas and nuts. Perhaps 120 rials worth.

---

[4]The notion of *baraka* is dealt with at great length in Westermarck (1968, vol. 1, pp. 35–261). See also Geertz (1971, pp. 44–45).

That blessedness, the blessedness of what people buy at the Amouggar, from what does it come?

People call "blessed" what they want to eat.

Isn't there something special about it?

What's special about it? Someone who wants to eat finds you coming back from the Amouggar and says, "Give me some of that blessedness, you've just come from the Amouggar. Give me a bit of what is sold in the Amouggar." But he's just filling himself up, just getting his fill, that's all.

But those dates, for example, that so many people bring back from the Amouggar, is there nothing more to them?

No, there is nothing besides filling up your stomach.

Or in its taste?

No. The taste that it has, is all that it has.

Or on account of that saint?

Those who are ignorant, they say such things as, "Blessedness" and then they kiss the date and eat it. But in truth, you just want your stomach to be fed. That's what is in it.

Are there many people who say, "It has blessedness"?

Yes, there are many, and many who kiss it and eat it. But all that blessedness just goes down to the stomach.

What is the difference between an Amouggar and a Moussem?[5]

In a Moussem, people just come together; they slaughter an animal, they eat it, drink, and amuse themselves. That's all. But in an Amouggar, there is buying and selling, and livestock of all kinds. People come from afar, from the farthest north. Merchants, buyers and sellers. They bring merchandise, and they take livestock back with them. The Moussem just attracts people from the near countryside.

Were you ever to a Moussem or Amouggar that broke up?[6]

No. What's that, "broke up"?

Where some fight started, and the festival was ruined.

That never happened to us. That happened in earlier times, when the land had no government. People would fight, and there would be robbers. With the government, you know, as soon as there is a theft or a fight, he who fought goes off to prison, and the market continues.

You mean it isn't the blessedness of the saint that protects the Amouggar, that keeps fighting from ruining it?

How can you ... we don't know. How can you know that? It might be working and we don't know about it.

[5]The Moussem is another form of religious festival; residents distinguish between it and the Amouggar much as the Faqir does. For a description of a Moussem, see Rabinow (1975, pp. 88–95).

[6]This question grows out of early ethnographic writings on Moroccan religious festivals that mention that festivals, even though taking place under the protection of a saint, sometimes are completely disrupted because of fighting.

Do you go to any other Amouggars?

Only this one, the one nearest to us.

Do you go to any Moussems?

I've no reason to, what would I do there? The others go, those who want to amuse themselves, and who want to party. I don't care about that.

How about when you were younger?

Yes. [The Faqir yawned again.] Then I'd always go, *toujours.*

What would you do there?

Well, I'd look around with my eyes, and speak with my mouth, and lie, and steal, and . . .

What do you mean steal?

I'd make off with women. All that I came across, I did. That's that.

How long has it been since you've gone to them?

Well, very long, perhaps thirty years or longer.

You mean, around the time of your marriage?

With my marriage, I stopped; that was all.

SCOLDING THE WOMEN . . .

When we arrived yesterday evening back here at the house, what was the matter with the livestock?

The livestock had had nothing to drink all day.

What was the reason for that?

The water was the reason.

What do you mean?

There was no water in the cement pool: the women had let the water out of it for the sheep to drink during the day.[7] And there was no one to start the irrigation motor to fill the pool again, for the cows.

Could the women have done something so that the cows wouldn't be thirsty?

They could have. As we came home, they wanted to begin drawing water from the well by hand, with the rope. But how long would that take? At least six or seven hours for the cows.

You yelled a bit when we returned.

I had to yell.

Why?

The cows were also starving, with nothing to eat.

---

[7]The irrigation pump nearest the house pipes water into a one-meter cubed cement pool above ground. From there the water passes through an aperture at its base into an irrigation canal. In the morning the men had filled the cement pool from which the cows could drink throughout the day, but before the cows came back the women had mistakenly let the water drain into the canal for the sheep to drink. The cows are unable to drink from the canal and had no water available when they returned from pasture.

But if the cows were starving, what could the women do about it?

They have to feed the cows, even if it means depriving the sheep; even just the hay in the storage room. The cows have to get their fill. Both with water and feed. They need all of it.

Do the women know what must be done in order to provide water for the livestock?

I told you, they must bring up the well water by hand. They made that mistake; they let the water out of the pool for the sheep, because the sheep can't drink from the pool, and the water has to be let loose into the irrigation canals for them to be able to drink. If the women had some intelligence, they would have filled some buckets of water for the sheep and left the cement pool full for the cows. But they let the water run into the canals and wasted it all.

Why didn't you tell them that before you left?

It doesn't matter what you say. You can say it, and the women still just do what they want. I didn't tell them anything, but even if I had, they would have done whatever occurred to them. I thought, you know, that we had filled up the pool in the morning and that the cows would drink from it. There would be no problem. In the afternoon, they'd drink from the water that remained, and in the evening we'd come back and fill it with more water.

But we were delayed. It was the pickup truck that put one over on us. Were it not for the pickup, we could have started up the motor and still have had time to go and cut feed grass.

We didn't get back until sunset.

What? Until the evening prayer, way past sunset.

What were the women doing while we were at the Amouggar?

They had their breakfast, and pastured the livestock a bit, and at midday they went to party at a close neighbor's compound.

At that time, was no one at home?

Mbiriku [his nine-year-old daughter] stayed; you know she was sick. And the little kids.

And who brought the women what they needed for the party?

They sent to the village for what they needed. They needed only meat, and they bought it.

From what money could they buy?

They collected forty rials from each.

And how many of them were there?

I don't know. Let's see: three of their women, two of ours, and two of another neighbor.

And when you came back from the Amouggar, did you talk with them about their party?

Why would I want to? I've no concern about them.

Don't you want to get their news?

Why would I want that, their news? What do I want with them? It's not my concern. What would I do with it?

HOLY MEN . . .

Who was this Sidi Ahmad u Omar?
A person.
But he has a tomb—he wasn't just an ordinary person, was he?
In early times he was a *mrabet*.[8]
What did he do to become a mrabet?
I don't know. He was a mrabet, and he died, and people buried him. He was one of the people who truly fear the Lord, that is, people to whom other people defer (*hshem*). They have real religion. A mrabet, that's all. That's the sort.
What is that, a mrabet? I still don't understand.
The mrabet, you know, is someone whom people take notice of. The mrabet does what . . . people do what he tells them to.
Is the mrabet like a sherif?
The sherif is one thing and the mrabet is another.
What is the difference?
The sherif, even if he's no good, is a sherif. You must call him Moulay. Even if he's no good. The mrabet comes, you know, from the fear of God. If you do ugly things, you are not a mrabet.
Is the son of a sherif a sherif?
Sherif.
And the son of a mrabet?
He remains a mrabet. He doesn't become a sherif.
But if the son of a mrabet does bad things?
Then he's not a mrabet. Because, we say, a mrabet comes from the fear of God.
And if his son doesn't show the fear of God, then he's not a mrabet?
Not a mrabet. And, if I truly fear God, I am a mrabet. Me. Or you.
But they don't call you . . .
No, I'm giving you the principle. If you do bad things, you're not a mrabet. You're like a thief, that's all.
So, there are mrabets who are known as such by others, and there are mrabets who are known only to God.
That's evident. That's what we call hidden knowledge and open

[8]Here, I am trying to have the Faqir elucidate two other central concepts: that of the *mrabet* (a holy man) and the *sherif* (a person claiming descent from the Prophet Muhammad). The Faqir's short, terse answers may indicate he feels some uncertainty on these issues, but I am pushing him to develop a coherent formulation. Eickelman (1976) discusses *maraboutism* at length.

knowledge. The knowledge that we see is open knowledge; that which is known but which we do not see, which only our Master knows, is hidden knowledge.

How's that?

Hidden, hidden knowledge: only God has knowledge of it. As if I say: "God knows what you are. I don't know you, whether you're a Muslim, or a Christian, or a *Rumi*, or an American. I don't know." Because I haven't spoken with you, you didn't tell me, I didn't tell you. But God knows you. That is hidden knowledge. Open knowledge is that I know that you are an American. So that you understand.

And hidden knowledge is what . . .

what God knows, and we don't know. That is what hidden knowledge is. And what we do know is open knowledge.

And those mrabets, who are known openly, what do they do that other people don't?

The mrabet must have respect, and deal well with other people, and not curse people with evil, and always be soft, with his eyes always lowered. He doesn't look at people a lot, and he doesn't argue, and if people are arguing he settles their arguments. That's what a mrabet is.

What do you mean, "soft"?

He's not nasty, his words are not nasty, not arguing, not cursing, not slandering. He must always be soft, and say, "Oh, Our Master, watch over these people; oh, our Master, provide for these people." That's all.

Do you remember the time we slept over at Muhammad the moqaddem's house and, in the morning, a mrabet came to visit?

Yes, that son of Ait Hmad, that one.

I understood very little of what he said.

He's ignorant. He has no knowledge. As though he had made himself a mrabet, all by himself, that's all. Just tied himself to his own head.[9]

But the people who were talking to him, they were . . .

they spoke with him, but their hearts weren't . . . they had no interest in him.

What was in your mind when you saw him?

I saw that he was just looking to get hold of something . . . just looking for something to eat. That is his sort.

And his answers?

Worth nothing; his answers were worth nothing.

How so?

Worth nothing, ignorant. His speech was rushed, and he knew nothing. His only aim was in the direction of food, only in the direction of getting a handout.

[9]The Faqir is here punning on the root of the word *mrabet: rbet* = to tie, fasten.

But people were laughing a lot.

They had to laugh, they were wise to his aims.

Why would they laugh if there wasn't something special about his words?

After all, they didn't want to make it obvious to him that he wasn't wanted there. And he was even believing that he was accomplishing something.

Did he curse people?

He curses, he always curses. That's all he does is curse.

If you give him something, is it because you are afraid of those curses?

Why should I fear him? Is he Our Lord? Those who are ignorant may fear him. Yes, most people will be afraid of him, but I'm not. I'm unconcerned. And he only talks to those who may, perhaps, give him something; as for those who clearly won't, he doesn't speak to them at all. You have to watch the people. He'll say, "Ah... Mister Kevin... dadadada... ," and to the Faqir he doesn't speak at all, because the Faqir isn't going to give him anything.

And then, whenever he goes on to another party, he'll say, "I have some friend, an American, ay, ay, ay, the best is provided." He always lets his mouth run.

What about that Aissawi who visited our place at the Amouggar?

He was all right, not too bad. He made people laugh, and spoke only of what is proper in God's domain. He was all right, all right. And that Aissawi, if you went to visit him, he'd serve you all that he possessed. What he had, he'd bring you to eat.

He said to me, "You and I have been fighting a long time." What did he mean?

That meant that he was taking a liking to you. By opposites, speaking by opposites. In other words, he liked you.

Where does that meaning come from?

He found you there and he liked you. As soon as he saw you, he wanted to get to know you.

But he said, "fighting."

By opposites. As if a thing was standing upright, and you turned it over.

Is it understood that way by all?

It is understood. He wanted to joke with you, to open the door with you. That is what his language is about. He wants to open the conversation with you, so that you and he will continue talking until he arrives at the money part. [The Faqir laughed.] That's what's in it.

At that moment, I didn't understand that meaning, although I understood his words.

When the meaning escaped you, his money died. But had you not lost the meaning and continued speaking with him, he'd have pursued you until you gave him money.

I said, "It has been such a long time that I don't even remember it."

You closed the door, that's all. But had you talked with him, and asked him, "Why fighting?" he would say, "No, not fighting, not fighting at all." And he'd follow you with speech until you gave him money. You stopped the talk, locked him out. That was good for you.

Why was it good?

It was good for you because you kept your money. You gave him nothing.

But with reference to my good will?[10]

With reference to good will, Our Master gave birth to you and to him, let each shift for himself. We owe him nothing and he owes us nothing.

How will that appear to others? You know, will they say, "He closed off the conversation; he has no good will?"

Those who are ignorant, that is what they'll say. Those who know the Law know that you owe him nothing. If he is overstaying his welcome, he should go. He shouldn't come to us at all, because there is nothing between us. But we wanted to let him stay at his pleasure; four rials is nothing. You can't go far with it.

Was he making fun of the people?

No, he was just measuring his words, in his head, tying them together. There are words that lead into other words, and he strings them together. There are some who can do this even better. There are those whose skill lies in that kind of speech. The fellow just looks at you and starts, "You are like this, and like that," and all the words come in accord with one another. And they have many jokes, many more than the one we saw.

Are there still people like that around?

There is one in a neighboring village.

Does he ever come here?

He might. If there is some party, some celebration, he comes. He makes the people laugh, and then he leaves. He really knows his words. He's now an old faqir, aged. He used to ride a horse. He'd put his hands in the stirrups and ride upside down. [The Faqir laughed.] Yes, there was a lot of fun in that. His brothers too were like that, and his father, in earlier times. But nothing of that remains in his children. No, nothing.

---

[10]I have translated the Arabic word *niya* as "good will," or "good faith," throughout the dialogues.

6

The Bicycle Theft

As I arrived at the Faqir's compound one day in mid-July—I had been away in Rabat for several days—the Faqir himself had just returned from a visit to the chief of police. Four days earlier, only hours after my departure, the Faqir discovered that a worker he had hired for a few days, who was an outsider to the village and to the region, had stolen his bicycle. The thief had been apprehended, and the Faqir had been summoned to the police station for questioning.

Although the theft of the bicycle was by most standards a minor incident and would not occasion much local storytelling or the consequent elaboration that accompanies more memorable events, such as a serious accident on the roads, or as had recently occurred, the theft of a neighbor's cow, the loss of the bicycle would disrupt the usual routine for several of the people in the Faqir's household. It would mean, for example, that trips to the village store, requiring perhaps five minutes by bicycle, would have to be made by donkey, which took longer, or by foot, which took at least fifteen minutes; the frequent daytime coming and going between the fields and the compound would be less easily done; in the evenings, both Ali and Mehdi would miss the vehicle when they wished to visit their friends in the village or in neighboring ones. And the Faqir's weekly trip to the one particular local market where communal leaders met and the sheikh held audience, and where he might encounter some of his long-time friends, would now require more than an hour by donkey—and he did not often need the donkey, because here his marketing was usually limited to buying one kilo of meat to bring home. (The Faqir marketed most of his crops in the larger markets of "44" and the Medina.)

The theft also permitted some villagers to underscore their definite yet restrained pride in a certain honesty within Ouled Filali; in this village, unlike many others, farmers were able to leave their tools out in

109

the fields overnight, unguarded; whatever other faults the villagers might possess, such thievery was not one of them. Some remembered when this was not the case; when, in earlier days, people feared to travel alone; when, at night, even in your own home, an unknown robber might climb over the wall and steal chickens or other goods while you slept.

In this instance, there was no doubt over the identity of the thief. Tahami—an Arabic speaker from a region north of the High Atlas Mountains (what southerners, with the implication of "rustic," "rural," call an "'Arobi")—had arrived at the Faqir's home the afternoon before I left, brought by the pickup truck driver, who was returning empty wooden crates that the Faqir had used to market that day's vegetables. The driver explained that Tahami had flagged down the truck about fifteen kilometers outside of the Medina and had said that he was coming to work for the Faqir. (It was common for the Faqir, as for many other landowners in the region, to hire outsiders to assist in the agricultural work. In the hot, semi-arid plains of the south, crops matured earlier than in the lands to the north; this encouraged Berbers from the mountains, as well as other Moroccans from farther north, to work in the southern plains until their own harvests were ready. Also, the work necessary to grow irrigated crops, such as pepper and watermelon, was uneven and at times quite intensive, and occasional laborers were often in demand.)

The Faqir evidently knew Tahami and received him with no great fanfare, inviting him to come in and eat dinner. During dinner that evening Tahami had appeared a very likeable sort, easy-going and full of good humor. After dinner, the Faqir told him to sleep in the tool shed in the fields, where he had apparently slept before, and to start work in the morning. The Faqir later said that Tahami could be a splendid worker when he needed the money, and that with Tahami working, he could probably dispense with the two Berbers he had hired just the day before. When I mentioned Tahami's winning manner, the Faqir cautioned that he was not to be trusted and reminded me of a story Tahami had told that evening: Tahami had been traveling, walking along a road, when he encountered a man making a meal, and he was invited to join in the meal. As the cooking was finishing, the man went off to gather a bit more wood and Tahami seized the occasion to run off with the pot of meat.

The Faqir's previous experience with Tahami had been mixed. Both he and his brother, Ali, agreed that, on the one hand, Tahami's farm work was excellent: quick, efficient, and knowledgeable. But he preferred to work alone, independently. He had first worked for them some months ago and, on the second day of that stint, had clashed with the Berber working alongside and told him that his work was worth nothing. The Berber answered that Tahami was not the boss; the words between them became angrier, and Ali had to come over to keep them apart. Each refused to work with the other, and Ali sent the Berber to work on the peppers while Tahami remained with the watermelons.

On the third day, Tahami had claimed that he deserved a day's rest, but that his food that day should still be at the Faqir's expense. "The work I do in one day," he had said, "is equal to what another does in two. So I should be entitled to take it easy on the third." He had gotten up late that day and had spent the rest of it working lazily, often filling his pipe with kif. The Faqir had challenged this behavior, of course, and they reached an accord: Tahami would not work for a daily salary but would instead contract to complete a specific task for an agreed sum—a common practice. Ali then estimated that it would require twelve days to finish the work on the watermelons, and they agreed upon one thousand two hundred rials. Tahami finished the job in half that time—in a manner that all agreed was superb—collected his money, took his leave, and set off for the Medina.

Some weeks after this, the Faqir discovered Tahami roaming around in his fields. When the Faqir asked him what he was doing there, Tahami answered that he was only looking for a gourd to have for breakfast. The Faqir gave him one and added twenty rials, as did the owner of an adjacent plot and Tahami went on his way. More recently, Ali came across Tahami in "44." He was playing on a one-stringed violin and begging for money. Ali passed him by and turned a deaf ear to his requests for a handout. A week after this, while I was staying at the Faqir's, Tahami drove up in the pickup truck and invited himself to work for the Faqir.

I left for the capital early the next morning and when I returned four days later it was not difficult to piece the events together. On the morning I left, as Mehdi was about to go down into the well to start up the irrigation motor, Tahami had asked him for the bicycle in order to ride up to the village to buy some cigarettes. A couple of hours later, at the morning meal, Tahami had not yet returned; they waited for him a short time and then ate. When he still had not arrived by lunchtime, everyone felt certain that Tahami had stolen the bicycle and ridden off with it. Yet, because no one knew in which direction he had gone, there was little that could be done then and there to pursue him.

Two days later, Abdallah, the son of the Faqir's sister, stopped by for supper. He casually mentioned that he had seen Tahami earlier that day in the Medina. Actually, because Tahami had come up to him and greeted him, Abdallah had assumed, wrongly, that the bicycle had been returned, and he did not even inquire about it.

Early the next morning, Abdallah rode to the Medina on his motorbike to find Tahami. Abdallah spotted him among the men in the labor marketplace; he grabbed Tahami and demanded to know where the bicycle was. Tahami replied that he had sold it in a market to the east of the Medina for four-hundred rials. Abdallah threatened him and convinced him to ride on the back of the motorbike; they would search out the buyer, Abdallah said, return his four hundred rials, and get the bicycle back. But, as they set out on the road east, Abdallah turned abruptly through the entrance to the police station, and Tahami was trapped.

The police refused to take any action against Tahami until the owner of the bicycle appeared before them. Abdallah returned to the Faqir's house with this message and the Faqir told him, "Tomorrow morning, you yourself will take me to the police station." Tahami was held in custody overnight. The Faqir presented himself the next morning. He had just returned from the police station when I arrived; we were able to discuss the episode that very evening.

🔲 SOME QUESTIONS ABOUT EVENTS

I was by now quite conscious of several reasons why I was finding the dialogues stimulating and why I wished them to continue. First, the dialogues not only showed people expressing themselves but also showed them doing so as a response to the behavior of others. Second, these particular dialogues, carried out as an inquiry, showed me, assisted by the Faqir, seeking knowledge and understanding; this epitomized the usual relationship between anthropologist and informant and therefore might enable me to confront and articulate my dissatisfaction with academic anthropology. Finally, the dialogues, together with my draft version of the events, might provide a relatively solid record of the summer's experience and my involvement with the Faqir, one that would not decompose as rapidly as my memory of them.

Although I was now convinced of my interest in the dialogues and beginning to formulate the reasons why, the "event" continued to pose nagging questions. I had started to work with the notion that both the Faqir and I would witness and participate in the event and that it would present itself self-evidently to us. Yet the Faqir had not been present at the encounter with the migrant worker and, now, the theft of the bicycle had occurred in my absence: twice in the last three events I had had to modify that early notion of the "event."

Both incidents, however, raised questions I felt were worth discussing, and for the moment, fortunately, the two anomalous incidents could easily be accommodated; after all, at least one of us, either the Faqir or myself, had been present at each of them, and that provided a sufficient basis for a conversation. But my deeper feeling of unease at the notion of the "event" would not go away. Perhaps I was fundamentally misconceiving the "event" and, in so doing, turning away from what might be very salient elements in our mutual experience.

Now that I had faced the fact that my own concerns inevitably affected how I questioned the event, I was able, during the dialogue, to direct my attention more freely and with fewer second thoughts to those matters *I* felt to be important. First, because I was not present when the bicycle was stolen, I wanted the Faqir to tell me what had happened ("The theft..."). But, more significantly for me, Tahami was an outsider to the region and, by the very nature of Moroccan society, the Faqir would frequently come into contact with such outsiders, with people who were different from him by their regional, ethnic, racial, or religious background, but who, unlike Europeans, were not foreigners. I was from New York, with its great variety of ethnic communities; from the United States, where a major cultural theme was the mixing of racial and ethnic differences in the "melting pot," but where social practice consistently contradicted this theme; and engaged in a profession that took as its central issue the differences and similarities between various human groups. How could I fail to focus upon, and ask the Faqir for, his views on the human diversity he encountered?

Consequently, I planned to question the Faqir, briefly, about Arabs from other regions and, more thoroughly, about Berbers ("Arabs and Berbers... "), and finally about Jews ("Jews... ").

▨ SIXTH DIALOGUE

THE THEFT...

Tell me what happened with that fellow who took the bicycle.

They have him now at the city police station, outside of the Medina. My sister's son and I went there this morning. I entered and went up to the secretary, who said, "What is it?" I told him: "Fellow, you know that bicycle thief who was brought here yesterday? Well, I'm the bicycle's owner." We continued talking, and then the chief of police came out. He said, "What is it?" And the secretary told him, "Here's the owner of the bicycle."

The chief said to me, "Come over here. How did you lose that bicycle?"

I told him, "This happened, and this, and this."

He said, "And why didn't you take this guy to the regional police, those who are in charge of your district?"

I told him, "I didn't have the time to take him there."

He said, "What do you mean, you didn't have the time?"

I told him, "I'm not like the government, which is able to take people from one place to another, to drag them from here all the way to the regional police. Now he is under your rule, on your land here. And as for the government, we think of it all as one. I don't have the power to take the fellow over to the regional police."

The chief of police said, "Well, you had the power to bring him here, didn't you?"

I told him, "I brought him here by trickery, not by force." I had changed the story now. Now I was the one, not my sister's son, who had accomplished this.

He said, "How's that? What trick did you do?"

I told him, "I asked that fellow about the bicycle, and he told me that the bicycle had been sold east of the Medina. So I said, 'Let's go and take the money to its owner and get the bicycle back.' Now he thought we were on the way east. But I turned in at the police station, and suddenly he found himself at your door."

The chief said, "This is not our affair, it's for the regional police in your district."

I told him, "I can't take him there now. I'm afraid he'll hit me, or run away from me, or whatever. You were the nearest, so I brought him to you. You may send him wherever it pleases you. The thief was caught in the Medina and that is under your jurisdiction. Now he is in your hands, you're in charge of the matter. I can't do anything more. With my hands, I can't take him anywhere, or make him do anything. Wherever it pleases you, send him."

He said, "O.K. I'll see."

Then he said, "But the bicycle was stolen days ago. Why didn't you report it then? Now you've added problems to problems."

I said to him, "I didn't come sooner, because I didn't want to add problems to problems to problems!"

"How's that?"

I told him, "Until yesterday, I didn't have the receipt that showed that I had bought the bicycle. I had no proof that the bicycle was mine. I have two bicycle receipts, and some time ago I gave one of my sister's sons one of my bicycles. But he needed the receipt because he was living in the Medina. I gave him both receipts because I don't have anyone here to read them and tell them apart. He took both receipts, and they remained with him. Then the bicycle was stolen. I looked for the receipt, but discovered that my sister's son was now in Marrakech. When he came back he gave me the receipt, and I went out and found that fellow who stole the bicycle and brought him here. If the Lord had made it so that the police caught the bicycle thief and summoned me and I didn't have the receipt, I'd go to jail. You would have said that *I* had stolen the bicycle! So I decided: I wouldn't declare it stolen until I had the receipt; and if I didn't get the receipt, I wouldn't declare it stolen at all. Otherwise I would be taken for the thief, not he. Better a problem upon a problem, than a problem upon a problem upon a problem."

The chief said, "Well, now there is no problem. Because you have this speech, all of these answers, I'll have to do something. Come here." We went to the telephone. He called the regional police at "44," and he awakened the commander from sleep, you know, from a sitting sleep. He told him, "So and so, living in your area in such and such a village; his bicycle has been stolen, taken by a day laborer. Now they are both in our hands."

They said, "Why are you calling upon us?" He told them, "Should I work on this business, or do you want it?" They told him, "Send the owner of the bicycle to us, and sent the thief to us tomorrow."

I took a taxi and went over there. I entered the commander's office and he said, "What is the matter?" I told him, "The bicycle owner— about whom the police chief from the Medina was just this morning talking to you, who awakened you from sleep—it's me." He said, "Go to the secretary and have it written down."

I went to the secretary. He wrote down what had happened with the bicycle and said to me, "Take this receipt and have a picture made of it." I had a picture made of the receipt, he took it from me and said, "Go away, God watch over you." And that's it, that's all.

What do you think they will do with the thief?

Oh, they will probably push him onto the public prosecutor, or whatever they do in such cases.

And the bicycle?

Well, the bicycle has been sold to someone far away. We'll probably never get it back.

ARABS AND BERBERS . . .

Was Tahami an 'Arobi?

Yes, from Asfi.[1]

Are there many 'Arobi around here?

Many come as workers; it is very common.

Do they speak Berber or Arabic?

There are some who speak Berber, there are some who speak Arabic, and there are some who speak Arabic and Berber. That one, Tahami, he didn't know any Berber.

Do they often steal?

Yeah, they steal! Yeah, they have even been known to kill people! Sometimes they enter homes at night and kill the people in them.

Do you mean the 'Arobi especially?

Yes.

Sometimes you have Berbers who work for you; are they also deceitful?

No. Berbers have more good faith, but in a special way: they put confidence in you even before they know you. But if you try to outsmart them, then they become deceitful too. And they do well in fulfilling their

---

[1]A coastal city north of the High Atlas Mountains.

religious obligations. But the Berbers just don't know how to work, they just don't know our farm work. They don't work a lot, and they don't know the work.

How can that be? They have farming in the mountains.

Their farming is worth nothing: they don't know about irrigation canals, they don't use a hoe, they don't have large-scale farming. You know, it is said that their fields are so small that they measure it in frogs' leaps, and use dogs to carry off the harvest. Their properties are tiny, what's to them?

But there are some who have worked for a long time on the modern farms. Those know how to work.

How many different kinds of Berbers are there?

Berbers, just Berbers.

There is just one type?

Just Berbers, that's all. But from many different places, from many regions: there are Berbers from Marrakech, there are Berbers from these mountains. [The Faqir pointed north.] Those from Marrakech know how to work; those from these mountains don't. And so on.

And how about from the mountains to the south?

None come from there now. But from the east, from the southeast, those Haratin come, from the Sahara, from among the Blacks of the Sahara.[2] There are plenty of them in the Medina.

Do you ever take Haratin on as workers?

Some people take them on, but we haven't taken any on. We've only taken on Berbers and 'Arobi.

Why don't you take them on?

Well, we bring most of our workers from "44" or from the local marketplace. Most Haratin are found in the Medina.

But there are some in both "44" and the local marketplace. Why don't you take them on?

Its time hasn't been inscribed for us.

Do you intentionally keep away from them?

I don't run away from them but ... they don't seem very good to me.

Why?

Oh, your pleasure can hardly tolerate them at all. You don't know their measure: they appear servile, but you don't know what they are thinking. They are not like that black mechanic who was working on the well. You remember. He was black, but not a Haratin. If he had been a

---

[2]Most Moroccans from the region divide Blacks into two groups: *'Abid*, the descendants of slaves who used to form an important part of the retinue of the ruling classes and who are now looked upon with a mixture of admiration and fear; and *Haratin*, whose origins are less sure and who appear to have migrated from parts of the Sahara and may have been low-caste artisans attached to Saharan nomadic groups.

Haratin he wouldn't have said, "Give me that" when he wanted something. But his father was a black slave ('*Abid*), and his mother was a free woman, so he is a hybrid. But it would be an insult to call him that if he wasn't really a hybrid.

And among the Haratin, too, there are many whose work is worth nothing. They work only when you chide them. And they are not attractive.

Do you find them ugly or . . .
Oh, their ugliness is of no concern.
Well, it is of some concern, you know. But I'm just afraid they won't know how to work.

You mean you've never really dealt directly with them much at all?
No.[3]

When you deal with Berbers, at the time of the harvest or at other times, do you find them good, or not?
Some are good, and some are no good.

In what ways are they good, or not?
There are those who don't work, who don't know how to work. And there are those who know how to work. There are those whose mouths are always ugly; he never shuts up, always yells about food, and he does absolutely nothing. Another one will have no concern for this and will never mention the meal. And will be clean. And will pray, do all the prayers, and his clothes will be clean. But there are some who are sloppy, like a pig, like a beast. If he found a donkey, he'd eat it. The whole animal, he'd eat it.

And would he say ugly things?
He wouldn't say something ugly, and he wouldn't say something nice. He knows nothing about nice or ugly. Just like an animal, that's all.

When you have Berbers working here, where do they sleep and where do they eat?
They eat their meals from the same table as we do, and they sleep in that other room, or in the shed in the fields.

Why do you separate them for sleeping and not for eating?
Well, we have to separate them for sleeping; should I leave them here next to the money? And near our clothes? From these other places, they can just steal a rug and that's all. But as for the money, no thanks. Ay, ay! What, let them sleep here? And if they slept here, in this room, they'd bring fleas and bedbugs. They're filthy, their clothes are dirty.

But in eating we don't permit separating them. By the grace of our

[3]In pointing out to the Faqir that his views on the Haratin are not based on his own direct experience, I have obviously been trying to cast some doubt on the validity of those views.

Master—we don't yet know what the Lord will be doing with us either, so why should we separate them from us?

What is the difference between the Berber and the Arab?[4]

The Berber, I've said, does deficient work. But some of them are clean, better than the 'Arobi. And they don't eat a lot, the way the 'Arobi do. But as for work, very few among them work. Their work is little.

Are you counted among the 'Arobi?

No. We're counted as Arabs, but not as 'Arobi. 'Arobi is a different type of Arab.

What is an 'Arobi?

You just know it from his speech; you just hear it and know it.

Where do they come from?

They come from the north regions, and from places like Asfi. All those we call 'Arobi.

And what's the difference between the people here and the 'Arobi?

The 'Arobi make a lot of noise and are filthy, and they have little knowledge. Those of us here are somewhat clean, with respect to our meals, and our dealings, and the rest. But, on the other hand, we have a lot of lying here; they have less lying. It's just that they have a lot of dirtiness; and they eat a lot, and they work a lot.

Are the 'Arobi very shrewd?

No, the 'Arobi aren't all that shrewd. When it comes to stealing for example, we're much shrewder than they are. Compared to us, the 'Arobi are pretty simple. Now, look at what that fellow who took the bicycle did. He admitted, "Yes, I took it." If he were one of us, he would have said, "I didn't see the bicycle. I don't know these people." He would let you go round and round. But the 'Arobi are another thing. It's just when he has no supplies that he makes a lot of trouble.

I see a lot of Berbers who own stores in the Medina. Why is that?

Yes, they are patient.

How are they different from you people?

The Berbers are patient. They may spend the whole day in the store,

---

[4]A central tactic of French policy in Morocco during the protectorate was to emphasize distinctions between Arabs and Berbers and, through support given to Berber institutions, to encourage Berbers to become protégés of the French. This policy, known as "la politique berbère," was consecrated by the Berber Dahir (decree) of 1930, which formalized differences in Berber and Arab customs, making them into distinctions in civil law. This policy, rather than driving a wedge between Berber and Arab, brought them together in the struggle against the French for Moroccan independence. In fact, already in 1930, when the Moroccan independence movement first organized demonstrations, it included among its demands the repeal of the Berber Dahir.

In the remarks that follow, the Faqir's own view of Berber-Arab distinctions clearly challenges the rationale behind "la politique berbère."

and eat just one-quarter of a loaf of bread. If he has a lot of business, he'll eat one-quarter of a loaf; if he has no business, he'll eat one-quarter of a loaf. Or he may even eat nothing at all. Until he gets his capital. But one of us, spending his days in the Medina, will have exhausted his capital after three or four weeks. "I want watermelon, I want a soft drink, I want meat on a skewer, I want, I want." There isn't any profit yet, and still he is unable to keep to his store. That way he never gets his capital.

But the Berber is patient: he spends the day there, sitting, and won't even eat a peanut.

Is it better to be like that Berber who only eats one-quarter of a loaf until he gets his capital, or like that other one who eats up his capital?

Better is the one who is in the middle. He eats a little and he asks Our Master to bestow more munificence. He wastes nothing. The one who eats nothing is not better; the one who eats a lot is not better. The one in the middle is better. He eats a little to keep himself going, so that he needn't beg or look at other people's things and die from envy. Munificence is the Almighty's. The man keeps himself going, and works, and doesn't go astray.

Are there Berbers who have come to live in your village?

Yes, there are a few.

Like Abdallah b. Shluh ["son of the Berber"]?

No, he was just named after his father. But their people had been here a long time.

But didn't his forbears come from Berber country?

Yes, in the beginning, but it is four . . . four generations now: the Hajj, and his children, and his children's children, and his children's children's children. A long time ago.

Those who have been here a long time—do you still call them Berbers?

No. We just call them Ait l-Hajj. We don't call them Berbers.

Are they Arabs?

Why yes, Arabs. They don't know the Berber language at all!

If you are a Berber, is that from the blood or from the language?

Being Berber is just from language. If his origins are Berber, if his root is Berber, and if he knows the Berber language, only then is he Berber. But if he no longer knows Berber, he's become an Arab, he's no longer . . .

Even if his roots are Berber?

Even if his roots are Berber. What, are you going to call him a Berber when he is an Arab? He was born here—that is an Arab. He's no longer a Berber at all.

Will something still appear in his face or in something about him to tell you that he has a Berber origin?

No. If he grew up here, he appears with the blood from here. He doesn't have the blood of his region.

But doesn't the blood come from the parents?

It comes from the parents, but it comes in a special way. Here, his blood becomes wetted and soft like ours; it doesn't become like that of the Berbers.

How about the others who came here from the Berber country? How long have they been here?

It must be some forty years.

Do they still practice some Berber ways?

No, they don't.

Are their women also Berbers?

Yes, they are, but they don't practice Berber ways.

What customs do you mean? Which ones are different from yours?

The practices that are different from ours: ... the women wear their hair differently, they tie their hair in braids, high on the head. Ours don't. And they cut their hair, here in front, they take a scissors to it. Ours don't. There was one girl from here who married a Berber in the mountains and there she became a Berber, knew their language and wore their clothes. But then she remarried here and became an Arab again.

And are some practices different between Berber and Arab men?

As for the men, just the shoes are different: theirs has a back and ours doesn't. They always wear them. And they have their different language. We're different just in speech, they are known just from their speech, that's all.

And also from their dealings, from their dealings with one another. The Berbers, you know, don't award a reprieve, they don't allow whispering.

What do you mean, "whispering"?

They don't permit, let's say, bickering, an affront (*barasit*). The Berber has to be dealt with justly. He won't settle for a plea for God's pardon the way we do: "Oh, you promised this, and you reneged; it's all right, no problem. God watch over you until later." The Berber won't do that. You and I agree to come to a party—I'll come to it. If you didn't come, and you said you would come, we'd fight over this. That's the *demokrati*[5] that they have.

With us, the temper is tranquil: "Oh, you said you'd come. Wait you donkey, wait you Jew." Until the matter is settled.

That's the difference.

Well, what do you still want, now?

[5]See chapter 4 for more specific use of *demokratiya*.

JEWS . . .

Well, you mentioned "a Jew."[6] **I'd like to talk a little about the time when the Jews were still here. Were there Jews here in the countryside, or only in the Medina?**

They were in the Medina, and in some parts of the countryside. In some regions there were many of them.

What did they do in the countryside?

They farmed, they raised livestock, as we do. They did tasks like ours.

And if you saw someone, how would you know whether he was a Jew or a Muslim?

You'd know from his answers to you, and from his beard, and from . . . they had their own practices.

What do you mean, "from his answers"?

His speech always sounded different from ours.

Can you imitate it? Can you say something as a Jew would?

He'd say, "Shidi." He would always call a Muslim "Shidi." And the bastard, he would say "Shidi" but he would really be saying "Shidi-la, Shidi-la."[7] [The Faqir chuckled.] You'd hear "Shidi" but in his heart it was "Shidi-la."

Were there many Jews here in your district?

There were some but not many. About two or three families.

Were they well off, or not?

They were well off. There was one who would lease out his stock to be worked by Muslims, his livestock and his land. He would buy cows, sheep, and camels, and lease them to others. And he himself continued to farm. He had his own plots, which he had bought, and he also had stores in "44." When independence came, he joined the Independence Party and went so far as to attend their meetings. He was a shrewd one!

And were there many in the Medina?

Sure. You've seen their section of the city: that whole section, from one end to the other, was theirs. Not one Muslim lived among them. You know where the New Quarter is now? Well, all of that was theirs.

Why did they live in a section separated from the Muslims?

Well, you know, everyone goes to his brother. If just one Jew was there first, another Jew would come to live near him, and then another, and then another. Would one come to live where I was living? No, that wouldn't happen.

---

[6]The Faqir obviously felt the subject to be finished. But I had prepared questions on Jews and by a happy coincidence he had just mentioned them.

[7]Jewish dialects of Moroccan Arabic commonly pronounce the *s* as *sh*. So, instead of calling the Muslim "Sidi" (sir; my lord, my master), the Jew was saying "No Sir, No Sir."

What brought them to Morocco in the first place?

I don't know, I don't remember anything about that.

Have you heard anything about that?

Perhaps... some say that they may have had some troubles in early times and that the countries divided them up. That's what I've heard. It could be, it could be that way. Perhaps they were divided up and each country took a portion of them. And Morocco's portion was brought here. And you know that while they were here, the Jews gave something to the government, regularly.

What was that?

They gave something like a head tax, from year to year. And if a major holiday fell on Saturday, they had to pay for the firing of the cannon. You know, in the Medina, there is a cannon at the Fourth Gate; on the major holiday a cannon is fired and during Ramadan it is fired each evening, as a signal. It has been said that when a holiday falls on what's its name, on Saturday, that they pay everything.

Did they wear clothes different from a Muslim's?

They always wore black.

Why is that?

I don't know. Those black jellabas were very strong; that black material was very tough. Always a black jellaba, always a skullcap and, in the early days, they wore a silk cloth. Their women put towels on their head, and they wore those dresses that are popular now. Their women were all right.

Did you have a lot of dealings with Jews?

A lot!

What kinds of dealings did you have?

In cloth. You know that group of cloth stores in the Medina? Then, there wasn't a Muslim selling there; there were only Jews who sold cloth, that's all.

So, whenever you wanted to buy cloth, you would go to them?

Yes, whether I wanted it sewn or unsewn. And Jews, the very poor ones, used to wander through the merchant sections selling candles, or selling matches. "Matches, matches, matches, matches, matches." [The Faqir's sing-song intonation was an attempt to imitate them.] Always the same. "Candles, candles, candles." Yep.

And they'd come here and buy a lot of melons from us. They were fond of melons. And they'd buy argan oil and vegetables from us, and I'd deal with them. And they would lease out their livestock to people, but we never did that.

What were their dealings like?

Fine. Number one. There was no deception, ever.

No deception?

No.

Did you deal with any Jews in particular?

I dealt with one young man. He was named Dawid and was still young at that time. I had just been dealing with him for about two years and then he went off to... what's its name... to Palestine.

One day, as I entered his house, another Jew arrived, bringing him a jellaba like the one you have, bringing him two of them in fact. Dawid's eyes appeared unhappy to me. I said to him, "What is the matter?"

He told me, "I'm taking these jellabas away with me."

I said, "How's that?"

He said, "We're leaving, we're going over there."

I said to him: "Please tell me why. Is it the government here that wants to throw you out against your will, or is it your government that wants you over there? Or what?"

He said to me: "Sidi Muhammad, let no one lie to you about this. You know that well-to-do Jews come here and marry from among us and then go back, having become our in-laws. And here, those among us who are rich go over there, making those over there their in-laws. Little by little, one leaves, then another, and a little later yet another. I spend a full day here in my shop, and when I go home I say to myself, 'If you were a man, you'd go to your own country.' So we begin to follow one another, 'He left, so I also want to go; so I also want to go; so I also want to go.'"

That's what he told me, himself.

Well, the Jews began to sell what they owned. They sold houses then for 20,000 rials, which would today bring in 3 million francs. Gardens were sold for 30,000 rials, which would today bring in 7 or 8 million francs. Those of us who were lucky, who had money at that time, really cleaned up. There was a *tallib* who had once served in our village who bought a house at that time for 30,000 rials. Now it's worth a lot and he's still living in it. If he wanted to, he could get 2 million francs for it, or at the least, one and a half.

Were you happy when the Jews left?

I wasn't happy when they left, I wasn't happy when they stayed. They took nothing from me, and I took nothing from them.

Still, you know, when they left we weren't at all happy. It was no longer easy to find someone who could meet your needs. Cloth became scarce and more expensive. And the Muslim is a swindler: he wouldn't go easy on you, wouldn't be forbearing. There were Jews who, if you wanted three or four thousand rials worth of cloth, would give it to you, and you wouldn't have to give him a rial until later.

And when the Muslims started?

When the Muslims started they were poor, they had nothing yet, and they would take a rial off the price. And at first it was only Berbers who began to occupy those stalls. The Berbers bought a lot of what the Jews left in the Medina.

Did you often go into the houses of the Jews?

Yes, often.

Did their houses seem pleasing, or ugly, to you?

Well, a little dirty. Noisy and dirty. And, in their houses, they don't keep things hidden from Muslims. We'd be right in the middle of their family, they wouldn't keep anything back. Unlike us, they wouldn't keep the Jewess hidden, nor anything else. Everyone was right there in the house.

You mean you'd see their women and

and she'd be cooking right next to you, and talking to you, kissing your hand. Their ways were fine, and they'd take care of the Muslim, take care of him very well.

You consider their customs good?

Fine.

But you don't do things that way.

There are some of us who do things that way. As in Bukhensha's family, they do things that way, now. They don't lock their house; it is always open.

What Jewish practices are different from Muslim ones?

There is the slaughtering of animals, which is different from the Muslims'.

How do they slaughter?

There is only one person who does the slaughtering for all of them.

Do they slaughter with a knife?

A chicken is all that I've seen. I haven't witnessed a cow's slaughtering. As for the chicken, they do it with a knife. They hold the jugular, and he cuts it as though with a lance. He hardly even cuts into the meat of the chicken.

As they do this, do they say, "In the name of God?"[8]

Well, I don't know, I don't want to lie to you.

I've heard it said that the Jews drank.

They drank *mhaya*.

What is that?

It is made with the pits of prickly pears. And they drank other drinks; I don't know which ones. But they didn't all drink, only some of them did. As even today.

Was mhaya *forbidden for you?*

Yes.

Did many Muslims drink with the Jews?

[8]Muslims say this when they begin to slaughter an animal.

A lot. During those times no Muslims drank your drink, they drank the Jews' drink.

I've also heard that Jewish women were often prostitutes.

They do as we do. Just the same. They do, as we do, as you do.

What did your brother say the other day about the way a Muslim used to greet a Jew?

Well, you'd never greet them with "Peace be upon you." Nor with, "Good morning to you," although this might be said sometimes. My brother was talking about the time when there was forced labor, here in our district. We had to work a number of days for the government and, on those days, the Jews would be allowed to work on their own farming. My brother was working with others on the government's land and a man passed by and was greeted, "Good morning to you." They thought he was just one of the local people. When he turned around and said, "Good morning to you, Shidi," the one who had greeted him answered, "Keep on moving, God burn you!" [The Faqir laughed.]

There is another story like this. There was a guy who sold salt in the marketplace. He was sitting on the ground, selling his salt. A Jew passed nearby and he pulled on the Jew's jellaba, saying to him, "Come here sir, if you want some salt, come here." The Jew turned, and then he said to the Jew, "Go on you Jew, or let God curse your father." [The Faqir laughed again.]

During the colonial period, did the French favor the Jews?[9]

For them, the Jew was the same as a Muslim.

How's that?

The same.

Did the French prefer the Jews to the Muslims?

Well, in any event, if a Jew brought a case against a Muslim, the Jew would be given his due because he would be on the side of the law. Always, always, the Jew has to watch out for the other. And the Jew doesn't stir up trouble the way Muslims do.

Why doesn't he?

Well, he sticks to his laws. Always, he knows that he is beneath the livestock. Always he knows that he is a foreigner.

Is the Jew a foreigner here?

Yes. Why do you think he is fighting now? And looking for a place in the United Nations? In order not to be called a foreigner. From the time that they were divided they have been called foreigners. Always, he has been just "the Jew."

Here, for example, if you had a fight with a Jew and the Jew beat you,

---

[9]I am returning to a subject touched upon in chapter 4. The Faqir's answer here contrasts with what he said there but because the discussion takes a different turn, I do not pursue the contrast.

it was "a Jew" who beat you. And if you won, you had beaten practically nothing, you had beaten only "a Jew." That's how we'd insult him, by saying that it doesn't pay to get into a fight with a Jew. And it's the same with respect to a woman.

Since independence, how are disputes between a Jew and a Muslim settled?

It is settled as is usual; they are not unfair to the Jew; he is given his due.

If they fight, to whom do they go?

To the government. Always to the government. To the judge if it is his affair; to the government if it is the government's affair.

And if two Jews are fighting with one another?

To the court, always. But if it is a question for religious law, they go to their rabbi.

Who's that?

There was a rabbi in the Jewish quarter. He would pray with them, and show them what their laws were, and settle their disputes according to their law. But if it isn't a question for religious law, then they go to the government.

Were there any Muslims who married Jews?

No, no, no. There weren't. Never.

Is it prohibited?

Forbidden!

Someone told me that a Muslim may marry a Christian woman, but only if she converts. But a Muslim may not marry a Jewess even if she converts. He said that when a Christian converts you can trust her; the Christian's word is good. But the Jew is deceitful and you cannot take Jews at their word.

It is forbidden for a man to take a Jewess, unless she converts; and forbidden for a Jew to take a Muslim woman. The Christians took many Moroccan women, and they took mostly older ones. But as for the Jews, I've never seen that. Never.

Have there been many Jews who've worked for the government?

There were many during the colonial period, and there are still some now. The Jews are still working in the banks, and as secretaries in the courts, and so on.

Are there many Jews still in the Medina who were born there?

Just one.

What does he do?

He farms.

Is he old?

About the same as I am.

Are his children still here?

Yes, and he's very well off. He has olive groves, and he has olive presses, and he has a lot of gardens. He's all that remains. There are also the sons of another Jew who have gone to Casablanca and another coastal city; their sisters are working in the region, one in a bank, one in the courts as a secretary. They are still around, but no longer in the Medina. And they go, from Sunday to Sunday, to visit a shrine in the region.

They had a shrine? Was there any special concentration of Jews in the region—a tribe, or a village?

There were two places farther east, and, I told you, there were some in our district.

But here, you said, there were only two or three families.

But there were many in each family, thirty or forty in each. Children's children, and children's children's children. In one village. And there were many in the coastal city, and there were many in the Medina. Every town, every city, had some. There were a lot in Essaouira, and a lot in Casablanca. You've seen their quarters, there were a lot of them.

Do you remember when I rented that house in the Medina in what used to be the Jewish quarter? I didn't know that when I rented it. Could I have known from its construction that it had been a Jewish house?

No, it is just the same. There is no difference in the houses; they are the same.

Was there anything wrong about my renting that house?

No.

But I remember you once said that it would have been better had I not rented that house?

It would be no good for a Muslim to go and live among the Jews, because of our prayers and other practices. You, you know, don't do our prayers or anything, so it doesn't matter. And also, you weren't living among the Jews. They had already left. And this is just God's earth, it's neither the Jews', nor the Muslims', nor the Christians'.

The Jews had already left, but you still said, "Better you hadn't rented that house."

But there is nothing wrong with that. Only a Muslim must, if he bought that house after the Jew, purify it. That is: recoat the walls and have a Koranic recitation done. Do this in order to cleanse it. But the house is still the same house.

Let's say, if a Muslim bought the house of a Jew, and began to live in it
he'd have to whiten it, to whitewash it, and to have a recitation done. We say, you know, that the Jews have no angels. But I don't know, I don't know.

Do you think that it is better in Morocco now that the Jews are gone or better when they were here?

According to me, it was fine when they were here, and it's fine now that they're not here. Times were quiet then and times are quiet now. And, you know, there are Jews among Muslims even when there are no Jews. Always, there are Jews.

How's that?

Well, all those who don't hold to religion, who do ugly things—the Jew is better than they are.

Sometimes, when you refer to someone, you say, "Oh, he's a Jew." For example, about Hmed you always say, "A Jew, that one."

Oh well, the Jews, we just disparage them, we use them when we want to insult others. You know, when two people aren't able to perform a task, we say, "There are two Jews struggling with a sack of hay." But the Jews don't do the things that we do; we do more bad things than they do. The Jew avoids doing bad things. There are those among us who are ignorant; they think the Jew simply does as he wishes. Some of us who are ignorant now say, "Those Jews, they have no religion at all." And also say, "The Christian has no religion at all." But we don't know about matters on that level.

But what about the Jew's religion?

Everyone follows his own religion. Everyone keeps to his own religion, whether he be Christian or Jew or Muslim. But the Jews say that they occupy all of Heaven and that the Christians have just one corner there. And that the Muslims are at the feet of the Jews.

And the Jew, when he came to our houses, would not enter them. He would remain by the door with his donkey tied to a stake next to him. He would not permit himself to enter the house.

When was this?

In early times, before the French came. Only after the French came did the Jew begin to come and sit with people. But in those earlier times, he restricted himself to the doorway, and his meal would be brought to him at the door. People would even brew tea inside and then bring him his glass of tea to the door, unless he was brewing his own tea by himself.

Why did you do things that way?

It was the Jew himself who didn't want to enter. That's his religion. And we too have been told that he shouldn't enter our rooms.

And why did this change when the French came, when the colonial period started?

Well, it is as though . . . in the practices of the French, people were the same: the Jew was as the Muslim was as the Christian. All the same.

Also, we say: "The Christian, you may pray using his cloth, for it is clean. But don't eat his meals." His meals are unclean. "The Jew, you may eat his meals, but don't pray with his cloth." The Jew gives care to his meals but he pays no attention to his cloth. And only eat the Jew's meals if it is there when you arrive; do not eat it if he prepares it for you. That is also said. And you know, we may eat meat slaughtered by the Jews, but they will not eat ours. They will eat only bread and butter from a Muslim.

Now, you are continually being a thief! You never have your fill of stealing from me. Your stomach is always large. You hunger after my work, and you come from New York to deprive me of it and to disturb my affairs. I can't stay with you any longer now; I want to do my work.

I shouldn't deprive you of your work?

Why, you are continually stealing work from me, you are always a thief. But, we say, "a handful of bees is better than a hoodfull of flies." What does that mean? No, don't turn it off! [I had been about to turn off the tape recorder.] Its explanation is: two good words, or three good ones, with probity, are better than a tremendous quantity from someone who knows nothing.

7

A Fight

I had now been staying at the Faqir's for several weeks, and a number of hired workers had passed through his house. There were fewer Berbers this year than usual, because the grain crop had been poor and there was no need to employ one of the teams that come down from the mountains in summer to work on the harvest. Yet Tahami, of course, had made an unforgettable impression during his brief stay, and several villagers, one at a time, had been taken on for a few days to help with the watermelon crop. The villager would work from shortly after dawn until sundown and would eat breakfast and lunch with us. For the day's work he would receive one hundred rials, a little less than the standard wage on the larger and more modern farms in the region, but in addition would take home a full supply of vegetables and a sack of feed grass for his cow.

Faqir Hmed, who in my experience had always been the Faqir's most regular worker, had not appeared at the Faqir's house even once during my stay. Faqir Hmed, not quite fifty years old and a very animated individual, had always seemed to be a good worker—steady, fast, and with great stamina. He had worked for the Faqir for months at a time while I had lived in the village in 1970–71 and, during a previous summer, had been with us in the Faqir's house every day except for the weekly trip he made to market in the Medina. The past spring, however, he had apparently returned to cultivating his small village plot, which he had all but abandoned some fifteen years earlier, irrigating it with water from a neighbor's pump in return for one-third of the crop's income. Faqir Hmed supplemented this by taking on occasional jobs in the village.

Faqir Hmed's shift to working his own land might, in other circumstances, call for no comment. But Faqir Hmed himself had often told me that the meager output of his family land was far from sufficient to support his large family—he had seven children (two others had married and no longer lived in the village), his wife, and his mother under his charge. He would be better off, he had said, with a regular wage job on one of the modern farms in the region, but he wished to avoid spending his days too far away from his family. For him, then, his almost regular employment at the Faqir's had been a happy solution and one that he had actively promoted over the past several years.

Faqir Hmed's shift from steady wage labor to cultivating his own land was surprising for other, less personal reasons: although such a shift had been quite common in the past, it had become, under the pressure of contemporary changes in Moroccan society, rather exceptional. Villagers often told me that, in the past, most village families had been able to maintain balanced production. Most had had two types of land: parcels used for dry cereal agriculture, and irrigated plots for vegetables and fruits, which were located either on the banks of the *oued* and watered from the soil's natural humidity and irrigation canals, or were situated in the village and irrigated with water that a donkey, cow, or camel would draw from a well. There had been ample grazing land in the past, too, and most families had goats and sheep for occasional meat feasts, as well as a cow for milk. It was true that a young man might find himself in some difficulty before he gained control over his share of the family land at his father's death, and the share itself might be too small to be viable, but in such instances he was frequently able to find work in a family that had more land and fewer children or, in extreme cases, to emigrate for a shorter or longer time.

This Arcadian view of an almost autarkic village economy neglects two salient, interrelated features: first, the political subservience of the village, ever since its founding, to regional and national power; second, the slow erosion and reorientation of production patterns as the village became more tightly integrated into a world economic system and grew in population as well, with the consequent pressures toward production for a national and international market rather than a regional one, and toward the performance of wage labor.

The degree of village subordination was variable and the process of economic reorientation still inchoate before the establishment of the French protectorate in 1912; but, as French administration of Morocco solidified, this subordination was deepened and made more systematic and the village economy increasingly reflected wider national and international market forces. Since Morocco's accession to independence in 1956, these trends have become, if anything, more pronounced: on the one hand, the Moroccan government's efforts to create a pervasive administrative structure were not hampered by the stigma of foreignness; on the other, the cumulative effect of years of short-sighted technical and economic policy accentuated those trends and awarded to them the character of a force of nature—they seemed beyond human control.

The general trends in the village economy—unbalanced production patterns geared to external market demands and the increasing dependence of the rural population on wage labor—were accentuated but not inaugurated by the severe erosion of riverbed lands in the middle and late 1950s, all but eliminating these lands as an important productive resource.[1] Only a few farmers possessed sufficient capital (some used money they had earned working in Europe) to buy irrigation motors in order to convert some of their grain lands to vegetable production, and this avenue was severely limited by a governmental decree of the 1930s, still in effect, which prohibited the construction of wells on many large tracts of village land. By the late 1960s the conversion of cereal lands to vegetable production and the pressure of increasing village population forced many farmers to produce grain on land that had previously lain fallow or been used for grazing. Land scarcity was now experienced for the first time, and, as a result, livestock herds became more difficult to sustain: the last two decades witnessed the disappearance of goats from the village and a noticeable reduction in the number of sheep and cows per family. At the same time, and surely not coincidentally, the demand for cheap labor was itself expanding as new, mechanized farms continued to spring up throughout the region and as new opportunities opened for the young and healthy as migrant workers in Europe.

Those few who were able to remain farmers found themselves pushed more and more to pattern their own farms after the large mechanized ones, which had by now become the most visible model of what a successful farm should look like. This meant an increasing dependence on machines, particularly irrigation motors, but also tractors and delivery trucks, an increasing portion of production devoted to cash crops for the national and European markets, and a readiness to hire wage labor.

Yet, the village farmer who learned the lesson that the large farms were teaching entered into competition with these farms with very telling handicaps. First of all, the family farmer had a severely limited knowledge of, and greatly restricted access to, the lucrative national and foreign markets. The middlemen who transported his crop, the wholesalers who bought it, the packagers, and the shippers took most of his potential profit; the large farms on the other hand, performed many of these processes themselves. Also, much of the large-farm produce that

---

[1]Neither this severe erosion, nor even the lowering of the water table (see below), should be viewed as a first or primary cause, as an event of nature beyond human control. The severe erosion was itself a product of an irrigation policy that neglected the plight of the small farmer: the erosion could have been substantially lessened, if not completely averted, by an effective damming program. Similarly, the lowering of the water table, "caused" by the recent scant rainfall, might have been forestalled by a policy that limited artifical irrigation.

does not attain export standards is dumped on local markets and this pushes down the price that the small farmer might otherwise receive.

Second, the small farmer is in direct compeition with large farms, and with the politically powerful groups who own them, for control over basic resources: land, labor, and water. A substantial number of recent land disputes in the region have resulted in the expropriation of small holders to the benefit of wealthy, well-connected landowners; village farmers must now pay higher rates than before to their day laborers. Also, because large irrigation motors on the modern farms extract an ever greater quantity of water from the earth, the level of ground water has been steadily decreasing in recent years, and the water table now seems unable to replenish itself. Many small farmers now face the prospect of increasingly difficult access to water, and they must consider deepening their wells—dangerous and arduous work—and the expense of obtaining larger motors and pumps. The Faqir himself remembered that when he was younger, water could be found at a depth of five to ten meters; now, one had to exceed twenty and sometimes thirty meters. The First Ones [ancestors] had always said, he added, that this was one of the signs of the end of the world. The water table had risen markedly in the few years following the return from exile and subsequent enthronement of Sidi Muhammad (when Morocco regained independence in 1956), and the plentiful rains that accompanied his rule; but, more recently, increased tapping of the water by irrigation, coupled with the poor rains of the last several years, had caused the water table to sink several meters.

Despite the improved technology, there seemed good reason to agree with one old villager who, to show me that even with all today's material benefits, life now was much more difficult than in earlier times, cited the adage, "This is the time of toil, like chickens we all scratch the soil; We can no longer tell the rich from the poor." It seemed all the more surprising to me then, that the Faqir Hmed—a poor man with a large family, without riverbed lands, without the capital to install his own irrigation motor, and with only meager grain holdings—was now struggling against the personal and societal forces pushing him into the labor market and had instead returned to cultivate his own lands.

I asked the Faqir's brother, Ali, about Faqir Hmed the first chance I had. He said that there had been some kind of argument and that Faqir Hmed no longer wanted to work for them. I pressed him further on this, and Ali and I had the following conversation:

Tell me now—I want to know exactly—tell me what happened between Faqir Hmed and that other worker, the well-man. From the very beginning when it first appeared, until the end.

But we say, "Some people just strike at the shadow."

What does that mean?

It means: the reason for something may not appear, but we give to it a reason that does appear.

Well, tell me about the reason that does appear.

The reason that appears is this: that morning a neighbor had come by and said, "Please, Ali, I'd like you to give me some hedging for my fields." And I told him, "God greet you. Just come by around noon for it." And the Faqir Hmed said to me, "What's wrong with you, inviting people over at mealtime?" He said this jokingly, but he was serious. He meant, "Don't invite people over at mealtimes when we're going to be resting."

Do you understand how the thing is going now?

More or less. Go on.

I told him, "When you're working with us, do you think I'm going to cut off my relations with other people?" Jokingly—it was said jokingly—but there was something to it.

After a little while, noon arrived. The well-man was doing a mounting and hoped to leave the cement to set while we all went in to eat lunch.[2] Then he would be on his way. When noon arrived, he and Mehdi were inside the well working on this and Faqir Hmed and I were above, with the pulley. If the well-man yelled up to you to let loose a little, you let loose, until he said, "Stop." Or you'd raise it, until he said, "Stop." But, now it was noon, and Faqir Hmed yelled down to him, "Come on up, it's noon." But the well-man called back, "No, not until we get this mounted."

Now Faqir Hmed, according to his needs, has to sleep at midday because he is going to be working until sundown. He has to sleep for a couple of hours or so in the middle of the day. That other fellow, the well-man, was hoping to finish the mounting before lunch so that he could leave us right after lunch for either another job or to go straight home.

So I said to Faqir Hmed, "Should I work on the pulley alone, and then you can go rest, or the other way around?" He just answered, "Let it be." [Ali said this to me in a tone that indicated that the Faqir Hmed had become short-tempered.] So I told him: "Let go of the rope, I'll take over. Go off to sleep. I'll go inside once we've finished the mounting." But then Faqir Hmed became ashamed, and he said, "No, you go inside. You just go." I went back to the house to sleep.

Meanwhile, the well-man was telling Faqir Hmed, "Let go a little." But the Faqir Hmed let it go a lot, just to anger him. Then he'd tell Faqir

[2]The heavy, difficult task of mounting—lining the inside wall of the well with cement to prevent it from caving in—normally requires four people: two men above ground maneuvering the pulley to raise and lower the metal mold that presses the cement to the well wall, and two men below, inside the well, to position the mold and set it firmly in place.

Hmed, "Raise it." And he'd raise it a lot, higher than was called for because . . . the time for sleeping had arrived and the well-man wasn't letting Faqir Hmed go off to sleep.

Was Faqir Hmed doing this with the mold purposely?

His head was spinning, and he couldn't stand the fact that the well-man was keeping him from his sleep.

So the well-man climbed out of the well, and then I heard some shouting. I came out—my brother had gotten there just before me—and I found them arguing. "What's the matter with you, what's the matter with you?" They wouldn't say anything. Faqir Hmed stalked off and went and sat underneath a pomegranate tree. The well-man said, "Well, I'm not working here anymore." "What's wrong?" "I won't work here— that fellow is trying to kill me." "Work!" "I won't work. I'm not working, that's all." He told that to the Faqir. And then he said, "Let Mehdi tell you what happened."

Well, I knew already that Faqir Hmed had been pulling some stunt, because I know him. He's sneaky, and he's always trying to outsmart other people. So I told him, "By God, I just leave you alone and you create problems." And then Faqir Hmed, there under the pomegranate tree, went and got on his bicycle. He was in a huff. The Faqir called out to him, "Hey Faqir Hmed, take it easy. Come on, go in and take a nap." But I said to my brother: "What do you want him for? Let him stay away until he's tired of it. God has provided plenty of workers and plenty of work. There are other workers who will work for us, and other work that he can find. What do you want him for?"

And Faqir Hmed continued on his way.

That's all?

That's all. But if you saw us together now, you wouldn't know that anything had come between us.

Ali's tone throughout this conversation had been quite disdainful of Faqir Hmed and contradicted what he had just said—that there was no longer any ill will between him and Faqir Hmed. But there were other grounds for not accepting Ali's version at face value. It was not simply that Ali's characterization did not fit the Faqir Hmed I knew; in any event, I was not so naive as to assume a flat consistency in the Faqir Hmed's behavior toward me, on the one hand, and toward any one of his covillagers on the other. It was rather that I had already seen Faqir Hmed a number of times that summer and he had not once mentioned the dispute or, as far as I could recall, talked about Ali in any but the coldest, most impersonal manner.

I knew Faqir Hmed quite well, both from all the time he had worked at the Faqir's and from the many hours we had spent with one another, alone. I wanted to know his side of the story, so I went up to the village the next day to talk with him about it. I found him working on his plot; his neighbor's irrigation motor was temporarily out of order and Faqir Hmed was quite concerned that he might lose some of his vegetable crop, particularly because the weather was so hot. As I came up to him, he was covering watermelon fruit with its leaves. It was almost lunch time, and, when Faqir Hmed finished shading the watermelon, we went inside for a few hours. In the course of our conversation I brought up the subject of the dispute.

All right. Tell me what occurred when you were working on that well at the Faqir's.

Oh, so you've heard about that. There's nothing, there's not much to that [his tone indicated that, for him, this was still a sensitive subject].

O.K., just tell me about it from the beginning. Tell me what everyone said until the moment you left them.

This story is about the well-man, about Muhammad the son of Ali b. Hashmi.[3] He and I were working on the well; he was at the bottom with Mehdi, and I was at the top with Ali. The weather was really hot that day and the time for sleeping had arrived—you know, when the weather gets really hot. The Faqir came up to us and said, "Fellows, you've got to stop now. Enough of this, the weather is hot." The Faqir went off to nap and we were going off too.

But the well-man shouted up to Ali, "I'm not coming up. I want to work here until we finish this." Ali said to me, "Buddy, go off to sleep." I told him, "No, I'm not going off to sleep." He said, "Why?" And I told him, "I'm working for you. I'm not going off to sleep while you remain here working. If you want to go off to sleep, go ahead." So Ali left and I stayed.

So I was alone, working on the pulley. The well-man and Mehdi were underground, placing the mold. The well-man shouted up, "Raise it!" The mold seemed very heavy. I couldn't move it—it must have been stuck—and I put pressure on. Earth started to fall down on the well-man, and he shouted up, "Let it down, let it down!" I did. And then he said, "Raise it!" and I tried again. Again earth fell down upon them, and the well-man began to yell.

I shouted down, "What are you yelling for?" And he said, "You're trying to kill me." I said, "What do you mean?" He said, "When I tell you to raise it, you lower it; and when I tell you to lower it, you raise it." I told him, "When you said 'Raise it' I raised it; when you said 'Lower it' I lowered it." Then he came up from the well and said, "You are trying to kill me. You did that to me purposely. You did that purposely when you saw the others go off to sleep and you didn't go too." I told him, "Buddy,

[3]Faqir Hmed often presented his stories in a formal manner, in a recitative mode.

it's not like that at all. The mold must have been stuck." He said, "No." And then he called for Mehdi and told him, "Get your father over here. We have to settle our accounts."

The Faqir came out, "What's the matter with you two?" Then, to me, he said, "Go in to sleep." I said, "No." To the well-man, he said, "Go in to sleep." The well-man said: "No. Let's settle our accounts now, please. That fellow is trying to kill me. He was just raising and lowering the mold without reason and sending all that earth down upon me." I was now sitting under the pomegranate tree and still hadn't said a word.

Were you angry at that moment?

Of course I was angry.

Then the Faqir said to me, "What's the matter?" And I told him, "This happened, and then this, and then this." The well-man said, "He did this purposely!" And I said, "It wasn't on purpose at all." The Faqir said, "Go in to sleep." And I said, "I'm staying right here." And the well-man said, "Let's settle up." The Faqir said, "Please, stay here." But the well-man told him, "No, I'm leaving. I'm not staying here any longer."

Then Ali came out to us. As he came out, he didn't ask us anything. He didn't say, "What's between you, what's wrong?" He just said to me, "I leave you guys here for just a minute, and then you go and screw things up." Those were his words.

I told him: "Listen buddy. You didn't ask us what is between us. I didn't screw things up and we have so far said nothing to you about this. What's the matter is between me and the well-man; you have to ask us what is between us in order to understand what the reason is. But you come up to us and you don't ask us what happened; and then you say that we screwed you up?" Those were my words to him. He shouldn't just come to us and say that we screwed up, like animals.

I went for my bicycle, got on it, and the Faqir said, "Wait!" And I said, "I'm not coming any more." That's all, that's what happened.

And you left?

I left. That's all, from that day to this.

After that, did they ever come and ask you to work for them?

That fellow b. l-Hajj, who came back from France, visited the Faqir and then came to me to ask me to work for the Faqir. I told him, "With them, it's finished. No more." But the Faqir did nothing wrong. It was Ali who said those words, and he knew nothing. That's all. That's what there was.

❈ EVENTS RADICALLY IN QUESTION

The absence of Faqir Hmed from the Faqir's household appeared, at first glance, to be an event of a new kind, for here my interest had been provoked by something that was *not* happening. This is evidently a superficial observation, but it led me to question my notion of the "event" in new ways.

It was clear that Faqir Hmed's absence struck me as noteworthy only in light of my previous experience in the Faqir's household and in Morocco. Consequently, my seeing this absence as an event had rather less to do with its actual significance for the Faqir and rather more to do with my distinctive experience and perspective. I had already noted that the questions I asked the Faqir reflected my own concern with the colonial experience, my curiosity about relations between different ethnic groups, my desire to understand how individuals can be deeply religious. Now I suspected that my more than casual interest in the absence of Faqir Hmed from the Faqir's household was accounted for, in no small measure, by my desire to understand the relationship between social ties and economic motives. Was my special perspective, my particular blend of my own society's concerns, not only inseparable from the questions I would pose about an event, but also essential to what I thought constituted an event?

The opening, superficial observation had another sequel: it forced me to reflect on the role played by time in giving meaning to my experience in Morocco. During the first few weeks of my stay that summer, I had not been conscious of Faqir Hmed's absence; with the normal variation in the intensity of agricultural work and with what might be Faqir Hmed's other commitments, it would not be unusual for such an absence to last several weeks. It was only as this absence continued and as the Faqir at times took on one or two other workers that I actually began to perceive an absence. Whatever its other characteristics, this event had a significant temporal dimension and needed a period of gestation to become visible to me.

If the event became visible only when looked at from a particular perspective, and if it became visible only with the passage of time, how, exactly, was this event situated in the external world? What did my experience in Morocco mean if an event, standing out in relief against the particular background of my own experience, might appear significant to me, and yet to someone else merge indistinguishably into a background of very different color and texture? And if this kaleidoscope shifted differently for each of us with the passage of time?

The solidity and "objective" character of the event—its existence as something fixed, once and for all, and identical for all those who look at it—was disintegrating. The Faqir and I, it seemed, were not discovering the meaning of events in his life, nor was I uncovering the meaning he already had given to them. Rather, I was *constructing* events out of my own concerns and out of the tissue of the Faqir's life; and the Faqir, perceiving this construction in the questions I asked, worked out his own view as a response, a response that treated my questions constructively and creatively, just as I was treating his life.

Because, from my point of view, Faqir Hmed's absence had a background and prior history, I would first question the Faqir about the fight and the sequel to it ("The fight ... "); and because at least part of its significance for me lay in its illustration of the conflict between economic interest and social considerations, I would ask the Faqir, in this light, about partnership, friendship, and other social ties ("Partnerships, friendship...").

⧉ SEVENTH DIALOGUE

THE FIGHT...

Tell me, Faqir, where were you when that dispute between Faqir Hmed and the mechanic broke out?

I was taking a nap, right here in this room. The mechanic came in here and said to me, "Give me my pay. I'm leaving."

Tell me what happened from that moment on, until the matter was over.

Well, they were all working on the well: the Faqir Hmed, the mechanic, my brother, and Mehdi. When noon arrived, it was time to sleep and my brother left them working on it, fitting the mold into the well shaft. Faqir Hmed was working the crank outside, on the ground, and the mechanic was positioning the mold from the bottom, inside the shaft. Faqir Hmed was in a hurry to come in and get to sleep, and he kept yelling, "Hey, hurry up," and so on and so on. Then the mechanic yelled back, "Hey, are you trying to drop me into the well?" And they began to argue and the mechanic came up out of the shaft, yelling at Faqir Hmed, "Hey, you weren't doing what I told you. Are you trying to kill me?" And then he came for me: "That guy is going to kill me. Give me my pay, I'm leaving."

When you went outside, did you question them?

Well, I went outside—my brother saw me going and followed after me—and I said to them, "What's all this noise for, what's causing this noise?" Then one of them said, "He can stay here. I'm leaving!" And then the other said, "He can stay here. I'm leaving!" Well, I saw that neither one of them wanted to stay, so they both left.

Who told them both to leave?

They told themselves. Each said, "I'm going to leave, let the other stay."

Faqir Hmed and your brother still don't seem on very good terms with one another.

Well, when my brother came out, he said to Faqir Hmed, "I left you both here and you were going to work the crank and pulley. If you didn't want to, or if it was too hard for you, you should have come and told me." "Ah, you are just like that mechanic," Faqir Hmed said. "You just want to talk without finding out what happened." And so on and so on. I said to him, "Come back, come back," and I followed him as far as the apricot trees. But he left. The mechanic came back and stayed with us for lunch. And he said: "No sir, I don't want to be fighting with your worker. God help me and God help you. Tell the worker to come back."

Well, we didn't ask either one of them back, neither Faqir Hmed nor the mechanic. They both left.

Why didn't you ask Faqir Hmed back afterwards?

We weren't up to it. The money that we were always paying him—we needed it ourselves. You know, there are times when we don't have one rial coming in for a week, and we have to give him six hundred rials, from market day to market day.

But, we had been embarrassed (*hshem*); he had been with us for so long, and he has many children, and we were too embarrassed to say to him, "Go." We were bearing with him, we were used to him, and we laughed together, and had tea together, and played together. And his work was fine, so all that was no problem. But every week I'd be saying to myself, "Next week he'll have to go. Next week." Finally, this thing happened.

So, for you, I guess this happened at a good time.

Yes, it came at a good time. I couldn't just say to him, "You'll have to leave us." That's it, that's the reason.

PARTNERSHIPS, FRIENDSHIP...

So, that relationship is broken now. But what about the others that you have with people around here? First of all, how about your partnerships, in land and in machinery?

Well, I am a partner in three irrigation motors and also in that plot of land by the river.

How did those partnerships in the irrigation motors develop?

Well, they heard that I had put up the money for someone else's motor; then, when they needed a motor, they came to me and said, "Help me out, too, with a motor. I want to work this out with you as is customary."

How well did you know them before you started the partnerships?

I knew them all; they're all our neighbors. You think you know them well—you say, "I know him well"—but it's all luck. You don't know if it was "well" until you settle the account.

What was the arrangement in those partnerships?

I buy the motor for the fellow; I tie up my money in it. Then, each year for three years, he should give me back one-third of the money I put up. And, until the day this money is paid back, he must also give me one-fourth of the income from the crop.

Have those fellows been paying you back?

No. One of them has paid back one-third. For another it is just the first year and the time hasn't arrived. As for the other, two years have passed and he hasn't given me anything back yet. He keeps saying, "Tomorrow I'll be selling some land, I want to sell some land." He has given me nothing back so far.

What can you do about that?

I'll tell him, "If you don't manage to get me those two payments that you owe, I'm going to take my motor from you. Even though the motor isn't mine, I paid for it, and I paid for it in your name. We said, 'One payment each year.' Now, two have passed and you have given me nothing. You haven't given me even one-third. So I'm demanding now that the motor become mine." And the motor would bring in more now than I paid for it.

Is this partnership written down somewhere?

It is just his word and mine, in the presence of the previous owner.

But what if the fellow won't give you the motor?

Then I would just have to go and dismantle it and haul it away.

When did you begin to go into partnership with people?

Well, about six or seven years ago.

Had you become well off; did you have money around at that time?

No, we never have money around. When someone comes to me and says, "By God, I need a motor," or whatever, I begin to get hold of ten thousand rials from one fellow, ten thousand rials from another. And I sell some livestock, and I might have some twenty thousand rials in cash. I collect a little from here, a little from there, and I go and buy the motor, that's all. But we never have hard cash on hand.

If you want to borrow money from someone, how do you go about it?

Well, if I know someone to have money and I believe him to be generous—he won't turn me down—I'll go to him and say, "I need some money, lend me some money."

And what do you consider if someone comes to you and says, "I'd like this much"? What do you weigh in order to decide whether you will lend it?

I weigh whether he is honest. If I know him to be a liar, I'll say to him from far away, "No, I have no money." If I don't know him well or, perhaps, I see he's in trouble and under a lot of pressure, my heart might return to me a bit and I'll say to him, "Well buddy, O.K., how much do you want?" And if I have it, I'll say, "Here." If I don't, I'll say, "No, that's too much for us. I don't have it."

If you've gone into partnership with someone and the partnership has turned out well, might you say, "If he has a daughter, I'd like her to become my son's wife"?

But not one of the partnerships has really turned out well. Even with that fellow Hummad, who just paid me back, he had paid me nothing for two years. He borrowed the money "for two months," and it stayed with him for more than two years. Last year, at the time of watermelon, I told him, "Bring me my money." Now, he's finally given me my money back, plus six sugar cones.

At first, when he came to borrow, he told me, "Lend me the money until the crop comes in. I'll make you a partner in the crop too, as if you had bought the irrigation motor for me." I told him: "No. You and I, we've eaten together and drunk together when we were in partnership. Now I want to just lend you the money. You need not give me any portion of the crop. Go until you sell the watermelon, and bring me back my money." But that year's crop did nothing for him and he brought me no money back.

But if the crop brought in nothing, is it his fault if he doesn't give you your money back?

Hey, I didn't lend it to him on the success of his crop. If you are partners and the garden doesn't produce, then you receive nothing. But if I've just lent him the money, he has to bring me my money the day the term is up. He has to handle it himself, even if he has to steal it. That's not my affair. When he borrowed, he didn't say, "Only if the garden produces," or "Until things are going well." He said, "Only for three months," or "Two months."

If you don't have the ready cash, if you have to borrow for it, why do people come to you for partnerships?

People know... people remember two things: where they have eaten their fill, and where they been beaten their fill. That's all.

And with you they eat their fill?

With me, they eat their fill. And they see other people here: one fellow comes and becomes our partner, then another, then another.

Have you ever gotten into a long dispute growing out of a partnership?

If I'm looking for a dispute, I'll always have grounds for one. Because you always have to squeeze the money out of them. You have to be a little patient and give in a little here and a little there, until you get it all back. Otherwise you'll always be fighting. Even now, with respect to that river plot, we are in a dispute.

Tell me about that, the whole story.

The story is... I took on their land in partnership. I was going to cultivate it and give them one-fourth of the crop. A little later they came to me and borrowed some money, 35,000 rials, without a contract, without writing it down, based on the partnership. Then, a short time after this, one of their brothers—he had turned bad—came to me and said that he wanted to take half of the cane crop; we were planting cane there. But we had agreed that they would get only one-fourth. So we argued.

I told him, "No. A quarter is what you get; you don't get a half." And we argued. And once we had argued over that, they began to welsh on the money they had borrowed. But, don't forget, we were working on their land, occupying it, so they had a problem.

Well, first they tried to get the money elsewhere, to pay me back. But no one would lend it to them, so they came back to me and said: "God's blessing upon you; that brother of ours is crazy. If you could just lend us a little more money, we'll put it all down in writing, we'll have a contract." I said, "All right." We went and had a contract drawn up for a three-year period; I gave them more money and altogether they then had 75,000 rials of mine.

The day that the final payment to me was due, they didn't show up. So I went and started a case against them. Before that, I informed them of this: I sent them a registered letter and the post office sent for them. But they paid no attention. For two months they didn't go to pick up the letter. After the two months passed, I started a case against them in the regional court.

Why didn't you go to see them?

What would I still have to say to them? There was nothing more I could do. If I had gone to them, they would have said, "In a day, tomorrow." They would have meant, "Never."

I went to the regional court and started the case. When the court was about to meet to consider it, the brothers contacted me and said, "Oh buddy, we'd like to extend the contract . . . we're looking for the money, we'd like to do this," and so on and so on. I told them: "There are three ways I will deal with you, three ways out of this: bring me my money and you may come back to your land; or, we'll extend the contract but you'll have to pay the fee;[4] or, bring me your deed and cede your land to me— then the money is yours. It's as you wish."

After a time they said, "Oh, all right. But in a little while . . . give us some more time . . . and a little this and a little that." In short, they didn't come back with an answer.

Finally, the court came into session and summoned us. But the brothers didn't show up, and the case was delayed from week to week. Five or six times it was delayed, from one Tuesday till the next, as though they had pulled some trick on me. I'd wait from the morning on, until the court disbanded, and then the court secretary would tell me, "Come back next week," or "Come back on such and such a date."

Finally, we got all three of the brothers there before the court but then, again, the court didn't call us. So they said to me: "Now, we don't have the money to give you. You'll have to bear with us. You pay the money for the renewal and we'll extend the contract." In short, they weren't thinking of giving me anything, and I saw that the whole busi-

---

[4]This would have amounted to almost four thousand rials.

ness was going to require more money. I'd been to the court some six or seven times, and now we'd spent the whole day there and no one had called for us. So I went back to them and said, "All right, let's go for another contract."

We did another contract. They went home, and I took care of registering it; and now, here it is three years later, and the payment is due again.

And now, what's going to happen?

Well, the contract is up—it was up just at the time of the Amouggar— and they haven't come to me yet, and I haven't yet said anything to them.

And if they don't come to you?

Then, I'll have to go to them.

How do you know whom to enter into a partnership with?

Well, you don't really know. It is said, "You can't know a person unless you've traveled together on the same road, or been partners with one another."

Well, what qualities do you look for in a partner?

In a partnership, trust is the most important quality. Trust is the key. If there is trust, you win and he wins. If there is no trust, there is nothing.

To your mind, what comes first, the partnership or the friendship?

The friendship comes first, then the partnership. Why, if a fellow doesn't know you, what can he ask you for?

But from what I see, you've gone into partnership with people like those with whom you're now having the contract dispute, who were no friends of yours. And then, too, what about that partnership you had with Sessy's son?[5]

Well, Sessy's son came up to me, falling from tears, saying: "The land is good, and I need a motor in order to work it. But now I get water from a neighbor's motor, and it is always breaking down and he doesn't repair it." And we were greedy; "Maybe partnership in a motor will satisfy his need and we can make something from it too." But now he has come up empty again, his luck is no good.

But why did you go into partnership with him? I had heard you say that he was not a good man.

But at that time we were still talking with his father and with his brothers; we were on good terms with his family. Even if he was no good, his family was good, and so was our relationship with them.

Did you go into partnership with him because of his father?

Well, I said, "Even if his father is a tough nut, he won't consume what

---

[5]At a number of points in these dialogues, I confront the Faqir's generalizations with my knowledge of counterinstances, as I do here. Such questions could not have been posed at the outset of my research—they require a certain amount of prior experience— and they are thus situated, temporally, at a precise moment, as part of a sequence in which things are learned.

is mine." In partnerships, where things are out in the open, he won't consume the goods of other people. But where it is a question of boundaries, in matters that people won't catch on to, he might try to outfox them. But in other things, his father won't consume what belongs to a fellow. It was only later that the fighting occurred.

You mean that dispute last year that isolated you from the rest of the village? Tell me, how did it happen that all the village was united against you then?

They united against me because all of them are Jews. Sessy and Si Hassan just said to them: "That Faqir Muhammad won't help us on this matter; he's no longer one of us. He won't help us get this road opened through that other guy's property, so don't anyone speak with him." But what they wanted—to have a road go right through a fellow's land—was no good.[6] But the others were thunderstruck, as though they were in fear of Sessy.

But they didn't all agree with Sessy, did they?

No, but Sessy and Si Hassan, and then two others, ganged up on them and the whole village followed. From fear. A guy would come up to me and say, "Ah, those heathens, they're trying this and this." But then he'd just be offered a little money, or sugar, and he'd go right over and support them, and they could do what they wanted with him.

When you would go up to the village, would anyone talk to you?

Those few who were on my side would.

And the others?

If I saw just one of the others in a group, I would go straight past them. I wouldn't address them at all, not even to say "Peace upon you." I cut off ties to all of them. I was completely free of them. None of them came here any more; I was finished with all of their kind.[7]

But now things have turned around. Now it's Sessy and his family who are isolated.

Well, they are isolated to a certain degree: no one deals with them any more, or entertains them. And they no longer invite anyone. The people woke up.

Have villagers come to you in order to try and patch up your differences with them?

This doesn't happen any more. These modern people don't settle things, don't come to terms. In former times, when someone was missing, the others would come to look for him. But now, you know, people no longer fear anything. That's freedom for you. People don't care any

---

[6]Disputes over rights of passage to inaccessible plots through the land of others have become quite common recently, as a result of the increased demand for land and the need for much wider paths to allow pickup trucks through to reach the crop.

[7]The Faqir had cut himself off from the village in the past (see ch. 1). One should certainly wonder how his statements in chapter 1 are related to this recent dispute, even though they refer to an event occurring in the distant past.

more whether things are resolved or not, whether you go with them or don't.

You mean people are no longer concerned about other people?

They're no longer concerned; they don't look ahead or behind. They just see what is in front of their faces. They don't care at all.

According to you, is this situation better now, or was it better in former times?[8]

It's better this way.

Why is that?

Wherever you find a lot of people, you find only trouble. This bothers some of us, but most just sit back. If there are three or four there in good faith, the rest are just having a good time, joking and lying. They are saying, "Yes, yes, yes," but there is no good faith, and underneath they are saying, "No." A guy will tell you he'll meet you the next day in such and such a place, but the next day he'll be spending the morning in the Medina instead.

So it's from the time of that dispute that you no longer give your dues for the mosque?

From the time when they all got together and wanted to ostracize me—you know, what they call "ostracism." They all agreed that they wouldn't speak to me. So why should I help them? Why?

But now that dispute over the road is finished, and it seems that most of the village now agrees with your position on this. Why, then, don't the villagers talk with you and gather together with you?

I'm the one who won't approach them; but now they will all come up to me and try to speak with me. But I have no use for them and I don't address them. I know how their thoughts go.

Why do you still carry ill will from that time? Why is your pleasure in them still lacking?

Why lacking? Because I know those fellows are empty. Whoever gets to them first leads them around. You just knock on a guy's door and he's ready to follow you. That's worth nothing. No. A fellow has to stand on his own.

They have no mind of their own?

Nothing. Even now, if they had their own mind, they wouldn't speak to that Sessy any more. But they say, "Oh, he didn't do anything."

But they don't speak to him now; he's kept completely apart.

They are kept apart, that's true. So now the villagers have no mind at all, not even the mind that was leading them around. They don't grab that Sessy as they should. It's just as though nothing happened, as

---

[8]This question seemed, as I asked it, an empty one, perhaps meant more to keep the conversation going than to elicit a substantive reply. But the Faqir's answer was unexpected.

though they had done nothing. Just like the play of little children, that's all.

But now at least they've awakened to what happened.

They've awakened, that's true, but that's not worth anything. They still say, "Oh all of that was nothing at all." Even though there was tremendous expense, enormous waste. They think "It's nothing." Just like the play of children, that's it. [The Faqir's tone had become very bitter.]

Won't you forgive them?

What do you mean, "forgive them"? For what?

You know, you might say to yourself, "Look, they were led around by that fellow and left their senses. But now they've awakened and so there should be no more problems."

Well, for them now, it's all no problem. [The Faqir's bitterness continued. He was speaking in a very low tone.] You can see them running around already and witnessing for other people. Sure, there's no problem at all. That's that.

8

An Unhappy Marriage

On my first day in Morocco that summer, the Faqir told me that his daughter Zahara had married Bukhensha's eldest son, Muhammad, at the end of the previous summer, and that the couple was now living in Bukhensha's house in the Medina. This gave me some satisfaction, because in many respects the two families had grown closer to one another as a result of my presence in Morocco. As one villager had explained to me: "You know, before Bukhensha brought you out here, he and Faqir Muhammad used to greet one another in the marketplace, but that was all, despite the fact that years ago Bukhensha had lived in this village for a long while. But once you came out here, Faqir Muhammad and his brother began to visit Bukhensha often in the Medina, on market days, and would bring them vegetables, clarified butter, and milk. And then their families—their wives and children—got to know one another too." The cementing of these ties through the marriage of the two children seemed a natural, even desirable course for this relationship to take.

I hardly knew the couple. Muhammad, who was now about nineteen, had left school at an early age and had run away from home to stay with an uncle in Casablanca on at least two occasions, once when he was no more than fourteen. In the past few years he seemd to have grown more willing to stay at home, perhaps because his father was so frequently away on extended trading trips, but for as long as I had known him he had had great difficulty finding ways to earn money in the Medina. For a short time he had been an apprentice to an automobile mechanic and now occasionally helped an electrician. Zahara, perhaps fifteen years old, had often worked on farming tasks while she still lived with the Faqir; it had been at those tasks that I had most frequently seen her, her slight body bending over the irrigation canals. In my presence she had always been extremely subdued, and she would smile shyly and lower her eyes when I greeted her in the fields, "God assist you in your work."[1]

[1]This is the usual greeting to anyone at work.

My pleasure at the marriage was to be short-lived. I began to sense this when the Faqir said to me only a few days after I had arrived, "You know, Bukhensha's house is very near the marketplace, and many men from the market come to visit them. I have told my daughter, 'If men come into the house, don't serve them tea or food. Don't allow yourself to be seen!' And some of their neighbors have been saying that Bukhensha's two grown daughters often go out at night." This was the first hint I had of a problem that was to grow more and more complex as the days and weeks passed.

About one week after my arrival, on 27 June, Ali brought the subject up: "I had known, even before they asked for Zahara in marriage, that the mother and two daughters were no good. But I don't think the Faqir knew. People are too modest in front of him to tell him such things. So, when they came to ask for the girl, I told him, 'Those people are not good, they are not right for you.' And he answered, 'You don't know anything, you have no sense.'"

On 13 July, Mehdi talked to me about the trip that his mother and Ali's wife had taken to the Medina the day before, to see his sister. The problem had become more acute. "My mother told me when she re-turned from the Medina that Zahara wants to come home, that she has had enough of the Bukhensha household. So my mother said to me, 'Bring your sister back!' I refused and told her, 'You didn't listen to me when I told you not to marry her into that family, so I am not going to bring her home now.' If she wants something done, she will have to tell my father.

Mehdi continued, "You know, a while ago, I went into the Medina and talked with my sister Zahara, alone. I asked her then if she wanted to be taken home and she said, 'I'm afraid of my father.' So now she must fend for herself."

The next day, 14 July, Ali spoke to me again: "The women have told me that Zahara wants to come home. Zahara told them: 'They are always asking me to greet their guests and to serve the men who are present. I want to be back in our house or I will die.'" Ali continued, "No, I won't tell the Faqir, because when I criticized his intention to marry his daugh-ter into that family, he said, 'She's not your daughter.' So his wife may be the only one to tell him, and he may still answer her, 'Zahara is just being stubborn; she'll get used to it.'"

Ali had predicted the Faqir's reaction very accurately; on the following day, the Faqir seemed to make short shrift of the problem: "Oh, Zahara, coming from our house, thought everything there would be agreeable. She just doesn't want to get used to things there. She's like a cow among them; she doesn't know how they want things done in the city; and they often laugh at her." The Faqir did not explicitly indicate that he knew of Zahara's desire to return home.

On that same afternoon, Mehdi spoke of the situation with more alarm: "I'm seriously thinking of bringing Zahara back here on the next market day. I'll either do it with someone's motorbike or get her a ride in a pickup truck. I really love my sister very much, and I don't feel that way about my other sisters. But she is a bit naive, and the fact that she has been willing to stay in that wayward house has spoiled my view of her by one half. But still, I think I will bring her back here, and, even though her husband's mother will not want this, I am willing to brook her."

Two days later, on 17 July, Mehdi explained why he had not accomplished this: "I really can't, until their faults come clear out into the open. Otherwise, it will mean a real fight with my father."

That same day, for the first time, the Faqir seemed to recognize the urgency of the situation. He told me that the previous day, while at the market, he had visited Bukhensha's house: "You know, my daughter is very unhappy there. First of all, she doesn't get any tea to drink. They tell her, 'If you want to drink tea, get your husband to bring money into the house for the tea and sugar. Then you can drink!' But, of course, it isn't her place to get her husband to bring money, it's the place of her husband's mother and father.

"And then, the other day, her husband's sister 'Aisha said to her, 'Your husband is going out with another woman. Climb up here to the roof and you will be able to see for yourself.' But just when she reached the roof her husband entered, saw her up there, and yelled at her. She told him that his sister had told her to go up there, but the sister completely denied this. They are just having a good laugh at her expense. And yesterday, when I went to their house, Fatima stepped between Bukhensha and myself, as though she wanted to ensure that nothing of this would be talked about."

The Faqir, clearly not wanting to continue on this topic, concluded, "It is evident that Zahara wants to come back home, but if I bring her back here I will never get my money back from them." I assumed that the Faqir was alluding to the dowry, a sum of money settled upon by the fathers of the spouses when the marriage contract is drawn up and which, in the event that the husband divorces his wife, must be given to her family. If the wife leaves the husband, on the other hand, it is common for her family to forgo part or all of this payment in return for the husband's agreement to a divorce.

For much of the next day Ali and I were alone in the fields. He agreed to talk, into the tape recorder, about the entire episode.

Tell me the story, from the first to the last, of Zahara's marriage.

In the early days, Bukhensha was a good-for-nothing. Later he improved. But I always knew that he was no good. However, with people like that you must be a little patient, yet on your guard so that they don't outsmart you. You shouldn't close the door in their face.

The Faqir began by selling our gourds to Bukhensha. And one day, while visiting him in the Medina, the Faqir noticed that their young daughter ʿAisha was a sharp worker, and he told Bukhensha. "One day, I'd like ʿAisha for my son Mehdi." But Mehdi didn't want her.

We had begun to see them more and more. They'd come here, we'd go there; and they treated the Faqir like a suitor. If they could manage it, he would be taking their daughter. But then they began to see that we no longer wanted to take a bride from them.

So, finally, Bukhensha's two daughters found a couple of men from the south to marry them. And, just as they settled upon the wedding of the second one, at the end of last summer, they approached the Faqir and said, "Give us your daughter in marriage."

Why did they want the Faqir's daughter?

They wanted her for their son, so that she would help in the house now that the two daughters would be gone. And they figured, "We know you, your people have been good to us, and your daughter is good."

Then they started to work at convincing the Faqir. They sent people to him who said: "What is wrong with you? Those two girls will no longer be in the house. They don't concern you now." The Faqir came to me and told me about the proposal. I told him—I wasn't modest before him now—"Those people are good for nothing." He said, "No, those girls, they've now gone." So I told him, "Well, do you have to do this? Have to? If so, let's do it." This was a Sunday, and they wanted the wedding for that next Thursday already![2]

[2]The typical village marriage takes place in the following way, and this pattern should be borne in mind as the event unfolds.

Arranging the Marriage: (1) Two people, a man and a woman, will be sent by the boy's family to the girl's, to ask whether the girl is available for marriage. (2) If the answer is "Yes," the suitor and several people close to him (usually family members) will visit the girl's family to make a formal marriage proposal (*khetba*). They will bring with them small gifts of sugar. The proposal is most commonly made by the suitor's father to the girl's father; these two will act for the couple on official matters before the wedding. (3) If the groom is not in a position to proceed quickly with the wedding, he will visit the bride's family on all important intervening holidays, bringing with him gifts on each occasion. (4) When the prospective groom is ready to marry, he and his family will bring a sum of money (*dfuʿ*) to the bride's family. This sum, which may vary considerably from case to case, is now often in the neighborhood of twenty thousand rials. When the payment is given over, the families will agree on a date for the wedding. (5) The families will then go to the *qadi* (judge), who will direct them to a *katib* (scribe) before whom they will agree to a dowry (*sdaq:* the sum of money that should be given by the groom's family to the bride's should the couple later divorce), which will be written into the marriage contract. The marriage is then registered.

The Wedding: (1) On the day of the wedding, one celebration takes place at the bride's house, another at the groom's. (2) In the evening, the groom's family (but not the groom) and his representatives will come to the bride's house, participate for some time in the festivities, and take the bride to the groom's home. One woman from the bride's family (her *wazira*, or aide) will accompany her to the groom's house, as may several of the guests (but not her father or mother) from the bride's celebration. (3) Upon arriving at the groom's house, the bride will be brought into her bridal chamber. After some hours of festivities, her husband will then enter it and have sexual intercourse with her. When he

Why did the Faqir accept this?

They did witchcraft on him, that's why. Fatima [Bukhensha's wife] did.

When they came here, that Sunday, Fatima took me aside. The Faqir had told them, "Wait until I decide with my brother." She took me aside, and kissed my head, and said, "Guest of God, you must help me with the Faqir." I thought it over, until it made me tired; even if I went to the Faqir and told him, "I don't want this," he wouldn't listen to me. So I told him, "God make it well. And if they want the wedding on Thursday, let's do it Thursday." And, as they were leaving, they said, "On Thursday, we will come with only three people to take your daughter: myself; the Hajj, my brother-in-law; and my eldest daughter."

Now you have Thursday. Our friends from the village and all around came to our house, and we slaughtered a goat. Not a lot of people, less than a hundred; from Monday to Thursday only these people caught the news of it. We had dinner, and the people from the Medina hadn't arrived yet. We ate, and we waited, and it grew so late that many of our guests left and returned to their houses. We even sent someone into the Medina to find out what was taking them so long.

Finally they arrived, although by that time most of our guests had already left. They arrived with a crowd, with eleven taxis and one pickup truck. And they seemed like loose women, all of them, all friends of the younger daughter. And they came in here like it was the waiting room in the bus station. A real crowd of them. Entering the guest rooms, the single men and the women, just as in the Medina marketplace, beginning to create a real uproar. That kind of celebration we didn't want.

And, at first, they weren't even going to come inside. We invited them inside, but that elder daughter stood aside and said: "We must take the bride and return immediately to the Medina. My mother said that you should serve nothing for all the people we have brought. We must take the girl and go right back." She was making herself out to be very important, wearing those clothes that came from the south, from her new husband. And then the Faqir began to curse them out. He said to

---

leaves her shortly thereafter, her *wazira* will enter and care for her. The bridal sheet will be shown to the guests as proof of the bride's virginity. All the bride's people, except the *wazira*, will depart soon thereafter. (4) The bride will remain in her bridal chamber for seven days (in some weddings, she may participate briefly in rituals with other women), and her needs will be taken care of by the *wazira*. (5) On the evening of the seventh day, the bride's family (including her father) will come to visit the new couple, bringing with them an animal for slaughter, sugar, bread, oil, and other items for a feast. On that day, the bride will leave her bridal chamber definitively.

After the Wedding: (1) One year after the wedding, the bride will return to visit her own family for the first time since the wedding (in many instances, this year's separation is no longer strictly adhered to). She may spend several days there before returning to her husband.

her: "Keep in your place. Wait until the people eat. They have come to my house, not to your house." And he began to argue with the Hajj, who also said that they wouldn't stay to eat. And the Faqir said: "No, no, these people came to my house. If they came to your house, you may give them nothing. When they come to my house, I must feed them." But all this was in a jesting manner. Finally, they came inside to eat.

After they had eaten, I selected good people—not like those who had come to visit us—to go with me to take the bride to the Medina. Of the women, I just took my sister, who would watch over the bride and give her support. My sister remained in the Medina with the bride until the seventh day.

Once we got to the Medina, we waited outside the houses until the brides' hair was braided: Aisha too, the younger daughter of Bukhensha, was having her wedding that night. Then the two brides were driven around the Medina in a taxi, with singing, noise-making, horns blowing. One bride following the other, and the entire Medina gazing upon them. This kept on until it almost grew light, until almost the call for the morning prayer. We, from the countryside, know nothing of such things, and we don't like such fooling around. But we were stuck there.

Well, now it was almost light. And, you know, if the groom wants to go to the bride, he says, "Bring the bride." They brought in the brides, and they ushered in that southerner first, to Aisha. That worked out, or so they say. They show the evidence but... the Arabs have plenty of stratagems.[3] And then Bukhensha's son went in to Zahara.

And did that work out?

Yes. It was fine. After all, we had watched over Zahara. Not like that other bride. Then we returned home until the seventh day.

On the seventh day we filled up a pickup truck with twenty people at the very least, with a ram to be slaughtered, with bread, and we went off to the Medina.

Was it a ram or a goat?

A ram, a ram!

When did you begin to notice that this situation was a spoiled one?

I saw this even before the wedding. I was awake, I knew what was going on.

But the Faqir doesn't want to follow my thoughts, and he figures this is all a lie. And I'm too modest in front of him to tell him what I've just told you. So I have to tell him in different words, like, "Those people are no good for you. They won't make you happy."

---

[3] By "evidence," Ali meant the blood-stained sheet shown to the wedding guests to prove the bride was a virgin. Men often suspect that the bride and her *wazira* contrive to stain the sheet with chicken blood, to deceive the groom and the guests and to convince them that the bride was indeed a virgin.

How did you become aware that Zahara wasn't happy in Bukhensha's house?

I recognized this from the first day. I saw it. And on the celebration of the seventh day, many of them became drunk from alcohol. And even though the Faqir was there he didn't catch on. He saw all that laughing and thought it was for real.

And I also recognized it because Fatima told me herself. She said, "I want to teach things to your brother's daughter, but she won't learn." But that isn't it at all. She says to the girl, "Come over and laugh with people when they come in; they are our friends." But the Faqir's daughter would just see strangers come into the house and she would run upstairs to her room.

Then, last autumn, when the Faqir's son died, Zahara came back here to visit. In Bukhensha's house they were saying, "We'll let the girl stay there for a while; in her father's house she will exhaust herself. She'll have to cut the alfalfa, and fetch the wood, and irrigate the land. Soon she'll be saying, 'Just let me go back to the Medina where I can spend the day sitting. I'm tired, I've got to get back to the Medina.'" They allowed her to stay here for fifteen days, so that she would say, "Whatever they ask me to do in the Medina, I'll do." They wanted to teach her a lesson.

But out here, among us, once a girl is married she no longer does any work at all. Just the kitchen tasks. She doesn't go out into the fields like those who are still girls. So Zahara did nothing, no gathering alfalfa, no irrigating. Among us, that would be bad. Bad. Don't let her out, and then people won't see her. Everyone has passions, and she might make a mistake and end up carrying something in her stomach. And there is no trust in the women. You must not let her out. So Zahara did only house tasks.

And how are things between Zahara and her husband?

It is all over with her husband. Her husband never goes to her at all. He says: "Those who have brought her here can have her. If they want to keep her, then they can keep her; if they want to send her away, they can send her away. I bought no one here, and I'll take no one away. I'll just leave her alone, apart, crying."

And the women of our house are saying, "She's alone, crying, and there is no one to comfort her, no one." But the women in our house can say nothing to us about this. In our house, even more than in others, it is the man who decides. If the women talk back to us, they'll get hit.

And the Faqir, when he sees his daughter, probably says to her, "If you don't want to stay here . . . you are causing hardship. You have to stay, even if it is against your will." The Faqir has no idea that her husband doesn't want her, and no one will tell him. I'm modest before him and I don't ask what is in his mind. Perhaps his wife told him, I don't know. But I do know that Zahara told the women of our house, "I don't have any reason to stay in the house of Bukhensha."

I won't tell the Faqir this; it would be shameful. For us, that is bad. One of his friends would have to tell him, someone like you.

But I've seen nothing with my own eyes. I'm not even certain of what is occurring.

You were just an example. I meant someone from the land, someone who could tell him, "Those people are behaving in such and such a way." But now, everyone is laughing at him, that he gave his daughter to that family.

You know, if only Zahara were shrewder, she could start to act up, start to break dishes and so on. And if they began to hit her she could scream and bring the neighbors running. Whoever hit her could be put in jail, if she could provide witnesses to this. She could cause enough trouble so that Bukhensha's household would be happy to get rid of her, and they would give her the letter of divorce. But she is too naive for that.

If you were in the Faqir's place, what would you do now?

I'd just go to Zahara and say, "Wherever you want to go, let's go."

And the money that was due the Faqir?

I'd just say, "It is gone, like a gift."

By now, numerous inconsistencies had become apparent, and this was especially so in the accounts given by Mehdi and Ali. Yet uniting both their accounts was the attack on the virtue of Bukhensha's family, and on its behavior in the events related to the wedding. Before confronting the Faqir, I wanted to question Bukhensha's family—one that I knew quite well—in so far as I could. Bukhensha himself was only infrequently in the Medina during my stay that summer, but I was able to talk briefly with Fatima.

Fatima began her version of the events: "I immediately realized that with my two daughters married and out of the house I would need another woman to help me. So I decided to find a bride for my son Muhammad. When I first suggested this to the Faqir, he was taken aback, said that he needed more time, that he would have to get some money together for the wedding. I insisted that he wouldn't have to spend much money and that I would use the money that Aisha's future husband had given to me for their wedding, in order to defray the Faqir's expenses for the wedding of his daughter. I told him that it all would cost him almost nothing. And then the Faqir said to me, "All right, but don't bring a lot of people to my house when you come for the bride."

"Yet, when the evening of the first wedding day arrived, my daughter was also being married, and many of the guests in my house wanted to go to the Faqir in order to collect his daughter. But I knew that he didn't want to feed a lot of people, so I fed them all first, and told them to go and pick up the bride without eating there. They went in six vehicles, and when they arrived at his house he was sitting by the door and screamed at them, "What kind of *moussem* is this!" His house was completely dark; there were only a very few guests present. This is because the Faqir is so tight-fisted.

"Then the Faqir served them a typical country meal, just goat meat and some gourds. And when our people brought the bride back here, we saw that she had brought almost nothing of any worth with her. Just some pieces of old-fashioned clothing, which her mother had probably given her. And further, on the seventh day, you know that the bride's family is supposed to bring to the bride's new household all the food that is necessary for the celebration, and to bring it early enough to be cooked. But the Faqir arrived on the seventh day with a load of people, about forty in all, and he brought with him only one goat—not a ram— one sack of bread, and two sugar cones. And they all came quite late, after the sunset prayer. But I had expected something like that from him, and I had prepared a number of *tajines* beforehand. So we all ate with little delay, and the evening passed well.

"For a while, we kept hoping that Zahara would adjust easily to her new life here. After all, it is much less work here than in the countryside, where they have the work of the cows, and the irrigation and weeding. But Zahara was so slow, heavy like an animal, so slow to learn. She would leave the meat uncovered in the kitchen, and the cat would make off with a healthy chunk. That was a very bad thing. But at other times, we got a good laugh out of her behavior.

"Once however, just recently, she almost caused a real problem. She was sulking over something or other, and then she refused to wash her husband's clothes. So, one morning, my son said to her: "That's enough. I'm taking you back to your father." But I stepped in and said to him: "Shut up! It was I who brought her into this house, not you. And I'm the one who tells her what to do in this house, not you. And if anyone is going to send her back to her father, it will be me."

I now felt able to approach this subject, in depth, with the Faqir; I did this several days later, little more than a week before I was to leave Morocco.

⊞ TIME AND TRUST IN QUESTION

At moments during earlier conversations—for example, when I had been reluctant to inquire into the death of the Faqir's young son (chapter 3)—I felt I might be asking about essentially private matters and I wondered whether I ought to ask about them at all. However, except for the dispute between Ali and Faqir Hmed, which had a confrontational character that required me to seek out its various versions, the events I had singled out until now were of a relatively public and uncontroversial sort and could be addressed directly. But Zahara's marriage was not only controversial; it also touched sensitive points, and the Faqir had not been forthcoming when I had brought up the subject previously.

Time now took on new signficance. Certainly, events seen from any perspective almost always had deep roots in the past and, in this sense, a temporal dimension; also, I needed time to construct meaning from the various indicators, signs, and pointers that, before an event, may have seemed inconsequential and unrelated to one another. Now, in addition, it became evident that the Faqir too needed time, before he would bring himself to discuss certain matters with me, especially a matter as delicate for him as the marriage of his daughter.

For all these reasons, I began to feel strongly that any effort to appreciate my experience in Morocco and the experience others had of me, and to understand my relationship with the Faqir, would have to respect timing even if one could not hope to reproduce it exactly. At the very least, I suspected that such an appreciation would be irremediably deficient if happenings and conversations were reordered and their sequence destroyed, if long segments were eliminated, if the passage of time was ignored, neglecting with this the growing ease and familiarity so essential to the meaning of what was said?

As I began to prepare questions about Zahara's marriage, another thought occurred to me: given the sensitive nature of this matter, and that on each previous occasion that the Faqir and I had skirted it his manner betrayed a wound that was still raw, I knew I would have to be somewhat circumspect in raising it. My questions would have to do more than reflect my interest in the topic; if I hoped for extended discussion, my questions would have to express and incorporate, to some degree, his concerns as well. Again I thought back to my hesitancy in the matter of his son's death and how, in finally raising the issue, I had been very conscious of the Faqir's wishes. This, once more, seemed obvious, but questions remained with me: how much of my actual questioning and the structure of my questions was designed less to satisfy my curiosity than to encourage his sympathy and to maintain his interest? To what extent had I been doing this all along, without reflecting on it? To what extent were my expressions of sympathy sincere, or simply a tactic to elicit his response? How much of my voice had become an extension of his, and how well could I now distinguish between the two?

I thought it best to enter the discussion of Zahara's marraige somewhat indirectly, first asking the Faqir to recount his visit, the day before, to Bukhensha's house, and proceeding from that to a direct discussion of the problem ("The problem ... "). I was also interested in the wedding details, because there was such ill will and difference of opinion over this issue; and why the Faqir had agreed to the marriage in the first place, despite Bukhensha's family apparently being held in such low esteem ("Details ... Bukhensha's family ... "). Finally, once we had discussed all these points, I wanted the Faqir to indicate how he intended to resolve the matter ("More details ... what to do next ...").

✣ EIGHTH DIALOGUE

THE PROBLEM . . .

Can you tell me, from the beginning, what happened when you entered Bukhensha's house yesterday?

Nothing happened. I just entered, "How are you?" "How are you?" "All is well." I talked a little, and said to them, "The money?" They said, "We don't have any." [The Faqir had started hurriedly, as though he wanted to make the talk brief.]

Could you tell me more slowly, exactly?

I just entered. [Now he spoke more slowly.] I said to them, "How are you, are things all right?" They said to me, "Fine. Things are fine. Shall we make tea?" I said, "I don't want tea." I got up, was going to leave, and then I said to them, "The money?"

What money?

My money.

What do you mean, "your money?" How much of it is there?

Twenty-two thousand five hundred rials. Fatima told me: "He doesn't have any. He even needs some to go back to Casablanca. He only brought eight thousand rials back here with him, he's spent that, and now he even needs money to pay his trip back."

Wait a minute. Where does that 22,500 come from?

I had lent it to him. For the Tinduf Amouggar, the one before last.

Does anyone know about this loan? Your brother for example?

No. No one.[4]

And when Bukhensha came back from Tinduf that year, he told Fatima "Give the Faqir back his money." She said, "Oh, wait a while." But when he came back from the Amouggar last year, he came back broke; he had sold little and had brought almost all the merchandise back to his house. And he said, "There is nothing." But still he said to her, "Give him the money." And still she told him, "Oh, wait a while." And again they gave me nothing.

Well, then he went away, and the matter became quiet. So the matter remained, until another day. Then, she told me, "The Hajj has advised my husband to sell the farina; then I'll give you your money." Well, I

---

[4]The money that Bukhensha owed the Faqir had been mentioned previously, both by the Faqir himself and by Ali. Both Ali and I assumed that the money involved was simply the dowry and that the Faqir was concerned that he might have to forgo the dowry if his daughter left her husband. Here, we see that a substantial sum is due the Faqir as a result of his earlier loan to Bukhensha, money that no one in the Faqir's household seemed aware of, and that may be discouraging the Faqir from acting to further his daughter's interests. The fact that the Faqir goes on to explain the loan in some detail without actually being asked about it may be an indication of the importance he attaches to this money.

said nothing; she didn't sell the farina and again didn't give me my money. Then he returned here again. I said nothing to him. I said to myself, "Until he comes back from this Amouggar." He came back, said nothing to me. I said nothing to him, and again he left. Now, here he is again, and he has again given me nothing. And she says, "He brought with him just eight thousand rials, and he's spent it already."

Well, I went to him yesterday. I told him: "The money is needed. The new well we need is going to take so much of our money now, and the casing for it is going to take thirteen thousand rials or so." She told me: "He's got nothing, nothing at all, not even the white of his teeth. He needs money even now just to return to the Gharb. And here's the farina, which we were requested to sell, and you see it is still here." I kept quiet.

I was just about to leave, and my daughter came up to me and told me, "I want to go with you." "Why?" "Because..." but right away Fatima came over and squatted next to me. Then Bukhensha came over too.

Where were you then, in the doorway?

At the door. After a moment, Bukhensha said, "Come with us into the room; we're not going to speak in the street." We went back into the room, and all of them came over: the two girls, and my daughter, and Bukhensha, and Fatima. "We told her, 'Do this' and she didn't do it, we tell her 'Do that,' and she doesn't do it..."

Wait a minute. What did they say she hadn't done?

They said, "In the morning, she took the flour and sifted it, and was going to knead it, and then she turned around and went up to the room and just left it there, and didn't return to it."

And what else?

And also, "She doesn't want to wash her clothes." That's what they were complaining about.

Just those two things?

And they said: "She doesn't want to mix with people. She won't sit with people." I told them: "If there are men, I'm the one who told her not to sit among them. If there are women, that's all right, all people like to sit around and enjoy themselves. But only if they are in the mood. Well now, that's no problem."

That reminds me of something. You know, shortly after I arrived this summer, I went to Bukhensha's, and I was beginning to eat with them when Bukhensha called Zahara over and told her to come and eat with us. I could see even then that Zahara didn't want to do this, and I told Bukhensha that even in her father's house she and the other women did not eat from the same table as the men.[5]

[5]Here what seems to be a purely descriptive statement to Bukhensha about practices in the Faqir's home had other implications. I had meant to defend Zahara in her

You see. This is very bad. The bad thing is not that they want her to eat from the same table as you do. You will only be here a short while and then you will leave. The bad thing is that they want her to eat with the men in the house. What if some other man should come in? And then they say to him, "Come sit and eat." And the man then goes and sits next to the women? And perhaps leans a little on her? This isn't done, neither in the city nor in the countryside.

But yesterday, I told them other things. "Your son too has been saying things. I have heard this from other people." They said, "Who told you this?" I said: "People in the Medina. He has been telling them, 'They did it; I didn't want to get married, they forced me into it.'" So Bukhensha's family said: "No. We'll get to him, we'll show him, by God." And so on and so on.

I told them: "As for now, there is no problem. I'm leaving, and you can mull over what I've said. If the situation turns out poorly, I'm going to take my daughter back, Nothing more need be weighed." And I went out and came back here, that's all.

Did you speak to your daughter at all?

I said to her, "Tell me what is hurting you. What is it?" She wouldn't say. "What's the matter with you; what are they doing to you?" She wouldn't say anything. I told her, "Because you are not telling me what is the matter, I'm not taking you back."[6] Because then I'd have no just cause to take her back, if I didn't have the permission of that family. I can't just enter there and tell her, "Eh, up, let's go."

But if she wants to leave, do you need a reason or . . . ?

If she wants to leave without their agreement, a reason is essential. But if they agree, she can leave without a reason; she knows it and everyone knows it.

What can you still do about this matter?

I'll just wait until she tells me, "What they have done to me is . . ." If they've done something outside normal practice, I'll bring her back. Then I can recount their errors if I have to. What if they want to start prosecuting me and I can only say, "They did nothing, and I just wanted her back and took her back"? That couldn't be.

Do they talk about this now in your house?

As for such things, the women can't mix in them.

Wouldn't, for example, her mother say . . . ?

Her mother said, "Bring her back!"

---

discomfort, but I also, in effect, support the view that men and women should be strictly segregated (a view I clearly would not defend in other circumstances). And, in recounting this to the Faqir, I also appeared to be taking his side in this matter.

    [6]The Faqir has placed Zahara in what amounts to a double-bind situation: on the one hand, he will not take her back unless she speaks up and tells him what the matter is; on the other, she has been trained not to speak of such matters to her father and were she to do so, she would be breaking the rules of modesty and proper behavior.

And didn't she tell you any reason why Zahara is unhappy?

She said, "Zahara is unhappy." Zahara had told her: "I'm unhappy. They told me, 'Now your husband will have to buy the sugar for you.' So I no longer want to drink tea, and I no longer want to drink coffee." But, if she doesn't want to drink, can I force her, make her drink against her will? And, all things considered, if she hasn't raised a ruckus with them, or done something bad, then I can't bring her back. If there isn't a reason then I can't.

What would make you decide to bring her back?

She must open her mouth and say, "They did this to me, they did this, and this." In front of the Bukhensha family, in front of them! So that I know, so that their errors appear to my eyes too. Otherwise, . . . perhaps she is playing with me, and with them, with the both of us. That couldn't be.

If you brought her back here, what might Bukhensha's family do?

They might say, "We want her, and you took her!" Even if they didn't want her.

On account of the dowry?

Yes.

How does the dowry enter into it?

You know that if I take her away from them, I won't get the dowry. Even though, according to the Law, the dowry must never be forgiven. It must be paid. If you don't pay it now, you will have to pay it before Our Master.

But what might Bukhensha's family do?

If they wanted her, in good faith, they might say, "You took her, but we want her back." Or, they might say, "We don't want her," and then they would give their permission for me to take her back so that I wouldn't keep hounding them.

Would they want you to pay them so that they would give her the letter of divorce?

No, but they would say that I'd have to pay them for the expenses of the wedding—what they had spent. I'd end up paying for everything, if they'd agree to settle with me at all.

So, in that case, they would want you to pay them that additional money?

That, and then they would still eat up the money of mine that I had lent him previously. [The Faqir scoffed and laughed nervously.]

Ay ay ay!

DETAILS . . . BUKHENSHA'S FAMILY . . .

How did this get started from the very beginning? How did you do the engagement and so on? Begin the long story of it, and then we'll see where to go from there.

The story, as I told you, is that Fatima had never said anything at all to me about this until that Sunday. I went to their house and had breakfast. Or perhaps I didn't eat there; I don't remember. I was about to leave, and she said to me, "You're coming back here, aren't you?" I told her, "Yes." I came back and said to her, "What did you want? We're ready to leave the Medina." She said to me, "We want to go with you. We'll follow after you." I asked her, "Why?" She said, "We want to set an engagement for your daughter for a wedding this Thursday."

I told her: "No. You've never spoken to me about this, you've never spoken to me. In addition, I couldn't do a wedding on Thursday. I have my married daughters, and my sisters, and I have people, and I have other things.[7] I haven't consulted them and now you tell me, 'A wedding on Thursday.'"

She said, "Yes. I have my daughter's wedding that day, and I want to braid the two things together." I told her, "Well, so you have your daughter's wedding, you want to braid them together for yourself. But what about me?" She said, "You, you won't have to do anything, neither this nor that." I told her, "Why wouldn't I want to do something?" In short . . .

Wait—why did she say to you, "You won't have to do anything"?

She meant, "You won't have to spend anything."

That is, she would spend everything?

Well, what would she have to spend anyway?

But she said that, didn't she?

She said, "You have sheep, and you have this, and that." I told her, "What do you care what I have, what I don't have. But I need time for this." She said, "No. For us, now, if you want to help us out, do the wedding now." I said, "My brother won't want this." They said, "We want to go with you now to the village to see him."

We returned home and they came a little later, in the late afternoon. I went up to my brother and told him, "Well, fellow, those who are coming here now have said nothing to me at all about this until now, and now . . . they want to take my daughter." I told him this, and when they came, they began to talk with him. When the speaking was finally over, he came up to me and said, "Let's just give her to them."

Was he in accord with this from the first?

Who told him?! No one had told him, neither him nor me.

No, I mean when you first told him, did he say something about it or not?

There was no time, we had no time. One-half hour at most. He looked at me sideways and then kept quiet. After this, they came and began to

---

[7]The Faqir was referring to his need to tell friends and relatives of the wedding well in advance. He particularly had to inform one of his married sisters, who lived in a rather distant village and required notice to prepare her visit.

talk with him, and then he told them, "All right." And then I changed, and said, "All right" too.

Didn't he contradict you on that, didn't he say, "No, we don't want . . .
No. He said, "O.K., it's for the best, all things considered." It was sick.

What was "sick"?
His speech was sick: "It's unfortunate, this, but it's for the best." That is, "I like it but I don't like it." That's it.

In what respect did he mean this?
That can't be explained. [The Faqir paused, seeming to search for an explanation.] He meant, "O.K., it's not that bad; O.K., let her go."

Then they spoke to her mother and she said, "All right." For me, too, that was already all right, as long as they weren't cursing me, telling me, "You are the one who rushed us, you were the one who . . . " And then Bukhensha's family said, "Tomorrow, you and us, we'll go to '44' to set up the marriage contract."

We went to "44" on Monday. The judge was absent. We went to the scribes. And the scribes too, the ones whom we knew, were absent. During that period, for some three months, there was no judge and no official register; the scribes were just giving verbal permission and would tell you, "Go and set the date." It would stay written with the scribe until the new judge came and then . . .

it would be duly registered.
Yes, until the judge came to give you the certificate.

So, that day we went to "44" and found no one. We agreed that on Thursday, the day the wedding was to occur, Bukhensha and I would meet again in "44" to settle on the contract. That Thursday morning I had to go to the Medina to market, to search out what was needed, because the wedding was to be that evening. I went to Bukhensha's house, and he had already gone to "44." I did my business in the Medina, loaded what I had bought into a pickup truck to be brought back to the village, and I took off for "44" to find him. I found him there, just waiting for me.

His wife wasn't with him?
Of course not! What would she be doing there?

We went to look for the scribes, but again they were all absent. We talked for a while, and then the Hajj Muhammad, a scribe, arrived. He had just returned from Meknes.

"How are you?" "For the best." "Things are well?" "What do you want?" We told him, "Oh friend, this is what we want, and this." He said: "I've just now come back from Meknes, just now. I'll look into the court to see if someone is there. And now, if I hadn't come, you'd have had to keep sitting there just like this." He came back, gave us the permission, and we paid him.

Who paid the fee?[8]

I paid it. That Sunday, when they left us, Fatima said to me, "Here's a bit of money so you won't have to spend anything." And I told her, "You must give me some, because you said I will not have to go to great expense." She gave me six thousand rials, six thousand rials in all. Then I waited until that Thursday morning and I said to her, "If there is some money available, I need it now." She said, "Well . . . there is just one thousand rials here with us." I left her with what she had and went out.

So, after we finished in "44," Bukhensha went back to the Medina, and they didn't arrive at our home until halfway through the night. Those people who had come to our home had already eaten, we had talked until we tired of it, and still no one had yet arrived.

When they finally came, how many of them were there?

When they came, they came in seven taxis and two pickup trucks. And when they came, it must have been at least three, or almost four o'clock, in the morning.

How many of them might there have been?

I don't know.

About fifty?

That is about right. And just . . . experienced women, just . . . And with them was that l-Hajj.

We went out to receive them. Our household was already sleeping, and we had told them, "At most maybe fifteen will come, or ten, or even twenty." So they left four *tajine*s prepared for them.

Didn't you agree with Bukhensha beforehand how many people they would bring?

Fatima had said, "You won't have to spend anything, no one will be brought to you, and you won't have to spend anything."

And when they came, were you obliged to feed them?

Otherwise it would be shameful. They arrived, and sat in front of the door, and said, "We're not entering?" I told them, "That is shameful, why aren't you entering?" I had already seen that a crowd was arriving, I had wakened my in-law and he was slaughtering a goat—a goat bought for three thousand rials. But they persisted, "No, we're not going to stay, we're not staying." The Hajj himself was embarrassed to be among those people, those belchers and experienced women.

Did you know those people from their faces?

Well, from their manner it was obvious.

I told the Hajj: "Come here, Hajj. If you want to return to the Medina now, if you won't stay here at all, come and pay for that goat. Now, here it is already slaughtered. You've arrived, and this isn't the proper time for arriving, and you waited till now. We had already cooked enough for fifteen or twenty, but now that doesn't suffice. I saw you coming, and

[8]Twenty-five hundred rials.

had the slaughtering done. Now, pay for this, and you can continue on your trip." He said to me, "Well, uh, I'll pay you soon, with God's help." I said, "Give it here. Now. Here and now. [The Faqir was now chuckling.] And when you've paid me we'll do God's praise and you can be on your way." Well, we were partly laughing, partly joking, and finally they brought the women into the house, and the men came in here.

Were many people still in your house at the time they arrived to take the bride?

My in-laws [from a distant village] were still here, but the people from the village had already left.

They'd already left?

They waited until they tired of it and then they left. My brother had invited them all, saying that he wanted to take many with him over to the Medina.[9] Well, when it had become almost morning and no one had yet arrived, the villagers went to their homes.

Well, now they had all entered the house and the meat was cooking. Some of them were still standing. That daughter of his, the elder one, was just standing, just looking sideways, and saying, "My father said to me, and my mother said to me, 'Don't stay!'" I told her, "God curse your father's father's father, and your mother's father's father!"

You really weren't mincing words.

Certainly not. Everyone was sitting and she wouldn't sit. And her teeth were like a wolf's. [The Faqir muttered, imitating her.] But the others, as I've said, were sitting; I had pressured them with curses.

What's that, "pressure with curses?"

I insulted them, cursed them. They became embarrassed. And some of the women too, the ones who weren't bad.

Why did you insult them?

What's this! They come to me on such an occasion and they don't want to stay? Shameful. Finally, they drank tea and ate a hungry meal, and then they continued on and left.

How long did they stay?

Just as long as it took the meat to cook.

Well, that's the accounting of what happened, that's it.[10]

And when did you begin to think that your pleasure in this matter was less?

The pleasure was always less. From the very beginning it was less, from their trickery. Because they would be sitting, and they would speak among themselves, and you wouldn't be able to understand. I'd just be in their house and watch; they'd talk, and you'd understand nothing. This means that they are wayward. You'd be sitting around, and she'd talk to her daughters, and they'd understand what was happening, and you wouldn't. They thought I had no mind at all.

[9]The Faqir, as the bride's father, could not accompany her to her new home. But Ali could, and wished to take along a number of women to accompany Zahara.

[10]The Faqir meant this to be the end of the story.

But look, before they took your daughter, was all this in your head, that people were saying, "Their house is no good"? I remember you told me long ago, "Fatima is no good."

Oh, many people said to me that she was no good, both then and now. But they shamed me into it. I gave in because of the salt in their words.

How could you do that...

I said, "Look, their two daughters will be out of that house." One had already gone and the other was going to leave that night. So there would be no problem. "And my daughter, I'll command her—I won't even need to command her, because she knows nothing about such things. And Fatima will have to shift for herself. What do I care?" That's what I said.

Now, as it's turned out, both daughters have returned.

They've all come back, and now they all gang up on your daughter.

That's it, that's it.

Weren't you afraid when Zahara became one of their household, that it might turn out poorly once she entered a house that people said was no good?

Well, I also say that it's no good. But Zahara, she has turned out well. It's what they say that tries to make her out to be no good. But as for her, because she doesn't sit with them, doesn't deal with them, that is fine. But she doesn't have much pleasure.

If she were in agreement with them, that's when I would be afraid. That's when I'd say, you know, "I'm worth nothing." But because she isn't in accord with them, I understand that I have no worry. I'm just clean.

Well, you're clean, and her honor hasn't been sullied. But, still, she's unhappy.

Right. Now you understand. That's just where the matter is now.

And according to your thinking, why do they insult her?

They insult her: "She no longer will do anything; she won't wash her own clothes."

Do they say that she knows nothing?

They say that she doesn't know anything. Like that, too.

Does she lack these qualities because she is from the countryside?

She doesn't lack anything; it's just that they say she does. And if she lacks something, it's simply because she doesn't want to do it. From contrariness. I've come across that. And, in addition, there are some things that they require that she doesn't know. Such as the fish that the mother prepares, and the salads, and such things. We don't make those things here. But if she just sees that once, she'll know how to do it.

But with contrariness, she won't pay any attention: when you are doing something and someone tells you, "Don't do it!" you won't pay attention. What! You're doing it and he tells you not to? You just won't pay attention.

What did Zahara take with her on her wedding day? Was it similar to what your other daughters, the two who have already married, took with them?

My other daughters took more with them. There was more time for their weddings. But also, the weddings were more important; we were fonder of their husband's families. With Zahara, things were just not as important. She only took with her some bracelets, and these she has already returned, saying, "They don't wear these in the city." And she took some clothes, fewer than my other daughters because fewer women came to her wedding: she was given less.[11] And Fatima's family made fun of the clothes; Zahara returned them. My wife and my brother's wife now wear them.

What was Bukhensha himself like, from the first?

His dealings were fine. But now Bukhensha no longer has his thoughts. He's all emptied out.

What's that, "emptied out"?

Fatima has taken Bukhensha's mind, that dangerous one has.

She took it?

She took it, with some technique, some machination. Bukhensha doesn't leave the Medina of his own will and he doesn't come back of his own will. Bukhensha's mind is now like the four kif smokers whose mother has to be carried to the cemetery to be buried: whenever three of them are ready to carry, the fourth says, "Let's rest." They never get to the task. As with Bukhensha, who can never make up his own mind.

Was that like sorcery?

Like sorcery. Bukhensha is finished. He says, "Oh, my dear one, oh my little daughter, oh my dear one, oh my little dauther, oh my dear one." [In a sing-song manner, the Faqir was imitating Bukhensha.] I can't even stomach saying to my girl, "My little daughter." "Oh, my little daughter, go slowly my little daughter, do this my little daughter." And to his wife he says, "Oh, my dear one." And sometimes, she'll just drop something down in front of you, abruptly. Why? What for? He has no will.

Do you mean he no longer has any desire?

Not that. It is according to his desire, but his mind is gone.

Has his decisiveness left him?

Yes, it's gone. His mind has left him, his thoughts are gone.

I see.

Formerly, had you talked of bringing his eldest daughter, Mehjuba, here, for your son? No? Not at all? [I was responding to the Faqir's negative looks.]

No, no, no.

---

[11]At the wedding, visiting women will normally bring the bride a present, usually some clothing, which she will then take with her to her new husband's house.

I thought I had heard that.

Why would I want to bring Mehjuba here? Why?

Before all this had happened.

No! You didn't hear that in this house. We never discussed such a thing.

Fatima is the one who started the story about my bringing Mehjuba here. She told them, "The Faqir asked me, 'I want Mehjuba for Mehdi.'" She started that.

And you had said nothing? Had she said this so that perhaps you would change and want to bring her here?

Maybe, likely, probably.

MORE DETAILS ... WHAT TO DO NEXT ...

And now, where might this whole matter end up?

The matter will go where Our Owner wants it to.

I mean, what are the different paths that it might take, according to your thinking?

We don't yet know where the Lord wants to take it, where he will take it.

No, we don't know what will happen in the future.[12]

Now, if there is agreement, fine. Otherwise it won't be a long time before I'll bring my daughter back here. That's all.

When you saw them yesterday and when you spoke with them, did they seem agreeable or disagreeable?

Oh, my daughter's spirits were very low; she was doing nothing but crying.

No, I didn't mean to ask that. Did you find that they were in good faith, or not?

You'll never find good faith there. Not on your life! Always good faith is lacking there. They say one thing and do another. Never is good faith present. Impossible! Not on your life! Not present in Fatima, in any case. Yet that 'Aisha, even though she's a tough one, she's all right.

What do you mean, "even though she's tough ... "?

Even though, you know, she is shrewd, she's O.K., O.K. She doesn't hide things.

You mean, she speaks frankly?

Straightforwardly. And Bukhensha, he has his good faith.

And when he first brought me here, did you know that their house was no good?

No. I didn't know Fatima hardly at all. And Mehjuba, I didn't know her at all.

---

[12]I have had to phrase several times the question of what might happen, but on each occasion the Faqir did not answer directly. Now, when I agree that "The Lord will take it where he wants to," the Faqir begins to answer.

I still don't understand at all. You tell me this and I still don't...

        I didn't know them well. I'd go there, you know, and when I'd go there, Fatima would make a fuss over me. And I said, "There is nothing wrong here." And Mehjuba, I didn't even know she was there. I thought there was just ʿAisha, and ʿAisha was very young then. And the other son who is always away, I don't know him. And the other one whom they say she bore in the wilds, I didn't know him then, and I still haven't met him.

You must mean Mensur and Hmed.

And when you went to them on the seventh day, what happened then? How many of you went?

Well, enough of us to fill a pickup truck.

Was that many, or a normal number?

A normal number, just in one pickup truck.

And what happened when you got there?

Nothing. We supped, you know, until it was almost morning, and then we left. That's all.

Did you sleep there?

No, we didn't.

When did you arrive there?

Well, we arrived with the evening prayer.

Is that a proper time to arrive, or were you late?

It's proper. It is after the evening prayer that is no good; but if you reach there with the evening prayer, that's fine.

But perhaps they didn't have the time to prepare...

        No, they were prepared. Besides, they knew that we would be coming that day, and with other people too.

On the seventh day, you were supposed to bring everything?

Yes.

What did you bring?

We brought a round of meat.

What sort?

A goat. And bread. And *zemmit*.[13]

Sugar and tea?

Some sugar, a bit of sugar, two cones of sugar. Tea, no.

No tea, that's not on your shoulders?

That's all, that's all there is in it. That's all. [The Faqir had not shown much interest in the previous questions of detail.]

For the wedding, who is supposed to spend the money—the groom's family or the bride's family?

The groom's family spends it.

---

[13]*Zemmit* is a cool, refreshing drink made from ground barley and water.

And now, you reckon that you have spent a lot on this?

Well, I've counted that I threw away about twelve thousand rials on it. Just on supplies for the wedding.

And what about the twenty-five hundred rials that Bukhensha borrowed from you to pay the scribe?

There is that too. And then, what about the other twenty thousand rials, the twenty thousand for the Tinduf Amouggar? He owes all that to me too. And now the money for the scribe has become just like the Tinduf money itself.

What will you do about all this, now?

I don't know. I've got to find some way. I don't know. I don't know.

9

The Sheikh's Visit

Mehdi and I were standing beside the cement pool into which the irrigation motor pumps water, which then flows into canals leading to the fields. We were waiting for the motor to cough, which it would do when the water in the well became too shallow; Mehdi would then have to go down into the twenty-five-meter-deep shaft to turn off the motor. While we were talking, one of Bukhensha's sons rode up on a bicycle, carrying a bag of cookies. He asked for the Faqir and we said that he was still in the house.

The bicycle ride from the Medina took more than an hour, and, as Bukhensha's son left us and entered the house, I mentioned to Mehdi that this seemed a very nice gesture and that perhaps the difficulties between the two families were easing. Mehdi replied curtly that this was a fine opportunity for Fatima, Bukhensha's wife, to work sorcery on the Faqir: she certainly would have put a special ingredient in the cookies designed to deprive the Faqir of his will, of his independence of mind. Bukhensha's family could then do with him what they wished. "Just watch," Mehdi advised. "Tomorrow, my father will be sending them a full sack of corn in return." (Later, the Faqir also showed little appreciation: "I asked for these cookies several days ago, and they should have been here yesterday. In any event, they are store-bought, and they should have been homemade.")

Mehdi took the occasion, however, to ask me, "Who is coming over here this evening?" That neither he nor, as I soon discovered, his mother, his uncle's wife, nor even his uncle knew of the guest was not particularly surprising. Casual conversation within the family was infrequent and much information of this kind was normally not offered or directly requested. I felt uncomfortable when asked to report on other people, so I usually responded, as Moroccans often seemed to do in similar

171

situations, with "I don't know" or, as in this case, with "The Faqir hasn't told me anything."

But I did know: the sheikh was to be the guest that evening. The Faqir had told me this the day before, remarking that he expected the sheikh to ask him to become moqaddem (one of three who act as the sheikh's principal delegates to the population groups under his authority; a post that is distinct from the village moqaddem position, which the Faqir had held many years earlier).[1] The Faqir had no wish to be moqaddem and he had been making an effort to avoid the sheikh for this reason. But the previous Sunday, they met casually in the Medina marketplace, and the sheikh informed the Faqir that he would stop by for a visit the next Wednesday evening.

Although no one in the Faqir's house knew who the visitors would be, there was abundant evidence that important guests were expected. The Faqir had brought home vegetables from that morning's market—a rare occurrence in a family that grows most of what it eats and, during certain periods of the year, garnishes all meals with one and the same vegetable. The Faqir fulfilled everyone's suspicions when, in addition to potatoes, some gourds, and melons, he also brought a goat back from the market. (Goats could no longer be raised in zones that did not have free grazing land and, in Ouled Filali, this condition had already existed for some ten years. As several other villagers did, the Faqir usually had a few goats grazed for him by a friend in an uplands village, far distant from the riverbed and with ground water too deep to be pumped by an irrigation motor; here there was usually much free grazing land. But this year had been a particularly dry one, pasture was scant, and, when the Faqir had slaughtered his last goat a few months earlier, he did not replace it.)

The Faqir was using the sheikh's visit to bring together a number of his other friends; whether this was a gesture of hospitality or an attempt to avoid a direct encounter with the sheikh I cannot say. A couple of villagers would be coming: Si Hassan, now head of one of the village's wealthiest families and owner of a tractor, who as a young man had been a religious student (*tallib*) and a merchant; and Hajj Hmed, who had made the Pilgrimage to Mecca some forty-five years earlier, by boat (before it became quite common to do so by airplane) and who now, although quite old and indigent, still retained a certain moral authority and was charged by the village with supervision of its mosque. Two friends from a neighboring village were also invited: the Faqir Hummad and b. Krim.

The Faqir had returned from the market about 1:00 P.M. He took a short nap and then began to prepare for the evening with a burst of energy that affected everyone in the house and that he sustained for the rest of the day. He swept and rinsed the courtyard, pounded and shook

---

[1]See chapter 1, n.15.

out all the reed mats and rugs, readied the charcoal burners for brewing tea, and washed and set aside the various utensils that would be used to prepare and serve the meal: tea glasses, teapots, trays, tables, and kettles, some of which had apparently had not been used since his daughter's wedding almost a year earlier. The Faqir explained that he had bought many of these items during a dispute that had estranged him from other villagers, so that he would not have to borrow anything from any of them; yet now they all would come and borrow things from him. (Indeed, two days later, he lent numerous items to a neighbor for a wedding.) The Faqir particularly prized a set of variously sized three-legged aluminum trays, which had been given to him by a villager re-turning from work in France, in thanks for his support in a land dispute. Upon these trays he would lay an assortment of dates, almonds, and nuts, as well as the cookies that had been brought by his daughter's brother-in-law. In addition, he slaughtered the goat, skinned, eviscerated and quartered it, and gave it to the women to be cooked.

In the course of these preparations, the Faqir was losing some of the usual distance and reserve that characterized his conduct toward his family. He badgered the women too frequently, and this soon lost its force; they began to mimic him, laughing as they did so, once he was out of earshot. (Although he would often mercilessly upbraid the women and the children for their lapses, they saw him as essentially soft under-neath his harsh exterior and not as brutal as his brother. One of the Faqir's sons made this point when he told me: "When my father hits us, we all make sure to cry so that he will think he has succeeded in punish-ing us. But when my uncle, angry, sets out toward you from across the fields, you are already beginning to cry and tremble from terror.")

The guests began to arrive shortly before sunset. Then Qebbor, a village merchant and a good friend of Ali's, happened by and made no attempt to resist the Faqir's standard solicitation to stay for dinner. Final-ly, shortly thereafter, the sheikh arrived, bringing with him the two moqaddems of the three under his charge (one position was still vacant). The sheikh was tall, heavy but not ponderous, and clearly commanded the respect of his constituents. He loved to talk, and talked perhaps too much, for his friends on occasion chided him for not acting in the imperious manner of previous sheikhs. He was also distinguished by complete baldness, which he deliberately put into relief by removing his turban as he settled into a gathering, a practice that is very uncommon in Morocco and for which he was often good-naturedly joshed.

The evening was pleasantly cool, and we sat in the courtyard, prop-ping our backs against the walls. (During a heat wave, these walls would retain their heat even at night and we would then sit at a distance of at least several feet away from them. The rooms remained stuffy for sever-al days after hot weather subsided and rarely served for evening gather-ings during the summer months.) As the evening began we formed a right angle, branching out from a common corner but, after a short time, the sheikh moved to a position directly opposite the corner and became an easy focus for everyone's attention.

The usual jousting arose over who would prepare tea. The choices were somewhat restricted, because the task certainly could neither fall upon the sheikh, whose position made such a role inappropriate, nor upon the Faqir, who, as head of the household, would be kept quite busy with other chores. Qebbor was suggested first, but he declined firmly, saying that he worked with tea all day. Si Hassan was suggested, but countered: "No, I can't. My ancestors enjoined me never to make tea. Give it to Moqaddem Abdallah."

Si Hassan's response, which I had heard him repeat in exactly the same way whenever he was asked to make tea, was accepted and Mehdi deftly set down the utensils in front of Moqaddem Abdallah, who said, "No, I'm exhausted. Give it to the Faqir Hummad." Faqir Hummad retorted, "Once the table is in front of you, you must stay quiet." Abdallah tried again, "I already made tea for the sheikh at lunch today; let's give it to you or to Moqaddem Hussein." But Faqir Hummad immediately rejoined, "You continue with it today; the Moqaddem Hussein made it yesterday, and I'll make it tomorrow."

Abdallah, apparently sensing defeat, made a desparate ploy: he stood up and moved away from the tray. But no one would take his place and people began to ridicule him. Trapped and finding no escape, he finally went back to his place, called for the water to be brought so that he could wash, and started to prepare the tea. He paid throughout the evening for his reluctance: he was berated once for tasting the tea from the wrong glass, repeatedly derided for his tea-making technique in general, and mocked as the guests tasted and then drank the tea.

Food and drink punctuated the long evening: first dates, almonds, walnuts, peanuts, and tea; then *tajines* of goat meat, potatoes and gourds; then tea again; then couscous garnished with boiled goat and varied vegetables; then tea again; and finally melons and watermelons. Throughout, until about 2:00 A.M., talk darted from one topic to another; only rarely did the sheikh simply sit back and listen.

It started, as was often the case in similar situations, with a token overture to me. "What is this group that Muhammad Ali Clay is in?" the sheikh asked. I talked a little about the Nation of Islam (also known as "Black Muslims") but when I mentioned its members' belief that Elijah Muhammad was indeed a Messenger of Allah, the sheikh cut me short, "Well, then they are just playing games."

I mentioned that one effect of the Nation of Islam had been the spread of orthodox (Sunni) Islam in the United States, and that a significant number of one-time members of the Nation of Islam now accepted the Sunni view that Muhammad was the Seal of the Prophets; also, that these groups often disagreed with one another and, as in the history of many other religious movements, bloody fights on occasion occurred.

The sheikh objected: "But in Islam we, as brothers, never fight over religion." When I suggested that this had indeed happened in the history of Islam—for example, in the struggle for leadership of the Muslim community within Islam's first century—the sheikh countered: "But this was not a fight over religion; it was simply as if two brothers were struggling with one another over control of the government. As if, for example, President Ford died, and his son and Nixon fought to be president."

"But, is there no difference at all between the different groups within Islam with respect to religion?" I asked. The sheikh answered, "No, we are all brothers in the same religion." He then began a long account of the death of Ali, the Prophet Muhammad's son-in-law, and the struggle that ensued over the caliphate, in the early days of Islam.[2] But the discussion, I noticed, seemed to bore everyone, for these were questions that could be discussed only by those who had mastered history and had acquired knowledge of books, as the Faqir had often told me. "The rest of us", he had said, "know nothing about these things and we must leave it to those who do."

Of those present, only Si Hassan also had a claim to learning, and he succeeded in interjecting a few thoughts: "You know, all those Blacks in America are there because the whites abducted them from Africa, from *Sudan* [the term for Black Africa]. And the Whites put them in regions in America from which they could not escape." I could not help but wonder if I had been the source for these views, which had a certain—if exaggerated—ring of truth to them. Si Hassan continued: "And the Blacks don't buy their food with money, but have to use coupons. And the Whites didn't let them learn anything until just a few years ago, when they were first allowed to go to school."

The others again seemed bored, and the conversation turned elsewhere, moving in fits and starts. Throughout the evening, Qebbor, who was sitting on my right, peppered me with questions. "Do flies give birth to worms? Because when you hang meat, flies come to it; and then, where the flies were, worms grow." A little later, he asked, "Do ants see?" He mentioned the long files that ants formed between a food source and their nest. And then, "How is it that a person cannot see things that are near, but he can see things that are far away?" The Faqir frowned at such questions, "All of this talk is empty; everything comes from God." And Qebbor answered, "Well, that is what we are interested in, the work of God."

Later in the evening, Si Hassan became the butt of joking. The region-

[2]See chapter 2, n. 9.

al police had come looking for him a few days earlier, because he was late in his payments for the tractor. He had been forewarned, however, and had taken refuge in the mosque, where he would not be sought. Qebbor began: "Hey, Si Hassan, you're always running off to the mosque when you're in trouble and need money. During the rationing period after the war, when you were supposed to be our religious teacher, all you did was sit in your store that was built in the wall of the mosque and try to gyp us." Ali added, to the rest of us: "You know, he'd sell us sugar—he'd knock off a hundred grams for you and wouldn't even give you the extra crystals that splintered off. He'd collect them all throughout the day and keep them for himself." Qebbor echoed, "Yes, just sitting there at the mosque and cheating us." And the Hajj Hmed accused him: "And all that time, did you ever give the call to prayer? I don't think you ever called us to prayer, not even once, by God."

Si Hassan was unable to find a forceful reply and remained silent. Conversation continued, touching upon several recent land disputes and other local events.

The visitors who came from the village began to leave. The rest of us, including the sheikh, went to sleep in the large guest room. The next morning, as the sun was rising, we awoke and drank a thick broth of mashed corn. The workers went off to the fields, and the rest of the guests went home. But the sheikh, before leaving, took the Faqir by the arm and went off with him for a walk, away from the compound.

🕮 QUESTIONS ABOUT TEXTS AND RISKS

I needed no remarkably deep understanding of contemporary Morocco to recognize that with its political system, in which people are dependent upon, and exposed to, the whims of local and regional officials, discussions about political practices might constitute some risk for Moroccans. Yet the Faqir's life had been intensely political in the modest arena of his own village and, on occasion, outside it. In particular, he had filled the most important secular village post, the moqaddem, from 1957 to 1968. The visit of the sheikh testified both to the Faqir's continuing interest in politics and to his still strong ties to key local political figures.

If political matters posed risks for the Faqir, should I discuss them with him at all? I felt I could not systematically avoid them, for this would be to divorce myself from many of the Faqir's central concerns, and to turn away from a subject that he himself often raised and that held great interest for me. If we consistently kept away from topics of vital concern to both of us, on what basis would our relationship continue and what sense would such a relationship have? Yet, even if we were to discuss these topics, should our discussions be tape-recorded and written down?

I had not yet decided what to do with the material I had been gathering—the rough drafts of the events and the tape-recorded dialogues. My attention had been focused, instead, on a prior question: What were the characteristics and implications of my close relationship with the Faqir, a relationship between a New Yorker in his mid-thirties and a sixty-five-year-old Moroccan villager, between an anthropologist and an informant? I am not, I think, even mildly obsessed with subjective, personal experience for its own sake, and my prior question already embraced the aim of commenting upon the similar experience of others. At the very least, once I had felt the force of my relationship with the Faqir, I was interested in what that relationship might add to an appreciation of interaction between people of different backgrounds and what this would mean for anthropology, the discipline that dominates our effort to understand people from other cultures, systematically creates personal interaction between the people of different cultures, yet just as systematically excludes this interaction when it presents its analyses.

In considering how my experience might be put these purposes, I had been weighing various alternatives: perhaps I would try to write an ethnographic novel in the manner of *Return to Laughter,* a book quite well-known to introductory anthropology students; or a more historical one, like Chinua Achebe's *Things Fall Apart,* which I found very effective; or a play might provide an appropriate form for communicating the experience.[3]

I had no definite idea what the public might be for such a text. I knew I would want it to be read by anthropologists because, if I did articulate my dissatisfaction with academic anthropology, I would hope to be heard by those who practice it. Yet I also felt that interactions between people of different cultures should not be the exclusive province of academic anthropologists and that academic anthropology should also be examined critically by those who did not practice it; I therefore would want a text that could be read by interested readers with less specialized training. On a more personal level, I would like the text to help me answer people close to me who, once I had returned from Morocco in 1971, kept asking me, "What was it like in Morocco?" For them, so far, I had been unable to find a satisfactory reply. And, as well, any text would have to include the Faqir as part of its public: although he himself was illiterate and never would read it, the text would have to be faithful to his concerns and desires and neither put him in danger nor cause him undue risk.

With my visit to the Faqir nearing its end, I began to wonder whether the dialogues themselves, in one form or another and perhaps in con-

---

[3] I had heard of, although not seen, Peter Brook's stage production of *The Ik,* based on the anthropologist Colin Turnbull's study; also, an anthropologist friend of mine, Thomas Dichter, had used "drama" as the key metaphor in his study of Moroccan schools.

junction with the "events," might be used to convey the experience to a wider public in a way that was both relatively faithful to the experience and that might encourage readers to look at anthropology, and at my effort at it, critically. However, as I began to consider including a transcription of the Faqir's own words in such a text, I saw that the Faqir's expressed wishes and preferences might force me to include matters irrelevant to a normal anthropological argument, and to exclude what might seem most germane. I would be opening myself to new constraints, forgoing the protection that anthropological conventions afforded, making myself more vulnerable to the Faqir's demands.

The visit of the sheikh and the discussion of contemporary Moroccan politics which would inevitably follow forced me to pose these questions. I did not yet have to answer them.

Shortly after the sheikh departed, the Faqir told me that the sheikh had asked him to become one of the sheikh's three moqaddems. I decided to open the dialogue with this ("Becoming the sheikh's moqaddem? . . . "), and then ask the Faqir about his long term as village moqaddem ("Being village moqaddem . . . "). I would then move to a discussion of the politics of the independence period and to a more general talk on the Faqir's views of government and government institutions ("Independence politics . . . ").[4]

🔯 NINTH DIALOGUE

BECOMING THE SHEIKH'S MOQADDEM? . . .

So, the sheikh has asked you to become moqaddem. What did he say to you?

He said, "You helped me to become sheikh; now you must help me while I am sheikh." That is what he said.

---

[4]I knew I would have to talk to the Faqir about the advisability of publishing his words on these subjects should I decide to carry out my then uncertain intention to use his words in a book. My intention became more firm in the several years that passed after I left Morocco that summer, as I transcribed the dialogues and examined the reasons why the whole summer's project had continued to interest me.

I was able to raise this question with the Faqir when I returned to Morocco in the winter of 1978–79. He was quite aware of the possibility that his words about political matters, however they were intended and whatever they might say literally, could easily be twisted to cause him and his family harm. He therefore specifically requested that "words that have to do with the government shouldn't be in it. You know, it's not that we have said anything wrong, or anything bad about the government. It is that there are people who wish me ill, and people who wish you ill. Someone without good faith will take our words and twist them, and they will cause me trouble and they will cause you trouble." (The Faqir's full words on my using his words in this book are found in the preface.)

It should be clear, then, that the Faqir's desire to avoid mention of the government is not a result of anything specific he said about it, but rather reflects his fear that his words might be reinterpreted and used against him.

I adopted one basic rule in editing this dialogue: any remarks that the Faqir made that

And what did you say?

I told him, "No. I don't need the position of moqaddem."

Did he have any other reasons in order to convince you? Did he say, "Look, Faqir, if you become moqaddem, we could do this and that"?

What kind of "this" was there? There was none. He said, "Be moqaddem," and I said, "No." And I named several other villagers he could select.

Then he went to my brother and told him: "You all helped me to become sheikh. And now the Faqir won't become, moqaddem, and just suggests others to me. And I know those others won't work well with me. I can't allow the Faqir to refuse." My brother became agitated and came up against me and said: "What's wrong with being moqaddem? Why not help him out?" And so on and so on. I told him: "Go and be moqaddem yourself. What's holding you back? The path to it is before you."

When I was village moqaddem, the villagers didn't help me out, they didn't work with me. If I needed something I always had to go myself. And the moqaddem needs people's support.

What do you mean, "support"?

He needs people to help him out, especially his son and his brother. And here is my brother—he sits around with his buddies and makes fun of me. And I should become moqaddem? The moqaddem really needs support, and his family should be in good humor, even when they are out with their friends. It isn't simply that I welcome my brother's friends in my house and that he then goes and makes fun of me. But he doesn't help, he doesn't work with me, he doesn't give me news. Yet I should be moqaddem? What am I, crazy, *fou?*

If I were sheikh, and I wanted you to become moqaddem . . .

Yes, what would you do?

I'd think a lot and find some really good reason to convince you.

What kind of reason? Whatever the reason, I'd still have to follow the sheikh around wherever he goes and transmit his orders to others. He'd still go on pulling me around. I wouldn't even end up on good terms with him. He'd say: "Why didn't you come today? Why can't you come tomorrow? The qaid said this and that." And I couldn't get along with him, I wouldn't be patient with him. One hundred chances out of one hundred.

What do you mean you wouldn't be patient with him? You'd get angry?

No, it's not that I'd get angry. He himself would begin to upbraid you. He'd say, "You weren't here today" and "Why didn't you come earlier?"

---

directly or indirectly referred to the current government or local administration were excised; these excisions are indicated by ellipses in parentheses (. . .). This is particularly unfortunate for the reader in the one instance where the Faqir initiated a skit: he took the role of the local qaid, and I was made to play an individual asking the qaid for a service.

and "Tell the car drivers this and tell the car drivers that." And so on and so on. What am I?

And then you'd have to go to a guy who's a good-for-nothing, who's not worth a franc. You could be bringing money to him and he won't even come out of his house for you. And it's for him, for his benefit. Why? I should work for that guy?

How much do those moqaddems earn?

What can they earn? [The Faqir said this disdainfully.] They make some thirty-five rials a day, that's all.

Do they get some coffee money on the side?

No coffee money, nothing. Oh, perhaps some coffee money if they do a circus with someone naive, really naive. But someone with his wits about him would give nothing.

Might he give something to the sheikh, if not to the moqaddem?

No, there's no reason to give either to the sheikh or to the moqaddem.

[The Faqir and I had begun this interview just as he had told his wife to heat the water he would wash with to prepare for his prayers. The delay in bringing the Faqir his ritual water seemed a bit long to me, and my next remark was an attempt to joke about this.]

Perhaps the women had to go and fetch the wood from the fields.

What do you mean? They have to go and buy the water. And from Tangiers! [We both laughed.]

The longer it takes, the better it is for me.

Sure, it's good for you.

BEING VILLAGE MOQADDEM...

Tell me about when you were village moqaddem. When and how did you become moqaddem?

Shortly after independence. For two years we had no qaid here and no sheikh. Then a qaid finally came, and he appointed a sheikh. And the sheikh said to the villages that each one would choose its own moqaddem.

And during those two years when there was no qaid, no sheikh, how was the area run?

By the leaders of the Independence Party: four in each village. I was one of those.

And if there was a fight between people, or something of that sort?

Those four would settle it. And if they couldn't settle it, they'd go to the head of the party and they'd say, "Well, this one did this, and that one did this, and now record this dispute." Or perhaps the two opponents themselves would go to him, and he'd say, "Shame upon you, you are brothers; and now we have our freedom." And so on and so forth.

And they'd settle it among themselves, and they'd go back to where they came from.

During that period, when people disagreed with one another, were they forbearing or . . .

They were forbearing and they settled things with one another. Or others settled it for them. If one refused to settle, the head of the party would tell them, "I've recorded this dispute," and it remained thus. They'd go away and wait for the case to be called before the court. But for two years there was nothing.

There was no court? No judge?

For two years, nothing.

And what was the spirit of the people like during that period?

It was beautiful. Always parties; we were always slaughtering cows. We never sat for a week without having a party. And the party head would come here to tell us what to do. And there were many things, many things.

You know, you were involved in this, you were among the leaders. But what about those who had no interest in government activities, or in Independence, or . . .

Whoever was bothered by anyone would come to us—we were always to be found at the mosque. "So and so did this to me," or "He worked this on me," and we'd summon the other one there, in front of everyone, whether he was a leader or not a leader. Everyone would help out. And we'd say to him, "Shame upon you, that's not right, that's not right," and so on. Until we had settled it.

And how did those two years end?

It ended, you know, when the qaid arrived. The qaid was an outsider, an outsider to this region. And he appointed sheikhs, new ones.

What were you saying to yourselves when the qaid arrived?

We said to ourselves: "Rule has come, and everything is fine. All is for the best."

That it was going to help the region?

Yes. And, "The qaid has arrived, and he'll be working for the people, and we're all brothers, and now we trust in independence, and there will be order," and so on.

And when the qaid and the sheikhs were named, they told the villages to choose a moqaddem. How was this done?

The village said to me, "You be it."

Well, how did they say this? Who, and how?

The whole village said to me, "You must be moqaddem, you."

Where did they tell you this? Tell me exactly, how . . .

Exactly: it happened in the house of the qaid, where we had all gathered, all of our fraction. And every village got up to name its own moqaddem. And our village named me:

"Oh buddy, be the moqaddem." And I told them, "No." Well, some of them came over to me and exerted a lot of pressure on me.

What did they say to you to get you to change your mind?

I said to them, "No. This won't work out for me." They said: "No, it can't be anyone but you. We will help you, we'll stand with you, it will be all right." Well, I heeded their call and kept quiet.

And you stayed on for twelve years?

For about twelve years.

What did you do as moqaddem?

My work was to bring letters to the villagers, for at that time there was no postman yet. And every two or three days I'd have to go to "44." And if there was to be a meeting, I would let the villagers know. And if there was work to be done—for at that time we were still working on the roads—I'd tell them to work on the road.

And one year we had forced labor again, to build that road to the north, and I had to organize that.

How did you organize that?

I was instructed that the village must give fifteen or twenty workers, and I'd go and tell the village. Of those families who had three workers, I'd require one of them. When there were no more with three, I'd choose those with two. When those with two were used up, I'd take the "ones."

And no trouble arose from that?

It couldn't. I used that bit of cleverness so that no trouble would arise.

What do you mean?

Formerly, the moqaddems would just enter the houses and say, "The three of you there—all of you to work!" With me, just one of the three, and the rest could sleep.

Did you start that system?

Yes, I started that. And it turned out fine. I was at peace, and the government said to me, "Fine." And the people, those of the land, they said, "Good work." The poor ones who were used to going first—for they would always be taken first—said, "Good work."

Were there people who would say to you, "Here Faqir, don't you want a little something... ?"

There were some guys who'd say that. I'd tell him that I'd take nothing from him.

You wouldn't take anything?

No.[5]

---

[5]The Faqir's honesty and unwillingness to accept gifts may seem a pose. But it is not; later in this dialogue, the Faqir reveals why he refuses to take such gifts.

During those twelve years, did any problems arise that you were involved in because you were moqaddem?

The first problem that arose for me was that of the school.

Could you tell me, Faqir, the full story of this, without shortening it?

You know, people were beginning to build schools, and we didn't have one. And we wanted to begin working on one.

Wait a minute. Whose idea was this?

The Independence Party said this. They said, one school for two villages or for one village, according to the number of residents, so there would be an education. At first, we had none here. Some people bid for the job, and we sold it to the lowest bidder.[6] But they kept backing out, saying they couldn't build it for such a cheap price. We auctioned it again and this time I had the lowest bid, so I bought it.

And I took on a builder and we began to build it. Each week, each village was to bring me a portion of the money. The first week they brought it to me, and the second. But came the third week and they stopped bringing me anything. When they stopped bringing me the money, I began to spend my own. I went back to the work and finished the school with my money. I bought the supplies, I bought everything: the lumber, the wheelbarrows, the satchels.

And then I sued them. Those from our village had paid up, because I had offered them a dodge: I told them that those in the village who had no money could work it off. I'd take off his debt with his work. But the other village didn't pay up. And I sued them. We waited for over a year until the case was called.

You sued them in court?

I sued one of them, the guarantor.

The day when the court was going to rule, he took twelve people with him, from his village. They told him, "Don't give the money." When we entered the court, the judge said to him, "Well, give this man his money." The guarantor answered: "Sir, here are the men who are to give the money. But they say that the work was deficient; and I don't even know how much each one is said to owe. I'm just the guarantor. Here are the ones who owe the money."

The judge said: "I do not see those who owe the money. I see only you, the guarantor. Give him the money or go to prison." The others then said, "Sir, this man never finished the work we contracted; we agreed with him on a certain size, and the school isn't that large; wait until we measure it and then we can decide."

The judge said to them, "Outside! Let's go, get out! If this one hasn't carried out his contract, sue him. If you want to give your friend the

---

[6]This involves a process in which bidders undercut one another in offering to perform a task at a lower price. In this way, the village pays as low a price as possible.

guarantor money, fine. If you don't, he is going to prison. And if the one who built the school owes you something, sue him." Well, they collected the money and gave it to the guarantor. He put it on the table for me.

And then I said, "And my expenses?" For the suit, for what I had had to give the government for the suit. The judge said to me, "Leave here, and do another suit for that."

I went from there and had another suit initiated. I asked for my expenses of 250 rials. That guarantor gave it to me from his own house, alone. Then I was satisfied and I didn't lord it over them. But they couldn't stand me after that.

[Our talk was interrupted at this point when the Faqir's wife called out that the water had been heated and was now ready. We were able to continue the next day.]

You told me yesterday about that case of the school. Were there any disputes within the village which you were involved in as moqaddem?

Well, at the very first you know, after independence, the villagers couldn't tolerate Sessy. And they said: "Don't associate with Sessy. Don't talk with him, don't deal with him. He is an outcast."

Why didn't they want people to associate with Sessy?

He used to have them beaten up. He had them knocked around when he was moqaddem. During the colonial period. He'd send them off to work for the qaid, and to work for the sheikh, and he'd have them work in his own farming. He'd have them use their cows to do his plowing. (...) And Sessy would knock people around too!

He'd hit them with a club?

With a club, like this! [The Faqir made the appropriate motion.] He'd be carrying a club and club them. And slap them. And he would go to the qaid and lie about them, and the qaid would have them put in jail. Those who weren't sharp, who didn't get to the qaid first and complain, would go straight from the qaid to jail.

So why do you say that it was better for the villagers to be on good terms with him after independence?

It's better that they should be on good terms because, you know, Sessy helps us out, he makes bread with us. If someone from the government comes to the village, it is only my house, or Si Hassan's, or Sessy's, that will receive them. Just we three. He'd always say, "I'll help out," always. The others, they say, "No. I can't ... "

And how did you manage to bring them to good terms?

They had to. The disputing led to nothing and the entire government was saying, in one breath, "Order." The government and the parties and everyone was saying, "Order. Order." And that we all be brothers.

But, if he was no good when he was moqaddem, why don't you pay him with the same treatment that he paid you?

That means we would become worse than he was. Just take over his place, just sit in the chair, and then hit the other guy—is that it? If he had no sense, we have to have a little bit more ourselves.

And with Our Master everything is watched over: you, me, him, the other, and the other. It is said that forgiveness is beautiful, and that God replaces what is taken. If the fire burns the date palm, it grows again; but the one who burned it is given nothing by God. That's that.

So that's the reason. And

And the government itself wouldn't permit us to do anything to him: it would accuse us of rebelling.

And what do you think is the opinion of villagers about your term as moqaddem?

They liked it a lot.

Why did they like it?

They liked it a lot. If the government required something, I'd do it in an orderly way. And if our fraction had to donate money for some gifts, I'd see that all of our fraction paid and that our village only gave its proper portion; so that other villages could not say to us, "You people, give!" I'd stand fast for the proper proportion. Or if there was some business between ourselves and the rest of the fraction, I'd call for many villagers to be present, so that no one could say that I consumed anything for myself. I'd tell them: "We have to give one thousand rials, that is our portion. Get it together!" They would collect it, would give it over, and it wouldn't pass through my hands. Or even if it did pass through my hands and four rials were left over, I'd say, "Here are four rials; give them to someone." I wouldn't consume it.

Or someone would come up to me and say, "Here, take this." I'd tell him: "No. Don't give me, I don't give you. I've got my own problems."

But many people who want something want to give some gift so that you will help them. If you don't take it from them, they'll say you're not a friend. Won't you help them out?[7]

I don't help them. I'd tell him beforehand: "Watch out; what you want is not yours. If you want to, we'll go and ask for it. That's all right. But if you want to get it through a stratagem, that can't be done, because it's not yours."

[7]The importance of gifts of this sort, meant to encourage someone to perform a specific task for the gift-giver, should not be underestimated, nor should the gifts be understood simply as bribes. Although giving gifts to government employees and administrators is a common practice by people in need of a service, it is also common in such diverse arenas as the schools, where a parent concerned for his child's progress will present the teacher with a gift; in industry, where an unemployed laborer will offer the foreman a gift in the hope of being hired; in the hospitals, where money will be offered to doctors and doctors' aides, for services that, according to regulations, should be free.

And even if they gave me, it doesn't benefit me. Someone would just give me something at the marketplace, and one of my livestock would die.

How's that?

If someone gives me four rials at the marketplace, one of my livestock will be found dead even before I arrive home. It doesn't suit me; Our Master doesn't. . . doesn't. . . doesn't permit me this. [The Faqir chuckled nervously.]

Did you ever try it?

Yes.

What happened?

What happened to me? Once I bought the 'ashur.[8] The party had told us: "Collect the 'ashur in all the village. The government will buy it from you, and you may reap a profit from it."

We collected it, and we auctioned it among ourselves. It settled on me. And just as I was buying it, some of our sheep and goats were grazing on that plot of land where we now have the irrigation motor. A dog got loose and ate four of our goats. It ate their eyes and their ears, and they were still alive, alive and seeing nothing.

Some profit I made. After that, such things no longer attracted me.

Did those who were well off like your term as moqaddem?

People who don't nibble on others liked it. But those who do, didn't. And of those who know the Law, most of them wanted me.

During your leadership, what is the most important thing that you did?

Important for others, but not for me. Not one thing was important to me.

Well, what was important for them?

What was important for them? Well, take that other moqaddem: if he requires one thousand rials for some donation, or gift, he'll ask them for two thousand. I'd stick to the amount.

What would he do with the difference?

He'd eat it up. I didn't let anything slip through, that's all.

And why did you leave the leadership?

I wasn't. . . I wasn't. . . I was short-changing our house, I wasn't working for our house. I was just working for the benefit of others. And people had become free, and they knew that the government no longer took any notice: if you brought someone before the government, the government would do nothing to him. The jokers just want to stir things up, to concentrate on making trouble. They aren't heeding independence but just stirring things up.

---

[8]This is the one-tenth part of the harvest that, according to Islamic law, must be set aside to be given as alms to the poor.

And me, I should lead what is worth nothing? For what? And the sheikh had become nothing, and the qaid had become nothing.

What do you mean, "become nothing"?

Nothing! Everyone is equal; no one is in charge. There is no advantage to it. Even if I wanted to consume what belongs to others, that doesn't benefit me. And even if it did, it doesn't exist any longer: they give you nothing. And I'm short-changing myself.

And also, one day the sheikh visits, another day his assistant comes, another day the guards come: "Hey, moqaddem! Hey, moqaddem!" Always a chicken for them, always dates and nuts, always more expenses. Always. And for what?

There is no benefit to it, nothing at all?

Nothing, nothing, nothing. If you want people to give you gifts, and if the government is being forceful, then you can benefit. But if the government isn't forceful, they give you nothing.

What's that, "when the government is being forceful"?

You know, when it stands firm on its rules: he who does something wrong gets his punishment. Then people will start bringing gifts to you: if someone does something wrong, he'll start to say to you, "See if you can do something for me." But now, even if they do something wrong, even if they take a life, nothing is done.

But if the government were forceful, and a man wanted to give you something so that you would help him out, would you take it?

If I wasn't sure to lose by it, if it agreed with me. But that doesn't agree with me.[9]

How did you quit your leadership position?

I told the sheikh, and he kept saying, "Wait until tomorrow." And so on and so on. Then, one day in the marketplace, I said it to the qaid, and he told me, "I'll put you in prison." I said: "Go ahead, do what you wish. And after I come out I'll go into a style where you won't be able to rule over me at all." He said, "How's that?" I said: "I'll become like a *hadawi*[10]: I'll go right in front of the door of your very house, and I'll eat bread there, and I'll beat on a drum. And you won't be able to rule over me at all." Well, we went back and forth like that, and he said: "Deal with your sheikh, fend for yourself. Look to your sheikh."

I went to the sheikh then and said: "That's the end. From today on. For me, it's finished." He told me, "Call together your people in the marketplace." I called about twenty of our villagers who were there, and I told them, "The sheikh wants to talk to you."

They went to the sheikh, and he told them, "Decide on a moqaddem, for this one no longer wants to be one." And Qebbor answered him: "Let

---

[9]In a sense, then, the Faqir is taking no personal credit for his refusal of gifts.
[10]See chapter 4, n. 9.

him stay moqaddem. Why, did we say he had faults? What's the matter with him, what's wrong? Why, we haven't complained about him." I said to Qebbor: "Be moqaddem yourself; you too don't have any faults. What's the matter with you? Be moqaddem yourself."

The sheikh said, "That's enough." And Qebbor answered, "Let it be the Faqir, we ask the sheikh for this," and so on. I told them: "This one says to me, 'Work!'. O.K., if he'll pay me for it." Qebbor said, "How much!" I said, "Four hundred rials." Four hundred rials from them was very unlikely. I said: "What is this work? You say, 'Just work, and God will thank you.' Why should I work; what does this guy give me? And what does that guy give me? Or that one?"

Finally, the sheikh said, "Well, you'll have to select one of your four leaders to be moqaddem." I told him: "If we are to take turns as moqaddem, I've already had my turn. If we are to be obliged by force, I've been moqaddem in that way. And if it's to be based on desire, I've already done that, too. But still, I will draw straws with you. If it comes to me, I will do it; and whoever it comes to will do it."

And the sheikh said to them: "What more does he owe you? Here, he is even going to draw twigs with you."

The sheikh went away and then returned, and we had our names written on slips of paper. We crumpled them up and threw them down on the path. The sheikh said to the first person to come out of the market, "Pick up those straws, those papers." He picked them up; the sheikh selected one, opened it up, read it out; it was the Hajj Hmed. But the Hajj said, "No, no, not me."

Didn't the others try to force him to agree?

Oh, we have freedom now. How could they force him?

I mean, didn't they say: "Oh, Hajj, this is shameful. We drew straws and it fell on you . . ."

He didn't want it. And besides, the Hajj wasn't up to it. You know the Hajj isn't able to do all that running around.

Well, finally, the sheikh said: "That's enough for me. You've got to find me a moqaddem, I'm no longer getting involved." We remained there, trying things out, and found no way. Then there was no more movement. So, I said to the sheikh: "Go, sheikh, give us another week to decide, until we go back to our land and decide. And if letters arrive, Si Hassan will bring them. And in eight days, we'll send you a moqaddem and you can put him down in your book."

Well, from that time on Si Hassan kept on answering the calls and no one said anything more about a moqaddem or whatever.

What is the position of moqaddem like now?

(. . .)

Who in the village could become moqaddem?

No one wants it, no one.

I didn't say what I meant. Who in the village is the sort of man to be moqaddem?

(...) No one. And all of them have something lacking in their thoughts. There are some of them who see just three meters ahead, some who see four meters ahead; the best of them just see up to ten meters ahead.

That's all?

That's all. Your vision must see from here to the coast; it mustn't just see ten meters ahead, like a rat's.

INDEPENDENCE POLITICS...

All right. Now, could you tell me how independence came about, how it came about here in the region?

When colonialism was still here, the Qaid Bush'ib took six hundred of us to Casablanca, with rifles, and knives, and clubs, and bayonets, and pistols—everything.

O.K., we've already talked about that.[11] But what happened when you returned?

We returned here and then, when Qaid Bush'ib came back a year later, people were no longer willing to give the market tax, and they were no longer willing to do guard duty. So the qaid had two or three truckloads of the legionnaires brought here. And in the marketplace, he told them, "Beat up the people." He wanted to have everyone beaten up. But the French control officer told him, *"Non."* He forbid him to do that.

Then the king returned from exile, they let him loose from ... from Madagascar. And then, you know, they carried on negotiations concerning independence.

And at that time, what was Qaid Bush'ib doing?

Then, Bush'ib was hatching eggs in his house; he stayed inside his house like harvested grain.

And during that time, our leaders told us to close off the roads, and we all went, all of us! Even the women, some of the women went with us. And we closed off the roads with rocks and brush. So that not one Rumi would get through, not one. For at that time there was a lot of military around.

And we'd close off the paved road. They'd come up to the barricade, and they'd get out, look around, and then turn back. And we kept doing that for some weeks, and we did it on every route, every road. After a while, no more military appeared. They went north, finished up, went back to where they came from. The roads were opened up, and we stayed, you know, as leaders to lead the villages.

What was the first qaid's work like?

[11]See chapter 4.

That first qaid, his work was fine. He brought the conditions of independence. He ruled justly even though he was a military man; he was just like a family member who ruled over the people so that all of them would be brothers. His dealings and everything were fine.

How long did he last?

About two years.

And who followed him?

After him, for about two more years, we had just temporary qaids. They weren't official, there were just substitutes.

What about the elections that have been held?

The first election was for... for the communal council. After that there was one for Parliament.

About that first election: What was to be the work of the communal council?

It would meet over requests for irrigation canals, or if they wanted to fix up some marketplace. You know, the market levies and expenses were under the council's charge.

What do you look for in someone to be delegate to the council?

I look for probity, he should desire probity. For if he doesn't seek it, we can't force him to.

And what were the people saying then about the election itself?

(...)

Were there parties involved in that election?

No. At that time, you know there weren't parties.

And what about the second election?

(...)

Were there parties involved in that election in 1963?

They were involved. The parties arose at that time. They became what steered the countryside. If things go so far as to have parties develop, the parties then run things in that respect. (...)

What was in your mind about the Parliament at that time?

It was going to have some 333 members from all Morocco. And we were told that they would be meeting and deciding on matters that concerned Morocco. And the king said that what the parliamentarians did, the king would carry out. That is, that they would be ruling and that the king would execute their rulings. And that we should struggle in order to install good people who would think about our livelihood, and our trade, and about the disputes between us and other countries, and... about the programs of the entire country. And how we should choose the people who would benefit us, who would be learned and knowledgeable, who wouldn't buy something for us too expensively, nor sell our merchandise cheaply. And always that, whatever they do for us, that it be good. That would be the work of the Parliament.

At that time, was the Union Party[12] *talking about people being partners (ish-tarku)*[13] *with one another?*

Always, they said that people should be partners with one another: that they should come and participate (*isharku*) in the government, and be partners in loans, and be partners in everything, in order to succeed.

Were they socialist (ishtiraki)?

The Union Party? It was trying to be . . . but they couldn't be ishtiraki all alone, they couldn't be ishtiraki by themselves. That's not possible. (. . .)

Is there something evil in that ishtiraki?

In capitalist ishtiraki, there is no evil, but the ishtiraki that is not capitalist is evil. Very bad. We wouldn't accept it, we won't accept it.

What is the difference between them?

With the capitalist ishtiraki, as you have in America, what you have remains yours. You work for yourself, that's that. But if we ended up in ishtiraki, a guy has nothing of his own, nothing.

I see. And what is the meaning of that word, "ishtiraki"?

With ishtiraki that is capitalist, you participate only in choosing the leaders. They are always made through voting. But *ishtirakiyya* is like Russia, and like Algeria. You understand?

Well, I see the example, but I still don't understand the difference according to your thought.

Now, the ishtiraki that you have is called "capitalist." What your family

---

[12]The Union Party, which made a very strong showing in the Sous region in the 1963 elections, was formed after a split developed in the Independence Party (*Istiqlal*) several years after independence was achieved. The Independence Party was the lineal descendant of the movement that had led the independence struggle during the protectorate period. As a result of this split, a faction whose dominant figure was Mehdi Ben Barka (who was later kidnapped in 1965 in Paris and killed, apparently by Moroccan government agents with the complicity of French security forces) and that had strong support in the urban working class and in selected rural areas, formed the Union Nationale des Forces Populaires, known to Moroccans simply as the Union (*Ittihad*).

[13]There are a number of words in the following discussion that grow out of the Arabic root *sharika*, to share, and for which translation constitutes something of a problem. In the text, I have translated *ishtarku* as "be partners" (in my question, I meant this word in its strong sense of "forming cooperative enterprises"; the Faqir, in his reply, uses it more as "working together") and *isharku* as "participate in."

Because of the way the Faqir uses the word *ishtiraki*, however, I have only given a translation in the first instance and have otherwise left in the original Arabic. Wehr, for *ishtiraki* (the adjectival form), gives "socialist, socialistic," but for *ishtirak* (a corresponding noun form) gives "partnership, participation, cooperation, collaboration" among others (1966, p. 469). In some of the Faqir's phrases, it seems that even the term *democratic*, as it is commonly understood in the West, might be an appropriate translation for *ishtiraki*. *Ishtirakiyya* unambiguously means "socialism."

As the Faqir continues, however, I think his use of these terms becomes quite clear.

left to you, you keep. You understand? What is ishtiraki in your system is just one aspect: you participate in choosing your leaders. They are only made through elections. You can't recall them without an election, or name them without an election. That is called ishtiraki, but capitalist: what you have is yours, and what someone else who is very rich has, he keeps.

But, in that ishtiraki of a special sort, you keep nothing! The government runs everything, and you receive your part. You, like the other, like another, like the next one. (...)

There was another election for communal council, wasn't there?

There was another election, five years later, for the council.

How did that work?

(...)

Do you consider the government and the rulers, and the court, important in your lives? Or do you say to yourself, "We don't care about that"?[14]

No, it's important. The courts are important.

Why?

It's important because it takes what you owe me from you, and gives it to me. And if I am unjust, it fixes me. It's not simply that if I am wealthy, I can clout you. Who would rule over me, then? For we say, "The representative of God the Almighty on earth ... the Lord is in the heavens, and his representative on earth is the government.

What was it like when there was no government, during a period of siba? What do people say about those times?[15]

During the time of *siba*, if you weren't on good terms with me and I met you on the road, I'd kill you. I wouldn't even bother to curse you out at all. There was no prison, nothing.

When was this?

I don't want to tell a lie, I don't know exactly when.

Could it have been during the time of your father?

When my father was a bit young, about Mehdi's age. It could have been then.

Did people say anything else about siba?

During *siba*, you know, every village had a number of people who were

---

[14]I would have liked the Faqir, in answering this question, to reject a governmental, administrative, and judicial structure, which, on the basis of my own political beliefs, I did not believe served his best interests.

[15]The distinction between *bled l-makhzen* (the land of government) and *bled s-siba* (the land of anarchy) is one that runs throughout the historical and academic literature on Morocco, being used there to differentiate between lands under control of the central government and those that were not subject to it. In current usage in the region, the distinction is more a temporal one—between periods when order was imposed from outside, and periods when the region maintained (or did not maintain) its own order; *siba*, used alone, often has the meaning of "disorder, anarchy."

leaders, like those we talked about before, about four or five of them. And they would mete out justice among the people. You know, if I stole a cow from you, they would come and take one away from me, and eat it themselves. Or they would decide that you had to give me a cow. They might come for it and then slaughter one of my rams and eat it that evening.

There would be, let's say, four here and four in the next village, and so on. And if there was something between village and village, they would all come together, from the whole region, in order to settle it. And if it was just within the village, the four from the village would decide it.

And if they meted out justice to a man, he'd submit to it at all costs. He had said, "Rule over me, by God and the Law"; and the Law is called "sacred" and "inviolable." If you came to ask me if something was permitted or forbidden, I'd tell you. The government didn't exist. Just justice, that means just knowledge.

Let's say they seized someone. If he said to them, "Rule over me, by God and the Law," one person among them would take him to the qadi and tell the qadi, "So and so, did this to so and so. Rule upon this." The qadi would judge, saying, "So and so should give to so and so, this and such." And he'd tell his decision to the court guard. And the court guard would return with them to the village and tell the decision to the group of village leaders. And the leaders would make things difficult for that one until he paid.

Is there anything like that group of leaders that still exists today?

No.

But, if there is some problem in the village, you say "We bring the group." What does that mean?

Even today, the group may be brought to someone who is ignorant. But, someone who is shameless pays no attention to the group. And the group doesn't have the power it requires. Because now there is the court. You can ask and ask, but if the other won't give in, you have to just go away. If the guy won't defer[16] to the group, the group has no power.

But don't people defer a lot?

There are those who defer, that's true. There are those who, if just one or two from the village come to him, he will defer. But if he doesn't defer, he'll pay no attention to the group. They would come, all of them, and put pressure on him, and he'd just curse them out.

And today, in the village, if someone wanted to bring the group, whom would he bring?

He'd go to those who have their wits about them, or those he'd find available by the mosque. He'd say to them, "Come with me. Look at this, at what that guy did to me." He'll say, "By God, be present with me," but

[16]The Faqir used the word *hshem.*

he knows that it's just their generosity, but that they won't be able to execute anything. They don't have the licence to.

Did you ever . . . [The Faqir yawned.]—we're almost finished now—did you ever bring the group?

Yes. You know, in earlier times, when I was disputing with the Agurram family, I'd often bring the group, those six, seven, or eight with good minds.

Have you done this in the last five years or so?

No.

Is the reason for that, that you don't have any problems for them to deal with or . . .

I don't have the problems.

And if you had them?

And it's unlikely that they would be able to settle them. They can't carry it out, they aren't able to accomplish anything. They just don't have the power.

Nothing at all?

That's it.

10

An All-Night Party

I frequently talked with Ali about women and sex, subjects that the Faqir shunned. While working in the fields, or lingering over a glass of tea (as he liked to, particularly on days when the Faqir was absent), Ali would recount the latest village gossip and often relate tales of his own exploits, at times seeming to boast. On everyone's lips this year was an especially abhorrent episode: one villager, upon his brother's death, had married his brother's widow, who was his own wife's sister; and he had done this without divorcing his first wife, but had simply thrown her out of his house. Marriage at the same time to two sisters constitutes incest in Islamic law, and comments on this incident would frequently terminate in the expression of extreme contempt, "Khkhkh."

One day, not long before I was to leave Morocco, Ali took me aside and, looking around circumspectly as he always did before mentioning matters related to women or sex, invited me to a party that he and some of his friends were preparing. The party would center around the participation of several unmarried women, known as *sheikha*, but Ali could not be certain who they would be, or how they would actually behave. Such a gathering, which differed radically from the weekly, all-male evening get-togethers that friends in a group would take turns hosting, would have to be kept secret, Ali insisted, and it was therefore to be held outside the village and to begin only after dark.

During the next few days, Ali and I met casually with the other party-goers to make the arrangements: two stopped by on their way back from the fields and another we met toward sunset at the customary gathering place near the village mosque. Qebbor, the merchant, would bring tea, sugar, and meat to the party; Ali would bring the cooking oil; Hashim, would drive to the Medina in his pickup truck to fetch the women and would also bring the wine and soft drinks; others, traveling by bicycle or motorbike, would bring assorted cooking utensils. After the party, we would total up the cost and each pay our share. The room in which we were to gather was situated on an isolated farm of one of the men and was large enough to fit the ten of us, as well as the women.

The next Wednesday evening, Ali and I set out on bicycles, shortly before sundown. We had told no one in the house where we were going. After a half-hour's ride, we arrived at the farm room. Hashim arrived soon after with two women and all three were already highly animated. Both women seemed in their mid or late twenties; one was full-bodied, high-spirited, and well-known throughout the region for her singing; the other, slighter, was much less expressive. Both were dressed in a headcloth, sweater, a thin full-length gown (*dfina*) and the usual baggy trousers that grip the calf; both had several teeth glistening with gold. Qebbor brought a third woman on his motorbike. With a finely sculpted face and tall, broad figure, she was much more imposing than the other two, and was wearing a bright green and red *dfina,* with no headcloth.

When Hashim and the two women arrived, the party immediately became livelier. Hashim admitted that they had already drunk three of the eight bottles of wine before joining us and that he himself had been drinking since ten o'clock that morning. He was boisterous and full of good humor, and his capacity to shock us all into laughter often dispelled a temporary lull.

Hashim began at once to joke with Qebbor, "Hey, do you want to fuck?" And then, as the laughter subsided, he began to test my knowledge of obscene Arabic words, insisting that I teach him the English equivalent. This was, in the spirit of the evening, difficult to refuse, and the two women Hashim had brought participated as actively in these lessons as the men.

About half the men and the three women were drinking wine diluted with Coca-cola, and Hashim offered me some: "Hey buddy, have a drink of this donkey piss." Alcoholic drinks are forbidden in Islam and half the men at the party were abstaining, Ali among them. Undecided between adopting this commendable stance and giving in to the openly condemned yet quite tempting Christian weakness for liquor, I hesitantly declined. Hashim continued: "But your prophet, Jesus, doesn't forbid it to you. And, you know, you Christians will end up in hell anyway!"

Hashim returned to the subject a little later: "What kind of Christian are you anyway? You don't drink, and you don't even smoke either." By now, my indecision had almost vanished and I dissolved what remained of it in the offered glass of wine. Qebbor, who was not drinking, interjected, "Now you're just like a Muslim." "If it's to be a Muslim like Hashim," I answered, "God help me!" For some reason, everyone broke into laughter. And Hashim retorted, still the buffoon, "I'm a Muslim, and a hypocritical one. Now we'll both go to hell!" The laughter redoubled.

The rectangular room was not a large one, perhaps three yards by four. We were all sitting or had stretched ourselves out upon the reed mats that had been laid on the dirt floor, bracing our backs against the earthen walls or leaning upon a pillow or jellaba. The middle of the room remained empty and every now and then, against the background of music from a cassette recorder, someone would break into a clapping accompaniment or stand and stamp his feet to the rhythm.

Hashim was in constant motion, now singing, now dancing; on occasion, someone would pull his feet from under him, and he would topple to the floor, laughing all the while. He continued to taunt Qebbor, "Hey, want to fuck?" Once, Qebbor tumbled him to the ground, rose above him, and began to unbelt his own pants, threatening to carry out the act. Qebbor was an enormous man, and, as he let his pants down, leaving his briefs on, we praised the size of his buttocks. Despite his size, he was very agile and a skillful dancer, and his feet kept perfect time to the music as he executed his mock assault on Hashim.

By now, several leitmotifs had emerged and were to echo throughout the evening: the wine drinkers were accused by the others of dominating the party, not allowing the others the chance to "warm their heads up," and Ali often chided Hashim in particular on this count; the wine drinkers, none of whom were taking their drinks straight, were also consuming the soft drinks, which the others thought unfair; and the two women other than the singer were contributing little to the ambiance and were frequently rebuked for their cheerlessness. The discord threatened on one or two occasions to break into an open rupture.

Finally, with Hashim temporarily at bay, the two women from the Medina took off their outer clothing and, wearing only slips and panties, began to dance together. Most of the time they faced one another, moving closer and then farther apart, their bodies erect and moving with restraint, and their feet marking the music's rhythm. At times they came so close to one another that their breasts touched. The men were now all seated, turned toward the women, and were clapping loudly, rapidly, rhythmically.

Soon, the slighter woman tired, or so she claimed, and the other took over in earnest. No longer did she limit her dance to deftly stamping her feet; now, her slip and panties began to reveal more of her body as she shook her shoulders and deliberately jiggled her breasts, and she began to roll her hips, first slowly, then very rapidly. Her belly, slightly less than taut, quivered to another rhythm, and Hashim joked that he had made her pregnant.

She faced each man in turn and danced her way toward him; he, still seated on the floor, would slowly look her over, from head to thighs. As she neared him, he might thrust his head between her thighs and nuzzle it there for several seconds. We all encouraged one another to do this, and when it was done and then noisily acclaimed by the others, the *sheikha* would laugh and perhaps repeat her approach. She might also turn around, her back now toward the man, and again dance toward him. She would not now come as close to him as before and he might simply make a gentle circular motion with his hands, outlining her buttocks although not touching them. Hashim seized the opportunity, when his turn came, to suddenly pull her red panties down to her thighs; her apparently shocked cry of "Shameful!" was, perhaps, completely incongruous, and the laughter only quickened.

The third woman, who had remained fully clothed and seated, and had taken charge of serving the drinks, was again and again encouraged to dance, but her response was unequivocal and impassive: "I don't know that kind of dancing." She parried all further objections by repeating, "I am free," and Hashim commented, ruefully: "You see, that's independence. Everybody is free and no one takes orders from anyone else. There are no rulers." Much later in the evening, when the mood had shifted, she did a short dance: only her feet moved to the music; her upper body remained almost motionless.

After the *sheikha's* dancing, the pace slowed. Hashim was still active, however, and he asked me, "Do you fuck your wife from the front or the back?", echoing the common belief that most Christians do the latter, a technique that Moroccans frown upon. Ali interceded, "Why don't you send him outside with one of the women if you want to find out?" Hashim responded, in a rare show of propriety, "No, he already has a wife." "So do you," Ali answered, "and that doesn't stop you. And anyway, Kevin probably does it just the way you do." "I'm not so sure," Hashim replied and, anticipating the laughter that was to follow, flashed back, "at least I've been able to make *my* wife pregnant."

It was by now about midnight, and the meat had been cooked and was ready to be served. Mehjub had been busy with this, under makeshift conditions, for much of the past two hours, yet no effort was made to spare him from criticism: he had put too much oil in the *tajine;* the meat was not cooked enough and was not correctly spiced. After the meal, a vain attempt was made to muster support for a pot of tea, but no one yielded to the call that he take charge of brewing it (a very rare occurrence).

The *sheikha* had begun to complain that she had twisted her shoulder while dancing. Several men, each with his own prescription, took turns at trying to ease her pain. One rubbed the heel of his hand into her shoulder blade; another planted his foot, and the full weight of his body, upon her upper back; a third sat down behind her, made her clasp her hands behind her head, drew her elbows together in front of her face and then abruptly pulled them down toward her chest; a fourth told her to lie on her stomach, pressed his knee against her shoulder blade, and drew her straightened arm backwards and upwards in a wide arc. She felt somewhat better, but would not dance again that night; she was, however, very willing to lead the singing.

The singing appeared to bring the evening to its climax. For more than an hour, everyone actively joined in and interest never flagged. The *sheikha* would sing the lead, and her words would be echoed by the others in loud choruses. Almost everyone contributed some form of percussive accompaniment, tapping fingers and hands, or a spoon, on a tin can or on a metal cup or plate, or clapping vigorously in rhythm. The energy of the performance, which grew now and again more intense as the lead singer and chorus sang with increasing force and punctuated the short pauses with enthusiastic shouts, seemed to derive not from the words of the songs but from the complex musical tension generated by the participants in their various roles. Yet the words were sung clearly, and they often revealed, as in the following song, a concern with disappointed love.

Sheikha: I gazed down at the water spring, my spirits sad, how much
       I cried,
      My land no longer matters, it's the girl I left behind,
      I'm stricken oh friends with love, it has made me insane.
Chorus: *(repeats these lines)*
Sheikha: If this village supports me, I still won't stay,
      Love is chipping away at my heart, and I won't heal,
      I'm stricken oh friends with love, it has made me insane.
Chorus: *(repeats first verse)*
Sheikha: Why did you deceive me, and tell me, "I'm walking on air"?
      Yesterday I returned, and found you with head and feet
       bare,
      I'm stricken oh friends with love, it has made me insane.
Chorus: *(repeats first verse)*
Sheikha: I'll never love again, my feelings (*kebda:* Literally, "liver")
       have flamed up and burned.
      I'll never love again, and my senses will never return,
      I'm stricken oh friends with love, it has made me insane.
Chorus: *(repeats first verse)*

The drinking and the general exertion began to take their toll. When the singing finally stopped, the leading *sheikha* relaxed herself against the man next to her and rested her head in his lap; the other *sheikha's* body was now fully entwined, although motionless, with that of another man. The third woman remained seated, still ready to serve drinks, but the wine had been finished. Hashim was quiet.

It was almost daybreak. Several of the men wandered outside and sat by Hashim's pickup truck. Three of them had done the buying for the party, and they would add up the cost, to be divided among the men. Hashim refused to break down the sum he had spent, saying, "Just reimburse my twenty-five hundred rials; we can do the breakdown some other time." Qebbor responded, "Twenty-five hundred? Let's add up your expenses and see."

The mild antagonism that had studded the entire evening was again surfacing.

Hashim asked, "What am I, an outsider?"

Qebbor answered, "Have we ever not repaid all your money?"

"Then just give me my money," Hashim said, "Do you suspect me of something? We're all sons of the same land."

"What kind of behavior is this?" Qebbor demanded. "We always total up. Have you no sense left from your drinking?"

Ali replied, "Yes, we always total up. So let's do it now."

Hashim, who perhaps had no desire, at this moment, to perform computations, said, "No. Let's wait until we all come together one of these days."

Qebbor stalked off angrily and muttered that he had spent more than eight hundred rials of his own money and did not want this money consumed by the others: if they did not do the accounts now, it might be some time before he was repaid, for there were people here he would not see again for weeks. Hashim remained propped up against the pick-up. He insisted that only the total was needed, and that it was unnecessary to bother with all the little details of adding up the numbers.

Muhammad then came over to Qebbor. Muhammad was a good friend of Hashim's; they had once been partners in a clandestine meat-selling venture in their villages, and they still spent much time together. Muhammed broke down Hashim's total for Qebbor: this included six hundred rials for the *sheikha* who had led the singing, and four hundred rials for her friend. Qebbor accepted this, but with misgivings: "Who told that second woman to come along anyway? She did nothing all night but lean her body against that other fellow."

Hashim had now come over to us, saying, "Do you still think I'm trying to cheat you?" His tone had taken on an injured whine, and Qebbor said, "Just be quiet or things are going to become worse." Hashim now seemed very despondent, saying, "You said 'Quiet!' So now I won't say another word." He sank down silently against a nearby pile of wood. Ali added, with Hashim in clear earshot, "Yes, you can't talk to someone who has left his senses." On the way back to the room, Ali and Hashim were talking together. All evening they had alternately clashed and avowed a deep mutual love, and now Hashim said, "It looks as though, after all this, we'll no longer be friends." This seemed to me, somehow, unconvincing; Ali simply answered, "How can I be the friend of someone who has no sense?"

The room had cooled off considerably while we were outside. Tea was now being brewed. We all sat down, except for Hashim, who remained standing next to Ali, facing the wall, and quietly crying. For a long while, no one seemed to notice. Then they began to badger him: "Hashim, sit down," "Hashim, drink some tea," "Hashim, relax. You can't rush off until your head cools." He stood silently and wiped his tears with a handkerchief.

Finally he turned around and sat down and his mood seemed to lighten. Tea was served, and talk was less strained, almost compassionate. But Muhammad soon began to chide Hashim: "One thing about you, you don't know how to be patient. If you had not been so bull-headed, none of this would have happened." Now Hashim confronted us all: "Everyone has been attacking me, all evening. Everyone except Mehjub. The rest of you think I'm not worth a franc. But it's not you who are donkeys, it's me. I'm the donkey here." He abruptly told the two women to get into his pickup truck. He grabbed his work jacket and stormed out, not heeding our strong protests.

It was dawn, the tea was finished, and we all prepared to leave. "I knew from the beginning that this party would be a failure," Qebbor said. "Liquor ruins it." And Mehjub added, "We would have been better off sleeping than coming here." Ali suggested: "It's because you guys don't know how to deal with drunkenness. You have to tell them straight out to sit down against the wall. Otherwise their carousing ruins everyone else's enjoyment."

As Ali and I rode back on our bicycles, he again insisted: "And, in any event, don't tell the Faqir where we were, or what we did. Just say we were in the next village, at the house of Muhammad, son of so-and-so, and that you don't remember his name." When we arrived at the compound, people were starting out for work. L-'Aribi had already noticed that our bicycle tracks led from the main road and not from the next village. He asked where we had been, and I simply said, "Ask your father's brother." The Faqir, fortunately, had left earlier that morning for the market in the Medina.

▨ QUESTIONS ABOUT DIFFERENCE AND DECEPTION

From the moment Ali approached me suggesting we both go to the party, I knew I faced a difficult decision. If I went with Ali, I would have to refuse to tell the Faqir about it—Ali was certainly going to insist on this, and my telling the Faqir would not only betray Ali's confidence, but I would also meet the Faqir's stern rebuke. If, on the other hand, I did not go, I would not only be rebuffing Ali, with whom I had always been, and wanted to remain, on good terms, but I would also be going against my own inclination.

That such a choice had to be made at all confirmed the obvious fact that here—as everywhere—varied practices and attitudes toward life coexisted. On occasion the people who held such views were indifferent to or even intolerant of one another; sometimes the differences were strictly incompatible. I had seen persistent evidence of this throughout the summer, perhaps most clearly in the context of the brotherhood seance, in the theft of the bicycle, and in the contrasting versions offered to me of both the fight between Ali and the Faqir Hmed and the marriage of the Faqir's daughter. But now the contrast was not between people with different religious standpoints, different ethnic backgrounds, distinct rural as opposed to urban habits, or between employers and employees, but between brothers who lived in the same house, worked the same fields, ate together, and were raising their children together.

Furthermore, I could neither keep myself at a distance from these conflicts, nor maintain the neutrality that many scientifically minded anthropologists recommended—I had to make a choice. From my first moments in the village, I had had to make such choices again and again, sometimes unconsciously, sometimes deliberately, attempting to accommodate my immediate preferences (toward enjoying myself and having a good time), my more remote career objectives (which required me to pay attention to traditional anthropological concerns), and my strong desire to appreciate what it is to be a Moroccan and to interact as fully as possible with some individual Moroccans. These choices were made even more difficult because my aims were not independent of each other, not necessarily conflicting, and not always easy to specify. In any event, whatever decisions I had made to reach an accommodation eventually led to my close relationship with the Faqir and, to a lesser extent, other members of his household. I could not help but wonder whether I would have become close to any villager had I consistently attempted to remain aloof from conflicts and avoid difficult decisions.

One such decision I had taken was to not discuss sexuality, in even a general way, with the Faqir; this was a topic that his sense of propriety placed out of bounds. I would chat only briefly with the women of his house: I had learned, early on, that to sit and talk with them at length was likely to make the Faqir uncomfortable. And, of course, I would certainly not discuss with the Faqir the more intimate details of his own relationships with women. Fortunately for our relationship, I myself was not particularly curious about the Faqir's sexual life. Our common reticence about sexual matters surely contributed, as did our mutual interest in politics, to the strength of our relationship.

In the event, I chose to go to the party and to not tell the Faqir. I now had to confront that I, too, was actively hiding things from the Faqir. Of course, there had always been many parts of my New York life that I could not fully explain to him because many aspects of New York life simply never crossed our minds in Morocco and because his experience did not provide a relevant context for understanding them. Nonetheless, we had discussed such remote issues often over the years, and I had answered his questions as thoroughly as I could, if still only partially.

Now, I saw that even with regard to my life in Morocco such secrets were inevitable. Not only would some portions of our relationship have to remain hidden from others if I were to remain faithful to the Faqir's wishes, and not only was our relationship built upon subjects we deliberately avoided, as well as those we explicitly addressed, but our relationship also found expression through our need to keep certain things about ourselves hidden from the other. It was as a common Moroccan saying that the Faqir would cite on occasion put it: "One third of what is in another's mind is unknowable." It would be a profound error, then, to claim that the strength of my relationship with the Faqir had its roots in our complete sincerity, honesty, and frankness, or that the relationship could be appreciated without taking into account, to some extent, the partial deception that necessarily ran through it.

This subject was not one that could be discussed directly, but seemed closely tied, here, to the character of the Faqir's relationship with his brother and to the secrets that this relationship seemed to inspire. I began to question the Faqir about the ill will that had surfaced between him and his brother, and whether they had considered dividing the household ("Brothers..."). I went on to ask more general questions about his feelings toward his brother and how these compared with his feelings toward his eldest son, Mehdi ("Brother and son...").

🔀 TENTH DIALOGUE

BROTHERS . . .

Faqir, I'd like to talk with you now about a subject that I think is a little difficult. I want you to answer slowly, to think your answers over. **O.K. I have in my classes a lot of students to whom I try to explain how people here live. I'm sometimes asked, "How is it that brothers"—like you and Ali—"remain living together?" We don't usually do that, you know. For example, my brother and I each live separately.**

Each stands on his own.

Yes, they fend for themselves. Each lives in his own household, raises his own children

he fends for himself. Once he gets his capital together, he fends for himself.

So I still don't understand why you and your brother stay together. People say that last year you and Ali were at odds with one another much of the time. What were you fighting about?

What about? Well, he'd say, "I didn't do what you accuse me of," or "Why didn't you do this?" Or I'd say, "Why didn't you do it?"

What things, what things? Tell me exactly.

For example, if he went off somewhere during the day, and when I returned in the evening he hadn't brought back feed grass, I'd say to him, "Why didn't you bring the feed grass?" He'd say: "Ah . . . and you? Why didn't you? I just didn't want to." That's the kind of thing.

Do you remember anything else and, in particular, how the words were exchanged?

Or, he'd say, "My son told me that you hit him." Even if I had only yelled at his son, even if I hadn't hit him at all, he'd say that. Those kinds of reasons.

At any time, did you really exchange harsh words?

Well, we'd exchange up to about ten or fifteen and then he'd go away, or I'd go away, and we'd be quiet.

When you argue, don't you begin to move closer to one another?

No.

You know, you might go up to him and say, "You did this and this and this!"

Yes, that's true. And then he'd say, "You too did this and this and this!" And then he'd go in this direction and I'd go in that. Because, probably, if we approached one another, we'd fight. The very meaning of approaching one another is to fight.

During that period last year, what did all the ill will that you felt come from?

My spirit is ruined if I notice, for example, that you are doing something that is no good.

What do you mean?

If you go to people and say, "My brother does this and does that; he goes outside the house and carries on." And he was saying such things. You find this out and you know that what he says isn't true. You feel bad; really, your spirit is ruined.

How did you know he was doing that?

People tell you. Or you come upon him and see it for yourself. You do. You enter a group and you can see it with your own eyes.

[Here, one of the children entered and we stopped the conversation for a few moments.]

When you heard that he was saying such things, saying that you were carrying on outside the house, did you say something to him about it?

No.

Why not?

I wouldn't say it to him.

Why not?

I wouldn't say it to him. I would just talk to him about the things I've seen him do that hurt me. I wouldn't say, "You've said this" or "You've said that." Let him do what he pleases, until he learns to restrain (*hshem*) himself, until he tires of it. Let him follow that path until he realizes where it leads him.

And at that time, or at any other time, did you ever think of separating from him, of dividing your household?

I'm always thinking of separating from him, but I've figured ... what's the value? If I separate from him, it will be of no value. What will he attain, what will I attain? There will be no gain. If we separated, and if today I went to market, he'd have to go too. And if he went to summon the tractor, or wherever, each would have to go for himself. That's worth nothing. Well, I say, he may yet acquire some sense. That's that.

Did the word separation *ever appear between the two of you?*

It appeared just last year. Then, it even appeared.

How did that happen?

It appeared when he said "Hospitality, by God" (dif Allah).[1] He said that.

And what was the reason for that, at that moment?

The argument over what he was doing on the outside, that argument. And disputes over his boy. He said to me, "Why did you hit the boy?" And "Why don't you answer me?" and "Why this?" and "Why that?"

At that time, had you hit his son?

No. I hadn't hit him at all. I had just found them all in front of the doorway, as we came back from market, and I yelled at them, "What's wrong with you? Out of the peoples' way, get inside!" They were all in the way, in the way of the pickup truck and the work, so I yelled at all of them and pushed them inside.

And what does that "Hospitality, by God" mean?

That "Hospitality, by God"—I want to separate. It means "Give me room, I want to separate."

And what did you say then?

I went outside and left him there. That's all. I left.

And then what happened?

We were silent for some days, and the matter stayed quiet, that's all.

And afterwards, those words didn't reappear?

No.

When the dispute was over the children, as when he said to you, "You're hitting my boy," is it possible that the women in the house were involved?[2]

If they had been involved in this, we would have separated long ago. They don't get involved in this.

You know, perhaps his wife told him, "The Faqir is punishing our boy"?

---

[1] The Faqir explains this term below.

[2] A common explanation men offer for brothers dividing the household is that it is a result of disputes between the brothers' wives, often stemming from quarrels over their children. This is mentioned again later in the dialogue.

If the women had a say in this, we would have separated as so many others have. The others did so because of their women. Our women don't get involved in these things. If his wife says "What?" to him, he tells her "Quiet." If mine says something to me, I tell her "Quiet. You have no say in this."

What do you mean, she "has no say"?

If you follow what the woman says, you wouldn't even be living here, you'd probably end up in Belgium. [I laughed at this.][3]

Do the two women get along with one another?

Yes, they get along with one another.

They don't fight?

No. And if they do, their fights don't reach us.

Have you ever been present when brothers separated?

Often. It is common.

In which cases, for example?

Most recently, for Si Hsen and his brothers.

Were you present when they were fighting or ...

Even with that family, which is a very secretive one, we were present when they argued, and divided the compound, and measured the land, and apportioned the grain.

What led them to separate?

The women themselves.

How so?

The women were fighting with one another, and each said to her man, "Separate!" "We're the ones who do all the work"; or, "Our kids are the ones who earn all the money"; or, "We have many goods, and they don't"; and so on. And these thoughts begin to stick to the man, until his head begins to swell. He becomes someone who just wants space, a rest; he has no more strength and desires nothing.

BROTHER AND SON ...

Do you have confidence in your brother?

In one way I trust him, and in another I don't.

How so?

There is trust in what he takes to market, and in the money he brings back from it. It's exact. And he takes no money from the house. He has never said, "Give me some money." But whatever he spends on the outside—I don't know where it comes from.

---

[3]My laughter here contributes to the dialogue and implies my approval of what the Faqir has just said and agreement with his corresponding view of women. I could not easily control my agreement or disagreement: his view here I do not normally share, but my laughter was spontaneous and sincere.

You don't know from where

> I don't know, I don't know.

From where might he get it?[4]

My mind has suggested something, but I have only had this idea for about two weeks now. My mind says that perhaps he set aside some money from his outside work, when he was younger, and that perhaps he used it to enter into partnership with Qebbor. That is what my mind is suggesting to me.

I see. Why with Qebbor?

At that time, Qebbor had just begun to buy and sell. And perhaps they did a partnership for some share of that business. I don't know. But he is always spending money.

On what does he spend it?

On the outside, on parties, on women.

And that money couldn't come from the house?

No, no. If it came from the house, I'd notice. It's too much.

Could it come from what he sells at the market?

No, it's too much. He really spends a lot of money. A lot.

You sound as though you have just begun to wonder about this.

Well, you know, just the other day someone told me that he has been spending a lot of money.

And you can't figure out where this money comes from?

No. It's not coming from the house, not from here.

According to your thoughts, do you love your brother?

Well, ah, all things considered . . . from his words—if I think of the answers that he gives, he's nothing.

What do you mean, "he's nothing"?

With reference to his words, when he's angry. But if I think about death, which must occur, about parting from him, he becomes loved. He, or anyone else, or you, and so on. If I think, "We're all going to die, everyone," if I think on Our Master's Law, then everyone becomes loved. Even a beggar.

But if . . . —now I'm not sure of the right words—if you think of him, do you think, "I love that man, we've been through so much together, I really love him." Or do you say, "Well, God made us brothers, for better and worse; that is simply God's work."

Yes, it's like that. And then, I think to myself and say, "Perhaps, later, he will acquire a different sense, better than he has now." But if he is always going to have the sense he has now, what's the good?

When you were younger, how did you treat one another?

As now even, just the same. As now, just the same.

---

[4] I may, in effect, be raising or reinforcing his suspicions here.

When your father died, Ali was just an infant. As you grew up, were you like a father to him, or like a big brother?
Like a big brother, no more.
From the first, did you tell him what to do? You know, tell him, "You, go do that!"
Yes.
And you were the one who sent him to work?
Uh-huh [yes].
Did he go willingly?
When he was small, like l-'Aribi, he did. When he got older, he would do it if he wanted to. If he didn't, he'd tell you: "No, that's not going to work. That's no good." And he just didn't want to. If he's planning to be somewhere else, he'll tell you, "No... I can't do it, that is no good." He won't say, "I don't want to." And at those moments he doesn't seem sure of himself, and then I'm wise to him, to the fact that he intends to go someplace. And I tell him, "Quiet, that's enough, quiet." And I do the thing that he wouldn't do, and I leave him.
Have you ever talked much with one another?
No. We don't exchange words.
Was it always like that between you?
Then, and now too.
When he was younger, were you reserved (hshem) in front of one another?
We are reserved in front of one another now too.
With your son Mehdi, you are also reserved. And you don't speak much with him.
Well, of course. If we exchanged a lot of words, there would be a fight.
A fight?
Uh-huh. Just let the words mount a little and, if he doesn't leave, I do.
Do you love Mehdi?
Well, of course, yes. I love him because of his submission. To the extent of his submission.
I don't understand.
You love a fellow according to the submission that he shows... toward you. Love, let's say, or associations go according to the submission that one evidences. Do you understand?
Perhaps I understand. I'm not yet sure whether I understand or not.
If a fellow gave you a gift, you'll love him equal to his gift.
I see.
If he is patient with you, you'll love him equal to his patience.
I see.
If he takes your troubles upon himself, you'll be fond of him to the extent of those troubles. That's that.
And what distinguishes the relationship between you and your brother from the one between you and your son Mehdi?

The difference is: this one I count as my son, and that one I count as my brother.

But what is the difference in the way that you deal with them, in the way that you deal with your brother on the one hand, and with your son on the other?

We say, in our words, "Your brother is your brother, don't lean upon your friends." Do you understand?

No.

"Your brother is your brother, don't lean upon your friend."

What's that, "don't lean upon your friend"?

You talk to your friend, but there always remains something hidden. But from your brother there is nothing to hide, nor has he anything to hide from you. Brothers.

But you keep things hidden from your brother, and he keeps things hidden from you.

Well, O.K., even with brothers a little is kept hidden. But with friends, you must not give your full faith to one another. But there are people who straight away show their good faith. For instance, the way you and I treat one another. If I deal with someone, and we share good faith, I don't hide anything from him. I speak to him frankly, and he must find his own way. This is so even if he wants to damage me. I hide nothing of what is, and he must find his own way.

But your thoughts on this are atypical and aren't like the thoughts that others have.

Of course, of course. Here is an example. If you want someone's advice about something, and you say to him, "Tell me what to do," one kind of person will say to you, "That's good," but the thing's really not good at all. And one kind of person will say, "Oh, shift for yourself, do as you wish, I don't know." And one kind of person will tell you, "no, no, no, no—*non, non*—it's no good," even if the thing is good. But one kind of person becomes perplexed. He begins to think, as though he was considering it for himself. And then he will tell you, "good" or "not good." And he shows you three ways, "Do this, and if that doesn't work, do this, and if that doesn't work, do this."

I see.

That's all.

And that, you would say, is a good friend.

Yes, that is the fellow who is *famila*.[5] You know, when people have a common objective, like when they are in business together, they are all good. But the fellow who is *famila* is one who wants the best for the other.

---

[5] The concept *famila*, a relatively important one, might not have emerged if I had not pursued this line of questioning, or if I had pursued it in another direction. I might have probed the meaning of *famila* further, but I did not.

Here is another example. There are those who are always on the lookout: whenever he travels on the paths, and he finds thorns, he removes them. He may just be traveling alone; there may be no one to see him do this.

Yes, I've seen you do that.[6]

And there are those who move hedge in order to bound their entire plot, and they let many thorns fall on the paths, and they leave them there. And there are those who see the thorns, and move to avoid them, slowing down until they pass. They don't bring the thorns there, but they just leave them. That's all.

Three types.

Yes, three types. And are they all the same? That can't be. Look—everything is written down by Our Master: the one who leaves the thorns, the one who drops the thorns, the one who removes the thorns. That's like the other example.

O.K. Let's return to Mehdi and Ali. Do you love Mehdi more than Ali?

Well, in one way more, and in one way not.

In what way more, and in what way not?

This can't be measured. [There was a pause.] If someone said ... "Tell us which one you wouldn't part with, which one is more beloved," I'd say, "All of them, all of them."

I see.

I don't want to part with any of them. If you said to me, for example—if you were trying to outsmart me—"The one whom you love less, I'll take away," I'd tell you, "You can't take any of them."

When you think about them, do you love both of them?

I love both of them, but the one who is still young I love more than the one who is grown. For the young one doesn't yet know all things. I say, he must still learn things from me. The grown one can't stand it when I try to show him something. He says to himself that his knowledge is better than mine. Do you understand? That is why the young one surpasses the other. That's all.

That's all?

No more.

Do you remember a couple of weeks ago, when your brother had his friends over in the evening for their weekly party? Why did they spend the evening outside the compound and not inside?[7]

---

[6]My remark was illogical, unintentionally: the meaning of the Faqir's action depends on his performing it alone, and my witnessing it changes its meaning. This is a minor instance of a common anthropological fallacy: to assume that actions performed in the anthropologist's presence are also performed in his absence, and that meaning, in both scenes, is the same. This fallacy occurs frequently on a grander sale, with serious consequences (see chs. 12 and 13).

[7]That evening it had been Ali's turn to host a handful of friends for their weekly

He knows that I don't like that... he understands that all of those things are no good. And he understands that I don't want it.
But
but he's not very smart: hadn't I already laid out the rugs and mats, because I thought the sheikh might stop by? If my brother was smart, once I had spread them all out, he would have stayed. But, he's not smart enough to see that far. His eyes only see four meters ahead, that's all.

You know, he surely tells his friends, when it is his turn to host, that here it is as though he is in prison;[8] that I don't speak with them; that if I'm there, they can't have the conversation that they would like to have.

Would you say that things are better between you now than they were last year?

A little, a little (*quand même*[9]).

What makes you think that?

He works!

He works?

Yes.

You mean, he doesn't argue a lot?

He does his work, that's enough. As for arguing, he always contradicts. Always, when he sees that I want this, he says [the Faqir shook his head, indicating his brother's contrary response].

As, "I don't want that." And has his going outside the house ruined the spirit within his house?

I don't know. I don't...

You mean, it's none of your business?

No, it's not that it is none of my business, but that it doesn't show, that spoiling doesn't show up in the house. There is no one to tell him, no one to show him, that the spirit is ruined or not ruined. It is as though I told you, "Go and leave me alone. Do what you want."

---

party (*zerda;* see Ch. 1, n.13), which would be characterized by heavy eating, much tea drinking, and generally boisterous and shameless behavior. Rather than receive his friends in the *dwiria,* where the Faqir might appear and inevitably dampen their spirits, Ali elected to spread out the reed mats and rugs and lay out the pillows in the open air where we gathered, a short distance outside the compound.

[8]Ali had used the very words, "I feel like I am in prison in my house," to me a few days earlier. On that occasion, at least, the Faqir could not have overheard.

[9]The Faqir uses the French term *quand même* frequently, but believes it to be Arabic, unlike his use of other French words, which he recognizes as such. See ch. 1, n.19.

11

Departure and the Final Dialogue

My wife and I were to leave for New York on 8 August. I wanted to have one final conversation with the Faqir before leaving.

The day before our departure, the Faqir had awakened at 3 A.M. in order to take his crops to market early; he wanted to sell them quickly and then find a mechanic to repair a serious malfunction in one of the irrigation motors. He returned home in the early afternoon, and after lunch we recorded the final dialogue.

In the late afternoon, just before sunset, my wife arrived from the Medina. She spent the evening and night in the *dar* with the other women and the children. I slept, as usual, in the large guest room in the *dwiria*, where the Faqir also slept.

We awakened early the next morning and had a quick breakfast of hot corn broth. As we were preparing to leave, the Faqir took me, alone, back into the guest room. He went over to the locked wooden cupboard in which he stored, among other things, nuts, dates, and clarified butter, which would always be on hand for guests and which he might eat as a snack when he came home at odd hours from the markets. He also kept a box of ready cash there.

He opened the box and offered me two bills, each of one hundred dirhams (approximately fifty dollars in all). "Here, take this. You have given away a lot of money to come here." I responded, "No, Faqir. You yourself have said there shall be no question of money between us." He insisted several times, but so did I. He then offered me a new pair of yellow goatskin slippers, which also lay in the cupboard, although he knew I had my own. I accepted them, saying, "These will be fine for my brother, who has already worn out the pair he bought here when he visited us years ago." The slippers and five liters of local olive oil were the only local goods that my wife and I took away with us.

The Faqir and I went outside where the women were already waiting;

212

the pickup truck, mercifully, was for once arriving on time. We all said our goodbyes and wished one another the assistance of God and a peaceful future.

⊞ BOTH OF US, AND SELF AND OTHER, IN QUESTION

Before the final dialogue, I took some stock of what the Faqir and I had been doing together that summer. We had been involved, in one way or another, in certain incidents: both of us had observed and been party to some of them (the brotherhood meeting, the Amouggar, and the visit from the sheikh, for example), others had occurred when one of us was absent (the visit from the migrant worker, the theft of the bicycle, the fight with Faqir Hmed); in some I had been an active participant, others I had merely witnessed, and one—perhaps the most unfortunate—I had unwittingly facilitated (Zahara's marriage).

The Faqir and I had also found some satisfaction in discussing these incidents. However, all of them could not be discussed in the same way: some we talked about directly and freely, but others I had to approach with discretion; one I felt I could not raise with the Faqir at all.

In any case, in the course of the summer, we had been very much at ease with one another, and we had both sustained our interest and extended our relationship. As for my own feelings, this time I experienced less ambivalence about a number of things than I usually did in Morocco: I had not pushed myself into tasks that others had demanded—neither those called for by professional anthropologists looking for well-designed research projects, nor by Moroccans toward whom I felt little good will; nor had I subordinated the wishes of people I cared about to mine in the stark manner common to many social scientists whose primary purpose is to gather "data."

I had started from rather vague initial motives and prior experiences and had come to focus on a certain number of events and dialogues. In doing this, I felt that the Faqir and I had together been involved in an experience that was emblematic of the relationship between anthropologist and informant and that allowed us to express ourselves quite fully, each taking seriously into account the actions of the other.

Yet, as we progressed through the summer, and through the events and dialogues, I was continually forced to question this experience more deeply. On the most basic level, the timing of the events and dialogues, and of the whole experience, seemed to me inseparable from them. The events only became visible and took shape as time passed, and they were not static once they emerged, but had to be probed, questioned, and constructed. The dialogues, too, clearly developed in time: discussion was prepared, outlined, deepened, reexamined, redirected, closed—all of which had to be seen in proper sequence if one were to retain any hope of appreciating and understanding the experience.

I looked at events and dialogues again and again. It was clear now that happenings were not self-evident, that the questions they invited did not spring solely from the event itself, and that the Faqir's responses were not straightforward answers to my questions. The "objectivity" of the event, the neutrality of the inquiry, and the information contained in the discussion were all called squarely into question. Even more important, perhaps, was that as I questioned the experience, I was also forced to call into question the participants, the Self and the Other—that is, the anthropologist and the informant, and the societies whose interests they carried.

The event, which I defined at first as an incident happening within my and the Faqir's shared experience, lost its solidity over the course of the summer. As I listened to the various parties to an event offer interpretations of it, I did not see a clear, objective story emerge, but rather a number of convincing, internally coherent yet often indubitably opposed versions: specific elements were embedded in different interests and concerns; different backgrounds were drawn; some aspects were put into high relief while others receded. To what extent, then, was an event the same for the different parties to it? Was the anthropologist's vision of it not simply one among many, seen from a unique standpoint against the background of his own particular and societal interests and concerns, and not from a standpoint that had any claim to be more "objective," more true than the others? Was his view of the event more a construction of "reality" than an insight into it, a construction that stemmed from his explicit need to find meaning, to uncover a "topic" that could be probed, later, in more detail.

And I looked more closely at the dialogues. They were no longer instances of a technique the anthropologist used to propose, discuss, and revise the meaning he had initially imputed to the event. The questions, for one thing, did not simply ask for information but, also, defined and structured the event and offered, already, a tentative interpretation of it. Every question was launched from a specific moment in experience, by an anthropologist who had certain personal interests, some intellectual, academic, and practical knowledge of Morocco, a number of his own political, cultural, and social concerns, reflecting those of the society from which he came. In their style, his questions tended to move the informant to wordiness in some places, to terseness in others; the anthropologist would pursue some subjects in detail, others he left completely unexamined; at moments, the questions would promote great freedom in expression, at others they stifled it.

The answers themselves were not simply direct responses to the questions. Although in many instances the Faqir clearly meant to furnish "information," his answers were also launched from his own standpoint, from a particular moment in his own personal, social, and cultural experience. His answers provided, as well, a comment on and assessment of my questions: he might be interested or disinterested in them, open to further talk or reticent, agreeing with me on particular points or differing, approving my whole approach or rejecting it.

Consequently, although I had certainly initiated the whole process of formulating and articulating the meaning of our mutual experience, just as I had initiated our relationship by coming to Morocco in the first place, my control over that meaning was checked by his words and answers just as his hospitality in receiving me into his house had helped to structure my experience in Morocco.

Taken together, these considerations were, to say the least, disorienting. If events were not objectively given, but were constructed by participants with their own interests and concerns; if the Faqir and I, together, were constructing our mutual experience as a product of the complex purposes we each had, including our manifest desire to take the other seriously into account; if in this process we were not uncovering meanings that already existed but were continually creating a new experience, a mutual experience where much was now shared, but also where new differences had arisen and temporarily solidified: I now had to ask to what extent the partners to this experience were still distinct? How had each, carrying initially his own sense of Self and of Other, and his own particular constellation of his society's concerns, conceived of and worked with the other to create this new shared experience? To what extent was this experience, emerging in time and in a specific situation, shared in a complete, coherent, and durable manner? To what extent was the sharing partial, unbalanced, and fleeting?

I had often wondered about this shifting sense of Self and Other during the summer and particularly at certain points in previous dialogues. My questions and remarks, on several occasions, had sounded as though they were not strictly "mine," not simply an extension of my interests: for example, I had agreed with the Faqir on issues that I would have disputed had I been sitting in New York; I had laughed, sympathetically, where previously I would not have; and, of course, I had come to see many things in ways that never would have occurred to me had someone other than the Faqir been sitting across from me. Then, too, the Faqir's answers were not simply "his": often he anticipated my questions, phrased his answers with my purposes in mind, incorporated my questions, in some incomplete and revised way, in his speech.

Where, then, did the Faqir end and Kevin begin? Where, then, did the Self's influence on this shared experience end and the Other's begin? Had we not only seen the objective character of the event disintegrate and the purely personal nature of questions and answers dissolve, but had we also called into question the independence and integral nature of one another and, therefore, on however modest a level, the identity and direction of Self and Other, in their extended senses? Had Self and Other each become, in some uncertain, ill-defined manner, vulnerable to the other? In what ways had each come to embrace and yet, at the same time, reject the other?

The real subject, then, of the final dialogue had to be ourselves and our relationship, had to be Self and Other with regard to one another. Yet the Faqir and I had been discussing this throughout our time together: sometimes referring to our societies, as when we had talked about relations between Moroccans and Europeans; sometimes, more personally, to ourselves, as when the Faqir explicitly invoked our relationship; but, always, we were inevitably commenting on the relationship between us, and between Self and Other, as we made decisions all along to change or pursue certain topics, to question and answer straightforwardly or indirectly, to sustain our conversations and the relationship rather than to break off abruptly.

What could be added to this by explicitly discussing the relationship? What if exploring this relationship verbally, directly, inspired reticence and led to an impasse? What if this relationship, perhaps the fundamental subject of the entire experience, could better be explored by simply looking at it and hearing it again, rather than by talking about it?

To look at it, to hear it again: the relationship would then have to be transformed, in some way, into a text. Would such a text, then, not have to strive for completeness? Would it not need to preserve order and timing and to present the interpreted events, the speakers' questions and answers, the conversations' twists and turns, starts and stops, moments of enthusiasm and patches of boredom? Even if it was impossible to fully realize such aims, was it not necessary to attempt to achieve them?

Yet, within anthropology, there seemed no recognized way to transform such an experience into a text, even though such experiences constitute the very foundation of the discipline and are the key element in anthropology's method. Only very rarely, if at all, can one find a text where the reader can see the anthropologist's effort to define and order experience confronted by the informant's own interpretation; where the informant's views are shown as *responses,* as answers to the anthropologist's questions; where we can see that a crucial part of the informant's experience is the informant's experience of the anthropologist; where the very questions that provoke the informant's responses can themselves be critically examined; where the creation of new, shared meaning can be seen; where the central question of the effect of anthropologist and informant on one another is raised.

To pose such questions, to seek a text that might challenge traditional views regarding the objectivity of the event, the neutrality of anthropological inquiry, and the invulnerability of the anthropologist, would necessarily be to challenge anthropology itself and its role as the preeminent intellectual arena for articulating the encounter between people of different cultural backgrounds. It would also, inevitably, lead one to challenge the very validity of what one and one's own society had been doing. This was a challenge I would ultimately have to raise, and a kind of text I would certainly have to seek, now that my experience in Morocco had led me to them.

But, for the moment, I was more immediately concerned with how the Faqir and I might discuss our relationship and the relationship between Self and Other. Although I expected that there would be a natural shifting between topics, I planned to open the dialogue by asking the Faqir, first, about his views of himself ("The Faqir himself..."); then about his thoughts concerning my initial period in Morocco ("Early thoughts about me..."). Then I would ask, more specifically, about his attitude toward my work and my being with him ("Thoughts about my actions..."), about his views of himself as a Muslim ("Being a Muslim... reaching heaven..."), and, finally, about his view of the dialogues and the things we had talked about that summer ("The dialogues...").

🔀 THE FINAL DIALOGUE

THE FAQIR HIMSELF...

Now, I'd like you to think this over a little. I mean, don't answer immediately, without thinking. If people in my country said to me, "Show us the life, and the character, of one person whom you know very well," I would show them your life, your character. What would you like me to tell them about you, in a general way?[1]

Tell them what happened, what I've told you here. You have it all here.

I don't mean events, such as when you were born, or when you began to fast. But with reference to you yourself, in general.

But what has happened is what has happened. That's what there is. What is recorded there, that's what you should tell them.[2]

I mean, for instance, what kind of a man are you?

I didn't become a man until the latter part of my life. In the beginning, I was good, I was a man. In the middle, I was no good: for about eighteen to twenty years my life was in disarray. And from then till now, again, praise God, it's satisfactory.

What makes you say that now you are "satisfactory"?

Now, my mind is satisfactory, praise God. I never lie to anyone. And

---

[1]In this question, I not only recommend that the Faqir reflect before answering, that he *prepare* his answer rather than simply deliver it, but I also specify a potential audience for his thoughts.

[2]Whatever doubts I may be having at this point about "objective" events and about the way people perceive, define, and construct events, the Faqir clearly has none. I may also see certain problems in transforming our talks into a text; the Faqir for the moment sees none, but he will revise his view later in this chapter and upon my return to Morocco in the winter of 1978–79 (see the preface).

whatever road I take, I take it in good faith, whether it's a good road or a bad one. Even if I go on a bad road, I go in good faith; I don't go there lacking in good faith.

For example?

For example? You, for instance, say: "I went to this empty gathering, although I didn't really want to. I went there lacking in good faith." Not me, I go in good faith whether it is an empty gathering or a full one.[3]

I still don't understand that too well.

For example, when I am on a good road, I am in good faith, and when I am on a bad road, I am in good faith. Even on a bad road I deal straightforwardly with my companions. Even if they aren't, I am still going in good faith.

And what else should I tell people from my country?

Well, now you have what appears in my behavior. The things that happened, you already know them. And the situations—how I was a farmer, how I was a worker—you know them. There was just that one thing left, and now you have that too. Wherever I act, even if I went on the road of fornication, I was in good faith: I don't frequent this fellow today, that fellow tomorrow, and another one the day after. If I don't find fault with someone, I won't separate from him.

Do you see your life as having some underlying order?

Good faith orders my entire life; all my thoughts work in that way. And I find good people even along a path that is no good.

You find good people?

Yes. They don't abandon me, and I don't separate from them, even along a path that is not a pretty one. They don't keep anything from me and I don't keep anything from them.

You said that in the beginning you were on a good road, in the middle on a bad one, and at the last part good again. What was the reason for that detour in the middle?

It was for enjoyment and sex.

But what caused it?

Well, it comes from the force in your body and from getting the habit of having a good time. And from smoking.[4] I liked that pleasure and would say, "Tomorrow, again."

If you think about the past and about what you have done, might you say, "It would have been better had I not done that, better had I done something else"?

All things considered, that very path, those twenty years, better I had stayed home and paid attention to my work.

---

[3]The Faqir is putting forward a crucial distinction between my behavior and his, as he sees them.

[4]The Faqir was referring to the smoking of kif, which he had frequently done in his youth. This is a subject I did not pursue in the talks we had that summer.

Do you consider those twenty years wasted, or did you gain something from them?

No, I gained something from them. During those twenty years I went with a lot of people, I got to know a lot of people. Those who were upright, I knew them as upright; those of seven days, I knew as of seven days; and he of two days I knew as of two days; and he of a month I knew as of a month. And those of "just meet and leave," I knew them too.

Did you gain anything else?

That's all. There is nothing else to be gotten from that, nothing else.

And what do you think that others think about you? Si Hassan, for example, what might he think of you?

I reckon that he would always want me to be with him and to go around with him. But he doesn't find me with him any more, no more at all. He would very much like to go around with a person like me, but he doesn't succeed, he doesn't find one. Such a person would never frequent him.

And Sessy, what might he say about you?

He would like me to go around with him too, but because I don't, he says, "The Faqir is no good." He knows what I'm like, that's all.

And the sheikh?

The sheikh too. But if there is going to be some shady dealing, he won't want me there. He would love me to be with him if it's a good situation. But where there is something unclean, consuming people's money or whatever, he will say, "Let's do without the Faqir."

And what do you think that I think about you? What might I say to myself about you?

You're the one who understands that. Why, am I going to enter into your head?

But you can't enter the sheikh's head, or Si Hassan's, yet you said something about what they might think of you.

I don't know. That—I don't know about it. I don't know about that.

All right. [This was a somewhat uncomfortable moment.][5] **And what differences do you see between yourself and the other people of the region?**

Why, there are many kinds of people. What, are all of the people from this region the same? You know, of our neighbors here in the village, there are people who are like me and those who are better than me, whose work is good.

---

[5]The question "What do you think that I think about you?" was too direct an approach to the subject of my relationship with the Faqir, and he refused to answer, despite my insistence and my pointing out that he had answered similar questions regarding the views others had of him. I was well aware of the crucial difference and so, obviously, was he: *I* was posing a question about *our* relationship, not about his relationship to a third party; here, the Faqir would not be drawn into an answer.

Well, what differences do you see between the behavior in your house and in other houses?

I don't have a picture of that. Each to his own with what he does.

But don't you know what goes on in other houses?

I know a little about that but,... oh... it's all the same, the practices are all alike.

So nothing seems different to you here from what others in the village do?

The villagers aren't all the same. There are some houses run by the women. And there are those run by the men. And then there are those run by neither the men nor the women, where everything is mixed.

If you think about it, what would you still like to do in your life?

I want to do what I'm doing now, that's all.

Don't you think of things that you would still want to do?

Well, if I found a lot of money, of course I could do something with it.

For example?

With a lot of money I could get something that I've never obtained. But if Our Master leaves us as we are, praise God. We have everything; there is no problem.

But if it happened that you found a lot of money?

If God brought us some money... we could use a tractor right now, and a large irrigation motor with a pump. Or a diesel pickup truck. Why, we could use a lot of things.

And how about going on the Pilgrimage?

With the will of God.

I mean, is the Pilgrimage on your mind now?

Yes, it is on my mind, because the Pilgrimage is one of our duties. If a fellow has the wherewithal, he must make the Pilgrimage. For me, now, it is an obligation. But I'm cooling my heels. I say, "Later, later, later."

Is that some sort of sin?

Well, all things considered, the Pilgrimage is a duty, that's true. But when I think about it, I say, "Until tomorrow." When the day for decision comes, I say, "Until tomorrow."

But, look how much time you spend every day on religion. You do the prayers, and the brotherhood litany, and the office. Why do you say "Until tomorrow" for the Pilgrimage?[6]

Tomorrow the kids will be able to take care of the work here and there will be spare time. And the house will have to be in good shape, because whoever goes on the Pilgrimage has a large celebration. And the bones should feel good, and one should be healthy. And all affairs should be settled: we say, "settledness."

[6]In the preceding questions, it is almost as though I am trying to convince the Faqir to go on the Pilgrimage to Mecca.

Have you talked to people about going on the Pilgrimage?

No, no. A fellow doesn't talk about the Pilgrimage until it's near. Until there remains a month, or two months, or at least until that year has begun. Then he begins to think about the Pilgrimage.

And before you go, would you go and talk about the Pilgrimage to someone like l-Hajj Hmed?

Yes, l-Hajj, or Si Hassan, or others. Because he who makes the Pilgrimage has to go to everyone he knows and say to them, "Peace upon you, and forgiveness." For he may die and perhaps his body will never even be found. It's like when you leave, now, "Peace upon you, and forgiveness."[7]

And we say, in our laws, "He who doesn't tell you of his departure, do not wish peace upon him."

How's that?

When someone departs without taking his leave, do not greet him with "Peace upon you" when he returns.

That is, if I leave and do not say to you, "I'm going

then I too, won't say to you, "Peace upon you," when you come back. That's the example. But today, the Arabs have no use for this example. They say, "Peace upon you," no matter what the situation. But that's the true way, that's in truth. If you and I were going around together, and I just left without telling you, I would have to act as though I hadn't really been absent.

O.K.

EARLY THOUGHTS ABOUT ME...

Now, I'd like you to think about this question. When I came here for the first time, when Bukhensha brought me here, what did you think then?

I wasn't thinking anything. Just, "welcome," that's all. What would be on my mind?

You must have thought something.

No.[8]

Let's see ... what did Bukhensha say to you then?

Well, he said it in front of you: "All things considered, this Rumi wants to come here and wants to rent your little room in the village. I have

---

[7]My departure, in the Faqir's view, creates a discontinuity in our relationship similar to that created when people leave for the Pilgrimage. The Pilgrimage, and my departure, carry with them the possibility of never returning, and the idea of finality, of definitive departure, is an important element in views of the Pilgrimage: not only must the pilgrim say goodbye to everyone, but he should also ensure that all his affairs are in order and that his family can sustain itself should he never return.

[8]This question leads to an immediate dead end. But it is an important issue, and I pursue it further by entering into detail.

gotten to know him, and I am making his concerns mine. He told me, 'I want to go to a village in the countryside.' I thought about you and about your empty room, and that perhaps you would rent it to him, and he would be able to live in it."

I thought then that you would come to live here with your wife. When you came, I showed you the room and I told you, "Here is the dwelling." Then I told you, "Living in this room is no good." Do you remember? *Vaguely.*

I said to you, "It would be better to come and live in our house." You said, "No. Why?" And I told you: "That room is far from here. And you don't know how the kids in the village will behave. In any case, traveling back and forth so much isn't good."

And when I first came here, what did you figure I would be doing here?

I didn't think about it. What could I figure? In any case, I didn't know. But we know that those things are of many sorts.

What do you mean?

We know about writing down what people do and about... writing down secret things. There are those who are, you know, spies, and there are those who write down what we do.

And what if I were a spy?

That's no concern of mine, that is the government's. Once you have the permission of the government, what do I care?[9] Let the government take care of its own business. What do I care?

But did you say to yourself: "Ay, ay, ay. This is going to be a real bother now. Someone will be coming to us, an outsider. We don't even know him, and he'll be eating with us"? What did you say to yourself?

But we hadn't talked about your eating here yet, or about an outsider coming to us. We had just talked about a room for you to live in: you up in the village and us down here. Why, what's the matter with you, are you *fou* or something? [The Faqir was mocking my lapse of memory.]

What did you think my relationship to the government was?

I wondered if you weren't a fake.

What do you mean?

If you were doing not what you said you were, but some other work that you and the government were in on together, with me on the outside. But you had obtained their permission, so that was none of my business. Do good work, or work as you deserve; fend for yourself.

And if you hadn't wanted me here, if you had said to yourself, "What do I need this for?" could you simply have said, "I don't want to rent you the room"?

Without a doubt. If it had seemed that something might cause me trouble, say with regard to the government or, perhaps, some treachery

<hr>

[9]To do research in Morocco at that time required formal permission from the Moroccan Ministry of the Interior.

or whatever, I would have said: "No, I can't rent that room to you. I've told someone else he can live in it. And I can't be lying to him." That would be all. And after all, I never charged you any rent for that room.

That's true.

And before I settled in here, did the qaid say anything to you?

[The Faqir yawned.] The qaid said: "Be careful, a Christian is going to come to your village. The sheikh and the moqaddems will be paying attention. No one should be disrespectful to him and no one should pick a quarrel with him. People should be upright and honorable with him."

What did he mean, "Be careful"?

"Don't joke around with him, don't provoke him, don't insult him, don't curse him. . . . Deal fairly with him, or take leave of him." That's all.

Did you ever speak to the qaid about me after I arrived?

Why, I never went to see him at all after that case I had over the water rights, and that was before you came.

Did people in the village ask you about me?

Yes. They asked, "What's he doing, what is his work?"

Si Hassan, for example, what did he think?

He just asked me once, that's all. He didn't keep at it. The others were saying, "He's surely doing some treachery . . . surely spying, and so on and so on." I paid no attention to that. It didn't matter to me.

But you didn't really know what I was doing then, at the beginning.

What am I supposed to do, beat them up? What did I care? Let them say what they want, let them fend for themselves.

You mean you have to tolerate what they say?

It has nothing to do with tolerance; I'm not patient with them. If someone who is my friend questions me, I tell him what you do. And someone who comes here sees what you do, I don't even have to tell him. But those who want to go on and tell tales, let them do it. What do I care? There is nothing that ties me to them.

Well, what kind of people in the village seemed to have no confidence in me and said, "That one is a spy"?

All of them. A guy like Si Hassan, you know, had some trust in you. But l-Hajj, for example, for a long time had no good will toward you.

Do you remember when someone went to the qaid and accused me of scheming with the sheikh? What was that all about?

There was that problem. And then you caused the sheikh another problem.

Tell me about them.

First there was the trouble when Si Tahar and the sheikh were disputing. Si Tahar went to the qaid himself and told him: "That Christian and the sheikh are spending all day in the marketplace, writing things down. I don't know what they're intending, I don't know what they're doing." Tahar thought that the qaid was ignorant, that he knew nothing.

I see. As though the sheikh and I were stirring up some trouble. How was that settled?

The qaid told the sheikh: "Be careful. Si Tahar is out to get you, he is saying this and that about you. He thinks I don't know what the Christian is doing. So he told me this and this and this." The qaid said this to the sheikh, so that was no problem. But the sheikh had another problem with you.

What was that?

Once you went to the qaid. And after you, the sheikh went in to the qaid. And the qaid began to talk to the sheikh looking at him with red eyes. [The Faqir scowled, imitating how the qaid must have looked.] And the qaid began to talk to him in a special manner, in a certain way. As though when you had been with the qaid, you had said something to him about the sheikh.

As though I had said something bad about the sheikh?

About the sheikh... "The sheikh and I have talked about this and this." As though you had told him about those discussions that you and the sheikh used to have, when you and he would sit and talk about "New York"[10] and so on. And the sheikh suspected that you had told the qaid, "The sheikh knows about this, and about this, and about this." Because it seemed that you had told the qaid, and that the qaid knew what was in your notebook.

I see.

And the qaid had changed his manner toward the sheikh, although he hadn't said anything to the sheikh straight out. The sheikh just found him in a bad mood, found him a bit changed. The qaid asked, "What's that Christian's name?" And "How is it going with him? All right?" And "How is his behavior?" But the qaid was looking at him with red eyes, and the sheikh became suspicious. He began to doubt you.

As though he was thinking

that you had told the qaid what you and the sheikh talked about. Because you and he would talk about New York and your government, and so on. We talked about all such things here.

Yes, I know. So, the sheikh

became suspicious.

---

[10]The term *New York* had become the Faqir's code word for discussions of world politics. The Faqir knew very little about this subject. He would hardly ever listen to the radio and never watched television: in both media, news transmissions are in modern standard Arabic, which differs considerably from colloquial Moroccan and which the Faqir understood very poorly. The sheikh, on the other hand, was very knowledgeable about events in other countries, and when he and I were together, talk would range far and wide, from discussions about U.S. politics to events in the Middle East. The Faqir jokingly referred to all this conversation as talk about "New York."

He probably thought, "That fellow is tell-ing the qaid everything that we say."

Yes. I told the sheikh, "That is impossible."

What did he answer?

He said, "It's possible that he said something to the qaid." I told him, "That would never happen. That's not so."

Did he think I was involved in some intrigue?

No, not an intrigue. He said, "It's as though he told the qaid what we say." As though you told the qaid of that understanding that the sheikh has, as though you said all that to the qaid.

What I think I said to the qaid was, "The sheikh and I have talked, and I find that he has a good head on his shoulders."[11] And now, as you're telling me about this, I'm saying to myself, "It's better that I don't visit the qaid anymore."

Why not go to the qaid?

Because—I don't know—I say one thing, and by the time it gets to the sheikh, it sounds like something else.

That's true, yes.

And

and, you know, if you go to the qaid, he's going to say, "You said . . ." even if you didn't say anything. That's the thing.

So, it's better if I never go there again. You know I don't want trouble for you, and visiting the qaid has never been a thing I enjoyed anyway.

Was this the reason that the sheikh no longer visited you?

Oh no, no. It was because of that dispute we were having over the road. Not at all because of you. What, are you kidding?[12]

THOUGHTS ABOUT MY ACTIONS . . .

Could you explain to me what you think I'm doing here?

My thoughts about that are what you've told me yourself, that's what I've put in my thoughts. What you write down is what you understand, and you try to understand a lot, so that you make the others understand, those whom you teach. That is as far as my thoughts go.

Well, I ask you about a lot of things. **To your mind, what is the most important subject that we talk about? You know, for some subjects you might say to yourself, "What is the sense of talking for so long about such a thing?" Or, on the other hand, you might think, "Oh, that's really interesting."**

As for me, I know that I'm not concerned with a single one of your questions. I know that these questions serve your purposes, not mine. I

---

[11]This remark now strikes me as patronizing and presumptuous.

[12]If the illusion was growing that I had an important effect on political action at the local level, the Faqir here clearly disabuses me of it.

think about the questions, whether they are small questions or large ones, and I think about them because they serve your purposes, not mine.

Well, what do you like me to ask you about?

It doesn't matter to me, you could even ask me about snakes.

But on some subjects your talk is more enthusiastic, more lively, as though you felt, "Ah, this is something I like to talk about."

If I had the time, I would always talk, I've told you that. Even about turtles. This is your goal, not mine.

But let's say I started to question you about, say, that pillow you're leaning on. Perhaps I'd ask, "How is the sewing done?"

Yes.

And how much does the thread cost?

Hmmmm.

And how are the flowers sewn?

Fine.

And are the colors natural ones?

Yes. We'd finish all that, and then go on to talk about the stuffing inside the next pillow. All of this is good, all of it, because it serves your purposes. But for me, not one single thing serves mine.[13] That's all there is to it. But it's good, because it's good for you. That's that.[14]

But if I continued in that way, you might get bored.

If I'm bored, or if I have work, I'd say, "O.K. [sic] Until next time."

And what if we started on a subject that began to turn bad?

But I asked you about this that day. I said to you, "What if the talk is not good?" And you said, "If it's bad, we'll turn the recorder off," if we want to continue talking about it.[15]

I don't like to talk about those things.

---

[13]The Faqir had said almost the exact same thing, that his work was important for others and not for him, when he described his term as village moqaddem (ch. 9).

[14]The preceding portion of dialogue, beginning with the question "Could you explain to me,..." has already been published in Dwyer (1977). In that article I saw this text as important because "the Faqir has been asked to conceptualize and evaluate my project, and to juxtapose that project with his own" (1977, p. 144). I then summed up his view by stating: "The Faqir has refused to identify with the specific implementation of my project, while at the same time establishing a fundamental bond between us by accepting this project as mine and, on that basis, acting positively for its fulfilment. He renounces a discriminating attitude towards the partial and incomplete implementation of my intent [i.e. towards my specific questions], while actively working to bring that intent to fruition" (1977, p. 145).

[15]We have just pointed out two possible ways to interrupt and break off our conversation. Although in the course of the summer the Faqir did not ask that the tape recorder be turned off at particular moments, the decision not to do so, the decision to continue, has been made in one way or another throughout the dialogues; such decisions are essential to the meaning of the dialogues.

O.K. But when you're sitting with your friends—with the sheikh or with those people you are fond of—there are some things you like to talk about, and some that you don't. Why do you say, for example, that the talk of your brother and his friends is "empty"? What makes their talk empty, and the other talk "full"?[16]

You've seen their speech. Why is it empty? Well, they just say, "Oh, so-and-so did . . ." or "You fed me this" or "I fed you that": things that only have to do with the stomach. Or "Hey, you ass, hey you bitch, hey!" Why, do we speak that way? And with them, doesn't the meat fly around the table? Everyone is trying to get as much as he can, they don't split it up. Do we grab for the meat that way? With them, everyone talks and grabs for it. And, in the middle of the meal, they get up, "Hey you ass, you bitch. *Tffu!*"

O.K. Now what is better in your speech?

You understand that yourself, you know what is better about it.

I know what I think about it, but I want to hear your thoughts.[17]

My thoughts are that they talk only about things that cloud the mind. "I ate enough" or "I didn't eat enough"; or "I outsmarted you" or "you outsmarted me"; or "We did that thing" or "We will do that," and that thing is no good. We don't say such things.

Well now you're telling me what is empty in their speech, but you still haven't said what is full in yours.

We question about religion, about things like that. And about our holy Moses and our holy Jesus; and about what the qaid said and what the sheikh said; and about how work is going and whether people are suffering or not. Those are the limits of our words.

They just say, "I ate, I didn't eat; I outsmarted you, I didn't outsmart you." Or "She did this" or "She didn't." Or "She stole" or "She didn't." Or "I saw her do this" or "She didn't."

So, if you and I talk about religion, or about history, or about the work of the sheikh: is that better than if we talk, say, about that reed mat and how it's made?

Talking about the reed mat is good too, that makes a good subject, that would be a nice conversation. [I chuckled.][18] There is no offense in its relationship to God. If we wanted to construct a mat, I'd show you

[16]I have now changed the topic from his evaluation of my project back to a subject raised in "The Faqir himself . . .": an evaluation of his project with respect to that of others in his society.

[17]Here the Faqir is refusing to play the role of "informant" instructing the anthropologist and has said, in effect: "These things are self-evident to any righteous human being and you claim to be one. Therefore, you must know the answer." But I insist and take refuge in an "anthropological" attitude. The Faqir, then, gives in.

[18]I laughed somewhat uncomfortably, because I now saw that I had missed his point and not correctly grasped his distinction between "empty" and "full." I had drawn an unwarranted parallel between empty talk and the details of making a reed mat, betraying my own unstated preference for "deeper," more philosophical issues, over detailed, minute explanations.

how we do it. If I had the equipment here, I could show you everything about its manufacture. When we had the equipment, I used to make them here in this very room. But now we don't have the equipment. But it is good to talk about the reed mat—the reed mat isn't said to be "orphaned by God."

Would you enjoy it more if we talked about the government, or about a pen—how the pen is made, and so on?

It's all fine, whether or not it's about the government. If we were able, we should talk about everything in this world.

When I lived in that room in the village, that first time I was here, I spent most of my time in the village. Now, I don't go there much at all; I stay at your place for four or five days in a row, without ever leaving.

Yes.

What effect has that had on your house? For example, when I'm not here, you all eat in the dar. Why, when I'm here, don't we all eat in the dar?

What, eat in one small room, with the children making all that noise? Sometimes we don't even spread out the furnishings: we just eat without sitting, and go on our way. And most often, even if the others eat in the dar, I still eat here. For dinner, I don't even eat there. They bring my dinner here.

You eat alone?

Yes. I eat here and then go to sleep.

And the rest of them all eat in the dar?

They eat there. And such noise: the kids go around fighting and yelling, "'ah! 'ah!'" What do we want that noise for? What, would the kids let us talk? Never!

So, we're not eating in the dar *because of your wishes or because of my wishes?*

Because of all of our wishes.[19] And that way, the women don't hear us. There is talk that the women shouldn't hear. What if we wanted to talk and the women would hear it? That should not be.

That's no good.[20]

No, that should not be. And they want to talk too, and we would hear their talk. That also should not be. Why?

What else changes now that I'm here?

That's all. Nothing else but that.

Think a little. Isn't there something

Nothing. There is nothing that changes—nothing, nothing. That's all.

If you and your brother are disputing, do you tone that down when I'm here?

---

[19]Although I have initiated and structured much of the interview situation, the Faqir, too, has clearly made important decisions in this respect.

[20]I agree with the Faqir here, although I certainly would not if the conversation were with someone from New York.

We don't decrease anything. What there is, is, whether you're here or whether you're not. Wherever the event happens, it's the same.[21]

Do you speak less in front of the others when I'm here?

It's just the same, I always speak a small amount.

Always?

Hmmm.

Do you speak less to your sons?

With them I always speak a small amount, because they don't have thoughts.

If you search your mind now, you don't see anything else that changes when I'm here?

No. Just the meal that moves from there to here, that's all.

And even when I'm not here, most of the time you still
eat here. Yes. Because in the evenings, I don't go over there at all.

You know, my customs are unlike yours, and when I came here I didn't know your practices at all. Do I do things that annoy you, that anger you, that you don't find good?

No. You always ask. Whenever you want to do something, you always ask, you say, "Can I do this?" You don't just go on your own thoughts, you always go according to mine. If you didn't ask, you might do something wrong.[22]

Are you just being polite with me, or what? I don't really know.

Well, up to now you've done nothing.

Do you prefer it when we work with a notebook or with a tape recorder?

For me, they are both the same. In both cases, it's *my* tongue that has to do the talking. You're the one who has to decide which is better. What I do in both cases is exactly the same. I don't do the writing, and I don't work the tape recorder.

So in both cases, you just talk, you don't
There is one thing, though, that distinguishes the recorder from the notebook. If we were discussing something suspect, or if you had some scheme on your mind, I wouldn't want to work with the recorder. In this the notebook is better, because it is somewhat artificial. It just has your own thoughts. But the recorder is

---

[21]The Faqir again rejects my questioning of the "objective" nature of reality and here attributes no importance to the role the anthropologist may play in forming or influencing the event. (See also ch. 11, n.2.)

[22]The reasons the Faqir gives here for approving my actions are similar to those he has offered in chapter 10 regarding the tie between love and submission (p. 208) and between love and a willingness to learn (p. 210). Both of these aspects should also be seen in conjunction with his previous discussion about the good faith and frankness between us.

sneaky, it doesn't take down falsely, it takes down reality. What is said is taken down.

But I think we're not saying anything suspect, and I think that you wouldn't take down something with the recorder that would hurt me, or with the notebook either. That would hurt me in any way. And that's why they are both the same for me.

But was there ever a time when you suspected me?

For me, there is no longer any doubt. If I reach the point of getting together with someone many times, it means that I no longer have any doubts.

But, you know, it is said, "One third of what is unknowable is inside men's heads."

I don't have any doubts about you. My mind tells me, and my heart tells me, that between you and me there is no longer any suspicion.

But above this idea, there is another one. There are two thoughts here. We want support from the Master who bore us. It is my behaving in good faith that will lead me to this. I can't count on your good faith. I rely on God and on my good faith, which directs me.

Because your good faith isn't going to benefit me, what benefits me is mine. So I have to struggle with myself to make mine good, and I don't struggle to make yours good. If you are lacking in good faith, the Lord will strike you, if not this year, then the next year, or the next year, or the next. Or he won't strike you at all until we all go before God the Almighty and are judged. Then we'll get our due.

I rely on God, and on my good faith, which I struggle for. You are on your own.

What if I started to appear suspect to you—then what?

If you began to appear no good, then I would slow down with you. My good faith toward you would decrease. But there is another thing here. If you were a Moroccan, I would know straight off whether or not you were good. But if you do something that is no good, I wonder if perhaps the customs of Europe, of America, are different in this from the customs of the Arabs. If you did something bad, I'd say to myself, "Perhaps in their country that thing is good."

So, if you saw me do something bad you would

I'd tolerate it until later, and then I'd try to get it explained. I'd ask: "Why was that? Did you forget how to do it? Are your country's customs like that?" And so on.[23]

And do you remember anything like that that I did?

No, no, I told you already, what are you making such a mistake for? Are you trying to outsmart me? What, even if you had twice as much

---

[23]The Faqir, too, has a certain "anthropological" perspective.

intelligence as you have, you couldn't outsmart me [the Faqir laughed].[24]

The first time that I was here, I spent a long time, about a year and a half. What were your thoughts when I left?

Well, I thought, "God help me, and God help you." You went off to do your work, and I stayed to do mine. And we parted in good will: I hadn't tried to outsmart you, and you hadn't tried to outsmart me. There was no problem.

Did you think to yourself, "Well, this fellow is never going to come back here"?[25]

I thought you might return, with the help of God, as we said when we had talked about this. You had said, "I'm not certain that I will return,— if I have a chance to, with the help of God." As you say, "With God", so I say, "With God."[26]

Now, for myself, I don't say, "I'm going to go to America." I say, "I'm not going." But if God the Almighty gives some cause for it, I might go. Because everything is the Lord's. Then I could obtain a passport and base it on my farming.[27] I wouldn't be going to look for work, I'd just be going to look around. I could do it even now, and just go and look around.

So do it.

---

[24]The Faqir knows well that I sometimes take several paths to get an answer, and he laughed sympathetically yet at the same time scoffed at my technique.

The previous portion of dialogue, beginning with, "You know, my customs are unlike yours..." was published in Dwyer (1977). In that article I commented: "In the discussion concerning notebook and tape recorder, the theme of the Faqir's acceptance of my total project is restated. At the same time, I now appear to submerge my judgment of his partial behavior in a way that corresponds to his attitude toward mine: just as he always responds without discrimination to my inquiries, I always ask his advice before acting.

"Beyond this, his discussion of behaving 'in good faith' indicates that his abrogation of craft and mistrust, his acceptance of my total project, is but one moment in a higher quest which defines his own project. On the level of partial action, the [Faqir's] suspension of judgment and the submergence of self for the other become preconditions for the transcendence of the partial self, for the realization of self on the higher level of total project.

"Just as importantly, this partial submergence of self for the other is facilitated by the presence and creation of a certain kind of other, one towards whom a sort of 'willing suspension of disbelief' can be maintained. A Moroccan, for the Faqir, is too obviously good or bad, his behavior is too transparent for interaction to provide an arena in which the important struggle, the struggle for his good faith through the other, can be carried forward" (1977, pp. 145–46).

[25]This continues the topic opened earlier, in "Early thoughts about me...."

[26]I have evidently moved somewhat into the Faqir's world by utilizing the notion "God" in ways the Faqir approves of.

[27]In order to obtain a passport, a Moroccan must show that he continues to be tied to Morocco by certain important interests and does not intend to leave the country definitively.

That was just an example. We were just imagining if there was money, and if the time was propitious, and if I was in a good mood for it, I could go. But the way things are now, I've got just enough money to take the trip, but then if something happened I'd be without relief. No.

As I think about it . . .

Or, if you'd begun to sprout wings, you a little, and me a little, then there would be no problem. But your treasury is still a bit small, and you have as yet no children. And no land. And your apartment is rented. And I should take what I have—seventy thousand rials or eighty thousand rials—and travel with it? The guy who starts out on that road has no sense. I'd need another seventy or eighty thousand for emergencies. A guy doesn't know what the Lord might bring and he should carry with him a lot to spare.

Perhaps if I was a landowner, and was able to invest my money in my land, perhaps then I too would not be in a position to spend sixty thousand or seventy thousand on this trip.

And when I returned here, the year before last, what did you think then?

I said, "That guy is of good spirit. He remembers what our being together was like." Because, one remembers what is important, not just what brings benefit. There are those who will remember a guy only as long as they get rewards from him. Once that is cut off, they forget. Or when they find a better reward, they forget the first. But some people remember probity, remember comradeship.

What do you mean, "comradeship"?

Fellowship: where there is no lying, no fooling one another, where people remain tied together for ever. That is, if you find no fault with me, you'll remain tied to me like your own property is tied to you. You'll always think of that.

And also, in the sayings of the Arabs, we say, "He who has died . . . whom people still talk about—it's as though he hasn't died, as though he was still alive."

And when I'm not here, do people still talk about me?

Yes. You know, just the other day, I went to "44" and that artisan— that black one—said to me, "Has that Christian come this time?" And I told him, "He's here right now; he has just come!" And he said to me, "Greet him for me." And if anyone comes to visit here, they always ask, "Have you heard from that Christian, has he sent you a letter, is he going to be coming again soon?"

You know, when I work with some of the villagers, when I spend time with them asking questions, I usually give them some money per hour. But you won't accept money from me.

I don't permit it. Why, I could take more money from you than they do. I could take more than just money. If I wanted to, I could get you to

give me anything, even your winter jellaba. But I just want Our Master
to give me my allowance and to give you yours.

So, you don't want to take from me.

No. And also, it would be shameful, to go around after you, to take
from you every day. "Give me, give me, give me," when I already have
enough. If I didn't, then there would be nothing wrong in taking from
you.

But, you know, I keep you from

and what if you do?

I don't allow you to do

It has nothing to do with allowing or
not allowing. Why, if I had something else to do, I would go and do it.
Money would not keep me with you. I am not concerned about your
money for a moment.

I see.

Faqir Hmed, on the other hand, needs the money. He has children,
and it's true, he needs those hours from you.

And he's poor.

And he's poor. And he's an excellent fellow too, . . . he's a good person. Sometimes, though, his mouth gets bad. When he becomes angry,
that defect of his immediately shows itself. But he's an excellent man. He
spends a lot of money on his children—everything that comes in he
spends on them. And he doesn't go out to other women. And he takes
care of you if you go to his home as a guest—both he and his mother do.
It's just that if you get into an argument with him, his mouth becomes
bad.

BEING A MUSLIM . . . REACHING HEAVEN . . .

**What differences do you see between yourself and the other people around
here?**[28]

The others, they all follow their advantage. If they are going to glean a
profit, then they will keep their appointments. Otherwise, there is nothing you can do with them.

And you?

Me, I go according to my pledge, not according to my advantage. If I
hang around with someone, perhaps I'll get something from it, perhaps
I won't. We'll stay together as long as there remains integrity. For example, why did you, before this, always spend so much time in the village,
and now you are almost always here?[29]

---

[28]This repeats a question I posed earlier, in "The Faqir himself. . . ."

[29]The Faqir here turns the tables on me, and again contrasts my "bad faith" and
my behaving according to the demands of traditional anthropological research tasks, with

234 / A "RECORD" OF FIELDWORK

*Well, I've told you this already. Before this, I had to pass an examination, in order
to finish my studies. And to pass that, I had to learn as much about everything in
the village as possible. I had to ask all those questions about land holdings. And I
had to talk to people I didn't like. Now I can do what I want to and talk to whom I
want to. And that's why I stay here.*

So, before this you followed your advantage. You went to people in
less than good faith, which I try never to do. Now you go according to
your pledge.

According to you, what do you have to do to reach heaven?

I have to . . . always take the good path, and never lie to people. And
never consume what is someone else's.

**But what is the difference between Muslims and Christians? If you are a
Muslim, is it easier for you to reach heaven?**

Yes. But easier only because the Muslim has the witnessing of the
Messenger of God. But if the Muslim lies, and steals, and is adulterous,
he'll still go to heaven, but before that he'll go to some other place until
he suffers for the amount he has sinned.

And if I'm not a Muslim, but a Christian, how can I reach heaven?

Well, in our books, Jews and Christians don't have heaven. In our
books. But only God knows. For the reason that the Prophet doesn't bear
witness for them. According to our books.

They don't have a heaven?

Not according to our books. But don't hang a lie upon me! I don't
know what is said in your books.

But according to your books, I cannot go to heaven.

Not unless you are working on your good faith. Can I look inside you?
What if you are following the laws of the Prophet, and no one has caught
on to this? There are Christians who do this.

*But I haven't taken the Credo, and if I haven't then I'm not a Muslim, right?
Perhaps I do behave in good faith, and I do what is right, then can I*

                         No. A Christian is a Christian.

I can't go to heaven.

No. According to our books, no. Except for one thing: that is, you
don't even know yourself whether you are a Christian or a Muslim. On
the day you die, your mind might go over to Muhammad the Prophet,
and you might take the Credo. And I wouldn't even catch on to it.

I say I'm a Muslim, and that you are a Christian, but we don't know
that until . . . until we're at death.[30]

---

his "good faith." We have now moved from a comparison of his project with that of others
in his social field, back to the contrast between his and mine. This time, the Faqir has
initiated the shift.

    [30]The preceding portion, beginning "What differences do you see . . ." was cited
in Dwyer (1977). There, I suggested that, rather than adopt the typical anthropological

So, I could be

doing Muhammad's religion even if you knew nothing about it, nothing of our Prophet Jesus[31] and so on. But if you didn't know its practices, you wouldn't perform them. Because no one would give himself that difficulty. Our religion requires difficulty.

How does it require difficulty?

You have to get up early, you have to pray and to cleanse yourself all the time. And you have to give away a portion of what you have. If you have just one loaf of bread—just enough for you and Daisy [my wife]—would you give it to someone else? If someone came to you and said, "For God," would you give it to him?

Well, I'd have to.

But then you and Daisy wouldn't have enough. [The Faqir chuckled at this dilemma.]

------

procedure of *extracting* the informant's cultural views from the dialogue (as I had in my interpretations, given above in notes 14 and 24, of the Faqir's words), we should remain attentive "to the dialogical and temporal character [of the field interaction] . . . and [refuse] to reduce it to monological, atemporal form" (1977, p. 146). In trying to do this, I proposed that this portion of the dialogue "begins with one of my questions which creates otherness by objectifying it.... I reject the Faqir's attempts to provide initial formulations of otherness... in various ways, most often through hypothetical proposals... and factual insistence.... We must recognize that this postponing of reconciliation, this prolonged insistence on otherness, creates an otherness and selfness of a particular sort,... in the sense that within and through the encounter each develops concepts of self and other which do not deny difference but rather affirm, elaborate, and articulate it. Yet, this articulation of difference cannot be divorced from its source in concrete, mutual experience nor reduced to some atemporal and/or soliloquized abstraction from that experience.

"One symptom of this otherness... is that the ultimate possibility of reconciliation between myself and the Faqir, projected forward to the time of entrance into the next world, is generated through the encounter rather than posited independent of it. Only an encounter where the reconciliation of difference is continually delayed can provide newly created potential, from the Faqir's standpoint, for self-realization and for the other's self-transcendence. I, for my part, find it impossible to definitively reject this potential, which epitomizes his project, precisely because it encompasses my project, the possibility of self-transcendence and ultimate reconciliation with the other.... What emerges for the Faqir is a greater potential for self-realization, for me of self-transcendence; for one the development of the self, for the other its mutation" (1977, pp. 147–48).

I then went on to argue that, if my quest was phrased in terms of self-transcendence, and the Faqir's in terms of self-realization, this phrasing was not accidental, but intimately related to the way in which each of us, "within his particular cultural and historical context, phrases his relationship to the world," and to "a world historical situation which [has witnessed], as one face of imperial domination, ... the consequent emergence of "center" and "periphery," and the inequality that has characterized interaction between people from these two spheres" (1977, p. 148).

[31] Muslims admit Jesus as one of their prophets, and Moses too. Moroccans often point to the tolerance in Islam evidenced by its acceptance of the prophets of the Jews and the Christians, and to the narrowness of Judaism and Christianity in not admitting the Prophet Muhammad.

236 / A "RECORD" OF FIELDWORK

Well, better the two of us should go a little hungry. What, should we let him die of hunger?

Like that, like that.

And if a Muslim has lied and committed adultery, where will he spend his time of suffering?[32]

In hell. Until you pay for those sins and until Muhammad takes pity upon you and brings you.

Can someone pay for the sins of someone else?

How could you do that? That's impossible. But if you kill someone, his sins will be added to your sins. That's all.

Everyone is on his own. You have no father, there is no mother. And you have no brothers. Everyone is on his own.

Was there ever a time when jnun entered you life? Did jnun ever do anything to you?[33]

We don't know if that's the case. Why, can we see them? We can't identify them.

But, if something happens, can you know whether jnun *caused it?*

For example, these two toes were hurting me, for no reason. And now they no longer hurt, not at all. That we call *jnun*. And if you get cramps in your legs, we call that *jnun* too. But I don't know.

But if it's something important? Say, for example, you did something evil to someone. Could you say, "Well, I didn't do that, but jnun *entered my head and forced me to"?*

But that is the devil. We say, "The devil entered my head." But your own head acted, not the devil. The devil just told you, and you acted. What, are you going to say, "It wasn't me who did that, the devil did it"?. No, that's not possible.

So, the devil told you, but you acted. So you are responsible.

Yes, you are responsible. If you think about it, you will say, "That devilish work, I did it." Devilish work. But the devil doesn't say to you, "Come and do this," or "Come and do that." It just goes to the fellow's heart and says to him, "Hey, that thing is nice." Until the fellow does it. But you can't say, "Ah, the devil said to me, 'Do this!'" No. You didn't see the devil. You took your own counsel, and thought it over, but you acted on the side of the devil.

---

[32]I was interested, here, in notions of responsibility and retribution for bad behavior. Underlying this question is my lack of sympathy for religious systems that counsel proper behavior yet often seem to easily accommodate evil behavior as long as repentance is timely.

[33]*Jnun* are malevolent spirits. I was continuing here my questioning into the notion of responsibility.

THE DIALOGUES . . .

With all that we've talked about now, is there anything we have left out?

If so, we just didn't think of it. We may have forgotten something that happened in my life, but all that we remember we've talked about.

And now, what do you think about all that I've been asking you in these days, these months, that have passed?

I think that there will be a lot to talk about with those people in your land. As you said to me earlier: "What will I tell the people in my country if? . . ." That's what I imagine. From this they will learn, from this you will tell them what is, in fact. From it they will learn the situation itself, as it is.[34] That's what I think.

[I had a few more questions to ask the Faqir, and I looked down at my notes for several seconds. When I turned toward him again, he was asleep.]

---

[34]Again, the Faqir has none of the questions I have about what has happened throughout the summer. (See also ch. 11, nn.2 and 21.)

Epilogue
Return: Winter, 1978–79

I was unable to return to Morocco until December 1978, more than three years after my departure, and was able to stay only three weeks. I was no longer teaching anthropology but had begun to do research on political imprisonment in the Middle East for an international human-rights organization. I expected that the longer I continued to do this, the more difficult it would be for me to visit Morocco and the Faqir freely. So, although my stay was to be a short one—my shortest ever in Morocco, after my longest absence since I had first met the Faqir—I felt I should not postpone the opportunity.

After I had left Morocco in August 1975, the Faqir and I exchanged infrequent letters, perhaps one a year, as we had before that summer. Our letters always pass through third parties: mine, written sometimes in Arabic script and sometimes in Arabic transcribed into the Latin alphabet, must be read to the Faqir; his, translated into French or written in Arabic, are put to paper by one of the scribes who frequent the marketplace or by one of the Faqir's literate acquaintances. The Faqir has told me that he dictates some letters; for others, he just mentions a few points and the scribe amplifies.

Our letters are always brief, no more than a page, and contain little more than formal greetings and wishes of good fortune; at times, the Faqir will tell me the price his vegetables or grains fetched in the market, or mention the death of a villager, or note a significant event. Such details are never accompanied by any explanation or discussion.

Because I decided almost on the spur of the moment to visit the Faqir in December 1978, I had been unable to write informing him of my arrival as I had been able to do when I returned in the summers of 1973 and 1975. I approached the compound on foot from the east, under a clouded sky and a light, irregular rain. A young boy in the distance was tending a flock of sheep on the Faqir's land and, although I couldn't

238

identify him, it was surely either one of the Faqir's sons or one of his brother's. The shepherd caught sight of me and began to run toward me, seeming to recognize me immediately. As he drew closer shouting, "Kevin, Kevin," I began to make out Hmida, Ali's eldest son, now perhaps ten years old, who, when he reached me, kissed my hand, and jumped on me.

As Hmida and I walked together toward the compound, I could see that a new wing had been added to the north and that the eastern wall was now almost twice as long and had two large wooden doors rather than one. I recalled two short phrases in one of the Faqir's letters, "My brother, Ali, has separated from us, each of us now goes his own way. Each to his own."

Both brothers were already waiting for me in front of the house by the time I reached it—the children who usually cavort around the front of the house had probably gone inside and warned the adults of an arrival. The Faqir looked well although he had lost some teeth. Ali, who had formerly been so robust, was now much thinner and more subdued. We all spent a good quarter of an hour inquiring after one another's health and the health of our respective families, and I learned that Ali had been seriously ill with a stomach ailment that had required a month's hospitalization in the Medina and constant treatment since.

The women of the house and all of the children had now also come outside to greet me, among them the Faqir's daughter Zahara, carrying her own infant strapped to her back. Despite the unexpectedness of my visit, the welcome from the adults was quite matter-of-fact, although warm. (Some days later, a villager insisted he knew of my arrival beforehand because one of his sons, three days before I arrived, had dreamt that I was there for a visit.)

I fit rather easily and quickly into the Faqir's daily routine and felt quite natural living with his family on this, the fourth occasion that I had come to stay with them. During the three-week period, I spent most of my time either in the Faqir's house or in his brother's, taking my meals with one or the other or with both together, and sleeping in the Faqir's guest room, where the Faqir slept too. I would rise with the Faqir in the morning and perhaps accompany him to market or, if he planned to spend the morning working in the fields, stay indoors and do some paperwork I had brought with me or sit talking with Ali. I spent most afternoons with the men in the fields, bantering with them and helping in some of the easier tasks. I managed to walk up to the village a few times in the course of the three weeks, saying brief "hellos" to the people I knew best, partaking of the occasionally offered glass of tea, and spending a few hours chatting with some of the men who gathered around the several small village stores and near the mosque. In any event, it was wintertime, days were shorter than in summertime and people less given to parties and socializing.

With my stay in Ouled Filali so very short, and with certainly no occasion to do sustained research even had I wanted to, we—villagers and myself—spent most of our time together simply amusing one another, relating gossip, talking over the economic situation, and filling my head with details of life in the region, in the village, and in the Faqir's and his brother's household.

The Faqir and Ali had separated their households in the fall of 1975, only several months after I had left, and had also divided all their lands and livestock. Each was now directing a family and economic enterprise independent of the other's.

It is difficult, perhaps impossible, to say why the brothers separated their households, and why they did it when they did. Ali told me that problems arose when the Faqir's wife, claiming that all the children together gave her too much work, began to insist that Ali's children—the three of whom were all then seven years old or younger—not mix with her seven children inside the house. Ali told me that this was merely an excuse, that she was actually seeking to avoid his authority, his scolding and his hitting her. Ali could not tolerate such restrictions: he would lose direct control over the Faqir's children and he would have to live with a sister-in-law who would not obey him. He feared, he said, that under such an arrangement he would grow so impatient with her disobedience and willfullness that one day he would lash out uncontrollably and hit her too violently. Better, he said, to separate households completely before such a misfortune occurred. The Faqir, Ali said, was reluctant to separate, and every time Ali raised the matter with him, the Faqir ignored it. Finally, Ali was forced to ask some of the Faqir's friends to intercede and settle the difference between the brothers. After long and at times bitter discussion, the separation of households and division of wealth was agreed to.

The Faqir told me that he had indeed been reluctant to separate. He had grown used to the way things were, and with his advancing age it would be difficult for him, and for his brother too, to oversee all the farming and household tasks unassisted. In addition, there was sure to be serious disagreement over how to divide the wealth: on the one hand, the two brothers had rights to equal shares in everything they had inherited (their two sisters each had the right to one half a brother's share, but when sisters have married into other villages, as the Faqir's had, such claims are usually not exercised); on the other hand, Ali at the time had only three young children, whereas the Faqir had ten surviving children, seven who still lived with him and had to be fed and, more importantly, six of whom had contributed substantial labor to the farming. As the Faqir said: "So many of my kids worked, ploughed, and shepherded; all of our land except our small village plot was bought with the fruits of this labor. And, with all the mouths in my household, I will have to mill as much grain in one week as he mills in three months."

The Faqir knew that according to Islamic law, wealth acquired by a household during its lifetime should be divided according to each family's number of workers. The Faqir, however, said he had decided not to insist on his rightful share, but simply to seek some compromise with his brother so that, as he said, "We will separate in good spirit."

The Faqir told me his version. First, he sought to break the stalemate by suggesting that Ali find the answer to the problem in Islamic law. Ali, too, knew the relevant provisions and declined. Then the Faqir said, "All right. You decide how we should divide our wealth, but let the justice of your decision be on your shoulders, between you and God." Again Ali declined. Finally, the Faqir offered: "I propose a solution, but don't hold it against me. We will divide all lands in half and with regard to everything else, I will take three shares to your two." (The Faqir, according to Islamic law and the respective sizes of his family and Ali's, would merit in effect, two shares to Ali's one, both in land and in everything else.) The Faqir said that Ali breathed a sigh of relief upon hearing this offer and agreed at once. The brothers then divided the wealth over the course of the next several weeks with the help of the mediators Ali had first brought to the Faqir.

After seeing the tensions in their relationship prior to and during the summer of 1975, and after hearing of the disputes they had had as they divided their wealth, I was relieved to see the Faqir and Ali getting on reasonably well together during my three-week stay. They visited one another frequently, and they spoke with one another in a relaxed manner, although still with propriety. Ali remarked to me that their relations were indeed better now: neither told the other what to do and each ate only what he had worked to produce. Ali admitted that before the separation he had to defer to the Faqir and would almost never speak openly with him. Now, while he would not say bad words in front of the Faqir, he could at least sit at ease with him and they could talk and laugh together. The two men often helped one another out, bringing back crates from the other's marketing and sometimes marketing one another's crops, and even on occasion lending the other a substantial sum of money.

The Faqir, too, agreed that relations between them were much better than before. His view, however, was more measured than Ali's. They did treat one another more as equals, he said. Each was working for himself, and each assisted the other when able. Ali had lent the Faqir more than fifty thousand rials toward the purchase of a new irrigation motor. But the Faqir still disparaged Ali's good sense and cited a dispute, now settled, they had had not long before over the Faqir's right of passage through Ali's land, which Ali had closed to him for a time.

Both agreed, however, that their families functioned more smoothly, although Ali admitted that he hardly ever spoke to the Faqir's wife and, of course, never hit her or disciplined her in any way. The two wives still

242 / A "RECORD" OF FIELDWORK

were very friendly to one another, as they had always been, and now the children were easier for them to control. Previously, there had been too many children for one hearth: too many had to be fed at one time, and one of the wives had to spend all her time at the hearth, cooking for them; also, the children were now able to get closer to the warmth of the hearth in winter and consequently squabbled less with one another. Now, according to the men, each woman spent only part of her time cooking, and a proper period doing other tasks. And Ali mentioned that he now asked rather than ordered the Faqir's children to help him out; he found they willingly did this and even seemed to derive some pleasure in satisfying their uncle's requests.

The Faqir and his wife and children were all in good health. Mehdi, the oldest, was still unmarried although he had almost taken a wife the previous year. His engagement to a girl from the village into which one of the Faqir's daughters had married had been agreed to in principle by the parents, but the girl changed her mind shortly thereafter. Ali said that some of the girl's friends had told her that in his household the men ruled tightly over the women and that there would be no parties and few visits, and for this reason she refused the marriage.

Mehdi's married sister, Zahara, had left her husband and definitively returned to her father's home during the autumn of 1977, shortly after her daughter was born. The Faqir told me he had sought to bring her home before that but had been unable to find a way. He felt for a long time that she was not being properly fed by her husband, who only supplied her with market-bought bread while she was nursing her child. The Faqir had tried to bring her home to help care for her uncle after he had been discharged from the hospital, but her husband and mother-in-law had not allowed him to. They had also refused Zahara permission to visit her uncle even once during his month in the hospital, and the Faqir found this inexcusable.

However, in autumn 1977, Zahara's younger sister had married a man from a neighboring village, and Zahara returned to the Faqir's house to participate in the festivities. Once in her father's house, she refused to return to her husband, and the Faqir took her side. Twice her father-in-law had come to visit him to ask for Zahara's return, but on both occasions the Faqir was not at home and the father-in-law had to return to the Medina empty-handed.

According to the Faqir, Zahara was now very unlikely to go back to her husband's household. That household had become more suspect in his eyes: her father-in-law was said to have deserted the house for good, and rumors were heard that Zahara's two sisters-in-law were receiving gifts from men. If her husband were to set up a separate household, perhaps the Faqir would allow Zahara to be taken back. For the moment, he was weighing the utility of suing her husband's family for support for the child—not for the money, but simply to encourage them to grant her a divorce. Then, at least, she would be free and could marry again, if someone suitable came to ask for her.

Since 1975, the Faqir had had serious setbacks in agriculture. His vegetable farming had been hurt by irrigation-motor breakdowns; as a result, he had been unable to market crops since the past summer but hoped that a solution was in sight, now that he had just invested almost five hundred thousand rials in a new irrigation motor, which he had put in operation barely three weeks ago. He was sinking a deeper well for this motor to secure a more assured water supply. The Faqir was also quite concerned about rumours that the government was considering installing a meter on every irrigation motor and charging a price for water. One villager remarked to me that the farmers should unite and oppose this, perhaps even beginning a strike, but that farmers never unite. He continued, saying that often one farmer was so at odds with others in his village that he would ask the government to introduce the meters simply to bring misfortune on the others, despite the hardship he himself would suffer.

For the Faqir, grain farming had been a problem too. The years of 1976 and 1977 had been very dry, and 1978 had not been much better. The Faqir's grain stocks were now almost depleted and if there were no improvement this year—and as yet no good, solid rain with which to begin plowing and sowing had fallen—he might have to begin to buy grain from the market, a catastrophic eventuality. Yet again, the Faqir emphasized that his livestock had carried him through the difficult period. As he had often said: "Farming without livestock, or livestock without farming, is worthless. It is doing both together that makes it pay." Now, with Mehdi and l-'Aribi both working full time on the lands (although l-'Aribi, now fifteen years old, appeared to be growing increasingly unhappy with farm work), younger children pasturing the cows and sheep, and with new wells and irrigation motors beginning to go into operation, the Faqir was in a reasonably good position for the coming spring and summer seasons.

Ali had been seriously ill over much of the last two years. In the winter of 1976 his stomach suddenly began to swell and cause him great pain. Initial treatment by local healers brought no relief, and his first visits to doctors in the Medina also led to no improvement. At one point, he had to have his stomach drained of several liters of liquid every month. Finally, he was admitted to the hospital and was operated on, remaining there one month. Ever since, he has been taking medication and experiencing some discomfort.

Despite these difficulties, Ali and his wife had two more children; they now had five in all, and his oldest son, who was now ten, would soon be working productively in the fields. Ali himself now did little more than oversee the work of men to whom he had leased his land in partnership, in return for which he received a portion of the proceeds from the crop.

Ali was no longer able to maintain the same active social life he had during the summer of 1975. He still gathered with a small group of male friends every Tuesday evening as each took his turn feasting the others. Ali, unfortunately, was always served a separate *tajine* on a separate table, because his diet required all his food to be cooked without salt. He no longer went to parties with women, which may have been just as well, because one party that he otherwise probably would have attended, ended tragically: four men and two women (one of whom had been the lead singer at our party in 1975) died of asphyxiation. Someone, it was said, had not completely closed a butagaz container, the party-goers all fell asleep, and only one survived; he (a man who had also attended our party) was still hospitalized and suffering brain damage.

The village of Ouled Filali had changed visibly in a number of ways. Several families had now moved away from the village clusters and founded relatively isolated homesteads like the Faqir's. Almost all village land that I saw had now been leveled and plowed and there were more and larger irrigation motors, a couple of which could be heard from the Faqir's house. I do not know to what extent this meant that irrigated farming was becoming more successful or, instead, that farmers were going into greater debt; or, whether differentiation was increasing between those whose farms were successful and those whose were not. The Faqir was certain, however, that there were fewer households than before—he cited the figure of twenty of the approximately one hundred in the village—that now made their livelihood primarily from farming, and he named several that were heavily in debt for their machinery.

Wood fuel had become very scarce. Because all land had been cleared and plowed, wood, which most families preferred to use for cooking, was no longer available. The Faqir still had enough wood for another year from a field he had cleared the year before, but many villagers had adjusted to the shortage by buying butagaz burners and stoves. Still, the Faqir mentioned that there had been numerous disputes between villagers and the local police, who guard forest land to see that is not depleted of its wood.

There were a pair of new stores in the village. Store owners no longer went to the Medina or "44" to buy their merchandise, but waited in the village for the truck that would deliver. Villagers were happy with the new arrangement: it meant that prices in the village were now almost identical with those in the towns. Prices on the whole, however, had been rising markedly, and most villagers attributed this to the continuing war in the Sahara.

There had been a few deaths in the village while I was away, but no one I knew well had died. Faqir Hmed, though, who used to work often for the Faqir until 1975, had had severe back problems and was now able to work only occasionally. Fortunately, his eldest son, who had left home in anger as a teenager some ten years earlier and had refused to visit even for major holidays, had now relented and was sending money home regularly. Saleh, the migrant worker, still behaved strangely in the eyes of villagers, sitting alone in his house and cooking for himself, and speaking his own peculiar language. His brother, who had also worked in France and whom I knew as the leader of a group of villagers who regularly played cards for money, had been arrested in Marseilles for transporting kif and was now serving a ten-year jail sentence there.

Throughout the three weeks, there was continuing dispute in the village about an inheritance, and the sheikh made several visits to help settle the matter. Once he came to visit the Faqir. The sheikh was as impressive as ever: his awareness of world events was still exceedingly sharp, and he was able, in addition, to give an interesting first-hand account of the Green March that took place in the fall of 1975, when more than three hundred thousand Moroccans were sent on foot into the Western Sahara in a large government-organized operation to seal Morocco's claim to the territory. The sheikh said he was hoping to retire soon, to busy himself with his own affairs; after he left, the Faqir and I nodded to one another, saying, in effect, that the sheikh had been telling us that very thing for years.

My departure was almost as unexpected as my arrival. I had planned to leave on Monday in order to fly from Agadir early Tuesday morning. But we woke up early Sunday morning to the pounding of rain that seemed likely, if it continued, to make the village roads and paths all but impassible: in such conditions, people on foot often slip and fall and vehicles can at best only run in place, at worst sliding down the uneven roads into the gulleys and ditches on the sides. So, with the rain still coming down, and after goodbyes that were hasty and somewhat anti-climactic, Mehdi and I together walked for almost an hour to the main road, where I hitched a ride to Agadir.

Photographs

Faqir Muhammad, praying

The Faqir's eldest son

The Faqir's brother

Midmorning breakfast with a worker

The Faqir's brother plowing, the Faqir's daughter sowing

The Faqir's brother and workers harvesting grain

Winnowing

A moment's release from the winnowing

A regional market

251

Children
of the village

A view of Ouled Filali

PART TWO

ON THE DIALOGIC OF ANTHROPOLOGY

The reconstitution of the unity of the subject, the intellectual restoration of man has consciously to take its path through the realm of disintegration and fragmentation.—*Lukacs,* History and Class Consciousness

12

Disintegration and Fragmentation: A Critique of Anthropology

🟦 INTRODUCTION

Anthropology has now gained about a century's experience as an academic discipline and is, on the face of it, a secure field of study with its own modest place within Western institutions. Indeed, it probably attracts a disproportionately large share of Western society's interest, if not of its spoils, for it still holds the important trumps of personal adventure and a close encounter with the "exotic" and bids to convey, as well, a hint of humanitarian good works.

Yet many anthropologists are unsure of their profession's worth and for good reason. Aiming to understand human experience, they must often feel the despair of the bettor throwing good money after bad: even as they try to understand human experience, anthropologists are part of it, contribute to it, affect its variety, and make it all the more difficult to grasp. And, perhaps dismaying them even more: as human experience changes so does anthropology and its place within that experience and, consequently, so does the anthropologist too. Anthropologists certainly cannot hope to fix human experience and their own activity and comprehend it all, once and for all.

There is, then, a necessary tie in anthropology between what is studied (the "object" or, for the anthropologist, the "Other") and who studies it (the "subject" or the "Self"): each is affected by changes in the other. And, too, because all individuals necessarily carry and express their own society's concerns, the terms *Self* and *Other* must be understood in an extended sense, as embracing yet going beyond individuals, and standing also for the cultural and societal interests expressed in individual action.

To stress the tie between subject and object, between Self and Other, has lately become something of a commonplace; the implications, however, still need to be carefully traced. One clear implication is that if we are to engage in an honest effort to approach and understand the Other, we must, as we do this, pursue the Self and try to expose it. Yet anthropologists, perhaps sensing that to expose the Self is to place it in jeopardy, have for the most part been unwilling to take such a gamble. Avoiding this risk in a variety of ways, they have usually refused to admit that the very possibility of dealing squarely with the Other is tied to the capacity to put the Self at stake.

The practice of anthropology is therefore rooted in a vulnerability of the most fundamental sort, because to expose the Self and to open it to question means not merely to question the individual anthropologist or anthropology's specific theoretical hypotheses. Rather, it is to question the Self in its extended sense: that is, the anthropological effort itself and the interests and social system that give that effort its force.

Although anthropologists are certainly not flush with their own success, they have consistently turned away from this vulnerability with something of a poker face and have failed to make it central to their work. Anthropology has thus projected, deliberately or not, a false image of strength. The effects of this go beyond anthropology itself, for the discipline, in refusing to discuss its inherent vulnerability, forgoes the chance to question itself and its own society. It thus inevitably attracts the accusation that despite its overtures toward the Other, it is little more than another self-serving field of study working to strengthen Western institutions.

To appreciate the force, however unfounded, of an anthropology that neglects its own vulnerability, we might best begin by examining briefly the development of the discipline's basic conceptual tools.

▩ CONTEMPLATION

The particular epistemological debate that governed the formation of anthropology around the turn of the century concerned the relationship of the "human sciences" to the "natural sciences." Some writers distinguished the two realms, either claiming that each was governed by a distinctive kind of causality or that the "human sciences" were characterized by a distinctive methodology of "studied empathy." Other writers saw no essential difference: both the human and natural sciences were carried out according to the tried and true procedures of the latter. Nowhere, however, were the principles of the natural sciences directly challenged, even though a few scholars sought to limit their domain.

The salient effect on anthropology of this discussion was the discipline's acceptance of the central, "contemplative" premise of the scientific attitude: the object of study—in anthropology's case the nonwestern Other—would be "observed" by the subject, the western Self. This central premise, variously phrased in language that either embraced, rejected, or sometimes ignored the discipline's kinship to "science," had two main corollaries: that Self and Other were essentially independent of one another and that "observation" was an objective act that in no way influenced the object's true significance, a significance that existed prior to the act of observing it.[1]

The Self hides and shields itself easily when it adopts the contemplative stance. First of all, the presumed independence of Self and Other not only conceals the responsibility the Self assumes in initiating the confrontation with the Other but also denies that the Other may have any significant effect on the Self. Second, the Self's claim to objectivity places the Self beyond question: the Self may seek to refine and make more acute its vision of the Other but need never examine its own vantage point.

Although the assumptions of the contemplative stance are most strikingly evident in the natural sciences, the power of this stance within anthropology is not derived simply from the reflected prestige of scientific knowledge. It comes, too, from the fact that even where science was directly attacked, the contemplative assumptions were challenged only partially and not across the board.

▓ ABSTRACT, CONCRETE, AND PRACTICAL OBJECTS

To assess the contemplative stance's strength, we must first be able to identify its characteristic traits. These come into clearest relief in the two dominant, apparently opposed, anthropological perspectives: the "comparative" and the "relativist."

THE PURSUIT OF THE ABSTRACT OBJECT: COMPARATIVISM AND RELATIVISM

The comparative effort, whether using a vocabulary that is evolutionist, cultural ecological, cultural materialist, or structuralist, is avowedly scientific and seeks explanations for all crucial differences between human groups in terms of an objective language that transcends these differences, that permits difference to be interpreted as variations on universal themes. The relativist effort, most frequently voicing a humanist aim, stresses the particular and unique and seeks a faithful representation of the Other's culture, purportedly in its own terms (for Franz Boas, the relativists' seminal figure, the humanist perspective was a stage in the progress toward a scientific one).

Yet the two approaches have a common core: both the relativist seek-

---

[1]Lukacs's critique of the contemplative stance in his *History and Class Consciousness* (1971) has helped me to formulate mine. The reasons why I take Lukacs to be a pivotal figure—in part because of his relationship to Marx and Weber—and the philosophical roots of my argument are presented in Dwyer (1979).

ing a faithful representation and the comparativist trying to reduce human difference to a common scale define an object of knowledge that is "abstract." It is abstract in two distinct, but closely related senses: (a) the object is taken to be independent of and unrelated to the particular individuals seeking it—that is, it is disembodied and (b) the object is seen as strictly divorced from the specific situation within which that search is pursued—it is unlocated. In this way, both the researcher and informant are deprived, together, of their human dimension: the researcher is reduced to a more or less mechanical receiver, the informant to a relay, and the object—the disembodied, unlocated message—is insulated from them both. Such a vision, in which the researcher is "not part of the investigation or object he is studying" (as Goldmann notes, disapprovingly [1964, p. 94]) has as its aim "not to constitute man but to dissolve him" (as the structuralist Lévi-Strauss proposes [1962, p. 326]).[2]

THE SUBJECTIVIST PURSUIT OF THE CONCRETE

The search for a disembodied, unlocated, abstract object, although still dominant within anthropology, has not been uncontested; it has been attacked, on the one hand, by those who feel the loss of the Other's "humanity" and who long for a concrete expression of the Other's subjectivity; and, on the other hand, by several authors who, recognizing the limits of the dichotomy between "objectivity" and "subjectivity," have sought to move beyond it by focusing, in various ways, on practice.

The longing for the Other's subjectivity often focuses on the "personal document" and, most commonly, on the "life history." Yet the two most distinguished proponents of this approach, Clyde Kluckhohn and Paul Radin, each working with great sensitivity although with different ultimate aims, were not free of contemplative assumptions.

Kluckhohn's attempt to recover the humanity of the Other through the personal document was the first step in his quest for a scientific anthropology.[3] Kluckhohn argues that "until anthropologists can deal

---

[2]Also clearly adopting the contemplative stance, although in a somewhat modified fashion, are those anthropologists whose approach has been called "ethnoscientific." This approach involves an attempt to generate rules that, once learned and assimilated, would enable any individual to operate as a member of the given society. This basic premise uncomfortably merges the relativist impulse of searching for terms internal to a culture, with the comparative effort to describe a particular culture in a universal language; or, as Geertz remarks, in ethnoscience "extreme subjectivism is married to extreme formalism" (1973, p. 11). The unfortunate result is that the ethnoscientific approach has been plagued—as was perhaps inevitable—by the question of the "psychological reality" of the rules it formulated.

[3]Kluckhohn's 1945 review of the uses of the personal document in anthropology has not been supplanted, and several authors have attested to the currency of its conclusions: "Unfortunate as it seems, we can use virtually unchanged the summary statements

rigorously with the 'subjective factors' in the lives of 'primitives' their work will be flat and insubstantial" (1945, p. 162). He goes on to say that "the key to the problem of 'subjectivity'" is to be sought in procedures that, like "multiple techniques, carried out by multiple observors and ana-lysts" (1945, p. 162) would facilitate an "anthropological mode [that] must become more objective both as regards gathering and analyzing data" (1945, p. 163). Kluckhohn's assessment of various forms and in-stances of the personal document rests on the degree to which the form can be "developed, controlled, tested" (1945, p. 79) and on the extent to which it might furnish standardized and reliable information for broad-er cultural or psychological theories.

Radin attached himself more tenaciously and more exclusively than Kluckhohn to the personal document. Radin sought from the Other "the inside view of their culture from their own lips and by their own initiative" (1963, p. 1), and "[Radin] alone, among the anthropologists of his generation, insisted that the only accepted ethnology is the life histo-ry, self-told, by members of indigenous society" (Diamond 1974, p. 111). Radin pushes this argument to its logical conclusion and gives the re-searcher a fundamentally passive role: "The ideal collectors of data are the natives themselves . . . the ethnologist's role should remain predomi-nantly that of an editor and annotator" (1933, pp. 70–71). Radin's basic justification for this was his view that an account of an aboriginal society "need properly have no purpose . . . over and above that of being a spe-cific account of a given culture" (1933, p. 12).[4]

Yet both Kluckhohn's and Radin's opposition to the contemplative pursuit of the object is only partial: they do challenge the validity of an object that is independent of the informant but keep it independent of the researcher and still ignore the specific encounter between the two. In their work the contemplative stance appears in a slightly altered pose: Kluckhohn and Radin attempt to recapture subjectivity by locating the object within the Other, but they still refuse to see the researcher in anything but an ideally objective and therefore essentially passive role. The concrete subjectivity of the Other appears, falsely, in isolation, alone and arising spontaneously; it was, of course, a product of a specific encounter with the Self.

---

made by Kluckhohn in 1945" (Langness 1965, p. 18, quoted in Mandelbaum 1973, p. 179). For a more recent assessment of the use of the life history in anthropology and, in particu-lar, in French anthropology, see Morin (1980).

    [4]Where Radin did allow room for the pursuit of a disembodied, unlocated object—and he had to, for he himself developed a refined theory of the nature of the primitive—he would never allow this pursuit to relegate the concrete to a secondary plane, as he had seen happen and had criticized in the work of Malinowski and Radcliffe-Brown (Radin 1933, p. 255).

THE INTERPRETIVE AND THEORETICAL PURSUIT OF THE PRACTICAL

There has been a clear challenge not only to the pursuit of the abstract object and to the search for the concrete but, more fundamentally, to approaches that divorce anthropology from the lived, practical experience of the Other. Within anthropology, this challenge has perhaps been phrased to best effect, although in different ways, by Clifford Geertz and Pierre Bourdieu.[5] In common, they both reject conceptions of anthropology that tend to create what is for them a false dichotomy and unnecessary choice between objectivism and subjectivism.[6] But their views differ on where to situate the problem's causes and on how to resolve it.

For Geertz, the solution lies in drawing the consequences of his view that anthropology is "not an experimental science in search of law, but an interpretive one in search of meaning" (1973, p. 5). The aim, therefore, is to reconstitute what Geertz calls a "thick description... a stratified hierarchy of meaningful structures... a context, something within which they [social events, behaviors, institutions, or processes] can be intelligibly—that is, thickly—described" (1973, pp. 7, 14). Such an interpretive effort—the construction of a thick description—focuses on "the flow of social discourse" (1973, p. 20) and "the interpreting consists of trying to rescue the 'said' ['the meaning of the speech event, not the event as event'] of such discourse from its perishing occasions and fix it in perusable terms" (1973, p. 20).[7]

Central to Geertz's approach is his notion that the anthropologist's attention to the flow of social discourse is "microscopic," involving "exceedingly extended acquaintances with extremely small matters" (1973, p. 21). Geertz states this even more strongly: "To divorce it [anthropological interpretation] from what happens—from what, in this time or that place, specific people say, what they do, what is done to them, from the whole vast business of the world—is to divorce it from its applications and to render it vacant" (1973, p. 18).

---

[5]Both have written many specific analyses over the years: Geertz, a number of monographs covering Bali, Java, and more recently Morocco; and Bourdieu, numerous articles in a journal, *Actes de la recherche en sciences sociales*, which he directs. The most systematic exposition of their theoretical position is found, respectively, in Geertz (1973) and Bourdieu (1977).

[6]Geertz remarks that "the interminable, because unterminable debate within anthropology as to whether culture is 'objective' or 'subjective'... is wholly misconceived" (1973, p. 10), whereas Bourdieu stresses the need to "escape from the ritual either/or choice between objectivism and subjectivism in which the social sciences have so far allowed themselves to be trapped" (1977, p. 4).

[7]Geertz is following, here, Ricoeur from whom he takes the quote I have inserted in brackets (Ricoeur 1971). Geertz's term *thick description* is borrowed from Ryle.

As attentive as Geertz wishes to remain to the microscopic level, he nonetheless feels required to face "the problem of how to get from a collection of ethnographic miniatures . . . to wall-sized culturescapes," to move "from local truths to general visions" (1973, p. 21). Geertz thus clearly distinguishes two phases of the anthropological endeavor: ethnography and the elaboration of thick description on the one hand, and a theoretical, generalizing moment on the other.

The first—doing ethnography—"is like trying to read (in the sense of 'construct a reading of') a manuscript—foreign, faded, full of ellipses, incoherencies, suspicious emendations, and tendentious commentaries, but written not in conventionalized graphs of sound but in transient examples of shaped behavior" (1973, p. 10) and then inscribing this reading, "[turning] it from a passing event, which exists only in its own moment of occurrence, into an account, which exists in its inscriptions and can be reconsulted" (1973, p. 19). The second, theoretical moment involves rejecting what are normally taken to be the scientific aims of abstraction, generality, and prediction and seeking interpretive efforts that are increasingly "incisive," "closer to the ground," "inferential" (1973, pp. 25, 24, 26), where the "essential task of theory building here is not to codify abstract regularities but to make thick description possible, not to generalize across cases but to generalize within them" (1973, p. 26).[8]

Now, to what extent does Geertz's approach challenge the premises of the contemplative stance, the presumed independence of Self and Other, and the "objective" nature of the Self? To what extent does it allow the Other's voice to be heard and permit a thoroughgoing challenge to the Self?

On the level of theoretical activity, Geertz clearly rejects the contemplative assumptions, for he recognizes, indeed emphasizes, that the theoretical effort is not the passive act of an objective observor who uncovers preexisting laws, but is a constructive one. "The view of anthropological analysis as the conceptual manipulation of discovered facts, a logical construction of a mere reality, seem[s] rather lame . . . [it] is to pretend a science that does not exist and imagine a reality that cannot be found. Cultural analysis is (or should be) guessing at meanings, assessing the guesses, and drawing explanatory conclusions from the better guesses, not discovering the Continent of Meaning and mapping out its bodiless landscape" (Geertz 1973, p. 20). Anthropological analysis is a constructive activity because the anthropologist brings to the activity particular interests and concerns and *constructs* interpretations of social phenomena in the light of those interests. As Geertz remarks, "where an interpretation comes from does not determine where it can

---

[8]Geertz, however, believes interpretation, as he conceives it, to be a "scientific" enterprise, although for other than the usual reasons (Geertz 1973, pp. 24–28).

be impelled to go.... Small facts speak to large issues... *because they are made to*" (1973, p. 23, my emphasis).[9]

Yet, on the level of ethnographic activity, Geertz's opposition to the contemplative assumptions is much weaker. Certainly, the development of a thick description—the practical aim of ethnography—is also a constructive activity, for "such descriptions are [not] themselves Berber, Jewish, or French—that is, [are not] part of the reality they are ostensibly describing; they are anthropological—that is, part of a developing system of scientific analysis. They must be cast in terms of the interpretations to which persons of a particular denomination subject their experience, because that is what they profess to be descriptions of; they are anthropological because it is, in fact, anthropologists who profess them" (1973, p. 15).

But at the most basic level of the "small fact," of the informant's interpretation, Geertz systematically refuses to see the anthropologist in his or her human relation to the informant or to accept the inevitable interdependence of Self and Other at the very origin of the search for "information." For Geertz, the anthropologist is not a social actor or is, at best, a very marginal one: "We are not actors, we do not have direct access [to raw social discourse], but only [to] that small part of it which our informants can lead us into understanding" (1973, p. 20).

This refusal is perhaps best summarized in Geertz's own words: "What we call our data are really our own constructions of other people's constructions of what they and their compatriots are up to.... Right down at the factual base, the hard rock, insofar as there is any, of the whole enterprise, we are already explicating: and worse, explicating explications" (1973, p. 9). Or, to the same effect: "The culture of a people is an ensemble of texts . . . which the anthropologist strains to read over the shoulders of those to whom they properly belong" (1973, p. 452).

Here Geertz implicitly suggests that the Other's constructions, the informant's explications, are elaborated in isolation and not in response to an anthropologist who poses specific questions, who helps create a situation that encourages certain kinds of responses. But, contrary to Geertz's view, the anthropologist, in practice, does not simply overhear or eavesdrop upon an informant's interpretations that would have been expressed no matter what the context; instead, the anthropologist's actions clearly provoke those interpretations and help to structure them and give them content.

[9]It is perhaps useful here to cite Max Weber, to whom Geertz recognizes a great intellectual debt, who argued that scholars necessarily construct, rather than merely uncover, "data": "A description of even the smallest slice of reality can never be exhaustive. A chaos of 'existential judgments' about countless individual events would be the only result of a serious attempt to analyze reality 'without presuppositions.'... Order is brought into this chaos only on the condition that in every case only a *part* of concrete reality is interesting and *significant* to us, because only it is related to the *cultural values* with which we approach reality.... It is in brief a question of imputation" (1963, pp. 384–85).

Geertz, then, restricts the active role of the anthropologist to the moment of writing, denying an active role to the anthropologist in the direct encounter with the Other. In Geertz's approach, the anthropologist has again become a passive observor or recorder, and the interdependence of Self and Other is supplanted by the interdependence of the anthropologist and the text he or she constructs, a text in which the Other's constructions are treated in isolation and as having been expressed spontaneously. The dialectical confrontation, for Geertz, does not take place during the field encounter with the Other, but is restricted to the privacy of the anthropologist's study.[10]

One interesting corollary to Geertz's unwillingness to award a constructive function to the anthropologist at the very point where informant and anthropologist produce shared experience is that his challenge to the discipline of anthropology is limited to a challenge to theory, and does not question either the discipline or its society. Although Geertz recognizes that "one does not start (or ought not) intellectually empty-handed," he has a narrow view of the domain from which new ideas arise: "Theoretical ideas are not created wholly anew in each study ... they are adopted from other, related studies, and, refined in the process, applied to new interpretive problems" (1973, p. 27). Geertz, here, does not face the fact that new ideas and approaches emerge not merely from theoretical discussion but from the historical and social action of anthropology and from the way in which the discipline expresses the concerns of its own society as it confronts the Other. In this way, Geertz remains within the narrow confines of "science" and directs his attention away from topics that would lead, naturally, to questioning not only theory, but also anthropology and its society.

Bourdieu's attack on the abstract and concrete objects is phrased as an attack on "phenomenological" approaches "which set out to make explicit the truth of primary experience of the social world" (1977, p. 3), "objectivist" approaches which "construct the objective relations which structure practice and representations of practice" (1977, p. 3) (of which he sees structuralist hermeneutics as an example), and "subjectivism" or "lived experience" (1977, p. 4).

Bourdieu's diagnosis of the failings of these forms of knowledge comes close to a critique of the contemplative stance; in each form, "the 'knowing subject' ... inflicts on practice a much more fundamental and pernicious alteration ...: in taking up a point of view on the action,

---

[10]This same perspective pervades the work of a number of Geertz's students, such as Rabinow (1975), Eickelman (1976), and Rosen (1980), who tend to view the Other as a literary text and for whom, like for Gadamer, "written texts present the real hermeneutical task... [and] reading is the highest act of understanding" (1975, p. 352). Rabinow's more recent work (1977), which constitutes an effort to go beyond this, but is nonetheless still bound by the limitations of a "literary" perspective, is discussed at length in chap. 13, n.6.

withdrawing from it in order to observe it from above and from a distance, he constitutes practical activity as an *object of observation and analysis*, a *representation*" (1977, p. 2).

Bourdieu proposes, instead, to "make possible a science of the *dialectical* relations between the objective structures to which the objectivist mode of knowledge gives access and the structured dispositions within which those structures are actualized and which tend to reproduce them" (1977, p. 3). He feels this aim can be satisfied "only if we subordinate all operations of scientific practice to a theory of practice and of practical knowledge . . . and inseparably from this, to a theory of the theoretical and social conditions of the possibility of objective apprehension—and thereby to a theory of the limits of this mode of knowledge" (1977, p. 4).

As he attempts to do this, Bourdieu strongly emphasizes the constructive role of the anthropologist in both eliciting and producing, by his or her practical activity, certain kinds of knowledge and testimony.[11] But Bourdieu refuses to see the anthropologist as a full actor, for he insists on "his situation as observor, excluded from the real play of social activities by the fact that he has no place (except by choice or by way of a game) in the system observed and has no need to make a place for himself there" (1977, p. 1). Rather than recognizing that attention to these and other similar limits on the anthropologist's action might lead to a better appreciation of the vulnerability of the Self, Bourdieu stresses that by focusing exclusively on the Other, by directing attention to the Other's practical activity, by reintroducing time, by refusing to use models to "annihilate" practice (1977, p. 9), we may lay the foundations for an adequate theory of practice and of the possibilities of such a theory.

Bourdieu's critique has the merit of pointing to a weakness in the work of Geertz and of several authors working in Geertz's tradition,[12] for he emphasizes the need, as Geertz does not, to "question the presuppositions inherent in the position of an outside observer, who, in his preoccupation with *interpreting* practices, is inclined to introduce into the object the principles of his relation to the object, as is attested by the special importance he assigns to communicative functions" (1977, p. 2). Yet surprisingly, Bourdieu's approach fails in much the same way as Geertz's does, for in both their programs the anthropologist's own activity, and therefore the practical activity of the society that places the anthropologist in his peculiar relation to the Other, are on the shadow side of the effort.

SUMMARY

Although each awards to "science" a different role, the pursuits of the abstract, concrete, or practical Other each, in their own way, reveal

[11]See Bourdieu (1977, pp. 18–19, 105–6).
[12]See note 10.

contemplative premises: either the denial of the interdependence of subject and object at the moment of their direct confrontation, or the affirmation of an "objective" subject, or both. None of these approaches, consequently, allows scrutiny of the subject's activity on any but a theoretical level, or faces the possibility of calling itself and its own society into question; all proceed untouched by the action of the Other. In this way, the Self, unchallenged, continues to promote the illusion of its own invulnerability.

🏵 FIELDWORK

For anthropology to seek an alternative to the contemplative stance and to act on its own vulnerability it must oppose, then, not only premises that deny subjectivity or that, while avidly pursuing it, isolate the Other from the Self and from the specific situation of their confrontation, but also those that, although focusing on practice, refuse to see the Self in its practical role. To do this, anthropology must begin, at the very least, to see its "facts" as emerging from the research process and from the demands of the anthropological career.

The crucial moment in the research process and in the anthropological career is fieldwork, "the intensive first-hand study of small social units within the larger society" (Geertz 1963, p. 4). Fieldwork has assumed a position so central to anthropology that for many within and outside the discipline, it defines anthropology's boundaries.[13] The rising frequency of works devoted to fieldwork suggests that the effort to see the relationship between anthropological facts and the situation that produces them may already be underway. These discussions appear in the following guises: (1) as "manual"—a guide to how fieldwork *should* be performed; (2) as "anecdotal account"—an episodic rendering of the anthropologist's personal experiences in the field; (3) as "commentary on fieldwork"—an analytic investigation into what fieldwork is and how it is practiced; (4) as "representation"—a description of fieldwork in progress, "as it really happened." We can now ask whether these studies challenge the contemplative stance or merely offer new versions of it.[14]

The manual[15] seeks to present formal methods that will enable the researcher to purify his or her work of subjective elements and cast it in an "objective" mold. Methods here consist of impersonal, timeless tech-

---

[13]Nash, examining the views of classical anthropologists on the importance of fieldwork, concludes that fieldwork constitutes the "culture focus" of the anthropologist's culture (1963, p. 149). At least one sociologist sees the view that fieldwork defines anthropology as widespread among sociologists (Becker 1956, p. 11).

[14]The following survey of the literature on fieldwork does not claim to be exhaustive. Nonetheless, I have sampled it extensively and the general patterns seem clear.

[15]The early work by the Webbs (1968, first published in 1932) established the model. More recent examples are Edgerton and Langness (1974), Epstein (1967), Naroll and Cohen (1970), and Pelto (1970).

niques—standard tools that can be wielded by all researchers. The manual, in this way, fully and consciously embraces the scientific purpose and the presuppositions of the contemplative stance and therefore abandons at the outset the possibility of questioning directly the activity of the Self.

In the anecdotal account, to the contrary, anthropologist and informant may both appear as subjects, but the fieldwork experience is still used to erect a barrier between Self and Other. First, the anecdotal account is explicitly opposed to the "ethnography" and usually appears either as the introduction to the ethnography proper, or fills alone an entire volume.[16] Here, the anthropologist's experience is sharply divided into its "personal" aspects, exemplified in anecdotal "tribulations" (as Malinowski revealingly called them [1961, p. 4]), and "work," which produces the "data" in which personal experience supposedly plays no role. With this opposition, the author reiterates and reinforces the immunity of the Self: the activity of the Other remains the object of anthropological "explanation" and analysis while the Self's, restricted to the anecdote, is sheltered from them.

One revealing symptom of the distinction between, and the relative value attributed to, an "explanatory" approach grounded in objectivity, and an "anecdotal" mode grounded in "subjectivity" is the fact that where anthropologist husband and wife have worked in the same region, it is usually the woman who adopts the anecdotal mode and the man the explanatory one. This is not surprising given the general character of sexual ideology in the West. Furthermore, the status of the anecdotal account in the traditional hierarchy of anthropological genres has been quite low: one author, at least, felt this so strongly that, to protect her anthropological career, she wrote her account under a pseudonym and insisted for some time that her account was a fictional one.[17]

The commentary on fieldwork, neither adopting the normative aims of the manual nor splintering experience in the manner of the anecdotal account takes, instead, an analytic approach.[18] In this, the commentary might move toward an alternative to the contemplative stance, if not provide that alternative itself, by distilling the relationship between "fact" and research process, and by underlining the active role of both

---

[16]See the introductory sections of such classic works as Malinowski (1961) and Evans-Pritchard (1940); or, for example, Chagnon (1968). Bowen (1964) and Fernea (1969) are examples of the book-length anecdotal account.

[17]Bowen (1964). For the husband and wife pairs, contrast, for example, Bowen (1964), Fernea (1969), and Wolf (1968) with the work of their anthropologist husbands, Paul Bohannan, Robert Fernea, and Arthur Wolf. One may well ask to what extent the contrast between Daisy Dwyer (1978) and the present book fits or breaks this pattern.

[18]Freilich (1970), Golde (1970), Henry and Saberwal (1969), Spindler (1970), and Wax (1971) are examples of this genre.

anthropologist and informant. Yet the analyses themselves are informed by and bound to the contemplative stance.

This is signaled by the use of certain characteristic metaphors to describe the fieldwork experience. Two types, closely related to one another, predominate: "progressive" metaphors, where the authors highlight the stages the fieldworker must pass through as the experience runs its course; and metaphors of "discovery," where the focus is on the skills and tools the apprentice fieldworker must gain to allow access to the as yet unattainable Other. Wax, for example, likens the process to socialization and to learning a language (1971, p. 12); Freilich talks of "the natural history of a field project" in order "to facilitate the development of a formal model of fieldwork" (1970, p. 485); Golde, in an analysis of the themes developed by the authors in her edited volume, assumes a similar developmental perspective and charged those authors to reveal "the natural history of adjustment and acceptance that characterize fieldwork" (1970, p. 5). In Henry and Saberwal, the contributors, "assess their own responses during fieldwork in diverse circumstances" (1969, p. 1); and, in Spindler's work, the attempt is to show "how 13 anthropologists and other members of their families made this adaptation in 11 different cultures" (1970, p. v).

The root metaphor that unites these is that of fieldwork as a "journey"; the researcher, in all cases, is little more than a vehicle, sometimes noting the obstacles and detours as so many significant milestones, sometimes fixing singlemindedly what is needed to reach the destination. In any event, with the journey over, an essentially unchanged researcher returns to his or her origin, ready to unpack the experience as just so much new cargo.[19]

Some metaphors that appear in the commentary go beyond the contemplative stance and, unlike the two types mentioned above, assign active roles to both anthropologist and informant, even suggesting the interdependence of Self and Other. For example, in an edited collection Casagrande outlines the respective roles described by the authors: "The relationship between anthropologist and the informant has many of the attributes of . . . student and teacher, employer and employee, friends or relatives . . . psychiatrist and his patient" (1964, p. xi). Yet the authors in the collection usually do not examine the interdependence of anthropologist and informant closely and tend to judge their encounter by the yardstick of anthropological goals elaborated independently of the Other. Casagrande's metaphors themselves, if we take them to refer to

---

[19]The view of fieldwork as a journey should perhaps be seen in conjuction with views that see "culture" as a map. As Bourdieu remarks, the map "is the analogy which occurs to an outsider who has to find his way around in a foreign landscape and who compensates for his lack of practical mastery, the prerogative of the native, by the use of a model of all possible routes" (1977, pp. 22).

standard Western educational, economic, and psychoanalytic practice, also imply a clear hierarchy of goals: of the teacher's over the student's, of the boss's over the worker's, of the doctor's over the patient's.[20]

Where anthropology's goals are explicitly taken to be primary, even the "active" metaphors warp and shift easily into metaphors of manipulation where risks, gains, and losses are judged only in light of the anthropologist's "higher" goals.[21] On occasion, these shade into even darker metaphors of conquest and submission, where "learning a native culture" is viewed "as a procedure not unlike seducing a woman" (Freilich 1970, p. 31, and in slightly different terms on p. 539). Here, the treatment of the Other's subjectivity as object reveals, ineluctably, its fundamental impulse to control and ultimately subjugate the Other.[22]

In the representation, authors strive to portray fieldwork "in progress," "as it happened," and often take care to relate portions of dialogue as it transpired and events as they occurred.[23] Here the aim is overtly nonanalytical, the experience is presented as unique, and there is usually no division between the "personal" and the "professional." But the premises of the contemplative stance are neither surmounted nor even attacked; they are merely ignored. There is now no barrier between Self and Other, but the authors present Self and Other "naively," as though the nature of their mutual experience was simple and self-evident. Neither Self nor Other are shown to be products of the specific effort, initiated by the Self, to intrude upon and understand the Other; no attempt is made to display the relationship between "data" and the situation that shapes them. In addition, these authors refuse to articulate the ties between the representation and the genres to which their work is opposed, and they thus abdicate all responsibility to define the nature of "valid, meaningful" knowledge. Thus, Maybury-Lewis, for example, remarks that his work is "an account of our experiences ... our personal reactions to the various situations in which we found ourselves, and above all our feelings about the day-to-day business which is mysteriously known as 'doing fieldwork,'" yet he goes on to say that "*it is not an essay in anthropology*" (1968, p. 7, my emphasis).

---

[20]If we were to base these metaphors on other visions of educational method (Freire 1974) or therapeutic practice (Szasz 1965), for example, they might gain in force.

[21]As, for example, in Freilich's use of the "net profit analog" (1970, pp. 539ff.) and the "game" metaphor (1970, p. 533).

[22]Paul and Rabinow (1976) demonstrate the close relationship between the impulse to control the Other and a "scientific" project that attempts to impose Western rationality and make the Other an object.

[23]Examples of the representation are Griaule (1965), Lizot (1976), and Maybury-Lewis (1968).

▓ CONCLUSION

The contemplative stance thus pervades anthropology, disguising the confrontation between Self and Other and rendering the discipline powerless to address the vulnerability of the Self. We have seen many forms of this epistemological conceit: in the contemplative pursuit of the abstract or the concrete object, anthropology denies either the subjectivity of the Self, or of the Other, or of both, and refuses to examine the conditions that shape the pursuit; in those efforts that focus on practice or on the fieldwork experience, the authors either strive to turn attention away from their own presence and that of the society that has brought them into confrontation with the Other, or refuse to use their specific experience to explicitly attack the contemplative impulse that they tacitly oppose.

In this way, anthropology has confronted the Other in a manner that works to muffle the Other's potential challenge. This adds a regrettable new dimension to the dominance that has enabled the anthropologist to initiate encounters with the Other in the first place: that dominance, which consistently challenges the Other, is now buttressed by an epistemology that does not allow the Other to challenge the Self. Under the appearance of discord, the many anthropological genres speak in fundamental harmony and echo, again and again, their own invulnerability.

13

Toward Reconstitution: An Anthropological Wager

✜ DESPAIR AND DIALECTIC

The critique I have offered so far of an anthropology that shelters itself and its own social system has been phrased in almost purely epistemological terms. The epistemological critique, however, is not the starting point but is called for once one recognizes that modern anthropology owes its development to a particular social system at a critical moment in that system's history: the discipline emerged within a portion of the world that sent emissaries—military, religious, economic, cultural—who systematically intruded upon, plundered, and often simply destroyed other human groups. Anthropology, even though it contested specific aspects of this historical process, was nonetheless formed by it.[1]

The inability of anthropology to transcend this situation has been noted, on the epistemological level, by many authors.[2] Talal Asad has joined this to a critique that focuses on the political dimensions of anthropology's situation:

The plausibility of the anthropological enterprise which seemed so self-evident to all its practitioners a mere decade ago, is now no longer quite so self-evident. . . . The answer . . . is to be sought in the fact that since the Second World War, fundamental changes have occurred in the world which social anthropology inhabits, changes which have affected the object, the

---

[1]My arguments should therefore be seen as continuing the work of those anthropologists whose critique of the discipline has been tied to a critical approach to the project of Western society as a whole. See, for example, Diamond (1974) or, more recently, Barnett and Silverman (1979). Western studies of the Middle East have been critically analyzed from a similar perspective by Edward Said (1978).

[2]For example, Derrida has argued that "ethnology—like any science—comes about within the element of discourse. And it is primarily a European science employing traditional concepts, however much it may struggle against them" (1972, p. 252).

ideological support and the organizational base of social anthropology itself. ... We are today becoming increasingly aware of the fact that information and understanding produced by bourgeois disciplines like anthropology are acquired and used most readily by those with the greater capacity for exploitation. This follows partly from the structure of research, but more especially from the way in which these disciplines objectify their knowledge... anthropology has not very easily turned to the production of radically subversive forms of understanding... it is most easily accommodated to the mode of life, and hence to the rationality of the world power which the West represents. (1975, pp. 10–17)

Some anthropologists, unhappy with the way in which the discipline objectifies knowledge, have managed to express their despair but have left it for others to draw the implications. Radin, for one, regrets "the impossibility of obtaining an inside view.... A native informant is, at best, interested merely in satisfying the demands of the investigator" (1963, p. 1). Radin's own effort to convey the Other's true subjectivity confronts "limitations... [which] are further increased by the circumstances under which the knowledge is usually imparted, circumstances of a nature tending to destroy practically all the subjective values" (1963, p. 1). Kluckhohn voices a similar lament: "The anthropologist almost never works with materials which have been produced entirely spontaneously for confidential or indeed for no eyes other than those of the author. He must instigate his subject to produce the materials for his (the anthropologist's) purposes" (1945, p. 79). Geertz, too, labors under a like dilemma: "so far as it has reinforced the anthropologist's impulse to engage himself with his informants as persons rather than as objects, the notion of 'participant observation' has been a valuable one. But, to the degree it has led the anthropologist to block from his view the very special, culturally bracketed nature of his own role and to imagine himself something more than an interested (in both senses of that word) sojourner, it has been our most powerful source of bad faith" (1973, p. 20).

We see now that the source of this despair lies in the hopeless search for an Other who supposedly can be isolated both from the Self and from the conditions that shape the encounter between Self and Other. This search *must* fail, for the premises of the contemplative stance lead to unresolvable contradictions: between an "objective" Self without history and culture and one whose "questions" must, by the nature of language and human experience, be culturally and historically phrased; between a pristine Other untouched by the Self and an Other whose very "answers" arise during and through contact with the Self.

An anthropological project that stifles the dialectic of Self and Other and refuses to set that dialectic in its particular context leads it seems, in the best of cases, to personal despair. But there are historical consequences too, and they may be pernicious: such a project, however modest it may seem when set beside the movement of armies, the missionary enterprise, or the growth of centralized technology and the dominance of the nation-state, contributes, by sheltering the Self and the Self's origins, to disarming and rendering harmless the Other.

To challenge such consequences, anthropology must revise its task, which can no longer be one that allows the Self to disappear. Anthropology, rooted in confrontations in which Self and Other interact directly with one another, must be seen, instead, as a particular form of social action that *creates* historically and culturally conditioned encounters that *produce* an interdependent Self and Other. More specifically, anthropology must begin to demonstrate the tie between an Other that is created as a relation to Self, and a Self that emerges in its encounter with the Other. Furthermore, this dialectic of Self and Other must be situated in its particular cultural and historical terrain: both Self and Other develop as they do only as a product of the specific conditions that permit their confrontation to take place at all and, in this case, as the implementation of an anthropological project in which the western Self embarks on a search to understand the nonwestern Other.

⌘ THE WAGER: "YES, BUT YOU MUST WAGER. IT IS NOT VOLUNTARY FOR YOU ARE EMBARKED. HOW WILL YOU WAGER, THEN?"—PASCAL

We can now begin to seek positive answers to our earlier question: How is anthropology to make its own vulnerability central? This question clearly implies others: a project that is vulnerable is one that may fail; how, then, can anthropology consciously embrace the possibility of its own failure? How can it become able to articulate the nature of that failure? Furthermore, if the anthropologist initiates the project facing the risk of failure, it is on the basis of his or her hope that the project will be successful. Only with this hope would one become willing to stake an important part of one's own life on this specific effort.

Yet, no matter how much care the anthropologist devotes to his or her project, its success depends upon more than individual effort. This problematic success is inevitably tied to social forces beyond the anthropologist's control: at the very least, for example, it depends upon an anthropological community that accepts the project as meaningful, and upon a world political situation that allows the project to be implemented. This stake thus binds, indissolubly, the individual's project to particular forces in the social world, and the project necessarily contributes, in its own small way, to the power of those forces.

The anthropological project now no longer appears as "the observation of external events," "the uncovering of hidden phenomena," or "the contemplation of scientific facts." Its constituent elements are not neutrality, objectivity, and distance but rather, as in all human action, "risk, the possibility of failure, hope of success and the synthesis of these three in the form of a faith which is a wager" (Goldmann 1964, p. 301).[3] And, as "a wager on the success of his own action and, consequently, on the existence of a force which transcends the individual" (Goldmann 1964, p. 301), it is a wager that destroys the notion of an isolated and independent Self.

The wager aspect of human action is undeniable once we recognize that the contemplative stance, too, exemplifies a wager, although it explicitly argues for the independence of subject and object, for an objective Self whose standpoint is beyond criticism, and thus against its own wager character. It is necessarily a wager because those who hold the contemplative stance, who defend it or promote it, are acting *in* the world, are a force *in* the world, although they claim to make observations *about* a world that supposedly exists without them in the same way as it does with them. Contemplators are wagering upon and supporting forces in the world that seek to strengthen the Self and divorce Self from Other, that strive to immunize the Self and to paralyze the Other.

All wagers are therefore not of the same form and it might be useful to note Goldmann's comparison of Pascal's wager with the Marxist wager: "Pascal's position [is]: ... he wagers that God exists, and that He is independent of any human will. ... What characterizes Marxism is the wager which it places upon the reality that we must create" (1964, p. 91).

It is important to understand the distinction between Pascal's and the Marxist wager, because it is similar to the distinction between a contemplative anthropology and the alternative I am suggesting. It might help to contrast a bet on a horse race with one in a poker game. At the track, the influence of the actual bet on the outcome is, in principle, nil and, as in Pascal's wager, one is betting on a reality that is independent of one's will and action. In a poker game, on the other hand, each player's bet is not only a prediction of the outcome, but also an attempt to influence the outcome (through bluffing, forcing other players in the hand to drop out, perhaps underbetting one's hand to keep them in, and so on), and on this level is similar to the Marxist wager.[4]

However much the previous world situation may have called for a contemplative interpretation of human reality and human action that refused to recognize its own wager aspect, today's world challenges conceptions of an independent Self and Other and calls into question views that break the tie between individual action and its social context. For it is a world dominated by ideological systems that claim universality and governed by economic forces and institutions that weld geographically

---

[3]Goldmann's very important book, to which I am heavily indebted, uses the wager and, in particular, Pascal's and Marx's wager, as its central theme (1964).

[4]I have discussed Lukacs's particular exemplification of a Marxist wager in Dwyer (1979).

distant regions into tightly connected networks; a world where overt and covert political alliances work to transform smaller nations into provinces and substates of more powerful ones; where differences between, and variety within, human groups are remodeled into hierarchy and domination. A contemplative vision is neither simply blind to this world nor outside it but testifies, instead, to a wager upon social action, which, in denying its own vulnerability, seeks to reinforce domination and to consume and level what is different from it.

What must distinguish the anthropological project, then, is not that it is a wager; so, we have seen, is all human action. Rather, its distinctiveness and its significance should grow out of the fact that in its relationship to its own society and to that part of human experience it has sought to understand, and in the way it pursues that understanding, it is pushed to recognize its own vulnerability and its wager nature.

⊠ THE DIALOGICAL PERSPECTIVE AS A WAGER

To what extent, then, is the fieldwork "record" in part 1 a wager and one that recognizes itself as such? To what extent does the "record" show that the contemplative stance is unmistakably subverted in the fieldwork situation: in the personal confrontation between Self and Other, the barrier between the two is broken down as the parties interact, daily, with one another; also, the illusion of an objective Self becomes untenable, because mere participation in the confrontation inevitably locates the Self culturally as the "outsider" intruding on the Other's terrain, and historically as a representative of a society that has a prior history of intrusion.

Such confrontations, and indeed all confrontations between people, necessarily have certain "dialogical" characteristics—characteristics that run counter to, and are suppressed in, contemplative interpretations. First, the confrontation is "sequential": the confrontation unfolds over time and in a particular sequence; its meaning at any moment is "recursive"—it depends upon the meaning of what has preceded and may force a revision of earlier meaning. Second, the confrontation is "contingent": its continuity must not be taken for granted simply because a given confrontation has lasted, and its meaning at any moment must incorporate the fact that rupture has so far been averted but may yet ensue. Third, the confrontation is "embarked": it is necessarily tied to specific social forces that transcend personal activity, its success or failure depends in part on such forces and, in its own limited way, the confrontation contributes to those forces. These dialogical characteristics reflect in turn, if somewhat schematically, the fact that all human action refers to both past and future, constitutes a choice, and has social implications.

An anthropological approach that incorporates these characteristics will be posing a number of sharp challenges to traditional anthropology and, more generally, to prevailing Western conceptions of "valid" knowledge. To demonstrate the recursive nature of meaning is to offer an alternative to normal scientific argument based on events whose content is forever fixed and on logical progress from simple to complex, from known to unknown. To insist on the inherent, ever-present possibility of rupture is to counter views of the anthropological project that require continuity and demand goals and strategies elaborated prior to the confrontation; now, instead, the anthropologist will welcome rather than reject the incessant adjustment and modification that again and again are required in the course of the confrontation and that orient the original project in new directions. To examine the tie between the confrontation and relevant social forces is to undermine the view that individual action can be divorced from its tie to the social world: here, anthropologists might now seek to examine and articulate the tie between their action and the social world and thus go beyond merely accepting that world as it was presented to them. All this, taken together, would permit, at least in principle, an anthropology that is able to challenge not only its practitioners' specific actions and its own theoretical formulations (a limited challenge that every science prides itself on being capable of making), but also to challenge both the discipline itself and the society within which that discipline developed.

▓ WAGER, DIALOGUE, AND THE FIELDWORK "RECORD"

How, then, does the fieldwork "record" embody these dialogical elements? Perhaps we can begin to answer this question by contrasting this "record" with other similar presentations in anthropology.

The conversation and, in particular, the conversation with the "key informant" has often been seen as the cornerstone of anthropological fieldwork. One anthropologist has stated this quite baldly:

In the field the relationship most critical to the ethnographer, the one that actually changes him from tourist to ethnographer, is the relationship with his informant. Whenever you think of the ethnologist in the field, you think of him as an ethnographer talking long hours with his informant. The ethnographer does many other things. . . . But sooner or later, the ethnographer feels that he must spend more time with his informant, for the informant has the type of knowledge that the ethnographer must have in order to understand this community. (Richardson 1975, p. 520).[5]

---

[5]Similar assumptions underlie Casagrande's book (1964) and many others.

The fieldwork "record" in part 1 might well be accused of reflecting the same assumptions that, locating valid knowledge in the "isolated" individual, undoubtedly contribute to the pervasiveness of the contemplative stance. It is tempting to defend against such a charge by noting, first, the emphasis placed on the individual and on binary ties between individuals, rather than on the activities of various social groups, in recent interpretations

Yet even where anthropologists have focused on such conversations, their contemplative stance has turned them away from the dialogical elements and they promote a number of corresponding fictions. Paramount among these fictions, and corresponding to the "journey" metaphors that dominate interpretations of fieldwork, is the view that through long-term acquaintance and rapport, Self and Other transcend their differences and attain communication with one another that is free from distortion; that Self and Other ultimately become transparent to one another, and their differences, rather than continually creating new meaning and new forms of mutual understanding, require only the technical task of translation. This has corollaries that are symptomatic of the rejection of a dialogical perspective: (1) that the dialectic of question and answer is not an intrinsic component of meaning; it only dresses meaning and can be stripped off and discarded when the author bares the Other's hidden significance; and (2) that communication may be severed from its timing and sequence, that segments may be recombined

---

of Moroccan society (e.g., "The constant focus in Moroccan society [is] not, therefore, on corporate groups but on individuals; not on the sanctions through which behavior can be channelled and limited, but on arranging associations wherever they appear most advantageous; not on a widely ramified set of solidary groupings of which one is a member but on the customary ways in which personal ties to others can be contracted" [Rosen 1973, p. 158], a view echoed by Eickelman [1976, p. 120], by Geertz [1980, pp. 204–5], and by Rosen again and again [1980, pp. 20ff.]). Another line of defense that I might offer would be to draw a parallel between the individual pursuit in the "record" and the "intensive search" ("exploring matters in depth with particular partners [rather] than surveying widely through the market . . . a case approach rather than a sampling one" [Geertz 1980, p. 224]) that Clifford Geertz suggests characterizes the bazaar and its Moroccan counterpart, the *suq.* (Geertz recoils from proposing that "Maghrebian society is a big bazaar," yet suggests, nonetheless, that "in the details of bazaar life something of the spirit that animates that society . . . can be seen with a particular and revelatory vividness" [1980, p. 235].)

(It should perhaps also be remarked at this point that such interpretations as these, which focus on the individual, developed in part as a response to what now certainly appears as an overly rigid segmentary interpretation of Moroccan society put forward primarily by Gellner [1969]. Gellner's view has been very effectively questioned by Hammoudi [1980, first published in 1974]. Brown, in his study of the city of Salé, presents convincing historical information that challenges both the extreme segmentary and individualist views [1976, pp. 212–18].)

I might also defend against the charge of an "individualist" emphasis by simply stating that anthropology is structured primarily as an individual effort, with the basic methodological procedure being the encounter between individuals, and that the fieldwork "record" merely reflects this.

However, all such responses would beg the question and close discussion at a point where I feel it should be opened. One of the merits of the fieldwork "record" is, I hope, that it allows us to address to the "record" questions concerning the limitations placed upon knowledge by structuring it as an individual pursuit.

For comprehensive critiques of the notion of the "individual," see Dumont (1965) and Barnett and Silverman (1979). Goldmann (1971) has some interesting remarks on this issue.

and reordered and some eliminated, with no vital loss of meaning. These fictions promote a view in which Self and Other are only provisionally different, a view that posits an Other that can be tamed and captured, at some point, for good.

These fictions can be seen in some of the best known works that have tried to restitute the Other's voice: those of Oscar Lewis, of Sidney Mintz, and of Carlos Castaneda. Lewis, perpetually beset by the tension between subjectivity and objectivity, sought to resolve this in a number of ways but never saw the presentation of dialogue as one of them, nor ever recognized the significance of the dialogical elements mentioned above. In the *Children of Sanchez,* he employed a method (which recalls Kluckhohn) of "multiple biographies... to offset the subjectivity inherent in a single autobiography" (1961, p. xi); in *La Vida* (1965) he juxtaposed the autobiographies with "days in the life" of his subjects. In each case, Lewis allowed himself free reign with the material, reorganizing and editing and thus *creating* autobiographies. Lewis, besides, never appears as a character in his books.

Mintz admits explicitly that "creating autobiography" raises important problems, and he does not reduce dialogue to the appearance of monologue, as Lewis does. Nonetheless, although recognizing that he had to severely edit the final manuscript if it "were to be read as autobiography" (1974, p. 8), Mintz fails to address the significance his act imparts to the manuscript or the extent to which it poses basic theoretical questions.

Castaneda's Don Juan series closely sticks to dialogue (it should be noted, however, that a number of anthropologists have disputed its accuracy and the veracity of Castaneda's books). Yet, in the first work of this group (1969), we find the unresolved tension between a contemplative stance (as seen in the final "structuralist" chapter) and the "naive" approach of the representation (as seen in the "conversations") which plagues the series as a whole. The later works in the series allow the interviews to speak for themselves and simply stifle the contemplative moment rather than supercede it: there is no attempt to articulate the relationship between these interviews and other anthropological genres, and therefore the critical significance of the work is only too easily confined.

All three authors, whatever their differences and whatever the various merits of their work, betray one fundamental similarity: in hiding the operations that they have performed on the text, they effectively blind the reader to the fieldwork confrontation itself and thus deprive him or her of the chance to seriously criticize the author's work.[6]

[6]In two recent books on Morocco (Rabinow 1977, Crapanzano 1980—unfortunately, I came upon Crapanzano's only as mine was being readied for publication), anthropologists have tried to convey the encounter with the Other from perspectives close to mine; nonetheless, the differences are marked and some, perhaps, should be spelled out.

Both Rabinow and Crapanzano challenge, as I do, the dominant anthropological view

The conversation can, however, be looked at differently, dialogically. To do this requires, at the very least, that both the Other and the Self remain visible and that we attempt to set them in the situation of their encounter. As a first step, we should not suppress the question or make responses appear as spontaneous declarations; we should preserve the

---

that the discipline's theoretical statements can be divorced from the anthropologist's practical activity, from his or her direct encounter with the Other. Rabinow, for example, disputes the view that "under no circumstances is there any direct relation between field activity and the theories which lie at the core of the discipline" (1977, pp. 4–5), that "the enterprise of inquiry is essentially discontinuous from its results" (1977, p. 5); Crapanzano argues against anthropologists who "efface themselves in their descriptive ethnographies ... [who] deny the essential dynamics of the encounter and end up producing a static picture of the people he has studied and their ways" (1980, p. ix), and who therefore fail to portray the "ethnographic encounter ... [as] a complex negotiation in which the parties to the encounter acquiesce to a certain reality" (1980, p. ix).

Rabinow and Crapanzano each focuses on a different domain—Rabinow on the fieldwork experience, Crapanzano on the ethnographic encounter between anthropologist and informant—and each finds a different form of presentation.

Rabinow conveys the "enterprise of inquiry" as a "reconstruction of a set of encounters that occurred while doing fieldwork" (1977, p. 6), a reconstruction "made to seem ... neat and coherent ... so as to salvage some meaning from that period for myself and for others" (1977, p. 6). Rabinow's central goal is one of "interpretation" or "understanding" and more particularly, "the comprehension of self by the detour of the comprehension of the other" (1977, p. 5, where Rabinow is quoting from Ricoeur 1969, p. 20).

Rabinow's "reconstruction" attests to several assumptions radically different from mine. For Rabinow, the fieldwork experience, like a journey, moves forward (his progressive chapter titles are one symptom of this) and leads, ultimately, to an encounter with "fundamental Otherness" (1977, p. 161). One should certainly question the notion of "fundamental Otherness," a notion that implies an irreducible and fixed difference between Self and Other, and denies that the encounter between Self and Other may continually generate new meaning. Yet even if we suppose for a moment the existence of "fundamental Otherness," the reader of Rabinow's book notes with dismay that Rabinow skirts rather than confronts the "fundamental Other" and, more subtly, seriously disguises and distorts the encounter between Self and Other.

Two telling indications that Rabinow's gaze does not converge on the "fundamental Other" may be mentioned. First, Rabinow's final chapter, where he encounters the "fundamental Other," is rather brief—in fact, it is one of the shortest in his book, whereas by all rights it might be the longest. (The "record" of my fieldwork, in part 1, may be seen as an extension of, and as a challenge to, Rabinow's final chapter and to his notion of the "fundamental Other.") Second, Rabinow's "friend"—his concrete exemplification of the "fundamental Other"—disappears behind a number of cultural generalizations, as Rabinow does too, and a timeless, abstract Self and Other take their place.

A more serious criticism of Rabinow's approach is that he denies solidity to the Other. In his own words: "This book is a studied condensation of a swirl of people, places and feelings ... some informants with whom I worked are not mentioned, some are collapsed into the figures presented here, and others are left out altogether" (1977, p. 6). Rabinow's freedom to decompose and recompose the Other has its source in an epistemology in which the moment of "interpretation" dominates, in an extreme fashion, prior experience; in which, as Rabinow says, "the meaning of each chapter depends on what comes after it" (1977, p. 6); in which the meaning of the fieldwork experience can be fundamentally transformed by the anthropologist's later "reconstruction" of it, and where the reader is

timing of the dialogue; and we should listen to the dialogue in its own context and situation. At least then we keep open the possibility of hearing the challenges to the Self that the Other may voice.

The texts in the fieldwork "record" testify to such an attempt. Let me now suggest several ways to approach these texts which hold to the

---

kept more distant from the experience than necessary and allowed substantially reduced critical insight into the work. This epistemology, which contrasts with my own emphasis on the recursive rather than linear nature of meaning and with my attempt to bring the reader as close as possible to the experience, necessarily awards to the "interpreter" the role of the final arbiter of meaning and, in so doing, works to erode the integrity of the Other. The comprehension of the Other has become, indeed, a "detour" in pursuit of a higher goal, the comprehension of the Self.

Crapanzano presents a series of conversations with Tuhami, an "exceptional" Moroccan, an "outsider, an outcast even," who "was married to a capricious, vindictive she-demon, a camel-footed *jinniyya*, a spirit, named 'Aisha Qandisha, who kept a firm control on his amorous life" (1980, p. 5). These conversations, all held with Crapanzano's field assistant present, were, in effect, the only meetings that Crapanzano and Tuhami had; as Crapanzano notes, "to have extended our relationship from the privileged domain of the interview to that of everyday life would have been too disrupting for Tuhami, and perhaps for me" (1980, p. 13). Crapanzano's interviews offer him the occasion to reflect upon and interpret Moroccan life, his own role as an anthropologist, and his encounter with the Other.

Some substantial differences between Crapanzano's book and mine should already be obvious: for example, his focus on the "exotic" and mine on the more mundane, and his removing the encounter from everyday life and my insistence on confronting the dialogues with everyday life. Also, Crapanzano's attitude to the interview contrasts with mine: almost all of Tuhami's words occur in short extracts selected from longer conversations that do not appear in the book; Crapanzano omits sections he takes to be irrelevant and weaves together parts of interviews held at different times. As well, Crapanzano frequently offers summary interpretations of Tuhami's ideas and attitudes, and presents "objective" analyses of Moroccan life and culture that are as neutral and distanced as those given in more traditional works on Morocco.

Crapanzano's main aim, therefore, appears to be an eclectic rather than a critical one: to introduce a psychoanalytic perspective into an understanding of the encounter between anthropologist and informant. Crapanzano is well aware of this, for he notes at the outset that "the reader will recognize too, especially in my questions, a psychoanalytic orientation that I have found impossible to eliminate" (1980, p. 10). This orientation is evident, too, in the fact that Crapanzano's interviews with Tuhami are insulated, as are psychoanalytic ones, from everyday life; in the strongly "interpretive" nature of many of Crapanzano's interventions in the text; in Crapanzano's view that "Tuhami and I both negotiated our exchange into a therapeutic one" (1980, p. 133), and his emphasis, throughout the final chapter, on the theme of curing.

It is not surprising, then, that Crapanzano tends to see the encounter's development as an example of the transference and counter-transference that characterize, according to psychoanalysts, the relationship between psychoanalyst and patient: Crapanzano begins his effort as a seeker of information, confronting an informant primarily interested in "evocation" (1980, p. 14); he begins with a culturally based predilection for the "real" and faces a person for whom "the real was a metaphor for the true" (1980, pp. 129–30). Although Tuhami may come to use more and more the language of the "real" in his movement toward Crapanzano (1980, p. 143), it is Crapanzano who appears to be more deeply seduced by Tuhami's evocative mode (1980, pp. 140–41). One might even say that

sequential, contingent, and *embarked* aspects of the confrontation and which point to questions that might expose this anthropological project to its own vulnerability.

Sequence: the texts contain "utterances" that are clearly ordered in time and in relation to what has preceded; meaning is not constructed in a linear manner but is recursive, depending upon and calling into question what has preceded.[7]

If we return again to the poker table, we might note that successive betting rounds exemplify the sequential principle and give each bet its recursive meaning: to evaluate the meaning of any given bet, one must

---

Crapanzano has been so profoundly affected that, in his own book, the tone is strongly evocative and rhetorical. Here, Crapanzano shows more sensitivity to the Other than Rabinow, a sensitivity stated well when he qualifies the same quotation from Ricoeur that Rabinow cited (see above) with the sentence "There is also a value, coordinate with tact and respect for the other, in pushing the swing of comprehension back to the other" (1980, p. 139).

As sensitive as he has been toward the Other, Crapanzano, in at least one important respect, leaves the Self unexamined: he refrains from questioning the extent to which his own structuring of the encounter as a psychoanalytic one, his focus on the exceptional and his removal of the encounter from everyday life, in effect create the opposition between the "real" and the "evocative." Related questions should also be posed: to what extent does this specific kind of encounter privilege the "evocative" over the "real"? Does such an encounter raise the odds in the contest between "real" and "evocative" in the latter's favor? Has Crapanzano unwittingly "introduce[d] into the object the principles of his relation to the object" (Bourdieu 1977, p. 2)?

Crapanzano is well aware that his decision to structure the encounter in the way he has has important implications, for he states that "as anthropologists, we have a responsibility to the people we study... to recognize the ethical and political implications of our discipline. Every interpretive strategy... involves choice and falls, thereby, into the domain of ethics and politics" (1980, pp. x–xi). Crapanzano's effort, limited as it is to the domain of personal action and rhetorical interaction, poses only a restricted challenge to anthropology, to his own society, to the Self. It would have been helpful if Crapanzano himself had traced more explicitly these implications.

What I have said about these two books may seem deeply critical. Yet, it should be clear that I have given them so much space here because each author has gone far (although I believe not far enough) toward creating an anthropological work in which the Self is exposed as it searches for the Other. If in Rabinow's book Self and Other are too general, too abstract, and the Self shows a certain disregard for the Other; and if in Crapanzano's the encounter is too insular, too personalized, and his evocative homage to the Other is, more accurately, a self-fulfilling homage to the Self and the psychoanalytic interview: these are faults that are signposts of each author's character and interests and, therefore, marks of the success, albeit partial and equivocal, of their efforts.

[7]Bourdieu, criticizing objective knowledge and the construction of rules in anthropology, and arguing for renewed attention to strategy and practice, stresses the importance of time. His view is close to mine: "To substitute *strategy* for the *rule* is to reintroduce time, with its rhythm, its orientation, its irreversibility. Science has a time which is not that of practice. For the analyst, time no longer counts" (1977, p. 9). Bourdieu's remarks are even more germane, because they grow out of his discussion of exchange and the various time-related strategies that affect the meaning of exchanges (1977, pp. 4–8).

see it as more than an instantaneous prediction and interpret it in the light of betting on previous rounds. At the same time, each bet also contributes to the meaning of earlier betting. The *exact sequence* of bets, then, is an essential component of any particular bet's meaning. Contrast this, for instance, with the nonrecursive meaning of a move in a chess game: the possibilities of the game are wholly contained within the present position and it matters not at all, in assessing that position, what the exact sequence of moves was that led to it.

Questions relating to sequence and recursivity can, in principle, refer to any moment in the fieldwork "record." Most noticeably, perhaps, the final dialogue (in ch. 11), which directly examines my relationship with the Faqir, explicitly calls for a reinterpretation of all that has gone before it. Yet what has gone before must influence the meaning of that final interview and thus must affect the very basis for such a reinterpretation. We are now deprived of an Archimedean point from which "definitive" meaning, valid once and for all, can be established.

There are more specific examples. In the first dialogue, the Faqir frowned upon ostentiousness in referring to his second marriage (see ch. 1, n.18); in chapter 8, we learn that this very issue was part of the Faqir's quarrel with his new in-laws over the recent marriage of his daughter to their son. Again in the first dialogue, the Faqir refers in passing to the fact that he does little more than say "hello" to his newly married daughter when he visits her; in chapter 8 problems are aggravated by his and his daughter's reticence toward one another. In both instances, it would be a mistake to attribute to the Faqir static cultural notions; rather, his views respond to experience and continually call for a questioning and reinterpretation of the past and the present (for some other examples, see ch. 7, n.7; ch. 9, n.5; ch. 11, nn. 2 and 13).

More generally, if we wish to hold to the sequential nature of the fieldwork experience as we pose questions of the text, we must make every effort to avoid distorting the text irretrievably by cutting it into bits and pieces or by playing freely with its actual order in time, just as we have tried to resist doing the same to the fieldwork experience in transforming it into a text. Bearing this in mind, we must ask to what extent this text retains a wholeness, a substantiality, that reflects the sequential and recursive character of the experience and yet does not shield the text and so discourage the reader from actively responding to it.

It should not be necessary to add that the reader's active participation is crucial, because only in this way does the individual anthropologist move the Other's challenge beyond the realm of the anthropologist's own personal experience. In effect, the reader adds, in reacting to this book, a new public chapter to it. This chapter, too, both depends upon the meaning of what has preceded and calls that meaning into question. (The reader's chapter, to take an extreme but perhaps not unlikely possibility, may judge the arguments I have made to be unconvincing and the entire confrontation to be senseless.) In any event, the reader is necessarily forced into a creative role with respect to these texts and to the arguments made here: in agreeing with them, modifying them, or even rejecting them, the reader inevitably joins the dialogue and must recognize that he or she too is involved in the wager.

Contingency: the complex manner in which rupture is or is not averted is basic to the meaning of the text.[8]

How is the possibility of rupture part of the texture of the confrontation? First of all, my very relationship with the Faqir was a product of certain decisions that I took and that others took, sometimes deliberately and sometimes without thinking, which sustained that relationship, brought me closer to the Faqir, and made me more distant from other Moroccans. The fieldwork experience, therefore, was not the practical implementation of a prior theoretical plan but, instead, the product of my continually developing intentions and the resistance, acceptance, and opposition of many other people. We might then ask questions about the processes of accommodation and rejection that led to this particular experience, and how its meaning might be related to other parts of the fieldwork experience in which rupture was abrupt and final.

A number of further questions arise from this. First of all, if meaning is closely tied to the nature of the specific confrontation, then an understanding of the Self's confrontation with the Other should include examination of encounters in which continuity was of other sorts. For example, what about meaning in those confrontations where the Other has been someone who clings to the anthropologist and who is often broken with harshly? Or in those where the Other sets out to use the anthropologist instrumentally and faces the anthropologist's refusals? or in those where the anthropologist has been rejected outright by the Other? (There are several short texts in the fieldwork "record" of encounters with people other than the Faqir that are suggestive in this light.)

One should also ask if there is anything about the complex mixture of rupture and continuity, of the predictable and the unexpected, which made my encounter with the Faqir satisfying to both of us from the beginning, and which made us both anxious to continue it. Is such a mixture similar to that which other anthropologists have unconsciously sought in settling on "key informants"? Might this allow us to say something about a "threshold of the unexpected" that the Self and anthropology can tolerate?

In many ways, however, although total rupture was averted during my confrontation with the Faqir, the continuity of that confrontation is

---

[8]Rabinow phrases this well: "Interruptions and eruptions mock the fieldworker and his inquiry; more accurately, they may be said to inform his inquiry, to be an essential part of it. The constant breakdown, it seems to me, is not just an annoying accident but a core aspect of this type of inquiry" (1977, p. 154).

problematic and more complex than might appear at first glance. Each dialogue, for example, is separate from every other, and within the dialogues there are very clear shifts of topics: beginnings and endings do not follow inevitably from what preceded but are concrete results of the participants' actions and components of every text's meaning. How does terminating a discussion at a particular moment influence meaning? What, for example, is the significance of my not pursuing certain topics (e.g. ch. 4, n.4; ch. 11, n.4)? Who initiates any particular rupture, and what appears to bring such termination about (see, for example, ch. 11, n.15)? If I seem responsible for rupture at certain points, we may well ask whether there are similarities between the structure such endings give to discussions and the structure I have given to the events themselves. Do any of these considerations shed light on the structure of the book as a whole?

In addition, each dialogue contains "episodes," points at which I introduce prepared questions and effect rupture of another sort (these questions appear in boldface italics). What can be said of the succession of questions and their part in defining the subject under discussion (see, for example, ch. 5, n.8; ch. 10, n.5; ch. 11, n.8)? On the other hand, the Faqir does not passively yield to this inquiry, but also creates rupture by deflecting questions, by answering tersely (or at length), or by other tactics (see ch. 4, nn.5, 7, and 16). Our roles are far from symmetrical and we must question the effect of this asymmetry on the production of meaning.

Yet, although partial and incomplete ruptures inhere in the texts, total rupture is averted over the course of the confrontation. How, then, does the production of meaning evolve as the confrontation continues? Does, for example, the nature of the questions and answers and the relationship between them alter? What is the significance of moments where the style of the dialogue is more staccatolike, or more expansive, or conversational and symmetrical?

Embarkation: the confrontation is not simply between individuals but between the social, cultural, and historical interests these individuals carry with them.[9] The confrontation thus provokes a calling into question of the forces that make it possible and a calling into question of the Self (again, in its extended sense), and it allows us to probe the wager aspect of the effort.

[9]Bourdieu emphasizes the same point, that "'interpersonal' relations are never, except in appearance, *individual-to-individual* relationships and that the truth of the interaction is never entirely contained in the interaction.... In fact it is their present and past positions in the social structure that biological individuals carry with them, at all times and places.... Even those forms of interaction seemingly most amenable to description in terms of 'intentional transfer into the Other,' such as sympathy, friendship, or love, are dominated... by the objective structure of the relations between social conditions" (1977, pp. 81–82).

We must now begin to ask how this fieldwork experience and its text can provide a commentary on the confrontation between the West and peoples from other societies. How, for instance, might we examine the tie between a Western societal project that has been imperialist, intrusive, and disruptive, and an anthropology that has seen the West pose all the questions; between views of this historical process that tend to hide its violence and coercion, and an anthropology that has refused to recognize its own dialogical and wager nature?

The anthropologist, in the very act of singling out events for attention and asking questions about them, cannot avoid defining topics in ways that reflect the concerns and style of his own society. Specifically, many questions grow out of the western academic literature on Morocco (e.g., ch. 5, nn.4 and 6), or out of interests very closely related to western or American experience (e.g., as throughout chs. 4 and 6). There is ample evidence, too, of certain intellectual strategies on the anthropologist's part that tend to dominate academic anthropology and other "scientific" fields: the attempt to move from concrete instances to abstract rules (see ch. 3, n.2); the attempt to undermine general statements by suggesting counterinstances (as in ch. 4, n.12; ch. 7, n.5); the very setting up of categories themselves (e.g., "religious purposes" versus "health reasons" in the discussion of circumcision in chapter 3, "rural" versus "urban" in chapter 8).

Again and again, too, the anthropologist makes certain stylistic demands, only some of which are explicit (ch. 10, p. 203; ch. 11, n.1), that privilege his and his own society's needs. One demand, implicit throughout the "record" but never directly addressed, raises significant questions that are perhaps impossible to answer: How was the style and substance of all the dialogues limited by my knowledge of Arabic; although I was quite fluent, I could never have the facility of a native speaker. How, when talking to me, did the Faqir adjust, and inevitably betray, the force of his usual speech, which, when he was among his peers, was incisive and often spellbinding, and which seemed to command, from villagers and other people from the region, a respect rivaled, I thought, only by the Sheikh's?

In addition, one should certainly reiterate a question I posed earlier (see ch. 4, n.8): How does the solicitousness and tentativeness of the anthropologist's manner reflect changing relations between the West and other societies?

In all these ways, at the very least, the anthropologist is embarked on his own society's mission. Yet this embarkation is not static; in particular it is repeatedly called into question and transformed by the encounter with the Other: here, by the Faqir's own resistance to my intentions (see ch. 4, n.12, where the Faqir remains firm in face of counterinstances I present; ch. 6, n.3, where he may be sensitive to them; ch. 8, n.12, where he is moved to further elaboration). Also, the Faqir on occasion insists on

285 / TOWARD RECONSTITUTION

certain of his own categories (e.g., ch. 4, n.14; ch. 5, n.10; ch. 9, n.13); on his own stylistic preferences (ch. 4, n.7, or, on a very different level, ch. 8, n.12).

Yet, in the direct confrontation, in staking their respective claims, both Self and Other have become vulnerable to one another, although in very different ways. It is clear that the influence of each on the other is strong: the manner in which the Faqir invokes our relationship (see ch. 2, n.11 for two instances) and the manner in which his answers respond to my interests (e.g., ch. 1, n.12; ch. 2, n.10; ch. 4, n.9) testify to this; so, too, does the way in which my questions incorporate his concerns (e.g., ch. 1, n.9; ch. 8, n.5; ch. 10, n.3).

However, although we have each taken the other into account and come to incorporate, to some extent, the other; although we have each been sensitive to the other's concerns and have come to share, albeit very unequally, one another's world: differences between us have not been surmounted but have been, instead, more deeply articulated and have generated differences on a new level (see, for example, ch. 11, nn.2, 21, 30, and 34). It is important to keep in mind that these very differences themselves should be examined for a commentary on the way in which both Self and Other are embarked on their own society's missions, missions that are, too, related to one another historically (see ch. 11, n.30).

So, we must finally ask how, and to what extent, this fieldwork experience and the effort to transform it into a public text, how and to what extent this active wager on dialogue, challenge the pattern of hierarchy and domination that so clearly marks contemporary relations between human groups.[10] Does this wager, which promotes an interdependent Self and Other, allow each to attain a solidity that effectively conveys power and resists disintegration and, at the same time, permits an awareness of vulnerability to take root?

▩ CONCLUSION

I have tried to raise a number of questions that challenge the normal practice of anthropology and the usual interpretations of the encounter between Self and Other, and I have tried to show why such a challenge needs to be formulated at all. It should be clear by now that the initial step along this path, the step without which the effort to hear the Other's challenge would be hopeless from the beginning, must be to seek forms of social action that do not silence the Other's full "voice" at the outset, that do not abstract it from its context, and that allow it to be heard in a critical address to the Self. Only in conceiving such forms and working toward them can anthropology and social action in general begin to embrace their own vulnerability. The failure to do this leads, as we have

---

[10]I have made some suggestions on this issue (Dwyer 1977).

seen, to either a monologue, as with Radin's voice of the Other or the comparativist's voice of the Self, or an antilogue where, as in the relativist approach and the pursuit of the practical, both Self and Other speak, but not to one another.

The fieldwork "record" presented here suggests an alternative to these approaches, but it should be emphasized that this alternative is in no sense meant to be definitive or to be taken as a model. It cannot provide a model, because just as the confrontation between the West and other human groups is not summarized in all its complexity by anthropology, and just as fieldwork does not encompass all phases of anthropology, neither does this "record" of events and dialogues exactly reflect the fieldwork experience. The event + dialogue motif must thus be looked at not as a model but as a suggestive metaphor for an anthropology that embraces its own wager character. It is a metaphor, the interest of which lies in its capacity to highlight several aims: to convey the integrity of the Other; to push for a critical examination of anthropology and this "record's" own success or failure in achieving its objectives; and to demonstrate the need to seek new forms of the Western project that recognize their wager aspect and their inherent vulnerability.

Postscript

It may seem somewhat paradoxical that this book, which challenges anthropology and taxes it with taking itself too seriously, with remaining too close to and too full of itself, nonetheless expends so much effort on anthropology, and does so in an apparently serious manner throughout. Would an irreverent style (and with it a lighter subtitle—perhaps, "Anthropology, you bet your...") have been more appropriate?

To some extent, I am sure that the stress on anthropology and the earnestness of theoretical argument are superfluous and might have been avoided. Some readers, who need no justification or analysis to enjoy participating, even as kibbitzers, in an encounter between a New Yorker and a Moroccan farmer, may now have realized this, to their cost; some other people, for whom "dialogical" encounters are a recognized, although perhaps unstated, part of their daily lives, may already know this without ever reading this book.

However, to some extent, too, I am just as sure that this serious tone was inevitable. It is certainly not a game to take that moment of the West's encounter with the Other when the West's project is at its most vulnerable, and to try to penetrate the shield of immunity that surrounds it. To suggest that in doing this here one might become better able to expose the vulnerability of the Self and the integrity of the Other in arenas where the Other's voice is more distant and the Self more heavily protected—to suggest this while knowing that, today's world being what it is, one is not yet able to demonstrate it—is also no joke, for the punch lines are pulled. To wager all this in a text—to try to make book out of making this book—and to do this in a text of just so many pages with perhaps even fewer readers, is not only to play with words but at times seems as futile as placing a bet when only you are willing to cover it.

It is unsettling to both attack and defend at the same time the tone of this book, and disorienting to suggest that, in some ways, it is both serious and irreverent. It is difficult, too, either to say more or to become silent, either to put up or shut up in the face of these paradoxes and others like it, but it is as clear to me as such things can be that this book, and the effort that went into it, is constructed upon and from such paradoxes.[1] I can only end, then, somewhat irreverently, by returning with the reader almost to where we began—almost, because we can never call back, or renege on, the intervening time and effort we have each wagered—to Goldmann, who might have said of this book that, "consistent with paradox itself, we must both accept and refuse it at one and the same time" (1964, p. 212).

In his own way, perhaps this was what the Faqir meant (somewhat irreverently, too) when, tired from a shortened night and after a summer filled with serious talk, he ended the final dialogue by falling asleep.

[1] I have discussed some of these paradoxes (Dwyer 1977).

Bibliography

Abun-Nasr, Jamil M.
  1965   *The Tijaniyya.* London: Oxford University Press.
Asad, Talal
  1975   Introduction. In Talal Asad (Ed.), *Anthropology and the Colonial Encounter,* pp. 9–19. Atlantic Highlands, N.J.: Humanities Press.
Ayache, Albert
  1956   *Le Maroc.* Paris: Editions Sociales.
Barnett, Steve, & Silverman, Martin
  1979   *Ideology and Everyday Life.* Ann Arbor: University of Michigan Press.
Becker, Howard
  1956   Fieldwork among Scottish Shepherds and German Peasants. *Social Forces* 35(1), 10–15.
Bourdieu, Pierre
  1977   *Outline of a Theory of Practice.* Cambridge: At the University Press.
Bowen, Elenore Smith
  1964   *Return to Laughter.* New York: Doubleday.
Brown, Kenneth L.
  1976   *People of Salé.* Manchester: Manchester University Press.
Casagrande, Joseph B. (Ed.)
  1964   *In the Company of Man.* New York: Harper & Row.
Castaneda, Carlos
  1969   *The Teachings of Don Juan.* New York: Ballantine Books.
Chagnon, Napoleon
  1968   *The Yanomamo.* New York: Holt, Rinehart & Winston.
Cote, M., & Legras, J.
  1966   La Variabilité pluviomètrique interannuelle au Maroc. *Revue de Géographie du Maroc* 10, 19–30.
Crapanzano, Vincent
  1973   *The Hamadsha: A Study in Moroccan Ethnopsychiatry.* Berkeley and Los Angeles: University of California Press.
  1980   *Tuhami.* Chicago: University of Chicago Press.
Derrida, Jacques
  1972   Structure, Sign, and Play in the Discourse of the Human Sciences. In

      R. Macksey & E. Donato (Eds.), *The Structuralist Controversy,* pp. 247–65. Baltimore: Johns Hopkins University Press.

Diamond, Stanley
    1974   *In Search of the Primitive.* New Brunswick, N.J.: Transaction Books.

Dumont, Louis
    1965   The Modern Conception of the Individual, Notes on Its Genesis. *Contributions to Indian Sociology* 8, 13–61.

Dwyer, Daisy
    1978   *Images and Self-Images.* New York: Columbia University Press.

Dwyer, Kevin
    1977   On the Dialogic of Fieldwork. *Dialectical Anthropology* 2, 143–51.
    1979   On the Dialogic of Ethnology. *Dialectical Anthropology* 4, 205–24.

Edgerton, Robert, & Langness, L. L.
    1974   *Methods and Styles in the Study of Culture.* San Francisco: Chandler & Sharp.

Eickelman, Dale F.
    1976   *Moroccan Islam.* Austin: University of Texas Press.

Epstein, A. L.
    1967   *The Craft of Social Anthropology.* London: Tavistock.

Evans-Pritchard, E. E.
    1940   *The Nuer.* Oxford: Oxford University Press.

Fernea, Elizabeth W.
    1969   *Guests of the Sheik.* New York: Anchor Books.

Foucauld, Ch. Père du
    1888   *Reconnaissances au Maroc.* Paris: Société d'éditions géographiques, maritimes, et coloniales.

Freilich, Morris (Ed.)
    1970   *Marginal Natives: Anthropologists at Work.* New York: Harper & Row.

Freire, Paolo
    1974   *Pedagogy of the Oppressed.* New York: Seabury Press.

Gadamer, H. G.
    1975   *Truth and Method.* New York: Seabury Press.

Gatell, J.
    1871   Description du Souss. *Bulletin de la Société de Géographique* 1, 81–106.

Geertz, Clifford
    1963   *Peddlers and Princes.* Chicago: University of Chicago Press.
    1968   *Islam Observed.* New Haven: Yale University Press.
    1973   *The Interpretation of Cultures.* New York: Basic Books.
    1980   *Suq:* The Bazaar Economy in Sefrou. In Clifford Geertz, Hildred Geertz, & Lawrence Rosen, *Meaning and Order in Moroccan Society,* pp. 123–313. Cambridge: At the University Press.

Gellner, Ernest
    1969   *Saints of the Atlas.* London: Weidenfeld & Nicolson.

Golde, Peggy (Ed.)
    1970   *Women in the Field.* Chicago: Aldine.

Goldmann, Lucien
    1964   *The Hidden God.* Atlantic Highlands, N.J.: Humanities Press.
    1971   Reflections on History and Class Consciousness. In Istvan Meszaros (Ed.), *Aspects of History and Class Consciousness,* pp. 65–84. London: Routledge & Kegan Paul.

Griaule, Marcel
1965   *Conversations with Ogotemmeli.* London: Oxford University Press.
Hammoudi, Abdallah
1980   Segmentarity, Social Stratification, Political Power and Sainthood: Reflections on Gellner's Theses. *Economy and Society* 9, 279–303.
Henry, Frances, & Saberwal, S. (Eds.)
1969   *Stress and Response in Fieldwork.* New York: Holt, Rinehart & Winston.
Julien, Ch.-André
1966   *Histoire de l'Afrique du Nord* (Vol. 2). Paris: Payot.
Kluckhohn, Clyde
1945   The Personal Document in Anthropological Science. In L. Gottschalk, C. Kluckhohn, & R. Angell (Eds.), *The Use of Personal Documents in History, Anthropology, and Sociology,* pp. 79–173. New York: Social Science Research Council.
Langness, Lewis L.
1965   *The Life History in Anthropological Science.* New York: Holt, Rinehart & Winston.
Lévi-Provençal, E.
1934   *Encyclopedia of Islam,* vol. 4, s.v. "Al-Sus al-Aksa."
Lévi-Strauss, Claude
1962   *La Pensée sauvage.* Paris: Plon.
Lewis, Oscar
1961   *The Children of Sanchez.* New York: Random House.
1965   *La Vida.* New York: Random House.
Lizot, Jacques
1976   *Le Cercle des feux.* Paris: Seuil.
Lukacs, Georg
1971   *History and Class Consciousness.* Cambridge, Mass.: MIT Press.
Malinowski, B.
1961   *Argonauts of the Western Pacific.* Prospect Hts., IL: Waveland Press Inc.
Mandelbaum, David G.
1973   The Study of the Life History: Gandhi. *Current Anthropology* 14(3), 177–95.
Maybury-Lewis, David
1965   *The Savage and the Innocent.* Boston: Beacon Press.
Miège, J.-L.
1961   *Le Maroc et l'Europe.* Paris: Presses Universitaires de France.
Mintz, Sidney W.
1974   *Worker in the Cane.* New York: W. W. Norton.
Morin, Françoise
1980   Pratiques anthropoliques et histoire de vie. *Cahiers Internationaux de Sociologie* 59, 313–39.
Naroll, Raoul, & Cohen, R. (eds.)
1970   *Handbook of Method in Cultural Anthropology.* New York: Natural History Press.
Nash, Dennison
1963   The Ethnologist as Stranger. *Southwestern Journal of Anthropology* 19(2), 149–67.
Nuttonson, M.
1961   *An Introduction to Northern Africa and a Survey of the Physical Environ-*

ment and Agriculture of Morocco, Algeria, and Tunisia with Special Reference to Their Regions Containing Areas Climatically and Latitudinally Analogous to Israel. Washington, D.C.: American Institute of Crop Ecology.

Paul, R., & Rabinow, P.
1976   Bourgeois Rationalism Revived. *Dialectical Anthropology* 1, 121–34.

Pelto, P. J.
1970   *Anthropological Research.* New York: Harper & Row.

Rabinow, Paul
1975   *Symbolic Domination.* Chicago: University of Chicago Press.
1977   *Reflections on Fieldwork.* Berkeley and Los Angeles: University of California Press.

Radin, Paul
1933   *Method and Theory of Ethnology.* New York: McGraw-Hill.
1963   *Autobiography of a Winnebago Indian.* New York: Dover Press.

Richardson, M.
1975   Anthropologist—the Myth Teller. *American Ethnologist* 2(3), 517–34.

Ricoeur, Paul
1969   *Le Conflit des interpretations.* Paris: Seuil.
1971   The Model of the Text. *Social Research* 38(3), 529–62.

Rosen, Lawrence
1973   The Social and Conceptual Framework of Arab-Berber Relations in Central Morocco. In E. Gellner & C. Micaud (Eds.), *Arabs and Berbers,* pp. 155–73. London: Duckworth.
1980   Social Identity and Points of Attachment. In Clifford Geertz, Hildred Geertz, & Lawrence Rosen, *Meaning and Order in Moroccan Society,* pp. 19–122. Cambridge: At the University Press.

Said, Edward
1978   *Orientalism.* New York: Pantheon Books.

Spindler, George D. (Ed.)
1970   *Being an Anthropologist.* Prospect Heights, IL: Waveland Press, Inc.

Szasz, Thomas
1965   *The Ethics of Psychoanalysis.* New York: Basic Books.

Valensi, L.
1969   *Le Maghreb avant la prise d'Alger.* Paris: Flammarion.

Wax, Rosalie
1971   *Doing Fieldwork.* Chicago: University of Chicago Press.

Webb, Sidney, & Webb, Beatrice
1968   *Methods of Social Study.* New York: Augustus M. Kelley.

Weber, Max
1963   "Objectivity" in Social Science and Social Policy. In M. Natanson (Ed.), *The Philosophy of the Social Sciences,* pp. 335–418. New York: Random House.

Wehr, Hans
1966   *A Dictionary of Modern Written Arabic.* Ithaca: Cornell University Press.

Westermarck, Edward
1968   *Ritual and Belief in Morocco* (Vols. 1 and 2). New Hyde Park, N.Y.: University Books.

Wolf, Margery
1968   *The House of Lim.* Englewood Cliffs, N.J.: Prentice-Hall.

Index

Page numbers for definitions of Arabic words are in italics

Berbers (*continued*)
colonial policy toward, 118; differences
between Arabs and, 26, 118; in Ouled
Filali, 119–20
Blacks, 116–17, 175
Boas, Franz, 257
Bohannan, Paul, 266n.17
Bourdieu, Pierre, 267n.19; contemplation
in work of, 263–64; critique of Geertz
by, 264; critique of individualism by,
283n.9; opposition to subjectivism and
objectivism by, 260, 280n.7; theory of
practice of, 263–64
Bowen, Elenore Smith, 177, 266nn. 16,
17
Brown, Kenneth L., 276n.5

Capitalism, 191–92
Casablanca, 33, 75–80
Casagrande, Joseph B., 267–68, 275n.5
Castaneda, Carlos, 277
Celebrations and parties: various kinds of,
31n.13; with *sheikha*, 195–201; *zerda*,
31n.13, 210–11. *See also* Circumcision;
Festivals; Marriage
Chagnon, Napoleon, 266n.16
Christians, 221, 223, 224; attitudes toward
Moroccans of, after independence,
81n.8; compared with Muslims and
Jews, 128; conversion to Islam of, 52,
83; differences between Moroccans/
Muslims and, 234–36; marriage of Mo-
roccans to, 87, 126; in Morocco, 22–24,
71–75, 80–82; relations between Mus-
lims and, xx, 70; role in army patrol of,
77–79; words for, 73. *See also* Europe;
Moroccan history, independence
period in
Circumcision, 31n.13, 53–58, 70
Cohen, R., 265n.15
Colonialism, 31; author's attitude toward,
70; contrast between author's and Faqir's attitude toward, 85n.12
Colonial period. *See* Moroccan history,
colonial period in
Comparativism. *See* Anthropology
Concrete object. *See* Anthropology
Contemplation: in anthropology, 256–69;
basic premise of, 256–57; contradictions
of, 271, 273; in fieldwork, 265–69; in
Geertz's and Bourdieu's work, 260–65;
political implications of, 273–74; in
Kluckhohn's and Radin's works, 259,
264–65; and Self and Other, 256–57;

as wager, 273–74. *See also* Anthropology, science and
Crapanzano, Vincent, 36n.1, 277–80n.6

Dar, 14
Demokratiya, 86–87
Derqawa. *See* Religious brotherhoods
Derrida, Jacques, 270n.1
Dfina, 196
Dialogical perspective: characteristics of,
235n.30, 274, 280–83; characteristics
of, defined, 274, 280, 282, 283; in field-
work "record," 275–86; political im-
plications of, 235n.30, 283–85; versus
science, 275; as wager, 274–75. *See also*
"Event + dialogue" motif
Diamond, Stanley, 259, 270n.1
Dichter, Thomas, 177
Dirham, 29n.11
Disputes: between brothers, 211, 240–42;
between men and women, 65; in Ouled
Filali, 48–50, 133–37, 139–40, 145–47,
202; between wives, 205–6
Douar, *50*
Dowry. *See* Marriage
Dumont, Louis, 276n.5
Dwiria, 14
Dwyer, Daisy, 266n.17
Dwyer, Kevin, 226n.14, 231n.24,
234–35n.30, 257n.1, 273n.4, 285n.10,
288n.1
Dying, 59–60

Economy: economic and religious aspects,
91; economic and social ties, 139–45;
kanun, as household unit in, 27n.10;
Moroccan currency, 29n.11; of Sous
Plain, 4–5. *See also* Agriculture
Edgerton, Robert, 265n.15
Eickelman, Dale F., 50, 105, 263n.10,
276n.5
Elections, 190–92
Epstein, A. L., 265n.15
Ethnic groups. *See* 'Abid; 'Arobi; Berbers;
Christians, Haratin; Houara; Jews
Europe: emigration of Moroccans to, 9,
14; marriage of Moroccans in, 87; mi-
grant work in, 68, 132; migration of
Moroccans to, 83–89. *See also* Chris-
tians; Moroccan history, colonial period
in
Europeans. *See* Christians
Evans-Pritchard, E. E., 266n.16